ROBERT SAM ANSON

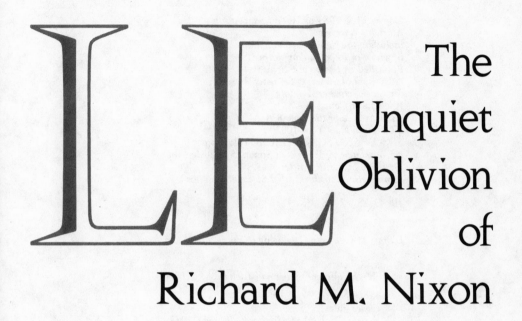

LE

The
Unquiet
Oblivion
of
Richard M. Nixon

SIMON AND SCHUSTER · NEW YORK

Copyright © 1984 by Robert Sam Anson
All rights reserved
including the right of reproduction
in whole or in part in any form
Published by Simon and Schuster
A Division of Simon & Schuster, Inc.
Simon & Schuster Building
Rockefeller Center
1230 Avenue of the Americas
New York, New York 10020
SIMON AND SCHUSTER and colophon
are registered trademarks of Simon & Schuster, Inc.
Designed by Edith Fowler
Manufactured in the United States of America

10 9 8 7 6 5 4 3 2 1

Library of Congress Cataloging in Publication Data

Anson, Robert Sam, 1945–
    Exile: the unquiet oblivion of Richard M. Nixon.

    Bibliography: p.
    Includes index.
    1. Nixon, Richard M. (Richard Milhous), 1913–
2. Presidents—United States—Biography.   I. Title.
E856.A25   1984   973.924′092′4 [B]   84–5431
ISBN 0–671–44021–7

The author gratefully acknowledges permission to reprint extracts from the
following works:
    "It Sure Looks Different from the Inside" by Ron Nessen, copyright ©
1978 Playboy Press. Permission PEI Books, Inc.
    RN: The Memoirs of Richard Nixon by Richard Nixon, copyright ©
1978 Richard Nixon. Permission Warner Books/New York.
    Breaking Cover by Bill Gulley and Mary Ellen Reese, copyright © 1980.
Permission Simon & Schuster, Inc.
    Special People by Julie Nixon Eisenhower, copyright © 1977. Permission
Simon & Schuster, Inc.
    "Richard Nixon Goes to a Party" by Benjamin Stein, copyright © 1976
Esquire Associates. Permission Esquire.
    "Reflections in a Wary Eye" by Bob Greene, copyright © 1980 Esquire
Associates. Permission Esquire.
    Palace Politics by Robert Hartmann, copyright © 1980 Robert Hart-
mann. Permission McGraw-Hill, Inc.
    I Gave Them a Sword by David Frost, copyright © 1978. Permission
William Morrow and Co.
    The Flying White House by J. F. terHorst and Col. Ralph D. Albertazzie,
copyright © 1979 J. F. terHorst and Ralph Albertazzie. Permission Putnam
Publishing Group.

For Amanda

Contents

"Let me make just one thing clear. I'm not just going to fade away and live the good life in San Clemente, listening to the waves and playing golf."

Richard Nixon,
Oxford, England
1979

1
Homeward

It was a few minutes past 9:00 A.M., August 9, 1974, and, like millions that morning, the people aboard Air Force One were watching television.

The image on the Sony picture tube fuzzed, rolled over once, then finally settled. In the First Lady's cabin, six of the aides who would be accompanying the President to California leaned forward as the scene from the East Room of the White House sharpened. The figure of Jack Brennan, resplendent in his Marine Corps dress whites, was unmistakable. "Ladies and gentlemen," they heard Richard Nixon's military aide saying, "the President of the United States of America!" The words were sharp, almost a shout.

There was music, the Marine Band playing "Hail to the Chief," applause, loud and emotional, and, at last, the familiar face. As usual when the cameras were on, he was sweating, perhaps this morning even more than usual.

"God," one of the men in the cabin said, "I don't know if I'm going to be able to watch this."

He stayed glued to the screen. The picture widened, revealing Mrs. Nixon, standing to the left of her husband, tight-lipped and controlled in a white dress and pearl earrings. Someone noticed that her hair had not been done, and that her face was masked in heavy pancake makeup. That was uncharacteristic of her; always before, nothing had been out of place.

To Nixon's immediate right stood his younger daughter, Julie, and, alongside her, her husband, David Eisenhower. Then came Tricia, and, finally, her husband, Edward Cox, a book tucked under his arm.

On the cabin loudspeaker, the applause continued, a minute, two minutes, four. Finally Nixon began to speak.

"I think the record will show that this is one of those spontaneous things that we always arrange whenever the President comes to speak, and it will be so reported in the press, and we don't mind because they have to call it as they see it." He sucked in his breath and smiled nervously. "But on our part, believe me, it's spontaneous."

Steve Bull, Nixon's appointments secretary, frowned at the screen. He was disgusted this morning, though at whom he couldn't be sure: those who had forced Nixon out, or Nixon himself for resigning. All the effort that had gone into the last year and a half now seemed a waste.

Standing next to him, Diane Sawyer, an assistant in Ron Ziegler's press office, shifted from foot to foot, battling exhaustion. Like many in the White House, she had not slept much during the last week, and last night, after Ziegler had told her that she would be one of the handful of aides going to San Clemente, almost not at all. She felt punch-drunk, emotionally drained, and it was only with effort that she gazed at the television. "My mother was a saint," she heard Nixon saying. Sawyer looked closely at the screen; there were tears in his eyes. The President paused and began to shake. "Yes, she will have no books written about her, but she was a saint."

At last, he caught himself. "Now, however, we look to the future." Cox handed him the book, a biography of Theodore Roosevelt. Putting on his glasses, Nixon began to read from Roosevelt's diary about the death of his first wife. " 'And when my heart's dearest died, the light went from my life forever.'

"That was T.R. in his twenties," he continued. "He thought the life had gone from his life forever—but he went on. And he not only became President, but as ex-President he served his country always in the arena, tempestuous, strong, sometimes wrong, sometimes right, but he was a man."

In the First Lady's cabin of Air Force One, Ann Grier and Jeannie Quinlin, two of the press office secretaries, were weeping. Frank Gannon, a former Rhodes scholar and the youngest of Nixon's speechwriters, looked at them, then turned back to the screen.

"We think, as T.R. said, that the light had left his life forever. Not true. It is only a beginning."

Grier and Quinlin were crying harder now. "Always remember, others may hate you—but those who hate you don't win, unless you hate them, and then you destroy yourself."

The applause welled up, the picture tube briefly darkened. In the cabin, the secretaries were still sobbing. Watching them, Gannon felt vaguely guilty. He wondered why he was not crying as well.

In the cockpit, Air Force One's pilot, Colonel Ralph Albertazzie, had completed his preflight checks and was monitoring the radio, waiting for the signal that Nixon had left the White House.

The course he had laid out for this morning's flight was the swiftest, most direct route. It would take Air Force One over central West Virginia, past Cincinnati, St. Louis, Wichita, and Liberal, Kansas; then on to Gallup, New Mexico, and Palm Springs, California, before turning for touchdown at El Toro Marine Air Station outside Santa Ana. At an average airspeed of six hundred miles per hour, Nixon would be back in California at noon, local time.

Albertazzie glanced at the manifest. Thirty-four passengers would be making the trip: the Nixons; Tricia, and her husband, Edward Cox; the usual Secret Service detail; Nixon's doctor, Air Force Major General Walter Tkach; the President's personal servants, Manolo and Fina Sanchez, and an abbreviated version of the White House traveling staff, including the President's official photographer, Ollie Atkins. Conspicuously missing from the passenger list was the press pool; after nearly six years of mutual hostility, Ziegler had extracted a last measure of revenge. Albertazzie noted one other omission: the warrant officer who carried "the football," the black satchel containing the codes that, on the President's command, would trigger a nuclear war. That power now resided elsewhere.

At 10:06, the radio crackled to life. "All cars and stations—depart, depart!" Albertazzie braced himself; the President was on his way.

A moment later, the voice of Ray Johnson, the aircraft communicator, came on the intercom. "Sir, Mr. Haldeman called and asked to speak to the President the minute he arrives here. What should I do?"

"Don't bother the President," Albertazzie instructed. "Give the message to Ziegler or Bull. Let them decide."

The pilot looked out the cockpit window. As always for a presidential flight, the fire trucks and ambulances were idling at their assigned stations. At the end of the deserted runway, a medevac helicopter hovered, waiting for disaster. The base was quiet. Albertazzie shook his head. He could guess the purpose of Haldeman's call; the President's former chief of staff was angling for a pardon. "The balls of him," Albertazzie muttered.

Sawyer was still watching television in the First Lady's cabin when she heard Nixon's helicopter roar past the tower, then bank to make its final approach. On the flickering screen, she watched the chopper settle onto the white hash marks of the helipad, as an Army sergeant came to attention and snapped a salute. The hatchway swung open, and, a moment later, Mrs. Nixon came down the steps, followed by Tricia. Several minutes passed. Finally Nixon appeared in the hatchway. Stepping down, he shook the hand of the base commander, then headed after his wife. The rest of his party followed quickly: Cox, then Ziegler, Fina Sanchez, and, finally, Manolo, carrying a cage with the family parrot.

Mrs. Nixon entered the airplane first, went immediately to her cabin and, beckoning Tricia and Eddie inside, closed the door. Outside, at the top of the Air Force One ramp, her husband had paused to wave good-bye to the small crowd of base employees and their families that had gathered at the terminal fence. His arms flung out in a V-for-Victory salute. As the hatchway shut behind him, Air Force One's engines began whining to life.

Within moments, the big silver-and-sky-blue plane was hurtling down the runway. Albertazzie pulled back gently on the yoke; the nose wheel lifted. It was 10:17 A.M. One hundred three minutes of Richard Nixon's presidency remained.

At the White House, the traces of his presence already were being stripped away. The Nixon family pictures that had lined the corridors of the West Wing had now been replaced by photographs of Gerald Ford. In the Oval Office, a clean-up crew was emptying the shelves and drawers of Nixon's possessions, wrapping them in plastic padding and packing them in cardboard cartons. The work moved quickly.

Across the alleyway, on the fourth floor of the Victorian pile that was the Old Executive Office Building, Gerald Ford was reviewing his inaugural address a final time. He had asked his chief of staff, a hard-bitten former newspaperman named Robert Hartmann, to write a speech matching his personality, and Hartmann had delivered. There was nothing particularly eloquent about the prose; the sentiments about "straight talk among friends" and truth being "the glue of government" were Midwestern in their common sense. Ford especially liked the passage Hartmann had composed about Nixon: "May our President who brought peace to millions find it for himself." The vice president drew on his pipe; he wondered if Nixon could.

As Ford examined his work, Hartmann himself was in the White House basement office of Bill Timmons, Nixon's assistant for congressional liaison. It had been an emotional morning for both men, Hartmann in particular. Half an hour earlier, he had been with the vice president and Mrs. Ford in the Diplomatic Reception Room as Nixon and his wife made their final farewells. No one had seemed to know quite what to say. Finally, Nixon had taken hold of his hand and said, "You won't have a lot of spare time, but when you get back to California, come and see me. We've got a great place there—you know, you've seen it, of course." It was not what Nixon had said, but the way he had said it that was so unsettling; he had seemed almost cheerful.

"You look like you need a drink," Timmons said.

He opened his desk drawer, pulled out a bottle of Scotch, filled two tumblers, and handed one to Hartmann.

"To the President," Hartmann toasted, meaning Nixon. "To the President," Timmons replied, meaning Ford.

Upstairs, in the press room, Judy Johnson, one of Ziegler's assistants, was trying to get hold of herself. She had been crying most of the morning, and was still weeping when Tom Jarriel, the White House correspondent for ABC, tapped her on the shoulder.

"What is it, Judy?" he asked with a grin. "I thought you told us yesterday that Nixon wasn't going to resign. Didn't you say that, Judy? Didn't you? Well, who was that we just saw leaving on the helicopter? Who was it, Judy?"

Johnson ran from the room, sobbing. Tom Brokaw of NBC caught up to her and put his arms around her. "It's going to be all right," he soothed. "It's all going to be all right."

A Ford secretary who had witnessed the scene from the doorway stuck her head in the room and announced, "We're going to have to get rid of these people."

Ziegler was on the phone to Haldeman for the second time since takeoff. Albertazzie's estimate of Haldeman's intentions had been correct, and Ziegler was having a difficult time fending him off. "I'm sorry, Bob," one of the stewards heard the press secretary saying in the staff compartment. "Sorry, but the President is not taking any calls. That's right, Bob, I can't put you through. I know it's rough. But that's the way it is, Bob. You understand. The President? Yeah, he's bearing up, but it's been tough, real tough. Sure, Bob, sure. You hang in there, too."

The phone in the armrest console buzzed again. Ziegler motioned for Sawyer to pick it up. It was one of the secretaries in the press office and she was crying. "You can't imagine what's happening," she reported. "They're literally throwing us out. It's awful."

Ziegler grabbed the receiver and ordered the secretary to get his deputy, Gerald Warren, on the line. "For Christ's sakes," Ziegler demanded, when Warren answered. "We're still President."

"I know," Warren replied wearily, "but what is there to do?" He was clearing out his own desk, making way for Ford's new press secretary, Gerald terHorst. The new team was coming in. There was nothing to be done.

Across the aisle, Steve Bull sipped on a bourbon. Normally, he concealed his liquor in a paper cup. This morning, however, he was drinking from a glass etched with the presidential seal. He didn't care who saw him.

Cox emerged from the First Lady's cabin, came down the aisle and perched on the arm of Bull's seat. Cox asked Bull for a rundown of what possessions of Nixon's had been packed in the cargo hold. Still dressed in his dress whites, Jack Brennan listened to them for a moment, then returned to his own thoughts. To the end, he had urged Nixon to "tough it out," dare Congress to remove him, damn the critics, Sirica and the press. Now that he hadn't, it probably meant the end of Brennan's career. The marines were a tight outfit; the generals he had ordered to do Nixon's bidding had long memories. They would make his life miserable, sixteen years of service or not.

He looked back at Bull and Cox still discussing the things Nixon had left behind in Washington. With the suddenness of the resignation, there were a lot of them, including nearly all of Nixon's papers and tapes. Bull, who had spent the last few days supervising the packing, told Cox not to worry. At the proper time, when the Nixon library was built, Ford's people would ship them to California. Bull sipped at his drink. "I'm quitting," he announced to no one in particular. "I'm going to see if I can make a living out there in the cold cruel world." He drained his glass and signaled the steward for another.

At the table across the aisle, Gannon was passing the time writing letters. He had written one to his parents, another to his tutor at Oxford, still others to the men who had given him his start in politics, sharing his thoughts as the final moments of Nixon's presidency counted down. As Gannon began his last note, to Kay Halle, who had been his friend and landlady in Washington, he paused and ran his hand over the embossed engraving of the Air Force One stationery. At thirty-two, and on the White House staff only a short time, he was new to such perks. Gannon touched the letterhead again. He guessed it would be the last opportunity he had to use it.

In the White House East Room, the Marine Band was playing mood music, low-keyed and unmartial. The chairs that two hours before had been filled with grieving Nixon aides had filled up with new faces, and, Hartmann observed, many not so new. Even with their chief gone, the Nixon men still occupied the choicest seats. At the direction of Alexander Haig, Nixon's chief of staff, most of Ford's aides, even his in-laws, had been consigned to the back rows behind the television cameras. It was a bad sign, Hartmann decided. Ford would have problems taking control.

At 11:35, Alexander Haig entered Henry Kissinger's White House office. Silently, he handed the secretary of state Nixon's letter of resignation. Kissinger studied it, and agreed that the signature on it was Nixon's. The constitutional process was complete.

"Ladies and gentlemen," one of the White House military aides announced, "The vice president of the United States and Mrs. Ford." Somberly, Ford entered the East Room stage left, his wife on his arm. The band stopped playing. It was no time for "Hail to the Chief."

"Is that clock right?" Nixon asked, gesturing at the three-dial digital display on his cabin wall. His black steward, Air Force Sergeant Lee

Simmons, checked it against his watch. The time read three minutes before noon. "Yes, sir, it's exactly right."

Simmons cleared his throat. "Mr. President, I'm really sad about all of this and I hope you and Mrs. Nixon and the family . . ."

"Now, Lee," Nixon cut in, "I've been wanting to tell you how much I appreciate all the good care and all the nice things you've done for me and Pat. Just remember, tomorrow is a new day. You can't let things get you down. You can't stay down. You have to pick yourself up and keep going. Life goes on."

Simmons started to say something more, but the words stuck in his throat. Nixon rose from his seat and gathered him in a hug.

The steward went out to the cockpit, astonished at Nixon's calm. A moment later, the sound of a buzzer summoned him back.

"I think I'd like a martini," Nixon said. The President shot a glance at the clock and half-smiled. "Ask Ron to come in. Better fix one for him, too. After that, I'll have my lunch."

It was twelve o'clock, Washington time. Air Force One was cruising at an altitude of 39,000 feet over a point 13 miles southwest of Jefferson City, Missouri. Albertazzie checked his position: 38 degrees, 35.5 minutes N, 92 degrees, 26.6 minutes W. "Kansas City," he radioed to ground control. "This is Air Force One. Will you change our call sign to SAM 27000?"

"Roger, SAM 27000," an unseen voice replied. "Good luck to the President."

"Mr. Vice President," Chief Justice Warren Burger intoned, "are you prepared to take the oath of office of President of the United States?"

"I am," Ford answered. His wife held out the family Bible, opened to a passage from the third chapter of Proverbs, verses 5 and 6:

> Trust in the Lord with all thine heart;
> And lean not unto thine own understanding.
> In all ways acknowledge him,
> And he shall direct thy paths.

Ford placed his left hand on the text, and, raising his right, repeated the pledge every President had made since George Washington.

The ceremony lasted only a moment. Burger shook his hand; his wife kissed him on the cheek. Then, trembling slightly, the new President turned to address the nation. "My fellow Americans," he said, "our long national nightmare is over."

Halfway across the country, a lunch of shrimp cocktail, prime rib, baked potato, green beans, tossed salad, coffee and cheesecake was being served on what was now Gerald Ford's airplane. Nixon, who had not listened to his successor's speech on the cabin loudspeaker, only picked at his food.

Seated across the table from him, Ziegler was struggling to keep his composure. Nixon tried to distract him by reminiscing about some of the morning's happenings, particularly the farewell to the staff in the East Room.

Nixon recalled looking out on the men and women who had served him, many of whom were strangers to him, and being startled to see that they were crying. He talked about Herb Stein, the chairman of his Council of Economic Advisers, how moved and surprised he had been watching the tears run down Stein's face. He had almost lost it right there, Nixon said. He hadn't realized how much people like Herb Stein had cared.

Nixon stared at his plate.

A moment later, he brightened. You know, he said to Ziegler, the strangest part of the entire morning was what Ford had said to him at the helicopter steps: "Drop us a line if you get the chance. Let us know how you are doing." Nixon laughed; the remark seemed so bizarre.

He was talking about California and the future when a call pulled Ziegler away. The Air Force advance agent had radioed from El Toro that a large crowd had begun forming. They were expecting Nixon to address them; some sort of remarks would have to be prepared. Immediately, Ziegler got on the phone to Washington and began barking orders to his staff. He wanted a complete transcript of the new President's inaugural address, not only what Ford had said, but how he had said it. He put Sawyer on the line and told her to begin taking dictation. As each page was completed, she handed it to Ann Grier for typing. Ziegler paced restlessly. "The President needs this," he kept saying. "The President wants it now." Bull watched the performance with amusement. *Poor Ron*, he thought to himself. *It's all over, and he still doesn't know.*

Albertazzie came out of the cockpit and walked back to where Ziegler was still supervising the transcription of Ford's speech. The pilot had begun to brief him on preparations for arrival at El Toro, when, behind him, Nixon appeared in the passageway. "Well," said the former President, rubbing his hands together nervously, "is everybody enjoying the trip?"

No one replied. Nixon turned to Albertazzie. "Ralph, when we get to El Toro, I'd like some pictures. You know, me and the crew. Then I'd like some of Mrs. Nixon and the crew, and of Mrs. Nixon, you and me—and, if you've got the time, one of just you and me. Think you can arrange that?"

"Of course, Mr. President."

Nixon paused. "Ralph," he said, "you know before we went to

China, I told you that when we got back, I'd make you a general. I really meant to do that. But like so many other things I meant to do . . ." Nixon's voice trailed off. "I'll just have to leave them all undone," he said finally. "I'm sorry."

"I understand, Mr. President," the pilot answered.

As Albertazzie headed back to the flight deck, Nixon began walking the length of the plane, pausing to say a few words at every seat. He saw Gannon sitting next to Sawyer and winked. "I see you remembered to bring along the good-looking girls."

He moved on, still bantering, until he reached the tail section, ordinarily reserved for the press, and now occupied by the Secret Service. "Well," Nixon said, at the sight of his security men. "It certainly smells better back here."

Everyone, including Nixon, laughed. Then Nixon turned, walked back to his cabin and closed the door.

On board SAM 27000, it was uncommonly still. Occasionally, a passenger made a desultory attempt at conversation, or attempted a joke. But for the most part, few people spoke. They looked out their windows, then at their watches.

An hour passed. In the cockpit, Albertazzie checked the weather at El Toro. The base reported clear skies, winds out of the west at fifteen knots and a temperature of eighty-two degrees; it was a perfect California day. Satisfied, Albertazzie leaned back and began considering his future. "The best job in the Air Force," as he used to call it, had lost its glamour and fun. When he got back to Washington, he decided, he'd put in his papers and retire.

At the White House, the new President was following the schedule drawn up by his transition team. Having inspected the Oval Office and met with leaders of Congress, he was now in the Roosevelt Room, being introduced to the White House staff. The meeting was not going well. Ford appeared halting and uncertain. Each time a question was raised, he looked down to the end of the gleaming conference table and asked Nixon's chief of staff, "Al, what do you think of that?" And each time, Haig answered, "If you think it is best, Mr. President."

"Okay," the President would agree. "Yes."

The process repeated itself, once, then again. The Ford men looked at each other; this was not the take-charge style they had envisioned.

Fifty miles east of Thermal, California, SAM 27000 was beginning its final descent. Slowly, the plane turned on a southwesterly heading toward Oceanside, then northwesterly up the coastline. As the ground came up, Gannon stared out the window, looking for familiar landmarks. He saw the ocher-colored cluster of buildings that until two hours before had been the Western White House; a second later, perched on a promontory overlooking the sea, the red tile roof of Casa Pacifica, Nixon's residence. Then, as Laguna passed underneath, Gannon saw the cars. There were hundreds of them, packed bumper to bumper, seemingly the entire route to El Toro. "Look out your window," he said to Bull. "Down there is the first spontaneous demonstration for Richard Nixon that was never planned."

There was barely a bump, as SAM 27000 settled down at the end of runway 34 right. In the bleachers the marines had erected alongside El Toro's terminal, a crowd of five thousand people broke into cheers and whistling applause. Mothers clutched at their babies; fathers hoisted children to their shoulders; teenagers scrambled into the branches of trees for a better look. As the plane taxied to a halt on the tarmac, Pat Hitt, a longtime friend of the Nixons who had been an HEW assistant secretary during Nixon's first term, fought her way to the arrival fence. She covered her ears from the shriek of the approaching jets. All around her, people were cheering. Unashamedly, she began to weep.

Mrs. Nixon, flanked by her daughter and son-in-law, stood in the passageway just outside the cabin where she had remained the entire flight. Her favorite steward approached; wordlessly, she reached out and embraced him. A moment later, the door of Nixon's cabin swung open. The former President appeared composed. "Well," he said to his wife, "it appears that we're here." She took his hand.

When he appeared in the open doorway, arms thrown up in V-for-victory salute, the crowd cheered again, more loudly than before. It continued cheering as Nixon, smiling and waving, came down the ramp and walked to the outstretched hands along the fence. Off to one side, someone began singing "God Bless America." Those around him took it up, and within moments the refrain, off-key, dissonant, overwhelming, had swept through the crowd.

From beneath the aircraft fuselage, where he had gone to retrieve his luggage, Steve Bull heard the singing and turned to Lee Simmons. The two men embraced; their bodies shook with sobs.

"Were you with him?" a woman near the fence called out to Gannon, as he hoisted his luggage into the trunk of a Marine Corps sedan.

"Yes," Gannon answered, "I was with him."

"Tell him we still love him."

Gannon turned his head, and, for the first time since he had been a child, began to cry.

A few yards away Nixon was standing at a battery of microphones. It took several moments for the crowd to quiet. Finally Nixon began to speak.

"Many statements have been made and this is not the time to bore you with another one. It is perhaps appropriate for me to say very simply this: having completed one task does not mean that we will just sit back and enjoy this marvelous California climate and do nothing."

At the mention of California, the crowd interrupted with another cheer. Nixon smiled and clasped his hands in front of him. He talked on, about California, about "this great plane that took us to China, to Russia . . . to the Middle East," about America being a nation in which "there is more freedom, more opportunity for all people, regardless of background, than any country in the world.

"With all the time that I have which could be useful," he continued, "I am going to continue to work for peace among all the world. I intend to continue to work for opportunity and understanding among the people in America."

There were more cheers, and Nixon's voice became stronger. "I am going to continue—we are all going to continue—to be proud of the fact that we, too, are Californians and we're home again."

With a last wave, he turned and walked back to the aircraft, where Albertazzie and the crew were waiting. They posed while Ollie Atkins took his pictures, then Nixon walked with Albertazzie across the tarmac to the small helicopter that would ferry him to San Clemente. "We covered a lot of miles together, you and I," he said, shaking Albertazzie's hand, "I'm sorry it's ending this way."

"I am, too, Mr. President," his pilot answered. "Good luck. Goodbye."

In the White House press room, Gerry terHorst was about to deliver his first news briefing. He smiled self-consciously at a group of reporters in front of him. Until this morning he had sat where they were sitting now, as Washington bureau chief of the *Detroit News*.

He gripped the lectern and grinned. "Any questions?"

One of his former colleagues held up his hand. "Can you check for us, as to if President Ford's position is still as he stated on the Hill, that he is not in favor of immunity?"

"I can assure you of that," the President's press secretary answered.

"He is not in favor of immunity?"

TerHorst repeated the answer, this time more emphatically. Gerald Ford did not favor a pardon for the former President. The press could be certain of it.

It was just before one when the marine helicopter bearing Richard Nixon and his family touched down on the helipad of the San Clemente Coast Guard Station. The strain of the day was at last catching up with Nixon; he was shaking as he got out.

Paul Presley, the owner of the San Clemente Inn, and Johnny Grant, a Los Angeles television personality, both of them old friends, greeted him with a hug. Nixon said he was surprised and glad to see them. There was a lot of catching up they had to do. They talked a few minutes more, posed for a picture, then Nixon got into a yellow golf cart for the half-mile ride to his estate.

Gerald Ford was in the middle of a long day that showed no signs of ending anytime soon. His once bare desk was now piled high with fat file folders, all demanding his immediate attention. There were appointments to be made, meetings to attend, matters that had to be decided. It would be well after dark before he made the drive home to Alexandria.

A few yards down the corridor, Hartmann was packing up his brief-case in what had been the office of Nixon's longtime personal secretary, Rose Mary Woods. He sniffed the air. It was heavy with the stench of papers recently burned in the fireplace.

Outside, the streets were nearly deserted. Across Pennsylvania Avenue, Lafayette Park, which for months had been home to dozens of anti-Nixon protesters, had suddenly cleared. Here and there a picket sign began softening under the evening damp. At the base of the statue of the Marquis de Lafayette, three men stood in silence, staring at the White House. Pat Hillings, who had known Nixon since his college days at U.S.C., and had taken his seat in Congress when Nixon was elected to the Senate, reached into his suit coat pocket and fumbled with some of the presidential cufflinks he had swiped that morning from the Oval Office. Such souvenirs were bound to be a scarce commodity, and he had taken as many as he could. He turned to the two men standing alongside him, John Sears, who had briefly been Nixon's chief political aide before being forced out by John Mitchell, and Nick Ruwe, a bluff, good-humored former advanceman who had risen to be assistant White House chief of protocol.

"I don't know about you guys," Hillings said, "but I'm going to go to Sans Souci and get royally drunk." As the trio turned in the direction of the restaurant, Sears looked back at the White House. That morning, he had won a considerable sum of money by betting his friends that Nixon would not be able to complete his farewells without mentioning his mother. That he had been correct cheered him only slightly. "God," he whispered, "it's so quiet."

In the red-walled master bedroom of Casa Pacifica, Pat Nixon was unpacking her husband's things. That morning, without telling anyone, she had gone to his sleeping chambers in the White House and removed his favorite personal possessions to bring with her to California. Now, she arranged them carefully, just as they had been placed in the White House. In the morning when he awoke it must seem the same.

Outside, unknowing, her husband stood on a bluff overlooking the Pacific. He lingered there a long moment, watching the waves crash on the beach beneath him. Then he turned back to walk inside. All at once, Richard Nixon felt very tired.

The First Month

$\mathcal{2}$

H e spent that first weekend trying to adjust.

Saturday morning, his two closest friends, Charles G. ("Bebe") Rebozo, the Key Biscayne banker, and Robert Abplanalp, the New York aerosol millionaire, who had flown in from the East the night before, aboard Abplanalp's personal jet, came to the estate for a consoling visit and a long talk. The consolation went better than the conversation. Nixon, who had had trouble sleeping the night before, was exhausted and in no mood to listen to Rebozo's urgings that he move to Florida, or to Abplanalp's that he move to New York. For the time being, he told them, California would be home base. Maybe later, after some months had passed, he'd put in roots elsewhere. For the moment, he simply needed time to relax and unwind.

The next afternoon, while the two dozen reporters who had been keeping vigil outside Casa Pacifica's gate were decoyed to Laguna for a noninformative press briefing, Nixon and Rebozo went out for a drive. With Bebe at the wheel of a white, black-topped Mercury, they first headed north, to Dana Park, where Nixon had taken Pat on their first date thirty-nine years before. They then turned back south, driving the Pacific Coast Highway to Oceanside. Around two, they arrived at Red Beach, a graceful stretch of sand maintained by the Marine Corps and off limits to the general public. Nixon slipped off his shoes, put on a blue windbreaker with the presidential seal and went for a long, solitary stroll.

Mrs. Nixon, Eddie and Tricia arrived some minutes later, bringing along a picnic hamper. They spread out a blanket and dined on the beach. Nixon munched on a sandwich and watched the waves roll in.

He rose early the next morning as usual, and, after a breakfast of coffee and orange juice, went to his second-floor, turret-shaped den to read. At eight, he began making phone calls to Washington, first to Julie, then to Rose Woods, who had remained behind to finish packing his personal things. Later, he began dialing old friends in California. One of the first he reached was Robert Finch, the state's former lieutenant governor and the manager of his 1960 Presidential campaign. During Nixon's first term, Finch had been secretary of what was then Department of Health, Education, and Welfare, until being muscled aside by Haldeman and Ehrlichman. Since then, Nixon and Finch had rarely spoken, and the conversation began awkwardly. Nixon talked at length about the welcome, describing how moved he had been by it. Finally, he said thickly, "Bob, a lot has happened, but I've realized something." There was a pause, then Nixon finished, "You don't realize until too late who your real friends are."

A few moments later, Nixon was saying much the same thing to Herb Klein, another old friend who had once been his director of communications and had suffered the same fate as Finch. "I appreciate how you handled that business about the tapes," Nixon said, referring to Klein's laughing reaction to the news that Nixon had said of him, "He doesn't have his head screwed on right."

"Think nothing of it," Klein assured him.

"No, I really mean it," Nixon protested. "It meant a lot. And your comments after the resignation, too. I'm very grateful."

Fearing that Nixon was about to turn maudlin, Klein quickly asked Nixon how he was and what were his immediate plans. Nixon was vague. The exhaustion in his voice was palpable.

The telephoning continued most of the morning. Then, shortly before noon, Nixon saw his first visitor of the day, Patricia Hitt, who had come down from her home in Newport at Mrs. Nixon's invitation. They spent an hour talking about California, and again Nixon mentioned how affected he had been by the reception at El Toro. He rambled on, not always making good sense. His body sagged and his face looked haggard. But his spirits seemed good and there was no bitterness in his tone. He said he realized that he'd never be involved in public life again, at least not as he had been in the past. But that was fine with him. He didn't want another public career. All he wanted now was time. To catch up on his reading, to perhaps do some writing, to allow, as he put it, "the wounds to heal."

A few hundred yards from where Nixon sat talking, in the compound of prefabricated buildings that had been the Western White House, Ziegler was waiting for a visitor from Washington, a bullnecked former Marine master sergeant named Bill Gulley. A career soldier and White House fixture since 1967, Gulley was administrator of the White House military affairs office, a little-known but well-positioned post that handled most of the logistics of the presidency, including communications and transportation. Gulley was also responsible for overseeing the needs of former Presidents, and since Thursday morning, when Rose Woods had told him that Nixon would be leaving for California the next day, he had been continually on the run. Until now everything had gone smoothly, but there were still countless housekeeping details that had to be worked out, among them the disassembly and shipment back to Washington of the vast communications network that linked San Clemente to the White House. Dozens of personnel also had to be reassigned and procedures drawn up for the administering of Nixon's postpresidential perks. What worried Gulley most was dealing with "the Old Man." Nixon was a stickler for detail and could become enraged at the smallest bureaucratic malfunction. Sensing trouble, Gulley had brought along a peace offering.

Friday morning, as Nixon was saying good-bye to his staff in the East Room, Gulley had slipped into the White House family quarters and removed eleven cartons of what had been described to him only as "Nixon's personal things." From their heft, Gulley guessed them to be papers, documents, he presumed, of the most sensitive kind. Without informing anyone in the White House, Gulley had had the boxes trucked to Andrews, and there placed aboard the Air Force Jetstar that had taken him to California that morning. Now, the boxes were in the backseat of his car.

As Gulley drove onto Casa Pacifica's grounds, he noticed that there was no guard at the gate. The parking lot, usually filled with cars, was almost empty. The place, Gulley thought, had the appearance of a ship that had been hastily abandoned.

Gulley went to Ziegler's office, and briefed him on the reason for his trip, omitting what was in his car. It was important, the sergeant added, that he see Nixon personally; there was something he had to give him. Ziegler told him it was impossible; the President was not taking calls. Gulley eyed Ziegler appraisingly. Like many on the staff, he had not liked the press secretary when they were in the White House; now, he decided, he liked him even less. Gulley shrugged and went in search of Steve Bull.

He found him in his office, conferring with Brennan. Gulley told them about the cartons he had brought to San Clemente. He wasn't sure what was in them, but he had a good idea. What was more important were the materials that had been left behind. There was a "shitload" of it, Gulley said, not only at the White House and in the EOB, but at a government warehouse at Fort Meyer, Virginia. If Nixon wanted any of it back, they had to move quickly. Things were confused at the White House, but they wouldn't remain so for long. Once Ford's people got themselves organized and noticed Nixon's papers were disappearing, they were sure to lock the doors. Brennan and Bull agreed. Could Gulley return to Washington and begin shipping the remainder out immediately? Gulley nodded. When he got back, he'd make arrangements with the Air Force to transport the materials on C-141s. The process should move quickly; each plane could haul fifty thousand pounds. Fine, Brennan said.

As soon as Gulley worked up a schedule, he'd have the marines meet each of the flights.

As Gulley headed back to Washington, Nixon's staff, which had spent the weekend collapsed in scattered motel rooms, was drifting into the compound and beginning to wonder what to do. In telling them to come to California, Ziegler had said only that the President "needed" them and that they should plan to stay perhaps six weeks. Beyond that, and the time they were to arrive at Andrews, there had been nothing.

The result Monday morning was dozens of questions, most of which Ziegler, who was spending the bulk of his time closeted with Nixon, was not in a position to answer. In the interval, men and women fended for themselves. Some retreated to the office complex, and there, behind closed doors, phoned old friends in Washington for the latest news. Others, like Sawyer, went through the motions of conducting business as usual, answering the phones, and telling the reporters who called, "There is no news. This is no longer a public operation." Still others passed the time exploring, poking into such hitherto forbidden precincts as the President's air-conditioned office, with its carved mahogany desk retrieved from the White House basement, and its magnificent, bulletproof, glass-protected view of the Pacific, or, when Nixon was away from the residence, ambling through Casa Pacifica itself.

The hacienda-style estate, built in 1925 by Henry Hamilton Cotton, a wealthy industrialist and longtime finance chairman of the California Democratic party, was modest by the standards of the California rich. The rooms, fourteen in all, including the nearby guest cottage, were smallishly proportioned and awkwardly laid out. Several of the five bedrooms opened directly onto an entrance courtyard, centered by a pyramid-shaped fountain, topped by a statue of Cupid and surrounded by four green frogs, spewing water to all the points of the compass. During the winter, when the fog rolled in past the stands of cypress, eucalyptus and palms that dotted the twenty-eight-acre grounds, it was a brisk, chilly walk across the courtyard into the main house. Within was the single sizable space in the house, a formerly gloomy 18 foot by 36 foot living room Mrs. Nixon had brightened with off-whites and yellows, her favorite colors. Next to a large, Spanish-tiled fireplace was a baby grand piano which Nixon had been fond of playing at the staff Christmas party. On the walls hung mementos of various travels, including two lacquer paintings, one of a Mekong Delta scene, the other of deer grazing in a mythical park, the then-vice president had brought back from Vietnam in 1953. With one exception, all the rooms were on the first floor. The exception was Nixon's hexagonal-shaped, 8 foot by 10 foot blue-carpeted den, mounted on the southwest corner of the house. Here, it was said, Cotton had played poker one night with his friend, Franklin Roosevelt.

Now, where FDR had gambled, a yellow easy chair and ottoman were drawn up next to windows overlooking the ocean. Nearby, on an embossed wooden desk rested a replica of a plaque the Apollo 11 astronauts had left on the moon. Works of history, biography and political philosophy filled the bookshelves. On one shelf, tucked beside some family photographs, was a framed poem Julie had written for her father as a child. "Handsome and kind," the opening lines went, "Always on time / Loving and Good / Does things he should."

The sight-seeing and idleness did not last long. Tuesday morning Nixon was in his compound office at 7:00 A.M., dressed in a blue business suit and ready for work. It irritated him that his staff was not similarly prepared, and by 7:30 he was placing calls to rouse the malingerers from bed. Nothing had changed, he told them; resignation or no, they would go on as they always had.

Nixon was not kidding. Within a week, he called the members of the senior staff together in what had been the National Security Council conference room. Pausing to glare at an aide who had shown up in Bermuda shorts, Nixon looked around the table, as if he were addressing his cabinet. "I've called you here to discuss an important topic," he announced finally. "And that is, what are we going to do about the economy in the coming year?"

In Washington, meanwhile, the confusion Gulley had described to Brennan and Bull was continuing. The transition planners, a hastily composed group of Ford's friends and political cronies, had foreseen that there would be problems dealing with an administration still overwhelmingly staffed by Nixon appointees, and they had recommended that he resolve them forcefully. Specifically, the planners had urged Ford to dismiss the entire cabinet except for Kissinger, and laid out procedures for physically clearing all White House offices within seventy-two hours. Instead, Ford, who admitted to hating to "hurt people's feelings," had called the cabinet together the morning after Nixon's resignation and announced, "I think we have a fine team here, and I'm looking forward to working with each and every one of you." As for the Nixon holdovers on the White House staff, with few exceptions, they, too, had been left in place.

Hartmann, who had been placed in charge of the presidential speechwriters (promptly and disagreeably, he fired them all), implored Ford to clean house.

"You don't suspect ill motives of anyone until you're kicked in the balls three times," Hartmann exasperated. "As a human being, that's a virtue. But as a President, it's a weakness."

But Ford was unyielding, and in the resulting chaos of orders and counterorders, Gulley was finding it easy to operate. Since returning from

San Clemente, the sergeant had been sending truckloads of Nixon's papers and belongings to an out-of-the-way hangar at Andrews. There, they were stored until Gulley, who was commandeering space on every available flight on the East Coast, succeeded in loading them for California. Ford's people finally became suspicious after one of them noticed dozens of bags of documents piled up outside the basement burn room, waiting for incineration. On inquiring, the aide was told that not only were "the Nixon people burning crap like crazy," but that the chemical paper shredder had been operating at five times its normal capacity for weeks. The destruction was ordered halted, and a short while later, Jack Marsh, a former Virginia congressman who was one of the leaders of Ford's transition team, pulled Gulley aside, and, as if guessing what Gulley had been doing, told him that henceforth nothing was to be shipped to San Clemente. Instead, Gulley, who sympathized with Nixon and was eager to court his favor, increased the pace of his shipments. It was only a chance discovery by Benton Becker, a young lawyer working on the transition, that finally put an end to the shipments. Arriving at the White House one Saturday night, Becker found three trucks loaded with Nixon's personal effects pulled up at a basement entrance to the West Wing. Learning what was in them, Becker told the Air Force colonel in charge of the loading operations, "This truck does not move."

"I take my instruction from General Haig," the colonel replied.

Becker retorted, "Let's go see him right now."

They found Haig in his office. Nixon's chief of staff claimed ignorance of what was happening and ordered the colonel to unload the trucks. To insure that he did, Becker, who like many of Ford's allies had become increasingly suspicious of Haig's loyalties, watched until the unloading was complete. By then, nearly 400,000 pounds of materials had been shipped to San Clemente.

In mid-August, Gulley flew to San Clemente, and this time had no trouble seeing Nixon. The former President was waiting for him in his office, and he looked ravaged. His eyes were red-rimmed and hollow, as if he had not slept in days, and his demeanor was tense. When Gulley walked in the room, Nixon, who had been complaining to Haig about the cutoff in his shipments, snapped, "What are those bastards going to do to me?"

"They're after your ass," Gulley answered. "Marsh and Hartmann are referring to you as a crook. But the buzz is that [NATO Ambassador Donald] Rumsfeld's coming back. If it's true, then things will get better. Rumsfeld's a pro."

Nixon was not mollified. "I'm not going to deal with those fucking bastards. I'm entitled to anything that any other former President is entitled to. Goddam, you know what I did for Johnson, and you know what I did for Ike and Truman, and goddam it, I expect to be treated the same way. When I travel, I expect military aircraft; I expect the same support I provided. I expect communications and medical personnel, everything they had. And, goddam it, you tell Ford I expect it."

Nixon talked on, increasingly agitated, demanding to know what was being done about his papers and tapes. When Gulley professed ignorance, Nixon said, "Well, you just tell those bastards that I'm going to keep my mouth shut. I'm not going to be talking to the press. I'm not going to be making comments about Ford or the administration, but, goddam it, I want them to know I'm here. And I want them to know there are certain things I expect from them. Briefing papers. Certain treatment."

They continued talking a half hour more. Nixon told Gulley there were only two people in the White House he trusted: Rose Woods, and Brent Scowcroft, an Air Force major general who was serving as Ford's national security adviser. "Be careful," he advised Gulley. "I don't want people knowing I'm close to Scowcroft. I don't want to do anything that will jeopardize his position."

As Gulley got up to go, Nixon said, "Is this going to present a problem for you, working with me?"

"I'm not here to pass moral judgments," the sergeant replied. "I'm here to do a job. It won't be any problem."

As Gulley drove to El Toro for the flight that would take him back to Washington, he felt he had been in the presence of a gladiator, a warrior who had not yet realized the implications of his own defeat.

A few days later, on August 20, Ford phoned Nixon from Washington. It was the first time the two men had spoken since the transfer of power, and the new President was still respectful of the old. Addressing Nixon as "Mr. President," Ford inquired about the state of his health and Pat's. He then announced some news. After consulting with party leaders, and careful deliberation, he had decided to nominate Nelson Rockefeller as his vice president.

Nixon said he was very pleased. Ford had selected "a big man for a big job." Rockefeller's name and experience would help him in foreign affairs, and, if anything happened to him, Ford could be confident that Rockefeller was fully qualified to take over. Of course, Nixon went on, the extreme Right wouldn't like the nomination, but Ford shouldn't worry; he had no hope of placating them in any case. All in all, Ford had made a wise decision. He was very happy.

In fact, Nixon was furious, not only that he hadn't been consulted, but at Rockefeller's selection. If there was a leader in the GOP Nixon disliked, personally as well as politically, it was the former governor of New York. Not only did Rockefeller represent the Eastern privilege Nixon detested, but twice he had tried to deny him the presidential nomination. Deepening Nixon's resentment was the fact that Rockefeller had snubbed and scorned him the years he was living in New York.

Still boiling, Nixon called Sacramento to share his resentment with Ronald Reagan. Reagan sympathized; he was no fan of Rockefeller's either. Afterward Reagan told an aide about Nixon's call. The aide talked to a reporter and, within days, the story was in the press. Its immediate effect, if any, was to boost Rockefeller's chances of confirmation.

Quickly and painfully, Nixon was coming to realize that his opinion no longer mattered. At one point, while Rockefeller's nomination was still pending, he called the White House to chat with a former aide. Ordinarily, the man would have come on the line instantly; this time, Nixon was put on hold. In another call to the White House, a former loyalist now working for Ford told him, "Those who served you best hate you most."

There were other reminders of how life had changed. Once secured for his exclusive use, the beach beneath Casa Pacifica's cliffs had been opened to the public, and to walk in privacy Nixon now had to drive thirteen miles to Camp Pendleton. During one such outing, while Rebozo was driving him down the freeway, a car full of young people pulled alongside and one of the occupants gave Nixon the finger. When Nixon and Rebozo returned home, they noticed the HOME OF THE WESTERN WHITE HOUSE signs at the San Clemente city limits were no longer in evidence; during Nixon's first weekend back, they had been stolen by vandals.

But perhaps the most telling incident came with the death of Charles Lindbergh, August 26. Nixon had been a great admirer of Lindbergh's and wanted to write his widow, Anne Morrow, a letter of condolence. All the stationery in his office, however, was emblazoned with the presidential seal. Deciding the paper would be inappropriate, Nixon commissioned Bull to find stationery with only his name on the letterhead. Bull searched the offices without success. Finally, he went into Nixon's den, picked up a piece of notepaper from his desk, and, as Nixon watched, scissored off the presidential seal. "That," said Bull, "is the new reality."

The friends who saw Nixon during those first days were telling him the present reality would change. Given time, the public would recognize Watergate for the aberration that it was, match it alongside the accomplishments of his presidency, see, then, that he was not only a good President, but a great one. Kissinger had said the same thing to him, even before he left the presidency, assuring him that his place in history was secure. Nixon had replied, "That depends on who writes the history."

In San Clemente, that question had already been decided: Richard Nixon would write it.

He was anxious to begin work as soon as possible, if for no other reason than that Cox, who had been going over the family budget with Abplanalp, had discovered that, with the recent payment to the IRS of hundreds of thousands in back taxes, the family bank account had been virtually cleaned out. Unsolicited, a number of literary proposals had already come in, promising various lofty sums. But the one that intrigued Nixon most was from Irving Paul Lazar, who promised only himself.

"Swifty" was an American original, an agent nearly as famous as the clients he represented. Short in stature (with benefit of elevator shoes, he stood five feet three inches tall), but long on chutzpah (he had been known to sell productions that did not yet exist, and was renowned for not reading the books he peddled for record sums), the bald-headed, pointed-eared little man in the thick, black-rimmed glasses possessed, as one of those who negotiated with him put it, "the legendary ability to enter a revolving door behind you and come out in front." His roster of talent, which ranged from novelist Truman Capote to composer Cole Porter to playwright Moss Hart, loved him for it, for however bizarre his appearance or unconventional his methods, "the Faustus with the Mostest" was unequalled at securing record advances. Without specifying how or how much, it was that talent Lazar offered to Nixon now.

Ziegler, who had been reviewing the various proposals, contacted him, and, on August 31, Lazar arrived at Casa Pacifica in a chauffeured Rolls-Royce.

What he told Nixon was encouraging, but blunt. A $2 million advance, spread out over several years, was a possibility, but only if Nixon was able to convince a publisher that he could be candid in dealing with Watergate. If Nixon had any other intention, they should abandon the project right then; he, Lazar, would want no part of it. Nixon smiled faintly. "Don't worry. That's not what I have in mind."

They talked on, discussing content and possible sales. Lazar felt strongly that Nixon had to account for literally every day of his presidency and Nixon agreed. "The full story," he mumbled. "All of it. Unvarnished." Nixon asked how the book would sell. "That depends on you," Lazar replied. "If you do your job, terrific. After all, you're the most controversial President since Lincoln." Nixon laughed.

After three hours, Nixon and Lazar shook hands on the deal. In spite of himself the agent had been impressed. Nixon had displayed none of the bitterness he had been expecting. Both his appearance and his spirits seemed excellent. Lazar had never cared for Nixon as President, but there was no denying his stamina. The man was tough. "You know," Lazar said, "there is one way you could make even more money than you can on this book."

"What's that?" Nixon said.

"Leave your body to the Harvard Medical School."

In dealing with Lazar, Nixon had been at his best, alert, bright, clear; as Lazar told a reporter "completely in command, of himself, his situation and what he wanted to do." Many who visited him during those first weeks came away with the same impression: Nixon was not only enduring, he was prevailing. True, he was tired, and, in some moments, distracted and depressed, but, on balance, his mood was good, indeed, extraordinary, given the rigors of the last two years. "Let me tell you," one of his dispirited aides confided to a reporter over a drink at the Surf and Sand, "I just wish the rest of us felt half as up."

But the private Richard Nixon, whom the visitors didn't see, was a different man entirely. That Richard Nixon had deteriorated drastically since the initial false euphoria. His body had worn down, and his mind with it. Unable to concentrate or work for more than a few hours, this Nixon kept to himself, the office door closed, the ringing telephone unanswered. There, in his solitude, the other Nixon brooded.

Gulley, who returned to San Clemente to discuss personnel matters, realized the change the moment he saw him. The combativeness Nixon had shown during their first encounter was missing and he seemed subdued and listless. In an effort to cheer him, Gulley fibbed that Ford and his wife had asked him to convey their best wishes. Still lying, he added that Ford was aware of the shipments he had made to San Clemente, and had given them his blessing.

Nixon seemed to perk up and inviting Gulley to sit down began recounting the conversations he'd recently had with a number of Southern congressmen. They had told him that the long knives were still out for him.

"I realize there's going to be bitterness," Nixon went on. "I expect that. But I want to know specifically what their plans are. I want to know when I get my papers. When do I get my personal effects? What are they going to do with my wife and daughters' things? And Rose's stuff? These are personal items, nothing to do with the presidency."

Gulley told him that the situation was still unsettled, but that at least one decision had been reached; with Ford's approval, he would be bringing him briefing papers and intelligence reports every two weeks. The rest of the news, however, was not so good. Gulley doubted whether, as Nixon had requested, the administration would make available military aircraft for his future travels, and, in fact, there had been talk at the White House about billing him for part of the flight he had taken to California aboard Air Force One.

Gulley tensed, waiting for an explosion. Instead, Nixon sat in silence a long moment. Finally, he asked who was behind the move to charge him for the flight to California. Was it Ford, he wanted to know, or his staff? Gulley assured him that Ford was not involved; the idea had come from his aides, Hartmann and Marsh in particular.

Nixon sighed. "Well, if that's what the bastards want, I'll pay."

He said nothing for a moment more, then thanked Gulley for his information. "You know," Nixon said, "I'm really sorry that I didn't spend more time talking to people in the White House like you. Bob [Haldeman], of course, always prevented it. But I've been thinking it over the last few days. If I had it to do over again, that's one of the things I would do differently. Talk to people like you, I mean."

Nixon fumbled in his desk drawer, as if searching for something. "I'd like to give you a memento." Nixon smiled self-consciously; the desk drawer was empty. He buzzed Bull and told him to bring in a presidential watch.

"I really appreciate your being available," Nixon said, as he presented Gulley with the gift. "I'd like you to know that nothing more can hurt me, but associating with me can hurt those who do. You should always remember that, because the media aren't going to let up on me. This is not going to satisfy them. They won't be satisfied until they have me in jail. You should keep that in mind."

"There are worse things than jail," Nixon said to an aide, late on the night before he left the White House. "There is no telephone there. There is, instead, peace. A hard table to write on. The best political writing in this century has been done from jail." He mentioned Lenin and Gandhi; maybe, he said, it would be that way for him.

His tone then had been fatalistic, almost offhand. Now, it was different. Nixon's comment to Gulley about his enemies not being satisfied "until they have me in jail" was neither casual nor hypothetical. The prospect had become a real one, and it terrified him. If he were brought back to Washington for trial, he told a friend, he would not survive.

But for Special Watergate Prosecutor Leon Jaworski, he would be there even now. The Watergate grand jury that had indicted Haldeman, Ehrlichman and Mitchell the previous March had been prepared to indict Nixon as well, but been dissuaded from doing so only at Jaworski's strenuous urging. Worried by the constitutional problems of charging a sitting President and concerned that such an indictment would make it harder to convict Haldeman, Ehrlichman and Mitchell, Jaworski had warned the jury that if it did return an indictment, he would not sign it. He further cautioned that if Nixon were indicted, the President, as commander in chief of the armed forces, might surround the White House with troops. The grand jury had been dubious but had nonetheless gone along, settling for naming Nixon as an unindicted coconspirator instead. Now, however, the basis for Jaworski's opposition was gone. The same grand jury was still sitting, and as the September 9 trial date of Haldeman, Ehrlichman and Mitchell approached, pressure was mounting to have Nixon join them in the dock.

The American Bar Association (ABA) had already gone on record favoring his prosecution, approving without dissent a resolution at its national convention that the law must be applied impartially "regardless of the position or status of any individual alleged to have violated the law." According to the polls, a majority of Nixon's countrymen felt the same. "Would it be just to permit [Nixon] to go untried while some two dozen of his agents have already paid the penalty of conviction or face trial for crimes committed on his behalf?" *Time* magazine commented. "What of justice for such as Charles Colson, Egil Krogh, Jeb Stuart Magruder, Herbert Kalmbach, Donald Segretti and the lesser Watergate burglars who already have been imprisoned? What of justice in a historical perspective, when so many have admitted to their guilt, if Nixon were allowed to cling to the fiction that he resigned only because he had lost his 'political base' in Congress?" In Congress itself, sentiments were divided. Massachusetts Republican Edward Brooke, who had been the first GOP senator to call for Nixon's resignation, had introduced a "sense of the Congress" resolution recommending that Nixon be spared prosecution, provided he made a full, public confession of Watergate guilt. Thus far, however, Brooke's resolution had found little support. Feelings were more hawkish in the House, where the Articles of Impeachment unanimously voted by the Judiciary Committee had, in effect, indicted Nixon of crimes that were punishable in the courts by more than thirty years' imprisonment and more than $50,000 in fines. On August 22, the committee released a 528-page final report. Approved by the full House by a vote of 412 to 3, it detailed "clear and convincing evidence" that Nixon had obstructed justice thirty-six times; "condoned, encouraged, and in some instances, directed, coached and personally helped to fabricate" perjury by his aides, and abused the powers of his office through misuse of such agencies as the FBI, CIA and IRS.

The final decision about whether to prosecute rested with Jaworski, and since mid-August, Nixon had made a number of calls to his remaining supporters in Congress, trying to learn his intentions. In some conversations, he was confident and controlled. Talking with Congressman G. V. ("Sonny") Montgomery of Mississippi, Nixon barely mentioned his legal problems, and spent most of the time chatting about politics and urging support for Ford. But at other moments, Nixon's composure fragmented. Phoning Congressman Dan Kuykendall of Tennessee to ask what he knew of Jaworski's plans, Nixon could not bring himself to utter the prosecutor's name. "We've got problems with that fellow, uh, uh . . ." Nixon fumbled. "Jaworski?" Kuykendall offered. "Yes," Nixon said. Then he asked, "Do you think people want to pick the carcass?"

Kuykendall had no answer, and it was that uncertainty that was preying on Nixon. Late in August, he called an old friend in the Senate.

They bantered for a few moments about politics, Nixon showing no sign of strain. Suddenly, his mood shifted, and he started talking about Jaworski and prison and what his enemies—"the jackals," he called them—might do to him. Finally, he began to weep.

When would they leave him alone? Richard Nixon asked. When?

3
The Pardon

The irony would always be that Richard Nixon had never really liked the one man who could spare him.

Gerald Ford had not been his first choice for vice president, even his second or third. If someone had to replace him, Nixon would have preferred Ronald Reagan, who, he judged, was "great on the tube," or, better still, John Connally, the slippery-smooth Texas tough guy whose passage to high office Nixon had been trying to arrange since 1970. Gerald Ford was not good on television. And certainly he was not tough. He was slow on the uptake, and slower still to comprehend the motives of the men around him. "A plodder," *The Wall Street Journal* called him, a "party wheelhorse who often speaks and apparently thinks in clichés." A man, it was said less kindly, "who could not fart and chew gum at the same time."

Jerry Ford took the gibes and grinned. "I am a Ford," he said of himself, "not a Lincoln."

What he really was, this former eagle scout, Rotarian and 33d-degree Mason who loved golf and wore double-knit suits, just as they did back home in Grand Rapids, Michigan—what he had been his entire public career—was nice. He made friends easily, and the ones he had made in Congress would see to it that he was confirmed.

It was enough, in the aftermath of Spiro Agnew's resignation, to gain the second-highest office in the land. Nixon hadn't liked making the appointment—"Can you imagine Jerry Ford sitting in this chair?" he laughed to Nelson Rockefeller—could not even bring himself to inform Ford personally that he was his vice presidential choice. Even afterward, the choice still rankled. Sending one of the pens with which he had signed Ford's nomination to his White House counsel, Fred Buzhardt, Nixon enclosed a note. "Here," it said, "is the damn pen I signed Jerry Ford's nomination with."

But in one respect, Richard Nixon could not fault Jerry Ford. The vice president was loyal—almost pathetically so.

"He's been my friend for 25 years," Ford said of the man who had appointed him. "He is my friend. I believe he is innocent of any charges." He traveled a hundred thousand miles saying it in five hundred public appearances in forty states, and he continued saying it, heedless of advice, even to the political damage he was doing himself, to the end. The night of July 25, 1974, as the members of the House Judiciary Committee were explaining on national television why they would vote the next day to impeach Richard Nixon, Gerald Ford was in Muncie, Indiana, telling a crowd, "I can say from the bottom of my heart that the President of the United States is innocent . . . He is right!"

But events had proved Nixon neither innocent nor right, and now it was Gerald Ford, and Gerald Ford alone, who could legally forgive him.

The idea of a presidential pardon, not only for Nixon, but for all the figures caught up in the Watergate net, had been percolating since long before Nixon left office. It intensified on July 24, 1974, with the discovery by White House lawyers of a taped conversation between Nixon and Haldeman June 23, 1973—the long-sought-after "smoking gun." The tape's contents—explicit instructions from Nixon on how the FBI's investigation was to be terminated—were damning, and, with a unanimous Supreme Court decision the same day, ordering Nixon to turn over the tapes Jaworski had subpoenaed, there was no way of holding them back. Impeachment was now certain; conviction by the Senate only slightly less likely. Resignation had become the only option.

After conferring with Haig, Fred Buzhardt, special White House counsel for Watergate, ordered his staff to draw up a list of all current and potential Watergate defendants who would be eligible for a presidential pardon. The staff came up with more than thirty names, among them, Nixon's. Buzhardt called Nixon, who was spending the weekend at Camp David, and while Haig and James St. Clair, Nixon's Watergate attorney, listened in, reported that the entire Watergate issue would be "mooted" if Nixon pardoned all the Watergate defendants and then himself. Nixon listened without comment.

A week later, on August 1, Buzhardt met with Haig to review the pardon possibilities. Buzhardt said Nixon had three options: he could pardon himself, then resign; he could pardon Mitchell, Haldeman and Ehrlichman and the other Watergate figures and then resign; or he could resign without doing anything, hoping that Ford would pardon him. Haig expressed surprise that the presidential pardoning authority was that sweeping. Buzhardt, who had researched the question carefully, assured him that it was.

In all of this, Ford, as usual, had been left almost totally in the dark. He had made only one public comment about the possibility of pardoning Nixon, that during his vice presidential confirmation hearings. Asked if he could conceive of any circumstances in which he might grant Nixon a pardon, Ford had replied, evenly and firmly, "I don't think the American people would stand for it."

But that had been in 1973, before the revelations, before the tapes, before the world, as Gerald Ford had known it, turned upside down.

It all began to change at three-thirty the afternoon of August 1, 1974. Alexander Haig was in Ford's office, and he was bearing bad news. A new tape had been discovered. It would contradict Nixon's version of events and likely tip the vote in the House; resignation was now a serious possibility. Was Ford prepared to take over the presidency within a very short time?

Ford, who had just returned from a Midwestern speaking tour defending Nixon and was about to depart on a similar swing through the South, said nothing as Haig talked on, describing the transition problems the new President would have to face. Emphasizing every word, Haig said, "A President has the power to grant a pardon."

Ford appeared startled and confused. Before he could say anything, Haig added that the situation was fluid; it wasn't certain that Nixon would resign. Some people on the White House staff, though, believed he would resign if Ford agreed to offer him a pardon in exchange. Haig emphasized that these weren't his suggestions, and that he wasn't recommending any one course of action over another. He simply wanted to know whether Ford's assessment of the situation matched his.

Still shaken, Ford said that it did, then asked Haig if he was certain about the presidential pardoning authority.

Haig replied, "It is my understanding from a White House lawyer that a President does have authority to grant a pardon before a criminal action has been taken against an individual."

Over the next twenty-four hours, Ford discussed what Haig had told him with a handful of intimates, including Hartmann, and Bryce Harlow, a veteran Washington lobbyist, who had been an adviser to six Presidents. Both were appalled by Haig's seeming offer of a pardon deal, and only slightly less dismayed by Ford's passive reaction to it. Hartmann was especially vehement. Ford, he said, "should have taken Haig by the scruff of the neck and the seat of the pants and thrown him the hell out of [his] office," then "called an immediate press conference and told the world why." Harlow, to whom Ford spoke the afternoon of August 4, focused on the likely background of Haig's visitation. He was certain that Haig had not broached the idea of a pardon on his own authority, and equally sure that the notion had not originated with "the White House staff." Nixon had to have been behind it, and, for Ford, that was the danger. Whether Nixon resigned or was forced out, sooner or later Ford would have to deal with the question of pardoning him. When he did, Harlow advised, "there must not be any cause for anyone to cry 'deal.'" It was crucial, Harlow added, to set Haig straight immediately.

Ford agreed, and, lest there were any mistake to his meaning, jotted down what he would tell Haig. A few minutes later he phoned the general at his White House office. Reading verbatim what he had written, Ford told him: "I want you to understand that I have no intention of recommending what the President should do about resigning or not resigning and that nothing we talked about yesterday afternoon should be given any consideration in whatever decision the President may wish to make."

"You're right," Haig replied.

Since then, the pardon question had remained on the White House back burner, simmering, but out of sight. The new President and his people were in the midst of a honeymoon. He was being pictured in the press toasting English muffins and swimming laps in his suburban backyard pool. His popularity in the Gallup Poll was at a historic high. With a great, collective sigh of relief, the country was beginning to trust him.

Apart from repeating Ford's quote that "I don't think the American people would stand for it," the White House had made no comment about the possibility of a Nixon pardon. But the time for silence was quickly passing. On August 21, Senate Republican leader Hugh Scott, reacting to ABA president Chesterfield Smith's comment that "no man is above the law," snapped to reporters, "For God's sake, enough is enough. [Nixon's] been hung, and it doesn't seem to me that in addition he should be drawn and quartered." Four days later, on August 25, during an appearance on NBC's *Meet the Press*, Nelson Rockefeller, whose vice presidential nomination was still pending, was asked whether he agreed with Scott's remarks. Rockefeller, who had not discussed the matter with Ford, answered emphatically that he did.

Two days after Rockefeller's television appearance, on the eve of his first formal press conference, Ford met with his aides to discuss what had suddenly become a problem. Playing the role of reporter, Hartmann asked whether he would put an end to all the pardon speculation. Ford ducked. He had heard no such talk, he answered, adding that, in any case, it was inappropriate for him to discuss such matters while cases were pending in the courts. Another voice inquired: "Does that mean that you disagree with your Vice-President designate, Governor Rockefeller, and your Senate leader, Hugh Scott, both of whom have stated publicly that President Nixon has suffered enough?" Not at all, Ford smiled. Both Rockefeller and Scott had a fine feeling for the public pulse, and, while personally he tended to agree with them, as President he had larger legal and constitutional responsibilities.

The answer pleased Ford's aides. If he hewed to that line during the actual press conference, they predicted, the talk about pardoning Nixon would soon blow away.

That night, as Ford went over his briefing papers for the next afternoon's press conference, two of the Nixon holdovers on his staff were talking on the phone. Both of them were anguished. Len Garment, who had been his counsel, and Ray Price, who had been his speechwriter, had once been part of the Nixon inner circle, New York branch. But their origins (Garment was liberal and Jewish; Price, a soft-spoken former newspaper reporter, had attended Yale) and decent inclinations had never really been trusted by the Haldeman-Ehrlichman axis, and when Watergate began to unfold, their access to Nixon had been drastically cut back. Nonetheless, they had remained loyal, and, after the resignation, increasingly worried over Nixon's fate.

Garment, who once had been Nixon's law partner, was all but certain that the former President would soon be indicted, and that, if he were, he could not possibly receive a fair trial. That evening, when he had come home from the White House, he had drafted a handwritten memo to Ford, arguing the case for clemency and putting emphasis on sparing the nation any further torment. Warning that Ford would "very likely lose control of the situation" unless he took action "by announcing a pardon today," Garment had written:

"The country is struggling to get on its feet. Public feeling toward Richard Nixon is extremely confused. There is a drift toward prosecution stimulated by a variety of reasons, but it has not yet crystallized. At this point most of the country does not want Richard Nixon hounded, perhaps literally, to death. Once the institutional machinery starts rolling, however, and the press fastens on Nixon as a criminal defendant, Presidential action will be immensely more difficult to justify and therefore, perhaps, impossible to take.

"The country trusts President Ford and will follow him on this matter at this time."

As he read his words to Price, Garment found a sympathetic ear. Price, too, was concerned, not so much by the legal aspects of Nixon's predicament, but whether he would be able, physically and mentally, to withstand the rigors of prosecution. Price doubted it. He had heard the tales about Nixon's alleged depression and erratic behavior, and they sounded correct. Garment, he told him, was right, especially about the need for speed. Nixon could not drag on in legal limbo. Ford had to be convinced to announce the pardon at tomorrow's press conference.

The next morning, Price arrived at the White House at 6:00 A.M. and immediately went to his office to begin preparing a pardon proclamation. With it, he attached a note, telling Ford that a Nixon pardon "turns on considerations that are essentially political . . . considerations of the broader public interest, not merely of the mechanical application of laws written for other purposes and other circumstances."

Garment, too, had gotten to the White House early. In his briefcase, stuffed in brown envelopes, were two copies of the memo he had written and rewritten most of the night. He gave one to Philip Buchen, Ford's general counsel, after the regular morning senior staff meeting. Buchen read it and handed the document back. A pardon now, he said, would be premature. Garment had better luck with the envelope he gave to Haig. Haig read its contents, told Garment he agreed, and added that Ford did as well. Garment, he said, should stand by. "It's all set," Haig told him. "He's going to do it this afternoon."

Gerald Ford was smiling as he went in to confront the press, and the men and women who had gathered to question him smiled back. There was a new atmosphere in the White House; the old adversarial bitterness had drained away. Then Helen Thomas of UPI got up to ask the first question.

"Mr. President," she began, ". . . do you agree with the [American] Bar Association that the laws apply equally to all men, or do you agree with Governor Rockefeller that former President Nixon should have immunity from prosecution? . . . And specifically, would you use your pardon authority if necessary?"

Ford started off well enough—"Now, the expression made by Governor Rockefeller, I think, coincides with the general view and point of view of the American people. I subscribe to that." Had he ended there, as he had during the previous day's dress rehearsal, the questioning might have turned into smoother channels. But Ford went on: "Let me add in the last ten days or two weeks I have asked for prayers for guidance on this very important point. In this situation, I am the final authority. There have been no charges made, there has been no action by the courts, there has been no action by any jury. And until any legal process has been undertaken, I think it is unwise and untimely for me to make any commitment."

After that, the press moved in, pushing Ford for specifics, and, ever genial, he obliged. "I make no commitment one way or the other," he said at one point. "It is an option and a proper option for any President."

Another hand popped up. "Mr. President, you have emphasized here your option of granting a pardon to the former President." Before the questioner could finish, Ford cut in, "I intend to."

"You intend to have that option," the reporter repeated. "If an indictment is brought, would you grant a pardon before any trial took place?"

Ford shifted uncomfortably. "I said at the outset that until the matter reaches me, I am not going to make any comment during the process of whatever charges are made."

Taken literally, Ford's words had committed him to nothing. He was merely biding time, weighing options, allowing the law to take its course. Their implication, however, was clear enough. A President, at least none the press was used to dealing with, did not air his thought processes aloud unless a decision had already been reached. What guileless Jerry Ford was doing was lofting a trial balloon.

In the East Room, where the ordinarily closed drapes had been drawn back, symbolizing the administration's openness, there was an audible stir, the buzzing commotion of people who had been told something they had not expected to hear. A moment later it was replaced by the scrape of pushed-back chairs as reporters raced for the phones.

Alexander Haig had watched Ford's performance over the television set in his office, and he was not pleased. Ford had come to the very brink of making a pardon announcement, then drawn back. In the process, he had confused everyone, including Haig. The general strode down the corridor to the Oval Office, went in and closed the door. Ford would require another push.*

The next afternoon, as the *Washington Star* was informing its readers that a pardon deal would soon be struck among Nixon, the White

---

* Ford later denied under oath that any such contacts had taken place. In an unprecedented appearance before the House Judiciary Subcommittee on Criminal Justice on October 17, Ford, who had volunteered to testify to present his version of the events leading to the pardon, stated: "At no time after I became President on August 9, 1974, was the subject of a pardon for Richard M. Nixon raised by the former President or by anyone representing him. . . . Nobody made any recommendations to me for the pardon of the former President."

Ford further denied—"There's no truth to it whatsoever, as far as I know"—that Kissinger had told him that Nixon might commit suicide. "Whatever information [about Nixon's mental condition] was generally known to me at the time of my pardon decision," Ford insisted, "was based on my own observations of his condition at the time he resigned as President and observations reported to me after that from those who had later seen or talked to him."

Later, after *Washington Post* reporters Bob Woodward and Carl Bernstein began looking into the circumstances surrounding the pardon, Ford, through Buchen, acknowledged that he had discussed the pardon with Haig the day of his first press conference.

Haig, for his part, was anxious to keep his role in securing the Nixon pardon hidden. In a report on the pardon prepared for senior government officials outside the White House, an aide who had seen Haig leave Ford's office on the afternoon of August 1, wrote:

"Haig spent the day in the White House trying to convince the President that he should not go up before the Congressional committee to discuss the pardon. Haig is concerned that the revelation that he, Haig, offered Mr. Ford a resignation from Mr. Nixon in exchange for a commitment that Nixon would be pardoned would cause Haig problems with regard to his return to uniform. Apparently, there are a number of points in which Haig will not look very good."

House and the special prosecutor, Haig was in Ford's office again. With him was Henry Kissinger. The topic of discussion was the pardon, and both men were upset.

The President, Haig said, could not afford to temporize further. National security was at stake. For eighteen months, Watergate had put the rest of the world on hold. Alliances had unraveled; crucial questions had gone begging. Already, State had picked up unconfirmed reports of Nixon writing "strange letters" to various foreign leaders. Unless Ford moved quickly, there was no telling what Nixon would do; the worst was entirely possible. There might be, said Haig, "a personal and national tragedy."

In a city like Washington, such meetings do not remain secret long, and, by the end of the day, Melvin Laird, Nixon's former secretary of defense, and one of Ford's oldest colleagues on the Hill, had heard of the Oval Office gathering. Hurriedly, he phoned Buchen to warn him that Ford was heading toward political disaster. He beseeched him not to allow Ford to be alone with Haig and Kissinger again.

But by then the advice reaching Ford was coming from all quarters, even from his Marine Corps aide, who was recommending a pardon to break, as he told his commander in chief, the country's "Watergate addiction."

Though Nixon himself had not called Ford, others around him were lobbying hard. Abplanalp and Rebozo had met with Julie, Tricia, Eddie and David and urged them to contact Haig about Nixon's health. That had already been done. Now, the appeals were coming to Ford directly from members of Nixon's family, in the person of David Eisenhower. After Ford's press conference, Eisenhower had called from San Clemente to report that his father-in-law was in a sorry physical and emotional state. One moment, said Eisenhower, Nixon was up, almost euphoric; the next, he was down, depressed and despairing. Something had to be done, Eisenhower urged; the burden had to be lifted. If it wasn't, Ford later quoted him as saying, Nixon "might go off the deep end."

Matters finally came to a head on Friday, August 30. That afternoon, Ford summoned three of his closest confidants: Buchen, his counsel, and the most instinctively cautious of his advisers; Hartmann, who was still pushing for a clean sweep of the Nixon holdovers, including Haig; and Jack Marsh, who, having finished with his transition chores, had taken over as Ford's legal adviser. When the three men entered the Oval Office, they found Ford at his desk, Haig sitting in front of him, squirming nervously in his chair.

Ford began by saying that he had been giving the possibility of pardoning Nixon considerable thought since his press conference, and that one of the things that bothered him was that even now he wasn't at all clear on the full extent of his pardoning authority. Turning to Buchen, he instructed him to research the point, though quietly, lest word of the enterprise leaked out.

Ford leaned back and very deliberately filled and lit his pipe. A moment passed. Ford tilted forward. He was inclined, he said casually, to grant Nixon a pardon and to do it quickly, just as soon as he was sure that he had the power to do so.

There was a silence in the room, broken only by the ticking of an antique grandfather clock. To Hartmann, it sounded like machine-gun fire.

Haig cleared his throat and asked to be excused. Considering the turn the conversation was taking, he thought his continued presence was inappropriate. Ford waved him back down into his chair. Then, one by one, he ticked off the reasons for granting Nixon a pardon: it would be degrading having a former President dragged into the prisoner's dock; if Nixon were prosecuted, finding an impartial jury to decide his case would be well-nigh impossible; the legal process would drag on for years; a trial would tear open the wounds that had been left by Watergate; and in the end the public would cry "enough," forcing whoever was President to grant a pardon.

"If eventually," Ford finished, "why not now?"

Again, there was silence. Finally, Buchen spoke up. "I can't argue with what you feel is right, but is this the right time?"

Ford answered. "Is there ever a right time?"

The meeting continued, though without Haig, who had used the excuse of taking a telephone call to leave the room. It was apparent to Ford's advisers that he had made up his mind and was in no mood to change it. Nevertheless, Hartmann made a passing attempt. "The fit is going to hit the shan," he warned. He then began reading from the transcript of Ford's press conference.

"Here are your own words, '. . . until any legal process has been undertaken, I think it is unwise and untimely for me to make any commitment.' And then they asked if you meant that pardon was an option you would consider 'depending on what the courts will do.' And you answered that 'until it gets to me, I make no commitment. . . . I am not going to make any comment during the process of whatever charges are made.' "

Ford's jaw tightened. "You didn't read the part about my not ruling it out. I refused to make any commitment one way or the other. I said that, too, every time, and I was very firm about it."

"Well, okay," Hartmann conceded. "Maybe that's what you meant, but that isn't what I heard or what most people heard. What everybody believes is that you may pardon Nixon someday but *not* right away. And not until there have been some further legal steps in the case. And, if you do, the professional Nixon-haters in the press and in Congress will go right up the wall. You are going to have a firestorm of protest that will make the Saturday Night Massacre seem mild."

"Sure there will be criticism," Ford shrugged. "But it will flare up and die down. If I wait six months, or a year, there will still be a 'firestorm' from the Nixon-haters, as you call them. They wouldn't like it if I waited until he was on his deathbed. But most Americans will understand."

Hartmann made one last effort. "I agree with Phil: This isn't the right time. It takes time for public sentiment to shift. Sooner or later, they'll get a bellyful of those people who keep hounding a former President and howling for more blood. Why can't you wait until some sympathy sets in? It's already begun. *Newsweek* says that 55 percent of the people think further prosecution should be dropped."

With visible irritation, Ford replied that he was not going to depend on public opinion polls to tell him what was right. A few minutes later the meeting broke up. As Hartmann left the room, he felt he had just witnessed a friend commit suicide.

If, as he told his advisers, Ford was "99 percent committed" to granting Nixon a pardon, there still remained a number of untied ends. One was determining the extent of Ford's pardoning authority.

Under Article II, Section 2 of the Constitution, the President's power in such decisions seemed absolute. The Constitution said nothing, however, about granting pardons to persons, like Nixon, who as yet had been accused of no crimes.

To find out whether Ford had such authority, Buchen commissioned Benton Becker, the young transition lawyer who had succeeded in halting Gulley's shipments to San Clemente, to hunt through law libraries over the long Labor Day weekend. Becker came up with several precedents, the most relevant of which was a 1915 case involving a New York newspaper editor, whose paper had published a series of articles about customs frauds committed by U.S. Treasury Department employees. Hauled before a grand jury, the editor refused to divulge his sources, and was thereupon presented with a document signed by Woodrow Wilson, granting him "a full and unconditional pardon for all offenses against the United States which he . . . has committed or may have committed or taken part in." As it turned out, the editor still declined to testify, was jailed for contempt, and eventually the case reached the Supreme Court, which overturned his conviction.

The analogy between the editor's situation and the Nixon pardon was not perfect, but, as far as Ford was concerned, it was close enough.

Meanwhile, there was still the problem of Leon Jaworski.

Since Nixon's resignation, the special prosecutor had been keeping an even lower profile than usual. Other than instructing his office to issue a statement saying that no deals had been made in exchange for Nixon's resignation, he had made no comment, pro or con, about the possibility of a pardon, or when or if he planned to prosecute Nixon. Like Ford, he was keeping his options open.

Very quietly, he was also keeping track of the opinion polls, as well as of the memoranda that flowed in from his staff, which were running heavily in favor of Nixon's quick indictment. In addition, he had been in contact with Mississippi Senator James Eastland, chairman of the Senate Judiciary Committee, and with whom Nixon had recently had a tearful telephone conversation about his legal problems. Eastland recounted the conversation and added, "He's in bad shape, Leon."

Jaworski's response had been noncommittal. As an officer of the court, he could not discuss cases that were pending, especially one involving a former President. And for Jaworski that was the rub: Nixon *was* a former President; trying him would be unprecedented. Simply selecting a jury, assuming an impartial one could be found, would require months, and once the trial commenced, there would be complicated legal wrangling every step of the way. Taken together—jury selection, trial, appeals—the process could stretch out for years, and Jaworski, who had been in Washington nearly a year, was anxious to return home. His law practice in Houston brought in $200,000 a year, and serving as special prosecutor had been a financial strain, one that was becoming increasingly intolerable as the months dragged on. Also, he had experienced chest pains and shortness of breath during a recent weekend in Texas. His health at the moment was fine, his doctor told him, but he was sixty-nine years old, and the sooner he got away from the pressures of his office, the better. Jaworski had told his staff of his yearning to retire, but he had also promised to stay on until, as he put it, "the big decision" was made.

Legally, the facts seemed clear cut. Even before the discovery of the smoking gun, Jaworski's staff had concluded that there was more than sufficient evidence to convict Nixon on a variety of charges. Jaworski, however, had hung back. "There are conflicting factors for us that [the] general public does not have to deal with," he told his staff. What those factors were, Jaworski did not spell out, but the staff got a hint when Jaworski instructed his press spokesman to put together an analysis of news reports during the week of Nixon's resignation to determine how pervasive had been the depiction of Nixon's guilt. It received a further clue when Jaworski asked Nixon's newly appointed attorney, a Kennedy Justice Department veteran named Herbert J. Miller, to submit a brief, arguing the case *against* indictment.

Without telling his staff, Jaworski had also been in touch with Buchen, with whom he was sharing the same hotel. On Wednesday morning, September 4, the two men met again and without mentioning the pardon directly, Buchen asked how long it would be before Nixon could be brought to trial. Jaworski refused to commit himself, but promised to send Buchen a letter on the subject later that day. The letter, written by Jaworski, arrived by messenger in Buchen's office a few hours later. It stated that, in view of pretrial publicity, it would "require a delay, before selection of a jury is begun, of a period from nine months to a year, perhaps even longer." Along with the note, Jaworski attached a memorandum he had received the day before from Henry Ruth, his chief assistant, listing ten areas of potential criminal liability for Nixon, none of which had to do with the Watergate cover-up. Ruth, who had already urged Jaworski to exempt Nixon from prosecution, had concluded: "One can make a strong argument for leniency, and, if President Ford is so inclined, I think he ought to do it early rather than late." The signal that Jaworski would not oppose a Nixon pardon had been delivered.

Only one matter remained outstanding: the custody of Nixon's papers and tapes.

By custom and historical precedent, a President's papers became his personal property the moment he left office. Nixon, however, was an altogether different case. For one thing, both the papers and the tapes (42 million pages of the former, 880 reels of the latter—enough to fill three 50-foot boxcars) were crucial evidence in any future Watergate trial, including Nixon's. For another, Nixon, in a move that contributed ultimately to one of the impeachment counts against him, had deeded the papers to the nation, claiming (and artfully backdating) a $432,000 income tax deduction in the process. Complicating the issue further was a letter Nixon had written to Arthur Sampson, administrator of the General Services Administration, on August 8, 1974, the last full day of his presidency, modifying the terms of the chattel deed so that "the undersigned [namely, Nixon] shall have the right of access to any and all of the Materials and the right to copy or to have copied any and all of the Materials by any means of his selection, and to take and retain possession of any and all such copies for any purpose whatsoever." Moreover, the letter went on, "Prior to January 1, 1985, no person or persons shall have the right of access to such Materials except the undersigned and those who may be designated in writing by the undersigned." In short, Nixon was claiming full possession of the papers and tapes against any and all challengers, including the courts.

Thus far, the White House position on the papers had been confusing. In a briefing for reporters August 14, terHorst said that while the papers were at present "in the protective custody of the Secret Service," they had been "ruled to be the property of former President Nixon." TerHorst, whose information had come from Buzhardt, said he was not sure who had made such a ruling, but added that Ford had not been a party to it.

A reporter asked, "Are you saying there was agreement among the different staffs, the Special Prosecutor, the Justice Department and the White House legal staff?"

TerHorst answered, "I am assuming there would be, because I am sure neither one would take unilateral action."

But there had been unilateral action—on the part of Buzhardt and the Justice Department—and Jaworski, who had not been consulted, was livid. He quickly communicated his unhappiness to the White House, and the next day terHorst admitted he had been "in error." A day later, terHorst announced that the papers and tapes would remain in White House custody pending "an orderly and more studied effort to resolve questions of when and under what conditions possession and sole control of the property would be transferred."

Ford, in fact, was anxious to be rid of the materials as quickly as possible, in part because maintaining them was presenting a sheer housekeeping problem. They were being boxed and packed on the fourth floor of the Old Executive Office Building, and, as the work continued, the Secret Service expressed worries whether the floor would stand the weight. Several of Ford's aides, including Haig and Attorney General William Saxbe, who had written a legal opinion to the effect, were recommending shipping them to San Clemente forthwith. The most heated opposition came from Becker, who had been working on the papers problem since Ford's inauguration. If the papers were given to Nixon, Becker told Ford, "history will record this as the final act of cover-up—there will be one helluva bonfire in San Clemente." Becker proposed several alternatives, from convincing Jaworski to subpoena the papers to placing them in a trust with Sirica as guardian. Each of them, however, was rejected. Clearly, something had to be done, and the prospect of the pardon presented the ideal leverage.

On Tuesday, September 3, Buchen and Becker met with Miller in an attempt to work out an agreement. Nothing about a pardon was said, but Miller, who had successfully defended several other Watergate figures, guessed what was in the wind. By the end of the conference, the two sides had fashioned a compromise. Under its terms, Nixon would deed the papers and tapes to the United States, and the government, in turn, would store the materials at a federal facility near San Clemente. Formal legal ownership would be shared jointly. For a period of from three to five years, all the materials would be subject to subpoena for use in possible court cases. When that time elapsed, Nixon could order the papers and tapes destroyed.

The next day, at another meeting to work out the language of the draft agreement, Buchen for the first time revealed that Ford was considering a pardon. "Look," he added, "I think it's important that there be a statement of true contrition from the former President. The President tells me we can't dictate the statement, but in the interests of your client and the President, I hope you would persuade your client to develop something that would tell the world, 'Yes, he did it, and he's accepting the pardon because he's guilty.' " Miller said he understood and promised to get Nixon's reaction. While he couldn't predict with certainty what Nixon would say, Miller indicated there would be no problem.

But there was a problem, though how large was not immediately apparent. All Nixon would tell Miller was that he wanted him to fly to San Clemente to work out several "technical points." Miller broke the news to Buchen, coupling it with a suggestion that someone from Ford's legal team accompany him.

Ford did not seem overly concerned. His more immediate worry was selecting the proper emissary to send. Contacts between the White House and San Clemente were a sensitive issue; the dispatch of a senior figure like Buchen was sure to be discovered. He needed a less visible presence, someone both trustworthy and discreet. He settled on Becker, who had performed a variety of unpleasant chores for him in the past, including assisting in his ill-starred effort to impeach Supreme Court Justice William O. Douglas.

Thursday afternoon, the fifth, Ford called Becker in to give him his instructions. Becker was authorized to say that, while a firm decision had not been reached, a pardon probably would be forthcoming. Above all, though, he was to resolve the question of the papers and the tapes. There was one other matter: Nixon's "statement of contrition." Becker had to extract it in the strongest possible language. Haig, who was in the office, cut in: "You'll never get it." As Ford walked Becker to the door, he put his arm around the lawyer's shoulder. "Be very firm out there," he counseled, "and tell me what you see."

No sooner had Becker departed than Ford, having read over the memorandum Jaworski had sent Buchen, summoned Buchen, Hartmann, Marsh and Haig into his office and declared that he was going to stop "horsing around." Ford said that he had decided to announce the pardon right away, the next morning, if possible.

"When's Benton [Becker] getting back?" the President asked.

Buchen told him the next night at the earliest, and, depending how negotiations proceeded, as late as Saturday.

"Well," said Ford, "I will not wait one day later than Sunday."

His advisers made little protest. All attention was now on San Clemente.

There, it developed, little had changed; the Nixon men were defiant as ever. "Let's get one thing straight immediately," Ziegler told Becker on his arrival late Thursday night. "President Nixon is not issuing any statements whatsoever regarding Watergate, whether Jerry Ford pardons him or not." Becker, who had said nothing to Ziegler about Nixon's "statement of contrition," wondered where he had gotten his information; he guessed it was Haig. Well, Becker replied, if that was the case, he would return to Washington immediately. Would Ziegler contact the pilot to make arrangements? At that, Miller stepped in and calmed both men.

The next day, the atmosphere improved only slightly. Miller had been wrong in assuming that Nixon would accept the compromise over the papers and tapes, at least as he and Buchen had drafted it. What Nixon wanted—indeed, insisted on having—was final authority on granting access, a condition that included the special prosecutor. Miller relayed the news to Becker, who suggested a series of counterproposals. Finally, after twenty-four hours of negotiating, largely between Becker and Ziegler, a tentative agreement was struck. The papers and tapes would be placed under a deed of trust, with Nixon as the grantor, the government as the receiver, and the GSA as the trustee. Third parties, such as scholars and journalists, who wanted access to the materials would have to subpoena the materials, and both the GSA and Nixon would have the right to object to the subpoena on various grounds. After five years, Nixon could order the destruction of any document or tape. In the interval any papers or tapes he wanted for himself would be copied by the GSA.

The arrangement was heavily weighted in Nixon's favor, but it was the most Becker thought he could get. Nixon had been adamant, and he had not been negotiating from strength. It was apparent that Ziegler not only knew that a pardon was a certainty, but that Ford was in a hurry to grant it. How he had come to his information Becker did not know, but there were a number of potential sources, including Haig, with whom both Ziegler and Nixon had been in continual touch. What mattered more to Becker was the leak's effect: Nixon, in effect, had seen Ford's cards before the bidding had begun.

Buchen, whom Becker called at the White House, agreed with his assessment and said that he would recommend that Ford accept. Increasingly anxious to get the pardon question behind him, Ford quickly did.

In the meantime, Nixon was beginning to suffer second thoughts about accepting the pardon at all. How could he accept, he asked Miller, when by accepting he was admitting guilt? Miller tried to reassure him: in and of itself, accepting a pardon was not a formal confession. Nixon was not convinced. "I'd just as soon go through the agony of a trial, so we can scrape away at least all the false charges, and fight it out on those where there may be a doubt."

Fine, Miller replied, but how was he going to get such a trial? Could Nixon tell him how they could find an impartial jury to hear the case? Could he pick a spot where there had not been overwhelming, negative publicity? He couldn't; it was impossible.

Nixon said he needed time to think about it and asked Miller to leave the office. An hour later, Nixon summoned him back. "Well," he said, "I'll sign it. I'm not sure it's the right thing to do . . . but I'll do it."

Negotiations now turned to Nixon's "statement of contrition." Ziegler was still resistant. "Contrition," he told Becker, "is bullshit." Finally, after Becker threatened that Ford would withhold the pardon, Ziegler wrote out one line: "In accordance with the law, I accept this pardon." Becker told him that no statement at all would be better than that. Ziegler went back to his typewriter. He tried again, then a third time. Finally, he gave the fourth attempt to Becker. The statement read:

I have been informed that President Ford has granted me a full and absolute pardon for any charges which might be brought against me for actions taken during the time I was President of the United States. In accepting this pardon, I hope that his compassionate act will contribute to lifting the burden of Watergate from our country.

Here in California, my perspective on Watergate is quite different than what it was while I was embattled in the midst of the controversy and while I was still subject to the unrelenting daily demands of the Presidency itself.

Looking back on what is still in my mind a complex and confusing maze of events, decisions, pressures and personalities, one thing I can see more clearly now is that I was wrong in not acting more decisively and forthrightly in dealing with Watergate, particularly when it reached the stage of judicial proceedings and grew from a political scandal into a national tragedy.

No words can describe the depth of my regret and pain at the anguish my mistakes over Watergate have caused the nation and the Presidency—a nation I so deeply love and an institution I so greatly respect.

I know that many fair-minded people believe that my motivations and actions in the Watergate affair were intentionally self-serving and illegal. I now understand how my own mistakes and misjudgments have contributed to that belief and seemed to support it. This burden is the heaviest of all to bear.

That the way I tried to deal with Watergate was the wrong way is a burden I shall bear for every day of the life that is left to me.

For Becker, there remained only the matter of seeing Nixon personally. Ziegler had initially turned down his request, but Miller intervened, and late Friday afternoon Becker was ushered into Nixon's office. The room, save for a desk and two flags, was barren, as if, Becker later told Ford, its occupant had just moved in.

Nixon greeted him with a weak handshake and slumped down into his chair.

"I'm sure," Becker began, "that Mr. Miller and Mr. Ziegler have told you that President Ford is considering a pardon, and I know they've showed you a draft of the document. Now, there are certain things you should know about pardons, and I should satisfy myself that you do know about them."

"Where do you live?" Nixon asked him.

When Becker replied Washington, Nixon said, "How are the Redskins going to do this year?"

Becker tried to bring the conversation back to the pardon, but it was useless. Nixon's attention span was short; what few remarks he did make ended in midsentence. Finally, after twenty minutes, Becker left the office.

He was outside, waiting for the car that would take him to El Toro, when Ziegler came out to say that Nixon wanted to see him again.

"You're a fine young man," Nixon told Becker when he came back in. "You've been a gentleman. We've had enough bullies." He paused and his voice faltered. "I want to give you something. But look around the office. I don't have anything anymore. They took it all away from me."

"That's all right, Mr. President."

"No, no, no," Nixon said. He opened his desk drawer and pulled out two small boxes containing a set of presidential cuff links and a tiepin. "I asked Pat to get these for me. She got these out of my own jewelry box. There aren't any more in the whole world. I want you to have them."

Becker took the gift and shook Nixon's hand. "I used to have an aide who'd stand by and hand me these," Nixon said, referring to the boxes of jewelry. "I used to have all kinds of things, ashtrays, you know, paperweights and all that. Lots of them. I'm sorry, but this is the best I have now."

When Becker returned to Washington, he recounted the scene to Ford. "I'm not a doctor," Becker said, "but I really have serious questions in my mind whether that man is going to be alive at the time of the next election."

"Well," Ford answered, "1976 is a long time away."

"I don't mean 1976," Becker replied. "I mean 1974."

The sympathy for Nixon soon passed. On Saturday, as Hartmann and Buchen were drafting the wording of Ford's pardon address, Ziegler called from San Clemente with changes in Nixon's "statement of contrition." Ford's face flushed. Angrily, he ordered that no alterations be made. Ziegler backed off. The statement stood.

Late that afternoon, terHorst, who was unaware of what had been going on, was shown a copy of the pardon proclamation. TerHorst read it in disbelief. He had known Ford since 1948, and counted himself one of his closest friends, yet Ford had excluded him from what was certain to be the most important decision of his presidency.

"You know what this means?" he shouted at Hartmann. "Jerry Ford is throwing away his presidency to do a favor for Richard Nixon." He flung the document across the room. "You guys walked into it. Well, that's fine. But I'm not sticking around."

Sunday morning, Gerald Ford rose early, as was his custom. By 8:00 A.M., he was sitting alone in the President's Pew at St. John's Episcopal Church, across from the White House on Lafayette Square. After Communion services, he returned to his office to read over the speech that Hartmann had written. Taking out his fountain pen, Ford wrote in several additional lines about the need for compassion and the state of Nixon's health. Hartmann, whom Ford had specifically instructed not to write anything about Nixon's health, began to protest. Ford cut him off: "I'm tired of arguing about the goddam thing. I just want to get on with it."

Then Ford picked up the phone to begin informing key congressional leaders of his decision. Massachusetts Congressman Tip O'Neill, an old friend with whom Ford often golfed, was stunned. "Jesus, Jerry, don't you think it's a little early?"

A few minutes before the scheduled taping at 11:00 A.M., terHorst entered Ford's office. Under his arm was a manila envelope across which was written in red, "The President—Eyes Only." It contained his resignation, and terHorst had been up all night writing it.

"Mr. President, I have something here that you need to see."

TerHorst tore open the envelope and handed Ford the letter. The President leaned back into his chair and began reading; his face showed no sign of emotion.

Finally, Ford put the letter down and gazed out the window toward the South Lawn and the Rose Garden.

"Jerry," he said, "I'm sorry you feel this way. But it was a decision I had to make. I've made it, and I'm going to stick to it."

Ford rose and shook terHorst's hand. The telephone began to ring. Carl Albert, Speaker of the House, was on the line.

A few moments later, the television crews came in. Ford did not engage in the usual banter; he seemed solemn and slightly nervous. Lying atop his otherwise cleared desk was a manila folder and a single pen. "Are you set?" he asked the technicians. They nodded, and Ford began to read:

"I have come to a decision which I felt I should tell you, and all my fellow citizens, as soon as I was certain in my own mind and conscience that it is the right thing to do."

Five minutes later, he came to the key paragraph.

". . . Now, therefore, I, Gerald R. Ford, President of the United States, pursuant to the pardon power conferred upon me by Article II,

Section 2, of the Constitution, have granted and by these presents do grant a full, free and absolute pardon unto Richard Nixon for all offenses against the United States which he, Richard Nixon, has committed or may have committed or taken part in during the period January 20, 1969, through August 9, 1974."

Ford swept his pen across the bottom of the proclamation with a flourish, got up and, without saying anything more, walked quickly out of the room.

Across the country in San Clemente, Richard Nixon was already awake. Walter Annenberg, the publishing magnate he had appointed ambassador to the Court of St. James, had invited him to spend the week at his estate outside Palm Springs, and he wanted to be on the road by the time the pardon was announced. Outside, Casa Pacifica's grounds were blanketed by a thick carpet of fog. There would be sun in Palm Springs. Nixon was looking forward to the trip.

Gerald Ford had a different date. That afternoon marked the concluding round of the annual Congressional Golf Tournament at Burning Tree, and he and his partner, Melvin Laird, were in the lead. Ford got to the club about one. Laird was waiting for him in the locker room.

"How do you think it went?" Ford asked.

Laird, who had learned about the pardon during an appearance that morning at the Women's National Press Club, shook his head.

"Jerry, don't ask me what I think. We still have a chance to win this golf tournament."

"Mel," Ford said, "I had to get it out of the way. I had to get it out of the way."

They went out to the links. That afternoon, the President of the United States played poorly.

4

Fire Storm

There was a brief pause, a momentary reflex of disbelief, then the fire storm Hartmann had predicted broke with full fury.

Overnight, Ford's popularity dropped twenty-two points in the Gallup Poll, the single sharpest plunge in the poll's history.* Thirty thousand telegrams cascaded in on the White House; by a margin of 6 to 1 they condemned the pardon decision. Across the street, in Lafayette Park, the pickets who had struck their tents only a month before put them up again. A bed sheet was draped across the White House fence: PROMISE ME A PARDON, the message scrawled across it read, AND I'LL MAKE YOU PRESIDENT.

In Congress, where Senator Howard Baker of Tennessee was predicting catastrophe for the GOP come November, there were calls for investigations and general stupefaction. "Difficult to understand," said House Judiciary Chairman Peter Rodino who pronounced himself "distressed and disquieted" by the pardon decision. It would, he added, "reopen a lot of old sores." Illinois Republican John Anderson growled, "Why were we ever stupid enough to think that this awful man would fade away like one of MacArthur's old soldiers? He was always going to be dragged kicking and screaming into oblivion."

The press was indignant. "Ford," declared the Long Island newspaper *Newsday*, "has embraced the demon of Watergate." The *Chicago Tribune* detected "a sour smell . . . in the White House." An editorial in *The New York Times* thundered, "In granting President Nixon an inappropriate and premature grant of clemency, President Ford has affronted the Constitution and the American system of justice. This blundering intervention is a body blow to the President's own credibility and to the public's reviving sense of confidence in the integrity of its government."

* As for the granting of the pardon itself, Gallup found that Americans opposed it by a margin of 62 percent to 31 percent.

That much was immediately apparent. When Ford flew to Pittsburgh to address a conference on urban transportation the day after the pardon, he was booed for the first time in the short life of his presidency, and greeted by demonstrators chanting, "Jail Ford! Jail Ford!" On the campus of the University of Wisconsin, students hoisted an American flag, across which was stenciled NIXON, FORD—THE SAME OLD SHIT. In Los Angeles, a Vietnam veteran who had held three hostages at rifle point during a supposed "combat flashback" was ordered released by Municipal Court Judge Gilbert Alston, who explained, "If a man who almost wrecked the country can be pardoned, this defendant can be released to get proper treatment."

Gamely, Ford tried to explain himself, likening the pardon to a round of golf. "I have never seen a tournament, regardless of how much money or fame or prestige or emotion was involved, that didn't end with the victor extending his hand to the vanquished," he told an audience at the dedication of the World Golf Hall of Fame in Pinehurst, North Carolina. "The pat on the back, the arm around the shoulder, the praise for what was done right and the sympathetic nod for what wasn't . . . are not limited to the 19th hole alone." Then Ford added with a grin, "This afternoon for a few hours, I tried to make a hole in one. Tomorrow morning, I'll be back in Washington, trying to get out of one."

Instead, Ford dug himself in deeper. Hardly had he returned to Washington than his acting spokesman, John Hushen, was announcing that pardons were "under study" for all the Watergate defendants. The statement was quickly retracted, but by then the damage had been done. By the end of the month, Ford would be forced, like Johnson and Nixon before him, to make his way to public appearances through basements and rear entrances, while young people called obscenities after him. At his press conferences, formerly friendly reporters would rise to ask if he saw any "conflict of interests" in granting a pardon to "his lifelong friend and financial benefactor." Rather than pictures of him toasting English muffins and splashing in the backyard pool, the cover of a national magazine would portray him as Bozo the Clown. LADIES AND GENTLEMEN, the headline would read, THE PRESIDENT OF THE UNITED STATES.

Meanwhile, the man he had pardoned remained in the seclusion of Walter Annenberg's Palm Desert estate, saying nothing and lying low.

Sunnylands, as the Annenberg retreat was dubbed, was not so much a residence as a small, elegantly appointed principality set down on 220 irrigated acres at the junction of Bob Hope and Frank Sinatra drives. Sunnylands had its own armed security force, its own golf course and lakes (twenty-seven of them, all man-made), even its own flag, a yellow Mayan rune set on a field of white. The main house, an overgrown California ranch, sprawled over 25,000 square feet, including a single

2000-square-foot master bedroom hung with Renoirs and Van Goghs and an only slightly less cavernous "Room of Memories" stocked with memorabilia from international celebrities and heads of state. Outside, beyond the 4000-square-foot patio, lay an enormous swimming pool, separate guest compounds and meticulously tended gardens, all of them surrounded by a barb-wire-topped, six-foot chain-link fence.

Nixon had come at an inauspicious moment. Annenberg himself was away on business, and many of the surrounding estates were deserted, for even without the pardon, September in Palm Springs was the cruelest month. By day, temperatures in the shade often topped 115 degrees while at night, the Los Angeles smog rolled through the San Gorgonio Pass and bathed the valley in a toxic mist. The San Jacinto Mountains took on strange colors, and frequently there were earthquakes —tremors, it was said, from the anger of Tahquitz, the great god of the Cahulla Indians. According to legend, it was to this valley, and the mountains that surrounded it, that Tahquitz had been banished for misusing his powers and dividing his tribe.

For most of the time since his arrival, Nixon had remained indoors, out of the heat, and away from the press, which ringed the estate's perimeter, telephoto lenses at the ready. One of the few occasions he ventured out, for a reflective pause at the edge of a motor-driven waterfall, a small plane that had been circling overhead swooped down for a closer look. Nixon glanced up, seemed to scowl at the intruder, then headed for the cover of an adjacent cabana.

The same day, a local reporter waylaid Manolo Sanchez as the former President's valet searched through a shopping center for Nixon's favorite pipe tobacco. His boss was fine, Sanchez insisted. "The pardon was a big relief to us all. He is in good spirits, thank you, God."

In fact, Nixon was not fine at all. The reaction to the pardon was troubling him. He hadn't expected it, especially hadn't expected the problems it was causing Ford. He was regretful about that, and a few days into his stay, he called Ford, offering, if it would help, to give the pardon back. Ford thanked him for the gesture, and then—a little curtly, Nixon thought—rang off. That bothered. What bothered even more was his leg. It was killing him.

The problem was thrombophlebitis, a common—and, in some cases, fatal—vein inflammation to which pregnant women and people who spent too much time at their desks or on long airplane flights are susceptible. Nixon had suffered from it off and on since 1964, when his left leg began swelling painfully during a business trip to Japan. Dormant most of the time, the phlebitis had flared again the previous June, two days before Nixon was to leave on a twelve-day, fifteen-thousand-mile trip to the Middle East. Prideful of his good health—he boasted he had not suffered so much as a headache in sixty years—Nixon said nothing to his doctors and departed on schedule, arriving in Salzburg, Austria, after a nine-hour flight. By then, he was in excruciating pain. After examining him, Major General Tkach recommended immediate hospitalization, warning Nixon there was an "outside chance" that a clot caused by the phlebitis might break off and kill him. But Nixon wouldn't hear of it. Instructing his staff to keep his condition secret, he continued with the trip and in Egypt hiked up to the pyramids despite a noticeable limp.

As a result, the phlebitis grew worse. At one point during his visit to Egypt, after he had been standing several hours on a train, waving to the crowds between Cairo and Alexandria, Nixon called Ziegler into his private compartment. Nixon's face was dead white. Momentarily, Ziegler thought that he might faint. "Ron," Nixon gasped, "I don't know if I can make it."

The phlebitis was still bothering him when, a week after returning from the Middle East, Nixon set off for the Soviet Union on what was destined to be his last official overseas trip. On the flight across the Atlantic to Brussels, his affected leg was encased in a tight-fitting support stocking, swathed in hot packs and propped up on the seat in front of him. That lessened the immediate discomfort; it also alerted the press, which began reporting on the phlebitis as soon as the plane touched down in Belgium. Irritated, Nixon instructed his doctors and spokesmen to minimize the seriousness of his condition. He recorded in his diary:

> It's amazing my health is as good as it is, and, as I told Ziegler, the main thing about this leg situation is not to let them build it up in a way that they think the President is crippled mentally as well as physically. I feel that at the present time we have it relatively under control but we must make sure that people never get the idea that the President is like Eisenhower in his last year or so, or like Roosevelt, or, for that matter, even like Johnson when everybody felt that Johnson was probably ready to crack up, and was drinking too much and so forth. I think we can avoid this by proper handling.

Medically, the problem was handled, at least for the moment. By the time Nixon left Camp David after a postsummit rest, the swelling in his leg had gone down, and the clot that had caused it had disappeared. But, having suffered a second attack, Nixon was now five hundred times more likely to suffer a third.

It struck three days into his stay at Annenberg's, following a round of golf. Over Nixon's protests, John Lungren, a prominent Long Beach internist and Nixon's longtime personal physician, was summoned to the estate.

Lungren was not happy with what he found. Nixon's leg was swollen nearly a third its normal size, indicating the presence of a substantial clot. Lungren warned Nixon that there was the potential of a life-threatening embolism and recommended strongly that he enter a hospital immediately. Nixon refused. Lungren, who had treated him since 1952, knew it was pointless to argue. Instead, having prescribed drugs to bring down the swelling and the wearing of a support stocking, he left it to Pat to argue the case for hospitalization.

Nixon, however, refused to discuss his condition with his wife, and by the time he returned to San Clemente the afternoon of the thirteenth, the swelling had increased. Worried, Mrs. Nixon called Tkach in Washington, and asked him to fly out as soon as possible.

Tkach arrived the next afternoon, phoned Lungren for his appraisal, then went in to see Nixon. Nixon's condition was worse than he had been led to believe. Nixon was refusing to wear the support stocking, and the swelling in his leg had reached dangerous proportions. Equally worrying was Nixon's mental state. In conversation with Tkach, he was sullen and remote, apparently uncaring about his health or the dire prognosis Tkach laid out.

"You have got to go to the hospital," Tkach ordered.

"If I go to the hospital," Nixon replied, "I'll never get out of there alive."

Tkach did not pursue the matter further. Instead he went to the press and, in a series of interviews over the next three days, repeated his conversations with Nixon, along with his assessment of Nixon's mental and physical health. According to Tkach, Nixon was "a ravaged man who has lost the will to fight." Nixon, the doctor claimed, was suffering from "severe physical strain and physical fatigue." His condition was "critical" and it was imperative that he be hospitalized and "not get under any more pressure." As it was, Tkach feared that Nixon was heading toward a heart attack. "The pardon did him no damn good," he told Helen Thomas. "It will require a miracle for him to recover," he added in an interview with *Newsweek*. "I don't know if I can pull him through."

Tkach's comments set off a free-for-all of medical speculation. During an appearance on the *Today* show, David Eisenhower said his father-in-law was "depressed," unable to relax. "Right at the moment, he is not feeling well," Eisenhower reported. "He has his leg elevated because [of the] phlebitis. . . . The clot has moved above the knee and his one leg is swollen about twice its normal size. His health is not good. He's fighting that. He can't golf, he can't relax, he can't unwind and so I would say his spirits are not great right now. There's no question about that." Julie Eisenhower insisted her father "seem[ed] fine, really well." "Dad," she said, "is in great spirits." Not so, said her brother-in-law, Edward Cox, who told The Associated Press that Nixon was "still way down, very depressed . . . in a deep depression." Donald Nixon, who hadn't seen his brother since the resignation, nevertheless proclaimed him "in good health and spirits." Herb Klein didn't think much of Nixon's spirits ("distraught," he called them) but did say his health was "good." Paul Presley went even further, declaring Nixon's health "super"—though not as far as Swifty Lazar, who, after briefing Nixon on the latest round of publishing negotiations, termed him "tanned, invigorated and in complete command." The White House, which had been asked for six days running to comment on how Nixon's health had affected Ford's decision to pardon him, declined to say anything.

At home in San Clemente, and still in pain, Nixon was finding life after clemency far from idyllic. While the pardon had removed him from immediate legal jeopardy, it had done nothing to counter the raft of civil lawsuits pending against him, solve his income tax problems, or, for that matter, eliminate the possibility, however remote, of his being criminally prosecuted in the state courts. Defending himself in any of these actions would be expensive—$500,000 in legal fees, at least, Miller estimated— and Congress was on the verge of making his already tight financial situation all the more precarious, by cutting in half the $850,000 Ford had requested for Nixon's upkeep during the official six-month period of presidential transition.

A storm was also brewing over a recent report in the *Washington Post*, which disclosed that the GSA had been intending to ship to San Clemente some 1100 crates and boxes containing gifts presented to Nixon and his family during his presidency. Nearly 200 of the crates, the *Post* reported, were packed with $2 million worth of gifts from foreign leaders, including a $52,400 matched set of emeralds and diamonds that had been given to Mrs. Nixon by Saudi Arabia's then Prince Fahd; a brooch of rubies and diamonds that had been given to Julie, and a brooch of diamonds and sapphires that had been given to Tricia. Under law, any foreign gifts worth more than $50 were to be turned over to the government. According to the *Post*, though, the Nixons had not only failed to turn over the gifts, but two days after the resignation, had tried to spirit both the crates and the records of their contents to San Clemente.

Embarrassing and troubling as all this was, Nixon's far larger and more immediate worry was Jaworski. Stung by press accounts of his role in the pardon, he had decided to resign to return to private law practice in Houston. However, the letter announcing his resignation would not be submitted until October 12, and, in the meantime, Jaworski seemed determined to go out on an aggressive note.

His first move, taken within days of the pardon, had been to announce that Nixon would be subpoenaed as a prosecution witness in the upcoming Watergate cover-up trial. His second, on September 13, had been to dispatch two of his senior deputies, Phillip Lacovara and Henry Ruth, to the White House to convince Buchen to kill the agreement

Becker had reached with Nixon over custody of the papers and the tapes.

The meeting had been heated. Jaworski had not learned of the papers agreement until the Justice Department had advised him of it in a memo, September 9, and Lacovara, who had already submitted his resignation in protest about the pardon, was in a combative mood. He accused Buchen of turning over crucial evidence in a criminal case. The deal Becker had made with Nixon was outrageous. The White House had had no right to make it, especially without consulting with the special prosecutor's office first. At the very least, Ford had to reopen negotiations with Nixon.

Buchen was adamant. Insisting the agreement was proper and the best they could get under the circumstances, he said that Ford had no intention of altering it. He added that he had a legal opinion from the Justice Department to back him up. However, Buchen did agree to one concession: the materials would not be shipped to San Clemente until Jaworski had a chance to persuade Congress to overturn the custody agreement.

Frustrated by the White House, Jaworski took his complaints to Congress, and, as a result of his lobbying, on September 17, a House subcommittee voted unanimously to delete from Ford's budget request $110,000 that had been earmarked to build a vault that would store the papers in Laguna Beach. The same day, a Senate committee began drafting legislation that would void the papers agreement altogether.

The White House, meanwhile, was distancing itself from Nixon as much as possible. Phone calls from San Clemente went unanswered, and when questions were raised about Julie's recent free ride to El Toro aboard an Air Force courier flight bringing Nixon's fortnightly intelligence briefing, Ford's spokesman had promised the practice would end. Soon, after additional pressure, the flights themselves would end.

Nixon was outraged. He sputtered, cursing, to Ziegler about it, the unfairness of it, the vindictiveness, the breaking of precedent—but there was nothing he could do. There had been a time before the pardon when such humiliations wouldn't have happened. He would have gotten on the phone and called Al, and Haig would have prevented them. But now Haig had problems of his own. In the wake of the pardon, the Ford loyalists had succeeded in pushing him out.

Temperamentally, Haig had never been cut out for the laid-back, fumbling style of the Ford White House. He was too brusquely efficient, too used to command and, after a year in which, in the opinion of some, he had been President in all but title, simply too accustomed to having things his own way. At first, Ford had deferred to him, seeking his input on every decision, or, more often than not, leaving the decisions for

Haig to make himself. But then had come a number of incidents, none of them major, but cumulatively unbearable.

The first blowup was when at Ford's direction terHorst announced the resignation of the ailing Fred Buzhardt as special White House counsel. Afterward, a red-faced Haig had nearly laid hands on the press secretary, calling him "the little executioner."

"Do you feel good?" Haig shouted at terHorst. "Executing a sick man?"

On another occasion, after Haig had finished briefing Ford on the workings of the White House staff system, Ford told him he would like to see the briefing book from which Haig had been reading. To the astonishment of the others present in the room, Haig informed Ford he couldn't have it because it was his only working copy. Ford acquiesced, and Haig continued to make decisions, including approving presidential appointments without Ford's knowledge. Nixon speechwriter Pat Buchanan, for instance, was appointed ambassador to South Africa, a fact that came to Ford's attention only after one of Hartmann's aides casually mentioned to him, "Why do you suppose the President is sending Pat Buchanan to South Africa?" Hartmann, who like the rest of the Ford transition team hadn't seen the Haig-initialed "decision memo," went to Ford and the Buchanan appointment—one of twenty-four for Nixon holdovers Haig had approved—was withdrawn.

The bad blood remained. Haig had assured Ford that all recording equipment had been removed from the Oval Office. Later it developed that the microphones Haldeman had installed—two embedded in the presidential desk, two others hidden behind brass sconces in the walls— were still in place, along with the wires that ran from them. Intentional or not, the deception snapped Ford's patience, and he called Haig in for a formal dressing down.

The tongue-lashing delighted Hartmann who had been conducting an increasingly vitriolic war of leaks with Haig in the newspaper columns. For his part, Haig had been threatening to resign unless Ford fired Hartmann. Ford, though, was unwilling to lose either man, and as the battling continued, the sense of Ford's incompetence heightened. Meanwhile, the two protagonists were refusing to speak to one another, or even attend the same meetings.

"Fuck Haig," Hartmann snapped when an aide asked why he was not attending the daily senior staff meetings that Haig chaired. "I work for the President."

Haig volleyed right back. Grabbing one of Hartmann's aides by the lapels, he warned, "If you have any influence over that fat Kraut, you tell him to knock it off or he's going to be the first stretcher case coming out of the West Wing."

But in the end it was not Hartmann or his own personality that undid Haig, but his ties to Richard Nixon. Around Washington, it was common knowledge that Haig was talking to Ziegler four and five times a day, and that he was conferring with Nixon frequently as well. It had also been reported that Haig had ordered the refurbishing of two plush suites in the Old Executive Office Building for Ziegler's and Bull's personal use. Then as the capper had come the Nixon pardon. Ford had denied being influenced by Haig, and Haig had denied trying. "Had I been asked to be an advocate," he claimed, "I would have been. I was never asked." The suspicions persisted, nonetheless, and finally in early September, Ford, under mounting pressure from friends on the Hill, decided that Haig must go.

Ford's first thought was to appoint him Army chief of staff. But the post required Senate confirmation, and there would be questions about Haig's relations with Nixon. Also, a number of senior Army officers still smarting over Haig's meteoric rise through the ranks (in promoting him from two stars to four in 1973, Nixon had jumped him past 204 more senior officers) and his politicalization in the White House were known to be opposed. So instead Ford decided to give Haig command of NATO, a comfortable European exile, but an exile nonetheless.

With Haig's departure from the White House imminent, a number of other senior Nixon holdovers began laying their own getaway plans, including Kenneth Clawson, a former *Washington Post* reporter, who had taken over from Herb Klein as White House communications director. During Watergate, Clawson had won minor notoriety by boasting to a reporter that it was he who had written the infamous "Canuck letter" that had doomed Senator Edmund Muskie in the 1972 New Hampshire primary. Clawson later denied the story, but the experience embittered him, and during the last months of Nixon's presidency he had been one of the most unbending opponents both of resignation and the press.

His stand did not make him popular with the new administration, and, after the pardon, Clawson flew to San Clemente to take up temporary residence with what Bull had taken to calling "the government in exile." Soon after his arrival, Nixon called him in to talk about his future.

Clawson found him sitting behind his desk, his ailing leg propped atop it. Nixon apologized for not rising. "The damn sawbones say I've got to keep it elevated. Helps keep down the pressure."

He clasped Clawson's hand in both of his. "I'm glad you came. Not that it's been all that bad, except for the leg. I just wanted to see you and hear the news. All bad, I suppose. . . . Don't bullshit me now. What's going on? What's happening to you, the others? How are the new people?"

In reply, Clawson began bitterly recounting recent events in Washington, how many of the Nixon holdovers on the White House staff were uncertain what to do: stay, and risk ouster by the Ford loyalists, or depart now, in hopes of finding a position in the private sector. Clawson added he was unsure of holding on to his own job. Already the Ford men had made it clear they wanted him out. But there were details to arrange, and Clawson was puzzled about what to do.

Nixon pulled out his pipe and began to fill it. His hands shook, and some of the tobacco spilled onto the desk. "We're all a little uncertain," he replied.

They talked on, gossiping about the new administration, Nixon sympathetic, Clawson angry at its incompetence. Sarcastically, Clawson described the self-consciously humble tenor of the Ford White House. It disgusted him, Clawson said, to see the Ford men falling all over themselves demonstrating how different they were from the Nixon people. According to Clawson, they almost prided themselves on their small-town incompetence. He, Clawson, had grown up in such an atmosphere. It bothered him then and it bothered him now to find it in the White House.

Nixon laughed. "Don't start quoting Sinclair Lewis to me again. After us, *Main Street* may be just what the doctor ordered."

Nixon shifted his leg on the ottoman. "I know you're feeling bitter, so am I. But we can't let it show, not now, possibly not ever. And don't draw conclusions now—wait. I'm a lot older than you and I know that five years from now, then maybe, who knows?"

Nixon's voice trailed off. "You've got to keep control," he said finally. "You know—discipline your mind to keep from taking on the whole thing now. How long has it been? It seems just yesterday, and then, sometimes, it seems like years ago already. We . . . I've got to let time go by, put some distance between then and now, break it into manageable pieces. You agree?"

Clawson protested, noting the good things Nixon had done.

"They'll never give us credit for that," Nixon snapped. His face suddenly hardened. "We're out now, so they try to stomp us . . . kick us when we're down. They never let up, *never*, because we were the first real threat to them in years. And, by God, we would have changed it, changed it so they couldn't have changed it back in a hundred years, if only . . ."

Nixon broke off in midsentence and looked past Clawson out the window toward the lawn and the ocean beyond.

"I knew what it was like. I'd been there before. That's one of the reasons I picked you and most of the others, my colleagues, your colleagues. What we all had in common was that we knew very young what the game was all about and how to win it. Being hungry helps, but it isn't enough, and, in some cases, it isn't even necessary.

"What starts the process, really, are the laughs and snubs and slights you get when you are a kid. Sometimes, it's because you're poor or Irish or Jewish or Catholic or ugly or simply that you are skinny. But if you are reasonably intelligent and if your anger is deep enough and strong enough, you learn that you can change those attitudes by excellence, personal gut performance, while those who have everything are sitting on their fat butts.

"You were a good athlete," Nixon went on, "but I was not, and that was the very reason I tried and tried and tried. To get discipline for myself and to show others that here was a guy who could dish it out and take it. Mostly, I took it.

"But once you learn that you've got to work harder than everybody else, it becomes a way of life as you move out of the alley and on your way. In your own mind you have nothing to lose, so you take plenty of chances and if you do your homework many of them pay off. It is then that you understand, for the first time, that you have the advantage because your competitors can't risk what they have already.

"It's a piece of cake until you get to the top. You find you can't stop playing the game the way you've always played it because it is a part of you and you need it as much as you do an arm or a leg. So you are lean and mean and resourceful and you continue to walk on the edge of the precipice because over the years you have become fascinated by how close to the edge you can walk without losing your balance."

Clawson interrupted. This time, he said, there was a difference.

"Yes," Nixon answered softly. "This time we had something to lose."

Clawson quickly switched the topic, asking Nixon about his leg.

"They say it's very bad," Nixon replied. "But I've already told them to go to hell. I've told them I wasn't setting foot outside the wall around my property no matter what. They can cut off the damn leg, let it rot, or just wait for the clot to reach the end zone. I don't care."

Clawson didn't know what to say. Nixon looked at him closely.

"You see, don't you? You've got to be tough. You can't break, my boy, even when there is nothing left. You can't admit, even to yourself, that it is gone. Now some people we both know think that you go stand in the middle of the bullring and cry, 'mea culpa, mea culpa,' while the crowd is hissing and booing and spitting on you. But a man doesn't cry."

Nixon clenched the pipestem between his teeth. "I don't cry. You don't cry."

There was a silence, and quietly Clawson began to weep. When he looked up, Nixon was weeping as well.

On September 16, Lungren arrived at Casa Pacifica to examine Nixon again. During the debate over Nixon's health, he had refused all comment, which, given Lungren's passion for privacy, was not surprising.

A former war hero and Notre Dame graduate, he was at fifty-nine a quietly owlish sort of man, stoop-shouldered, bespectacled, and in manner and outlook, perpetually dour. Examining his most famous patient did not improve his mood.

Nixon's condition had deteriorated drastically since his last visit. The swelling in his leg was such that he had difficulty putting on his pants. He also was exhausted, and the fatigue, combined with the sharp, near-continuous pain, made him cranky and irritable.

At least part of his irritation was traceable to Sirica, who had turned down requests from Haldeman, Ehrlichman and Mitchell that the charges against them be thrown out on the grounds of Nixon's pardon. Already impatient with the multiple delays, Sirica had also rejected a motion that the trial be indefinitely postponed because of prejudicial pardon publicity. Only after prodding from the U.S. Court of Appeals, had he agreed to set the trial date back three weeks. But at the same time, Sirica made it clear that when the period was up the trial would go forward—with Nixon on the stand whatever the state of his health.

But that had been before Lungren's latest examination. Unlike his last visit, Lungren was insistent. Nixon had to be hospitalized. If he wasn't, the prognosis was grave. Nixon looked at his doctor mournfully and finally agreed.

The hospital Lungren selected for Nixon's treatment was Long Beach Memorial, at 880 beds the West Coast's largest private medical facility and one of its best-equipped. Nixon arrived Monday afternoon, the twenty-fourth. The next day, as a light plane circled overhead, pulling a streamer that read WE LOVE YOU—GOD LOVES YOU TOO—he underwent a battery of tests, including two radiological scans of his chest, one of which revealed a dark area of approximately nine cubic inches on the outer side of his right lung. The dime-sized embolism that had put it there was the apparent result of a clot that had broken off in his left leg. Had the clot been bigger—no more than the size of a man's thumb—it might well have blocked the great artery through which blood is pumped from the heart to the lungs, almost certainly resulting in death. As it was, the clot was sufficiently small and the damaged area sufficiently confined that the only noticeable impact it had on Nixon's condition was a slight shortness of breath.

"This is a potentially dangerous situation," Lungren told reporters late that afternoon. "But it is not critical at this time. . . . There is a very good chance of recovery [but] it will take some time."

According to Lungren, Nixon had taken the news "as he normally takes anything else, it's another problem." His mood, said his doctor, "is remarkable, considering what he has been through." A few minutes later, with Lungren having added very little save that his patient "has a helluva will to live," the briefing was over.

The virtual news blackout continued the rest of the week. At each morning's medical briefing, the hospital's spokesman would announce, "Mr. Nixon's staff has allowed the Medical Center to release the following information." Then he would say there was not much new to report. Officially it was disclosed only that Nixon was receiving a combination of anticoagulants—Coumadin orally and heparin, a more powerful drug, intravenously—and that his recovery was proceeding on schedule and without incident.

The remaining tidbits came from a variety of sources: a nutritionist who reported that Nixon was forgoing the hospital fare of mahi-mahi and spaghetti with meat sauce in favor of meals brought up from San Clemente (asked to confirm it, a hospital spokesman replied, "The Nixon staff has not given me authority to talk about Mr. Nixon's food."); the head of the hospital volunteers who disclosed that Nixon, clad in a bathrobe and looking little the worse for wear, had walked four feet down a corridor to shake her hand; the hospital mailroom which announced the reception of two thousand get-well cards and telegrams; the delivery desk which said it was being swamped with scores of plants and bouquets.

There were also less welcome greetings, including a bomb threat and a promise of "salvation" from a self-proclaimed evangelist who, until the Secret Service picked him up, wandered the hospital hallways heralding the imminent arrival of the Messiah.

The few people in a position to know what was actually going on, including Ziegler, said very little, or, in Ziegler's case, spent their time denying reports of Nixon's alleged depression.

"He is not having any psychiatric problems—not at all," Ziegler insisted. ". . . He feels like anybody would feel after going through a great and severe loss and after going through the uncertainty of the last 45 days. . . . Sometimes [he's] very reflective, sometimes looking ahead. But he is physically very fatigued and the events of the past months have caused him not to be in good spirits, to at times be in a low frame of mind. But this should not suggest that his mind is not acute or that he is not working or that the state of his mind is not a healthy state."

In truth, Nixon's hospitalization was proving every bit as uneventful as Ziegler and Lungren were saying it was, and after a week, Nixon was not only up and around, but spending long hours on the phone in his $90-a-day room. The only bit of excitement came nine days into Nixon's stay when he was wheeled from the nuclear medicine department straight into the path of a photographer for one of the Long Beach newspapers. "You goddam son of a bitch," Nixon yelled, "get the hell out of here!" The photographer did, without clicking his shutter.

Later the same day, Nixon was paid a pastoral call by Timothy Cardinal Manning, the Los Angeles archbishop, and a Nixon friend since

1946. They spent two hours together, praying and talking about the Catholic school system. Afterward, Manning, apparently unaware of the strictures Nixon was placing on information, met with the press. "He looks good," the cardinal reported, "better than I've seen him in two years. He showed no sign of strain or illness. He said he was in no pain. I was amazed. He was in excellent spirits, very happy . . . as sharp as ever." Upstairs, in the Nixon suite, there was consternation. However well-intentioned, the cardinal's remarks were creating the wrong impression. Jaworski and Sirica might get ideas. Finally, Lungren was sent down to set the record straight.

Nixon was better, he told reporters, and he'd be going home soon. But there were still problems. He was "physically extremely fatigued" and would require at least a month of closely supervised recuperation. During that time and for two months afterward, he would have to avoid sitting, riding or standing for prolonged periods. That meant flying to Washington was out, unless, Lungren added sarcastically, the Watergate lawyers "have communication with the good Lord and can tell Nixon that he's going to have a perfect flight." As for taking written depositions in San Clemente, that, too, would be impossible for at least three weeks. "There are a lot of doubting Thomases, the country is full of them," Lungren concluded. "But this is my honest conception of what I think could happen to him during his recovery period."

Three days later, Nixon, smiling broadly and shaking the hands of hospital staff and volunteers, was rolled out the door through which he had walked twelve days earlier. "I feel great," he said, rising from his wheelchair to get into his car. "Just great."

5
Shock

For once the press was prepared to take Richard Nixon at his word. "Great" he said he felt and great he appeared to be. And that was the problem: Nixon didn't seem sick enough.

Certainly he had seemed reasonably well, both on his entry into the hospital and on his discharge from it, and what little was known about his stay seemed only to confirm it. Nixon might be ailing, but a man who talked long hours on the phone, bellowed at photographers and ordered special meals from his own kitchen was obviously in no grave danger. He was faking it, the story went, employing a minor upset to avoid appearing in John Sirica's court.

So was the impression of the reporters who gathered outside his gates, idling the hours eavesdropping on the Secret Service radio, following the movements of "Searchlight" (Nixon) and "Whaleboat" (Ziegler). Inside, hidden from their view, Nixon was going about his usual business. His attitude toward his illness hadn't changed—in calls to friends, he still was insisting he wasn't sick—but, however grudgingly, he was following his doctor's orders: taking his daily dose of Coumadin; soaking his leg in the pool; walking a prescribed four hundred yards each afternoon. He was also going into his office, just as he had before his hospitalization. Not only going in, but spending a full day at his desk: making calls and dictating letters; reading and underlining the memoirs of Charles de Gaulle, receiving occasional friends like Baruch Korff, the rabbi, or Clement Stone, the insurance billionaire.

His feelings about his enemies hadn't altered, either. He was still, in the words of one of his friends, "pissed"—about the Congress that was bleeding him, about the papers that were denied him, about "the goddam Marine Corps" that had decided not to let him play golf on the Camp Pendleton course.

And for what? he demanded of a visitor. Other Presidents had done the same as he, or worse—done it and gotten away with it, because they weren't Nixon. Take Lyndon Johnson, Nixon went on, rubbing his hands together. "Now there was an astonishing creature, a piece of work." The taping system Johnson had installed in the Oval Office? Made his own seem like junk. And the things Johnson said—"People said that my language was bad, but Jesus, you should have heard L.B.J.!" Yes, Johnson was something. The shenanigans with Bobby Baker, the way he played Hoover and the FBI, the financial and political skullduggery, the whole, slick business—talk about cover-ups; there was the champ.

Nixon shook his head. "People used to think I was on bad terms with L.B.J. Not at all. He came to see me right after I was inaugurated to see if I could do something to stop the publication of his brother's book. What could I do? I couldn't do anything. Now people say that Ed isn't a good brother. Ed is a fine brother. But, Christ, you should have heard what L.B.J. had to say about *his* brother. They kept the poor guy locked up on the third floor of the White House."

He shook his head again. People always judged him differently. Like the Jews. He knew they had always hated him, knew they never voted for him, knew they disliked him even now, despite everything he had done for them. "Christ," he said, "if it weren't for me, there wouldn't be any Israel. They know that in Israel. Golda Meir knows that even though they may not know it over here." That was the trouble: they didn't know it over here. And, because they didn't, they voted for liberals, Democrats like Johnson.

Do you know what Johnson had told him about the Jews? Nixon asked his visitor.

No, his visitor replied.

"Put a few Jews on your staff for window dressing, but know they'll never vote for you."

In his humor, and everything else, Richard Nixon seemed the same. If there was a difference about him since his release from the hospital, so far as the outside world was able to discover, it was only that he was rich, courtesy of Swifty Lazar and Warner Books, which had awarded him a $2.5 million advance for his memoirs, to be paid in stages as the writing progressed. "He sleeps beautiful," his valet reported. "His appetite is good. . . . He's the gentleman that he always was." There was pain, yes, but, according to Manolo, the boss was handling it in typically Nixonian fashion: "He gets angry at himself."

In Washington, meanwhile, the last and most spectacular of the Watergate trials had finally gotten under way, and already John Ehrlichman was causing Nixon trouble.

Unlike his principal codefendants, Ehrlichman had had no contact with Nixon since leaving the administration. He had not remained stoic, as had Mitchell, or scrambled after a pardon, as had Haldeman. Instead,

John Ehrlichman had gotten angry. His troubles, which were numerous (in addition to the current charges, Ehrlichman had already been sentenced to a term of from two and a half to eight years for his role in the break-in of the office of Daniel Ellsberg's psychiatrist, and, as a result, had been disbarred), he blamed almost exclusively on Nixon. It was Nixon, Ehrlichman claimed, who had involved him in the cover-up, who had schooled him step by step in the techniques of stonewalling and obstruction of justice, who had directed all the crimes of which he now stood accused and then—to use Ehrlichman's own phrase—left him "twisting slowly, slowly in the wind."

He was innocent, Ehrlichman insisted, like "Jesus . . . in the Garden of Gethsemane . . . facing trial and crucifixion . . . pray[ing] that the bitter cup of that experience be taken from him if it was God's will that he be relieved of it."

"I wasn't praying for a loophole," Ehrlichman would write later, "I was asking only for God's perfect result, whatever that might be. . . . I was putting myself in God's hands."

More immediately, the hands Ehrlichman was putting himself into belonged to Richard Nixon, the same Richard Nixon, Ehrlichman's attorney, William Frates, told the court, who had "deceived, misled and lied" to him—who, as Frates put it, had "had" him. If only Nixon would step forward, Frates went on, the matter could be quickly resolved. Nixon knew what Ehrlichman had told him, how he had warned him of the legal folly of it all, and surely, if Nixon could only be compelled to testify, he would affirm what Ehrlichman claimed he had told him that fateful day at Camp David when he had fired him: "John, you have been my conscience, but I didn't follow your advice. It is all my fault. If I had only followed your advice we wouldn't be in this situation."

Unfortunately for Ehrlichman, it did not appear that Nixon would be affirming anything of the sort, or, if his doctor had his way, testifying at all.

In an eleven-paragraph affidavit filed with the court in mid-October, Lungren stated, "It is impossible to predict . . . the duration of the therapy." However long it lasted, "the limitations on Mr. Nixon's physical activity will involve, first, the avoidance of prolonged periods of sitting, standing or walking which . . . might produce further clotting; and, second, the avoidance of any possible trauma which, given the coagulant therapy he will be receiving, could lead to hemorrhaging somewhere in the body." According to Lungren, if Nixon were compelled to testify, it "would pose a serious risk to [Nixon's] health."

Sirica, who was as anxious as Ehrlichman to have Nixon take the stand, was skeptical about Lungren's diagnosis. The doctor was neither an unbiased observer nor an expert on venous diseases, and the arguments he was raising seemed as much psychological as medical.* Sirica ordered Miller to prepare a complete medical report, hinting that if it did not satisfy him, he would immediately bring Nixon into court, and in a wheelchair if necessary.

The speculation about the seriousness of Nixon's condition became academic on October 23. That afternoon, Lungren examined Nixon again, took his blood pressure and observed that, despite the anticoagulants, the swelling in his left leg had returned. After consulting by phone with several specialists, Lungren decided to hospitalize Nixon immediately and, ignoring Nixon's protests, made arrangements to have him readmitted to Long Beach Memorial early that evening.

Ray Mackey, a sanitationman, was compacting cardboard cartons in the hospital parking lot a few minutes after 6:00 P.M. when Nixon's white Cadillac drove up. Nixon got out, smiling, but obviously tired, as Mackey called out a greeting. "Hi there," Nixon replied. Still on his feet, Nixon half-turned and walked a few paces to a waiting wheelchair. "I hope everything's okay," Mackey called after him. Nixon said nothing.

Within moments, Nixon was wheeled to a glass-partitioned room in a new and still-unoccupied intensive care wing on the hospital's seventh floor. After his condition was checked again, he was taken down to the hospital's X-ray department, where the inflamed leg underwent a series of radiological scans.

The tests, administered by Dr. Scott Driscoll, Memorial's cardiovascular radiologist, revealed that one of the main veins leading to the heart was, in Driscoll's words, "99 and $^{44}/_{100}$'s percent blocked." As a result, the supply of blood to Nixon's left thigh was almost entirely shut off, raising the possibility of gangrene. X-rays of the thigh also showed evidence of several small clots, any one of which might break off.

At a minimum, Lungren concluded, more tests were needed, as

---

* In fact, phlebitis did have a psychological component, and, according to a number of doctors being quoted at the time in the press, it was playing a crucial role in Nixon's case. Depression of the kind Nixon was suffering affected the body's hormonal secretions, and through them the clotting process of the blood. Moreover, patients like Nixon who were "feeling low" were both more susceptible to disease and less able to cope with it. That was especially true, according to one University of Rochester expert, "at times of changes in their life to which they cannot adjust." Such patients, said Los Angeles psychiatrist Ralph Greenson, were "poor surgical risks." Some doctors, like psychiatrist Samuel Silverman, a specialist in psychosomatic disease at the Harvard Medical School, went even further, claiming not only that Nixon's phlebitis had been caused by stress, but that the timing of his most recent attack, coming as it did within days of the pardon, was highly significant. As Silverman told *Time*, "I have no way of knowing whether Mr. Nixon has any unconscious guilt, but if he does, with the threat of legal punishment now removed, the only punishing force left is himself. That's why pardons can kill."

well as the presence of outside specialists. While Lungren placed a call to Dr. Eldon Hickman, a venous surgeon at UCLA, Nixon was wheeled out of the X-ray room and onto an elevator for the trip back to his room. Harold Twomley, a thirty-year-old carpenter from Buena Park, caught a quick glimpse of him and was shocked. Nixon's skin color was deathly gray; his face was pasty and cadaverous, like a figure, Twomley thought, in a wax museum.

There were more tests the following day, and, in a briefing for reporters, Lungren revealed that surgery was being "actively considered." "This hospital admission was imperative," Lungren stated. "We have had some difficulty regarding the oral anticoagulant therapy. If anticoagulant therapy cannot be adequately established and controlled, then surgical intervention is a real possibility."

As Lungren was talking with the press, Nixon's already large dosage of Coumadin was increased, and in addition he began to receive regular injections of heparin. The hope was that the drugs, together with bed rest, would make surgery unnecessary, and for a time the therapy seemed to be working. Thursday, the twenty-fifth, Nixon passed a quiet, comfortable day. He slept soundly that night, a marked change from his grumpiness of the night before, and felt well enough the next morning to dictate a note of apology to a group of student nurses, whose planned tour of the new intensive care unit had been put off by his presence. His one complaint was that because the anticoagulants had thinned his blood, his gums had begun to bleed. Otherwise, his spirits were excellent. With luck, his aides were saying, he would be home by the end of the weekend.

But Nixon did not go home. Tests on Saturday and again on Sunday showed that the anticoagulants were not working even at the higher dosages. On Monday, Lungren ordered more tests, including a "venogram," a particularly painful procedure in which a plastic tube approximately one millimeter in diameter was inserted in the femoral vein, and poked up, down and around while being injected with radioactive iodine dye for contrast.

To Lungren's horror, the venogram showed a large new clot in Nixon's left iliac vein, one of the channels through which blood passes on its way from the thigh to the heart and lungs. Some eighteen inches in length overall, the clot, said one of the doctors who viewed the venogram, was large enough "to kill not only Nixon but three other men as well." Equally dangerous was the fact that the clot was barely attached to the walls of the vein. On the venogram, it showed up as a lumpy, white snake, poised and ready to strike.

Surgery was now the only option. But there remained the problem of convincing Nixon, who was becoming increasingly irritable as his hospital stay dragged out. Worried that his recommendation alone would not be convincing, Hickman called Dr. Wiley F. Barker, chief of the surgical section at the UCLA Medical Center and an expert on venous diseases, and asked him to come to Long Beach to view the venogram and talk to Nixon. Barker, who was planning to leave for a medical conference in Hawaii the next morning, was not enthusiastic. A number of doctors at UCLA were as skeptical about Nixon's condition as was the press, and Barker himself, though once a Nixon supporter, had soured on him after Watergate. Hickman, however, was insistent, and finally Barker agreed.

One look at the films of the venogram convinced Barker that Hickman had not been overstating the seriousness of the situation. The clot was one of the biggest he had ever seen. Accompanied by Hickman and Lungren, he went in to see Nixon, whom he imagined would be sullen and depressed. Instead, the former President was chipper and alert. Propped up in his bed, he greeted Barker amiably and listened closely as Barker described his condition.

"If you look at this clot cross-eyed," he warned Nixon, "it will kill you."

"So, it's surgery, then?" Nixon asked.

"If you want to go on living, it is."

Nixon smiled. "I can assure you about that. I've got too many things to do to go on being sick. Let's just get it out of the way."

Nixon and Barker continued to talk for nearly three hours, reviewing Nixon's medical history, the coming surgery and the likely course of therapy following his discharge. Throughout, Nixon showed a detailed, sophisticated knowledge of his condition that left Barker impressed. It was apparent that his patient had done his homework.

"You know," said Barker as he prepared to go, "that venogram of yours is a classic. If you weren't who you are, I'd love to show it to my class."

Nixon beamed. "I have a feeling," he said, "that these X rays are going to belong to history anyway. Go ahead, use it."

That afternoon, Nixon discussed with his wife what Barker had told him, then called his daughters in New York. The decision to proceed with surgery was unanimous.

"When do you want to do it?" Nixon asked Lungren.

"Now," Lungren replied.

Nixon sighed and closed his eyes. "I'm so tired," he whispered hoarsely.

"All right," said Lungren. "Get some rest. We'll do it in the morning." Barker called to reserve an operating room. Surgery was set for 5:30 A.M.

The next morning before going down to surgery, Nixon called David and Julie in New York. He tried to sound upbeat. There was nothing to worry about; the operation was merely a matter of routine. Personally, he didn't think it was necessary—"I feel a little silly being here," he told David—but who was he to argue with the experts? Still cheerful, Nixon hung up. Half an hour later, the attendants arrived to take him down to surgery.

It was supposedly a relatively simple procedure, no more than a neat surgical incision just above the groin, followed by the insertion of a white, serrated, bobby-pin-sized, Teflon device called a "Miles clip" on the distal external iliac vein. Once in place, the "teeth" on the clip, like sluice gates on a dam, would allow blood to flow through, but would block the passage of clots. If all went well, the only hazard lay in the possibility of postoperative bleeding, a possibility enhanced by the very anticoagulants that had failed to work.

The actual operation, performed by Hickman, assisted by Lungren and two members of the hospital's surgical staff, went off as planned. Nixon took the mild anesthesia well, and his vital signs remained stable throughout. When Hickman made his incision, there was normal bleeding, but nothing to cause concern, and seventy minutes later, an already semiconscious Nixon was on his way back to his room.

"The doctors are looking rather pleased," a hospital spokesman told a crowd of waiting reporters. Hickman, looking nervous and chain-smoking cigarettes, expanded on the optimism. His patient, the doctor declared, was "doing well, post-op; stable, in his room undergoing a normal recovery period." It was, he said of the surgery, "a relatively uneventful procedure."

But even as Hickman was proclaiming the surgery a success, complications were beginning to develop. Thinned by the massive doses of anticoagulants, Nixon's blood was seeping, drop by drop, into a vacant cavity between his abdomen and his back. A pint oozed out, then another. Gradually, almost imperceptibly, Nixon's blood pressure began to fall.

At first his condition was not apparent. Twice since the surgery, one of the attending nurses and Bob Dunn, Nixon's Navy medical corpsman, had lifted him up from his pillows and swung his feet out over the bed. The exercise, designed to help clear anesthesia from the body, was routine for postoperative patients, and both times it had gone well. Then, at 1:15 P.M., Dunn and the nurse came into Nixon's room to repeat the procedure again. As they swung Nixon's legs over the side of the bed, his eyes suddenly rolled back into his head. Unconscious, Nixon sagged backward. Lowering him to the bed, the nurse pulled the pillow from beneath his head and leaned close. She said loudly, "Richard! Richard!" There was no response. At the foot of the bed, Dunn was cranking furiously, elevating Nixon's feet so that blood would flow to his brain. The nurse slapped Nixon across the face, once, then again. Still, there was no response. She placed her hand on Nixon's forehead; his skin was clammy and cold. She reached for his wrist to take his pulse: Nixon's heart was racing. Quickly, the nurse grabbed a blood pressure sleeve from the bedside table and strapped it around Nixon's arm. She pumped the bulb, trying to establish pressure. The count read sixty over zero. "Condition Blue Holding!" she called out. At the central nurses' monitoring station a few yards away, another nurse yelled into a phone, "*Condition Blue Holding.*" It was the signal of critical trauma.

At the sound of the alarm, Nixon's doctors, who had been conferring in an outer corridor, came running. One attached a plastic sack of glucose solution to a vein in Nixon's arm, then a bottle of whole blood in the other. Nixon's blood pressure kept dropping. Another doctor pulled back the bedcovers and placed his hand on Nixon's stomach. It was grotesquely swollen, a classic symptom of major internal bleeding. More blood was ordered—eight additional pints in all—and the drip of the glucous IVs was increased.

An hour slipped by, then another. Nixon continued in shock. Additional tubes were inserted into his body: one, through his nose into his stomach, to relieve the pressure on his abdomen; two more IVs in his arms, and a clear-colored catheter in his neck to monitor the flow of blood through his veins. Finally, three hours after the crisis began, Nixon's condition stabilized.

Seven stories below on the hospital's ground floor, a crowd of reporters, ignorant of what was happening above them, began gathering near the main entrance to await the expected arrival of Julie Eisenhower. It had been a boring day. Empty coffee cups and cigarette butts littered the visitors' lounge that now served as a makeshift press room. At one of the typewriters, a reporter pecked out an imaginary lead: "Richard Nixon received his first liquid nourishment today when his friend, Bebe Rebozo, paid a visit to his bedside." Pleased with his joke, the reporter read the passage aloud to his companions. There was lewd laughter. Someone looked at his watch. It was a few minutes before 6:00 P.M. Suddenly, out in the corridor, there was the sound of running feet, then the voice of the hospital public relations man yelling, "He's in shock! He's in shock!"

Beyond that there were few details, only an announcement that at that moment doctors were "fighting for that man's life." Finally, an hour later, the hospital put out an eleven-line statement. It reported that Nixon had suddenly gone into cardiovascular shock, and that "a team of physicians and intensive care nurses administered countershock measures for three hours until a stable cardiovascular condition was once again restored." The patient, the statement concluded, "is still considered critical." In New York, the headquarters of the major media began readying obituaries.

There was not much more information the next morning. In a

medical bulletin issued by Lungren and Hickman, Nixon was still reported as critical, though stable and slightly improved. The bleeding, which was attributed to the heavy doses of anticoagulants, had stopped, and, despite continuing pain and occasional nausea, Nixon had managed a few hours of uninterrupted sleep. But there were still problems. Among other things, Nixon had suffered partial paralysis of the gastrointestinal tract, and his blood count remained worrisomely low. The statement ended on an ominous note: "At this time, it would be premature to provide a prognosis."

Ziegler, who came down to meet with the press a few hours later, sounded no more optimistic. "There is no question about the fact that we almost lost President Nixon yesterday afternoon." He paused, as if struggling to control himself. His eyes were red-rimmed from crying. "I know President Nixon has not lost the will to live. He's a man of great strength and great courage, and he will pull out of it."

Nixon himself was not in a position to say anything. The first day of the crisis, he was groggy and semicomatose, only dimly aware of his surroundings. When he regained consciousness at 7:00 A.M. Tuesday and saw Lungren standing by his bedside, he said thickly, "Are we going to do the surgery now?"

Though the immediate crisis had passed, Nixon's condition remained critical. His blood pressure and pulse continued to fluctuate, and tests revealed that his red blood cell count had taken a slight dip. That, in turn, diminished the number of clot-producing "platelets," suggesting the possibility of continued internal bleeding. "There is very real danger lurking in the background, in the imminent background," Lungren told reporters; the next 24 to 72 hours, he added, would determine Nixon's fate. "Don't get your hopes up," another doctor told a member of Nixon's staff. "This man could die at any moment."

Nixon, who had been briefed on his condition, assumed the worst and began preparing for it. Calling his wife to his bedside, he asked her to get a notebook and pencil. He wanted, he said, to dictate some last recollections. He talked for two hours; when Mrs. Nixon tired, Ziegler took her place for another two hours, and Gannon after him for yet another two hours. The pace was slow, and for Nixon, still connected to various life-support systems, nauseous, feverish and in considerable postoperative pain, agonizing.

He ranged over the whole of his life, especially the events of his presidency. During most moments, his tone was reflective, philosophical; at other times, particularly in relation to Watergate, he was bitter and combative. Listening to him reflect on the past, Gannon felt both privileged and terrified: privileged to be present at so extraordinary a moment, terrified that every utterance he was taking down could be Nixon's last.

Slowly, however, Nixon's condition improved. The second night after his operation was more restful than the first, and the following morning he began taking liquid nourishment. The slight fever he had been running disappeared; the nausea that had convulsed him vanished. For the first time since he had slipped into shock, his blood pressure and pulse returned to normal levels. By Friday he felt well enough to eat some Jell-O and consommé, and to register some complaints at all the attention he was receiving. His spirits, Lungren reported, were excellent. "He is alert, oriented to everything going on around him and co-operative."

Meanwhile, the calls of good wishes flowed in: from Billy Graham and Norman Vincent Peale; from Imelda Marcos of the Philippines and Ardeshir Zahedi, the ambassador of the shah of Iran; from ninety Indiana University students, who each volunteered to donate a pint of blood; from the First Lady, Betty Ford, only recently released from the hospital herself, following an operation for breast cancer.

The President had not called. The day of Nixon's operation, Ford was at home in Grand Rapids, addressing a Republican rally at Calvin College, one of the stops on a three-week campaign swing of fifteen states. The trip had gone well, with friendly crowds and a minimum of pickets. The only reminder of the pardon was when the Calvin College master of ceremonies asked the band to play something suitable for the guest of honor. To which the band had responded with a chorus of "Nobody Knows the Troubles I've Seen." Then had come the call from the White House, with news of Nixon's condition. Politically and personally, it put Ford in an awkward position. In two days he was scheduled to travel to Los Angeles to address a major Republican fund-raising dinner at the Century Plaza Hotel, only minutes by helicopter from Long Beach. If he didn't visit Nixon, he would be seen as heartless. If he did, the pardon would be back on the front pages.

Ford's staff was still debating what to do when Air Force One departed for Los Angeles. The arguments continued throughout the flight. Finally, a few minutes before touchdown, with it all but decided that Ford should not visit Nixon, the President walked back to the staff cabin. Ron Nessen, his new press secretary, told him what they had been discussing and began to explain the political risks. Ford's jaw tightened.

"If there's no place in politics for human compassion, there's something wrong with politics. I'm going to leave it to Pat."

A few hours later Ford called Mrs. Nixon from his hotel suite. Nessen was in the next room, listening.

"Hello, Pat?" he heard Ford's voice boom out. "This is Jerry Ford. How's the President?"

There was a long pause while Mrs. Nixon described Nixon's condition.

Ford resumed: "I don't want to push it, but would it help if I came down there?"

There was another pause, a closing exchange and a moment later Ford hung up. He told Nessen: "She said, 'I can't think of anything that would do him more good.' "

The next morning, Ford choppered to Long Beach airport, then went by motorcade to the hospital. Ziegler and Lungren met him on the ground floor. "He's a very sick man," Lungren advised. "You can only have a few minutes. But, above all, don't say anything that will upset him. Just be quiet and general."

Upstairs, Mrs. Nixon and her daughters were waiting in a corridor outside Nixon's room. Ford embraced them, then, accompanied by Lungren, Ziegler, Nessen, Steve Bull and Richard Cheney, the new White House chief of staff, went into the intensive care unit. Through the glass-walled partition, they saw Nixon squirming uncomfortably in his bed. His hair was tousled, his jowls were flabby; his arms, one of which was stuck with tubes and locked in a splint, looked terribly thin. An air line extended from one of Nixon's nostrils, while a catheter protruded from his neck. Above his bed, a battery of emergency monitoring equipment blinked and flashed.

Bull turned the doorknob. It was locked. He tried again. Now it was jammed. Through the glass, Nixon shot him a disgusted look. Finally, after five frantic minutes, during which Ford kept wondering what would happen if Nixon's heart stopped, a carpenter was summoned with a hacksaw. "Hi, Jerry," Nixon slurred as Ford walked into the room. His voice was husky, barely audible. The sight of him, flat on his back, deathly pale, tubes running in and out of his body, rendered Ford momentarily speechless. Awkwardly, he tried to comfort him, talking about foreign policy and the upcoming congressional elections. "It looks like we're going to do fine," Ford fibbed. Nixon made no response. He seemed to be struggling simply to keep his eyes open. There was a long silence, then in a hoarse whisper Nixon said slowly, "My own situation is not too good . . . I'm not feeling too well, but I'm going to make it." Ford was on the verge of tears; he had never seen anyone who seemed so close to death.

"How are your nights?" he asked.

Nixon answered: "None of my nights are too good."

After eight minutes, Ford reached out and patted Nixon's hand. "Be well." Nixon forced his eyes open. "Mr. President," he said, addressing Ford by his title for the first time, "this has meant a lot to me. I'm deeply grateful." As Ford left, he wondered whether he would see Nixon again.

Ziegler, who had watched the entire episode from the nurses' station, pulled Nessen aside. Before Ford went downstairs and met with reporters, there were some things that needed saying. He didn't want the problem with the door mentioned. It could be, well, *misunderstood*. And it was important—very important—how Ford described Nixon's condition, that he not be too positive, give too much hope, say that he appeared better than he imagined. That, too, could be misunderstood. Nessen looked at him and wondered: was it the press Ziegler feared might misunderstand—or John Sirica?

Ford, in any case, was properly grave. "He's obviously a very, very sick man," he told the press afterward. "But I think he's coming along."

Gradually, Nixon did come along, though not without complications. On Sunday, November 3, he was taken off the critical list and spent a brief time dangling his legs over the side of his bed. The next day, at Lungren's direction, he took a few halting steps in his hospital room. However, he was still in pain and tired easily, and tests later the same day revealed that fluid was collecting in his left lung. Two days later, there was another setback when chest X rays disclosed that his right lung—where the embolism had shown up in October—had partially collapsed. In addition, Nixon, who was described by Lungren as "terribly physically weak," had come down with a mild case of pneumonia. Antibiotics and breathing exercises eventually resolved the problems, but Nixon was still far from well. His platelet count remained inexplicably low, and his blood pressure continued to fluctuate, especially during times of stress. The simple act of walking across his room left him exhausted and out of breath. According to Lungren, Nixon was still "physically quite ill."

Sirica, who was under mounting pressure from Ehrlichman's attorney to compel Nixon to testify, was less convinced, and, in mid-November, with Nixon showing steady improvement, appointed a three-member panel of doctors to conduct an independent examination. When Ziegler informed Nixon of Sirica's decision, Nixon's blood pressure immediately soared. Furious, Lungren snapped at reporters. "He's weak and he's very tired. There's simply no telling about possibilities of other complications arising. I don't know or care about politics or law. This is a medical judgment."

Nixon, meanwhile, continued to recover, and, on November 14, twenty-three days after he had been admitted to the hospital, Lungren declared him fit to go home.

There were no smiles the morning Nixon emerged from the hospital, no proclamations of "feeling great." Still clad in light blue hospital pajamas, topped by a navy blue robe, Nixon looked tired and drawn. He had lost fifteen pounds during his stay in the hospital, and, when he rose from his wheelchair, the strain was evident. He stood unsteadily for a moment, patted Lungren on the back, then eased himself into the backseat of his limousine.

The doctors appointed by Sirica arrived in California nine days later. They went first to Long Beach Memorial, where they met with Nixon's physicians and reviewed his medical records. By midafternoon, they were in San Clemente, examining Nixon. Their findings were unanimous: Nixon was in no condition to travel. However, barring further complications, he could be interrogated at home as early as January 6.

Determined to wind up the trial by the first of the year, Sirica was unwilling to wait, and, over Frates' objections, ruled that Nixon's testimony would not be necessary. On the afternoon of December 19, James Neal, the chief prosecutor in the case, began his final arguments to the jury. "Ladies and gentlemen," he said in a soft, Tennessee twang. "Justice and its pursuit is an elusive goal. The court system is a delicate instrument which works only if it is not impeded, not tampered with, and if it gets the facts and the evidence."

As Neal was speaking, Nixon was at his home in San Clemente, settling down to what would prove to be a long and difficult convalescence. Mentally and physically, he was exhausted. Simply speaking required conscious effort, and after a few sentences he had to pause to catch his breath. His appetite, never robust, was slow to return, and he remained thin.

Emotionally, the events of the past few weeks had left their mark as well. In conversation with aides, Nixon described how he had felt at the moment of slipping into shock; of feeling the slap of the nurse's hand on his face; of hearing voices calling to him, "Richard, pull yourself back, pull yourself back." Recalling the experience, he said he felt then almost as if he had a choice: whether he should give up or whether he should continue. And in that instant, he said, he had decided that he would go on, that there was more for him to do, that the moment to end his life had not come yet.

Nixon's tone was dispassionate, analytical. He seemed more fascinated by his encounter with death than moved by it. It left him, he said, with a deeper understanding and appreciation of what others in similar circumstances had undergone. "You mean religiously?" an aide asked. No, Nixon replied, intellectually.

Other aspects of his illness were harder for him to accept. The piece of plastic that had been inserted in his groin was now a permanent part of him, and so, too, was the phlebitis that had nearly killed him. Because of them, there would always be doctors hovering nearby; there would always be tests and periodic visits to the hospital; there would always be "it," as he called his illness, the enduring, unshakable token that he was vulnerable after all.

6

Transition

The New Year began badly. A few minutes before five, New Year's afternoon, as Nixon was watching the Rose Bowl on television in San Clemente, the jury in the case of his three closest aides came in with its findings. The verdict was guilty.*

Mitchell and Haldeman reacted stoically and immediately announced their intention to file appeals. Ehrlichman, however, was bitter. "If I had known Nixon was taping my conversations," he said sarcastically, "I would have acted differently."

Nixon, whose tapes had provided the prosecution's principal evidence, was not surprised by the outcome. Since the case had gone to the jury, he had been bracing himself for the verdict, as well as the stiffness of the sentences he was certain Sirica would hand down. Again, his estimation was correct. The terms Sirica imposed were long ones: up to three years for each of the defendants.

What Nixon had not foreseen was the impact the convictions would have on him. He was devastated, and for days afterward he remained moody and depressed. He found it difficult to sleep and had to be encouraged to eat. During the day he kept to his den, avoiding visitors and fending off calls. He wanted, he told his aides, to be alone.

Yet for all his anguish, outwardly Nixon remained detached. To Gulley, one of the few people who saw him in the days immediately following the verdict, Nixon's attitude about the convictions was like that of someone who had read of a terrible accident in the newspaper: interest in the tragedy, concern for the victims—even that "poor, poor woman" Martha Mitchell, who was daily lambasting him in the press—worry for the ruination of their lives and fortunes, but, so far as the sergeant could

---

* Two other Nixon administration officials were tried along with Haldeman, Ehrlichman and Mitchell. They were Kenneth W. Parkinson, a former CREEP lawyer, who was acquitted of all charges, and former Assistant Attorney General Robert C. Mardian, whose conviction was later overturned on appeal.

detect, no real personal involvement. Instead, Nixon talked in code words. Watergate was not the scandal, but "this business"; the prison his former aides faced was "what they are going through." Instead of his own agonies, he dwelt on the country's, as if as an innocent bystander he had been untouched.

Mrs. Nixon, who knew but too well the workings of her husband's defenses, had been watching him closely, and she was worried. Since Nixon's release from the hospital, it had been she, far more than his doctors, who had slowly been nursing him back to health. She supervised his diet—sometimes placing handwritten notes on his tray, informing him that "this fulfills your doctor's requirements for good health"—ensured he took his four-times-daily medication, did what she could to cheer him. But caring for a man who disliked being cared for was a struggle, and the verdict in Washington had not made it any easier.

Personally, she had little sympathy for most of those caught up in Watergate, especially Haldeman, who had treated her in the White House with only thinly veiled contempt and had at one point advised Nixon to divorce her as a political liability. Her husband could sometimes forgive those who had savaged him; Pat Nixon did not. Beneath the carefully controlled image of the quivering-lipped wife in the good Republican cloth coat was a woman of sharp, often acerbic, intelligence. She was fierce in her opinions and fiercer still in her loyalties, and she blamed Haldeman for her husband's troubles and for many of her own during the White House years.

It had been a difficult time for her, in some respects more so than it had been for her husband. Coming from a background even poorer and meaner than Nixon's—"I never had time to think about who I wanted to be or whom I admired, or to have ideas . . . or dream about being anyone else," she confessed to journalist Gloria Steinem in a rare, unguarded moment in 1968—"I've never had it easy. I'm not at all like you . . . all those people who had it easy"—she originally had been attracted to the excitement of her husband's political career. But by the time he had reached the presidency, the glamour had long since worn off. Deeply private and continually resentful of "the fishbowl living" of the White House, she termed politics "the thief," the thing that stole from her her husband and their marriage. Nixon had not helped. He was not an open or affectionate man even in the best of circumstances—Brennan joked that one of his duties was instructing Nixon how to kiss his wife—and once Watergate began to absorb him, the gulf between them widened. Dinners in the family quarters were rushed, the silence at the table glacial. Her one piece of advice—that Nixon destroy the tapes—had been rejected, and at night, when Nixon returned to his office to plot his defense, she frequently slipped out to walk the streets. When she came home, it was to sleep alone.

Doggedly, though, she had continued to defend him, excusing his coldness ("Nobody could sleep with Dick," she told a friend. "He wakes up during the night, switches on the light, speaks into his tape recorder or takes notes, it's impossible.") refusing even to consider the possibility of his resignation. Meanwhile, her husband appeared to go out of his way to humiliate her. During what was billed as a celebration of her birthday at the Grand Ole Opry in March 1974, Pat, who had just returned from a South American tour and was ill with the flu, walked out on the stage to find the President banging away a rendition of "Happy Birthday" on the piano. Arms outstretched, Pat moved to embrace him. Nixon turned his back and began playing with a yo-yo. Tears had brimmed in her eyes; Nixon kept playing with the yo-yo.

Publicly, she had not complained. "I keep it all in," she said of herself. "I never scream. . . . If I have a headache, no one knows about it. . . . If I were dying, I would never let anyone know."

It was only in private that her true feelings came out. An aide who was standing outside the Oval Office on Nixon's last day in the White House, heard her say through the wall, "You have ruined my life."

Since returning to San Clemente, she had slowly been trying to decompress. Apart from moments with her husband and visits from her daughters, she had kept mostly to herself, tending her garden, reading, or listening to show tunes on the stereo at night. Calls from friends had largely gone unanswered. The previous Christmas, for the first time in memory, she had neglected even to send out cards. One of the few times outsiders had caught a glimpse of her, at a small dinner party Nixon had hosted shortly after the resignation, had gone badly. Over dinner, one of the guests, a former member of Nixon's cabinet, had begun probing Nixon for the real explanation of Watergate. Before Nixon could answer, she excused herself from the table. Henceforth, all invitations were meticulously screened.

Ironically, it was the illness that nearly killed Nixon that succeeded in bringing them closer together. During Nixon's time in the hospital, she was seldom far from his bedside, and later Nixon credited her for, as he put it to a visitor, "leading me out of the depths. . . . If it hadn't been for her," he went on, "I might not have survived. [She] pulled me through . . . kept me alive. I doubt I would have made it without her." The experience changed Mrs. Nixon's feelings as well. "I used to catch myself resenting the fact that Dick's time with the family was so limited," she confided to Helene Drown, a friend since childhood, as the two of them walked the beach during a break from the hospital vigil. "But then I would say to myself, 'His work is what's important now—we can wait.' And I admired him for it."

Now, though, she was concerned. Dick was not getting better. His physical condition was poor, and since the convictions in Washington, he had resumed his brooding. He needed a break, to be surrounded again by friends. January 9 would be his sixty-second birthday. Pat decided to throw him a party.

Quietly, the calls went out: to Bebe Rebozo and Cy Mandel, the old friend and restaurateur in Florida; to Bob Abplanalp, the even older friend and aerosol millionaire in New York; to Victor Lasky, the jolly, right-wing journalist and Kennedy-phobe in Washington. Come, she instructed, but above all, keep mum. Dick, who despises birthdays, mustn't know.

It was midafternoon by the time they arrived at the estate, and Pat, who greeted them with hugs and kisses, was still in her gardening clothes. Putting her finger over her lips, she pointed in the direction of Nixon's office. The group nodded and tiptoed in. When the door swung open, Nixon's jaw dropped in surprise. "Well, goddam!" he exclaimed.

The evening was festive and intimate, just as Pat had hoped. First there were gifts: a kitchen apron from Abplanalp, inscribed with the legend "I got my job through *The New York Times*"; a fountain pen from Lasky, who claimed to have received it for his bar mitzvah; a chestful of steaks and lobsters from Mandel, taken from his Miami larder. Rebozo waited until Pat left the room to present his gift: a windup doll that, penis erect, walked to the edge of a table and "urinated" over the side.

Afterward, in the family living room, Nixon made the group drinks. A heaping silver bowl of caviar, a gift from the shah, was brought out, and Nixon urged, "Eat, eat—the shah won't like it if you don't." A fire crackled in the hearth. Outside, a cool mist rolled in off the Pacific. The family dogs—two poodles and the aging Irish setter, King Timahoe—pressed their noses to the window, begging to be let in. Dick, over Pat's protests, obliged. One of the poodles settled himself on his lap. The former President and his friends talked.

The conversation was bantering and easy, the sort Nixon seemed so incapable of in the presence of strangers. They joked about the shah and old times, and Nixon, a note of surprise in his voice, talked of the birthday greetings he had received. Chou En-lai had sent a note, and Ronald Reagan had called from Sacramento; even Ford had troubled himself to say hello.

Over dinner, Abplanalp related how, on the flight out, he and Lasky had encountered Gus Hall, the boss of the U.S. Communist party, knocking back bourbons in the first-class cabin with John Abt, who had been Lee Harvey Oswald's lawyer. They had chatted about the economy, then in recession, and Hall had teased, "When your business is bad, our business is good." Hall had also asked Abplanalp to convey his best wishes to Nixon, a bit of news that brought a smile to Nixon's lips. Finally, Nixon offered a toast. Looking around the table, he noted how each of them in his own way had been successful, and that all of them— or at least their ancestors—had come from different corners of the globe. This could only happen in America. His eyes moistened as he went on, describing the importance of good friends, how they were always there when he needed them. "Never dwell on the past," he said, lifting his glass. "Always look to the future."

While Manolo and Fina cleared away the dishes, the men went into the library for brandy and cigars, Nicaraguan ones, emblazoned with the presidential seal. Toward ten-thirty, Nixon, obviously weary, got to his feet. Lasky bear-hugged him and was startled by his frailness; he could feel the bones under Nixon's suit. All at once, Lasky, ordinarily boisterous, felt very sad. Here was someone who until a few months ago had been the most powerful man in the world. Now, he was sick, isolated, alone.

Nixon's situation was not good, and, as the end of the official six-month presidential transition period neared, it was not getting noticeably better. His fatigue and poor health made it nearly impossible to work. He could not read for much more than twenty minutes and had yet to begin dictating the memoirs that were due at the end of the year. For long periods he was sullen and morose. Then suddenly for no apparent reason he would become buoyant, telling one visitor of his plans to return to public life in the manner of Bernard Baruch and to another boasting that he was grooming daughter Julie for a career in politics. "After all," as Nixon put it, "she is both a Nixon and an Eisenhower."

He was still feeling upbeat when Barry Goldwater came to visit in late January. During Watergate, relations between the two men had been strained, especially after the Arizona Senator told the *Christian Science Monitor* that Americans were once again getting the feeling "Would you buy a used car from this man?" In San Clemente, however, all that was forgotten. Instead, having complained about the White House's continuing refusal to return many of his personal possessions, Nixon began discussing his future. He would like, he said, when the time was right, to become a spokesman for the Republican Party, declaiming on politics and world issues. Almost offhandedly, Nixon added that he would make a fine ambassador to the People's Republic of China.

Afterward, Goldwater repeated to reporters what Nixon had told him, and the next day stories of Nixon's diplomatic ambitions were being headlined—and denounced—from coast to coast. Nixon was incensed. "Did you see that report in the paper about Goldwater's visit yesterday?" he fumed to Gulley, who had. "Well, it's all a goddam lie. I never told

Goldwater a goddam thing about wanting to be an ambassador, to China or anyplace else. Goldwater probably went down there to the San Clemente Inn, got drunk, and made those goddam dumb statements." Nixon paused. "On the other hand, maybe he never said a thing. Maybe the goddam press printed it on their own. They might have taken whatever Goldwater *did* say out of context—that's what the bastards do constantly. They take things out of context; they print what they want to print; and you've got no recourse. Once it hits the headlines, there's no recourse.

"But I would never even speculate about a thing like being ambassador," Nixon continued. "Christ, I know how the American public would never accept a thing like that. Not in any foreseeable future can I see being able to participate in any way in government. There may be a few million hard-core Nixonites out there, but there are hundreds of millions of others who are anti-Nixon. I know that."

Brennan and Ziegler did their best to keep such outbursts from being repeated to the press, but it was not always possible, especially when Nixon was talking with Rabbi Baruch Korff.

Of all the characters who drifted into Nixon's orbit over the years, few were more improbable, and none so compulsively loquacious as the pint-sized rabbi from Rehoboth, Massachusetts. Born in the Ukraine (where, he claimed, his mother was murdered while shielding him from Bolshevik bullets), he grew up and was educated in Poland, before escaping to England at the onset of World War II. During the war he was active in the rescue of Jews from German-occupied countries, and eventually fell in with Menachem Begin's notorious Stern Gang. After an arrest in Paris on suspicion of complicity in terrorist activities (released after eleven weeks, Korff claimed he had been tortured and that his captors were "making another Jesus Christ out of me"), Korff departed for America. He ministered for a time to a small congregation in Portsmouth, New Hampshire, before moving on to Taunton, Massachusetts, where he became an outspoken backer of various Democratic candidates. Retiring in 1971 (among other ailments, Korff suffered from high blood pressure and ulcers), Korff settled on a small farm in Rehoboth. In the next year's presidential election, he voted for the Republican candidate for the first time in his life, and quickly became as enamored of Nixon—"the greatest President of this century"—as he had been of his former hero, John F. Kennedy.

The real turning point in Korff's involvement, however, was watching Sam Ervin's televised performance during the Senate Watergate hearings. Incensed by what he deemed to be Ervin's misquotations from the Bible, and furious about the media's coverage, Korff used $1000 of his vacation money, a few contributions from friends, and a $3000 bank loan to place an ad in *The New York Times,* accusing Nixon's critics of "lynch-mob psychosis" and announcing the formation of the "National Citizens' Committee for Fairness to the Presidency." More ads followed, and in time Korff's movement enlisted more than two million members. Appreciative, Nixon invited him to the White House, and soon Korff became a regular Oval Office visitor.

Since the resignation, Nixon and Korff's relationship had deepened, if only because Korff's committee—now renamed The President Nixon Justice Fund—was at the moment the sole source for paying Nixon's legal bills. By the first of the year, with help from such Nixon allies as the Teamsters, the campaign had gathered in nearly $100,000 and had pledged to raise hundreds of thousands more. Korff himself had been in frequent touch with San Clemente, contacts he ensured were well-known. "My ego," he admitted, "is larger than most. It requires near-constant feeding."

Following a visit with Nixon shortly after his return from the hospital, Korff called a press conference to denounce the White House for withholding "thousands of [Nixon's] letters." Two weeks later, as Christmas neared, Korff issued an appeal for "the suspension of all civil suits, all legal harassment" against Nixon, lest the former President "be hounded to death." After visiting Nixon on his birthday, Korff called yet another press conference to tell the scores of reporters present that the White House was continuing to mistreat Nixon by keeping many of his personal possessions and political mementos, not to mention Julie's wedding dress and Pat's inaugural gown. "Do we have to deprive the man of his last vestige of dignity?" Korff demanded. "He has been emasculated. The genius of medicine could in no way repair the incalculable damage being inflicted on this man."

A few weeks later, the rabbi returned to visit Nixon again, and afterward there was another Nixon-sanctioned press conference. This time, however, Korff went too far. After delivering Nixon's message that he had no aspirations for any quick return to public life and had "nothing but love and admiration for Jerry Ford," Korff began to delve into Nixon's more private affairs, including his feelings about Watergate. The former President, he revealed, "repeatedly said to me, 'I should not have allowed a climate to reverberate that would even lead to Watergate. . . . I should have acted differently. I should not have yielded to considerations.'" Nixon, Korff continued, "has deep regrets, profound regrets, and he agonizes. He is tormented." He added that Nixon was in poor "physical and emotional health," a fact, Korff said, Nixon sought to conceal from his visitors and staff. He is "a lonely, troubled man," Korff went on, ". . . at a low ebb emotionally," given to periods of "inertia, sadness and depression." "The trauma," Korff concluded, "still lingers on."

After that, the invitations from Casa Pacifica came less frequently. Korff, however, had been right about one thing: Nixon was troubled—not only medically, but financially. As one of his lawyers had put it the previous August, Richard Nixon was, for all intents and purposes, "almost broke."

It was the classic middle-class dilemma: too many expenses, too little cash. On the plus side of the ledger, Nixon had what at first glance seemed to be sizable assets. They included congressional and presidential pensions with a combined yearly total of nearly $80,000; $60,000 in federal transition funds, plus $175,000 paid to him by Warner's as the first stage of the advance on his memoirs. In all, the funds available to him between the end of the transition and the beginning of the next fiscal year, July 1, amounted to $275,000—not counting his equity in Casa Pacifica, which he had purchased in 1969 for $1.5 million, as well as his two homes in Key Biscayne, Florida, for which he had paid slightly more than $250,000 in 1968.

Against this total, however, were considerable expenses. The cost of defending himself against various lawsuits, either current or expected, was projected at a minimum of $500,000. Since he had neglected to take out medical insurance after leaving the government, he also had to contend with a $23,000 hospital bill from his stay at Long Beach Memorial. Upkeep on Casa Pacifica, where the yearly property tax bill alone amounted to $37,300, consumed additional funds, and the previous July Nixon had had to scramble to keep from defaulting on a $226,400 mortgage payment. The bank had agreed to renegotiate his loan, but it had cost him an additional $17,000 in interest. Now, the same payment was coming due again, and Nixon, who often recounted growing up in a family so poor he had to eat a candy bar for breakfast, wasn't at all sure how he would come up with it. After paying his medical bill, he had exactly $500 left in his checking account.

A major part of his problem was taxes. During Watergate, an IRS audit had found that he had evaded paying a total of $432,787 in back levies, the bulk of it when one of his accountants had illegally backdated the gift of his vice presidential papers to the nation. It had been one of the impeachment counts against him, and Nixon had partially settled the obligation before leaving office. Still outstanding, however, was $148,081 in taxes due in 1969, on which the statute of limitations had run out, but which Nixon had nonetheless promised to pay. In addition, there were back income taxes due the State of California totaling more than $75,000.

Finally, being a former President was proving to be an expensive proposition. Congress' postpardon budget cuts had left Nixon with $60,000 with which to pay his staff (including his valet and cook, who were going off the federal payroll February 9), phone, light, postage and heat bills and any traveling he might want to do between the end of the transition and the beginning of the next fiscal year. As it now stood, Nixon could not even afford to process the more than one million pieces of mail that had piled up since the resignation.

The most obvious sign of short rations was the condition of Casa Pacifica's once-magnificent grounds. With the departure of the small army of federally employed gardeners who had seen to their care, they were overgrown and tattered, and the weeds in some spots had grown to a height of three feet. Mrs. Nixon, unable to keep up with them alone, had dug out her prized collection of rosebushes and given them away. The estate, as a result, had a down-at-the-heels, seedy look, and some of Nixon's neighbors were grumbling that the ex-President in their midst was violating the zoning laws and hurting property values.

The neighbors quieted after Paul Presley prevailed on a local Boy Scout troop to spend occasional Saturdays policing Casa Pacifica's perimeter. Similarly, a start was made at getting rid of the mail by the arrival of a cadre of grandmotherly volunteers from an Orange County Republican club. To handle the larger picture, Abplanalp, who had taken on the chore of managing Nixon's budget, had ordered major cuts in expenditures. For one thing, the Key Biscayne houses would have to go on the block. For another, Nixon had to get out of the habit of spending so much time on the telephone. In the few days before Christmas, he had made more than two hundred long-distance calls. That, Abplanalp decreed, would have to stop.

Not so easily dealt with was the expense of Nixon's staff. In the first weeks after his return from Washington, Nixon had been served by a total of twenty-two persons, including drivers, secretaries, stewards and senior aides like Ziegler and Brennan. That number had dwindled substantially and with the end of the transition would dwindle still more. Salaries for the survivors would have to come out of Nixon's pocket, and, with the need to add editorial personnel for the writing of the memoirs, it was apparent that additional layoffs would have to be made. One obvious candidate was his former press secretary, Ron Ziegler.

He had never been an effective public spokesman, and Watergate, which Ziegler originally proclaimed "a third-rate burglary" (a statement, like his others on the break-in, that later became "inoperative"), had undone what little credibility he had. Both Melvin Laird and John Connally had unsuccessfully urged Nixon to get rid of him, and even Rebozo, normally the most taciturn of Nixon's friends, had conceded that "Ron knows nothing about public relations." He also had a problem with those of the human kind. Thrust into a position of major responsibility at the age of twenty-nine, with no skills save his own street smarts, he was, like his mentor, H. R. Haldeman, frequently rude and habitually arrogant, even with many who had been his friends. The consequence was that by the time Nixon was driven from office, Ziegler had become the object of popular loathing not only from the press, but from most of Nixon's own staff.

Since then, Ziegler had done little to ingratiate himself. He remained caustic in his dealings with reporters and had managed through frequent shouting tirades over the phone to Washington to alienate the Ford White House as well. While his San Clemente colleagues rallied around Brennan, a gregarious charmer and host of frequent backyard barbecues, Ziegler stayed to himself. He lost weight and let his hair grow long, so it curled around his ears. He bought a motorcycle and acquired a set of drums. Cut off from his family, who had remained in Alexandria, Virginia, he holed up in his Laguna apartment and fretted about his future.

He had expected when his White House days were over to be awarded with a major position in publishing or industry. But that was before Watergate. He had not been involved in the scandal except defending it, but his connection was unbreakable in the public mind. Ziegler thought it was perversely funny at first, seeing his name and picture included in every Watergate rogues' gallery; lately, though, his sense of humor had waned. The job offers he had been hoping for had not been coming. Apart from a brief stint in advertising and an earlier career as a guide on a Disneyland Jungle Adventure boat, his entire résumé consisted of service to a disgraced President. Ziegler was realistic. Professionally, he admitted to a friend, his life was "pretty much shattered."

Nixon had tried to help, buttonholing visitors to "try to do something to help Ron." He'd also arranged interviews with several friendly corporations, including Marriott Hotels. Ziegler, however, continued to hold out for something more substantial. In the interim, he made plans to write a book and tried to launch a career as a lecturer on what he described as "The Use and Abuse of Power." A booking agent was lined up, and several college speaking dates were tentatively arranged. In preparation for his debut, Ziegler allowed himself to be interviewed on NBC's *Today* show. Rather than displaying his usual aggressive cockiness, he seemed subdued, almost repentant. "We conducted probably the worst public relations and press program in the history of the United States in the way we handled Watergate," he admitted. "Of course I made mistakes, but a press secretary is only as good as his information. I did not have the facts, only those I could find out about or was told."

The contrition did not advance his career. Shortly before his first scheduled speaking appearance, Boston University cut his promised fee from $3000 to $1000 on the grounds that it would be "morally wrong" to reward those associated with Watergate. A few days later, the student government board at Michigan State withdrew his speaking invitation altogether, and Ziegler thereupon canceled the remainder of his tour.

The problem of how to employ him was thus back with Nixon, and

Nixon was torn. He was aware of Ziegler's limitations, including his inability to get along with Brennan, with whom Ziegler maintained a fractious, icy relationship. But Nixon was also fond of Ziegler. After the firing of Haldeman and Ehrlichman, he had been his principal sounding board, not only for recriminations about the press, but over a whole range of topics, from Congress to foreign policy. With the exception of Haig, no one had been closer to him during that period, and not even Haig had been so unblinkingly loyal. "They will never get that pound of flesh," Nixon had replied to previous calls for Ziegler's ouster. Now, however, the situation had altered.

Physically and emotionally, Ziegler was burned out. Unlike the rest of the staff who had come to San Clemente, he had not been able to relax. Nixon's demands on him were every bit as intense as they had been in the White House. He had had to make all the major decisions, deal with the press, lawyers, doctors and the White House. Most wearing of all, he also had had to deal with Nixon. It was he Nixon called in when he wanted a companion to rail at or brood with, he who had spent countless hours with him, alone, listening to his not always rational discourses. Now, the strain of it had caught up to Ziegler. For the last several weeks he had done basically nothing, and it was then that he began to sense a change in Nixon's attitude toward him.

Nothing had been said; there had been no change in his access or daily routine. When an aide fell out of favor with Nixon, the signs were always more subtle, no more than a gnawing feeling that the psychic ground had shifted. Ziegler had that feeling. He knew he had become expendable.

In mid-January, with the end of the transition only a few weeks off, Nixon summoned Brennan into his office to tell him he had made a decision. He had agonized over it, but had reluctantly concluded that Ron would have to go. Then he called in Ziegler. Nixon, who hated dealing with personnel matters, especially firings, was edgy. Finally he said, "Ron, Jack has something to tell you."

After Brennan had finished, Nixon paid Ziegler all the necessary courtesies, adding that he would, of course, be welcome to stay on as a "volunteer consultant" until he had lined up something suitable to his talents. Ziegler thanked him, and said he understood. He was calm throughout.

Afterward, Ziegler rode his motorcycle over to the bar of the San Clemente Inn to talk to two reporters from the *Los Angeles Times.* Nixon, he insisted, was still his friend, and he would continue to help him anyway he could. "I'll be around," Ziegler said. "I'll be in and out. I don't think he plans to replace me. I don't think he has to replace me." His own life, he added, was in "a recycling period." He smiled, as if amused by his own Zieglerism. "I have now to dial a telephone and pick up my own luggage at the airport, drive a car for the first time in five and a half years."

But as the drinking continued, Ziegler grew more bitter. Recently he had tried to use his Carte Blanche card in a San Clemente shop and been told that it was canceled. *Canceled.* Did the reporters realize how embarrassed he felt at that moment? Did they know why it was canceled? Because he hadn't paid his bill, and the reason he hadn't paid his bill was because the White House wasn't sending his mail to him. That was the way it was now at Casa Pacifica: to get your mail, you had to hire a lawyer. It was part of a pattern, a plan consciously and vindictively designed to punish Richard Nixon and anyone who had anything to do with him. Nixon could take it, but he couldn't. He was "fed up with Richard Nixon taking it in the ear."

What did people want? Ziegler demanded. How severe did Nixon's penalty have to be? He had resigned in disgrace. His friends had abandoned him. He was certainly a beaten man. Ziegler looked up from his glass. "If society wants to put him in a cell, there is a cell out there. Have you seen the size of his office? What more is wanted?"

The reporters did not answer. Two hours had passed and too much booze had been consumed. Even Ziegler was tired of talking about it. He simply wanted them to understand what had been happening. That had been his job, making the press understand, and in the past he had not done it very well. This time he described the situation with precision. What Richard Nixon was going through, his friend, Ron Ziegler, said, was "exile."

As the transition deadline of February 9 approached, the compound that had been the Western White House appeared more and more like a ghost town. The once-clogged staff parking lot was now all but deserted. Here and there, teams of GSA workmen, hammers and crowbars in hand, scurried to dismantle the prefabricated modules that had been the working quarters for Nixon's staff. By the ninth, all but three of the buildings —one for Nixon, his two remaining secretaries and senior staff; another, which formerly housed Kissinger and the national security staff, for the use of the mail-opening volunteers; the third, a Secret Service command post—would be gone, and most of the Coast Guard men who had patrolled the grounds and spent their off-hours planting flowers with them. Already, nearly all of the telephone lines had been disconnected, including the one that had linked Casa Pacifica directly to the White House. Across what had been the helipad, someone had strung a volleyball net. At the main gate, the sentry who had stood in dress whites had been removed, his place taken by a speaker box. Beyond, on the road that led into San Clemente, a vandal had defaced one of the street signs. Once, it had proclaimed AVENIEDA EL PRESIDENTE. Now it read, AVENIEDA EX EL PRESIDENTE.

Ex El Presidente himself was feeling somewhat better, sufficiently well in any case to ride a blue golf cart occasionally to his office. He also received a few visitors, among them Billy Graham, who reported he had prayed with Nixon, and that the former President was reading "an excellent Life of Christ"; John Lungren, who pronounced him "looking physically improved" for the first time since leaving the hospital; and Henry Kissinger, who dropped by for dinner on the way to a weekend vacation in Palm Springs.

The news that drifted in from the outside world was mostly bad. In Washington, a federal judge had ruled that Congress had acted constitutionally in laying claim to Nixon's papers and tapes. Though an appeals court had temporarily stayed the ruling, the prospects for overturning it did not look bright. Meanwhile, in another federal courtroom, Tim Babcock, the former Republican governor of Montana, had been sentenced to four months in prison for concealing the source of a $54,000 contribution to Nixon's 1972 reelection campaign. Elsewhere, Republicans were reacting with a mixture of ridicule and anger to recent reports that Nixon might one day serve as a party spokesman. "*Ich kann nicht Englisch sprechen*," Hugh Scott had answered to a reporter who asked for a comment—I cannot speak English.

Nixon said nothing. He was no longer commenting on the events of the day, good or bad. For the moment he was concentrating on matters closer to home, like the small farewell party that had been planned for the departing staff and a few friends the afternoon of Saturday, the ninth. He prepared himself for it all that morning. There weren't going to be any replays of the teary good-bye in the East Room; he was determined to keep up a brave front. "I can't let them leave and take with them a state of frustration," he told a friend.

Shortly before five, the guests began gathering in Casa Pacifica's living room. By the time Nixon came in some minutes later, the alcohol was freely flowing, and laughter filled the room. Nixon, his wife on his arm, worked the crowd, shaking hands and passing out autographed pictures. Many of the nearly sixty faces in the room were unknown to him. He mumbled his apologies to the strangers; it was hard, he said, for a President to keep track of everyone. He was sorry for that; he'd have liked to know them better.

Finally Nixon delivered a short speech. He teased Brennan with a few quips and told the others how much he appreciated everything they had done for him. They should be proud of themselves. However lowly their position, they had all contributed to the cause of peace, and he would miss them. But they mustn't be sad. When they looked back at the past, it should only be on the good things, the memories they would all treasure. There were many good things they had done together, Richard Nixon told them. Many.

Outside, it was quiet. On the beach, where armed Secret Service agents had formerly shooed away the public, a solitary surfer prepared to take to the waves. The sea was empty. The Coast Guard cutters that had monotonously churned its waters, ever on the alert, had been withdrawn. Now it belonged to anyone. The surfer glanced up the cliff face. Seventy-five feet above him, a sound-sensitive surveillance camera peered down. "Can you hear me?" the surfer whispered. Slowly, mechanically, the camera nodded yes.

Departure from the White House, August 9, 1974: "Always remember," he had told his staff, "others may hate you—but those who hate you don't win unless you hate them, and then you destroy yourself."

Demonstrators outside the White House reacting to the pardon decision: "There was a brief pause, a momentary reflex of disbelief; then the fire storm broke with a full fury."

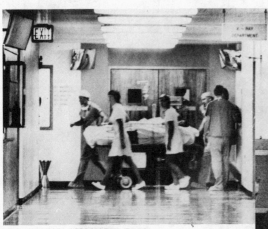

TWO PHOTOS: ASSOCIATED PRESS

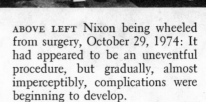

ABOVE LEFT Nixon being wheeled from surgery, October 29, 1974: It had appeared to be an uneventful procedure, but gradually, almost imperceptibly, complications were beginning to develop.

ABOVE Twenty-three days after being admitted to the hospital, Nixon goes home: "His illness would remain the enduring, unshakable token that he was vulnerable after all."

BELOW LEFT Nixon writing his memoirs in his San Clemente den: How history judged him, he had predicted to Henry Kissinger, would depend on who wrote the history.

ABOVE Nixon walking the grounds of Casa Pacifica, July 1975: Brooding, depressed, unable to relax, he was, said Ron Ziegler, "in exile."

LEFT As Teamster President Frank E. Fitzsimmons (right) looks on, Nixon tees off at the La Costa golf tournament, October 9, 1975: A reemergence in a setting and a company almost guaranteed to provoke.

BELOW Nixon and Pat touring China, February 1976: "If he wants to do this country a favor," Barry Goldwater said on the Senate floor, "he'll stay there."

WALLY MCNAMEE/NEWSWEEK

WIDE WORLD

Nixon addressing the faithful at the dedication of the Richard Nixon Community Center, Hayden, Kentucky, July 2, 1978—his first public speech since the resignation: "The crowd roared and continued to roar, not so much at Nixon's words, which were predictable and banal, but at the sheer, improbable fact of his presence."

Nixon with David Frost before the start of their television interviews, March 1977: "He thought he had handled himself well. He hadn't groveled; the dramatic requirements of the medium had been met."

While Jimmy Carter forces a smile, Nixon greets Chinese leader Teng Hsiao-ping at the White House, January 29, 1979: "You know," he said that night at dinner, "they're playing the same songs, the songs they played when I was here."

Nixon and the deposed Iranian Shah pose for pictures after their meeting at the Shah's Cuernavaca, Mexico, refuge, July 13, 1979: "You've got to keep fighting," the American exile told the Iranian one. "You could fade away, but that's the easy way out."

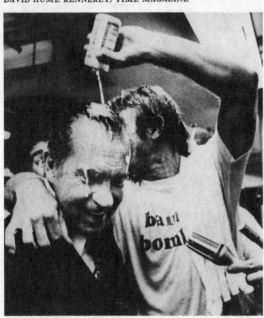

Nixon with Carter, Kissinger and Ford at reception prior to Capitol memorial for Hubert Humphrey, January 14, 1979: "He stood there a moment, head down and shoulders hunched, nervously shifting from foot to foot. To the others in the room he seemed aged and morose."

Nixon being doused with beer in the California Angels locker room after the Angels clinched the 1979 American League Western Division championship: "Something more than baseballs was in the air. After a long and difficult dormancy, the Exile of San Clemente was beginning to stir."

New York Mayor Edward Koch grimaces as he encounters Nixon en route to a funeral: "Not everyone was pleased by his return. According to the polls, the same margin of Americans as ever thought him guilty and unworthy of playing a role in public life."

Nixon greets an admirer as he emerges from his New York town house to take his morning stroll: "New York was the center of the action—'the fast track,' as Nixon called it. It was where he wanted, where he needed, to be."

Nixon in his library in New Jersey: "Of his essential blamelessness he remained convinced. 'Always dream of the future,' he wrote a friend. 'Never think of the past.'"

Nixon, Pat and Tricia with Julie's daughter Jennie (center) and Tricia's son Christopher (right): "He goo-gooed and baby-talked with them, did everything grandfathers are supposed to do, including spoil them shamelessly."

7

Watergate Redux

The limousines bearing the evening's guests began rolling through the wrought-iron gates of Walter Annenberg's estate just after sunset, the Palm Springs paparazzi craning after them.

Ronald and Nancy Reagan flashed by, then Bob and Dolores Hope; the futurist, Herman Kahn, came in, and right behind, scowling, Frank Sinatra and Barbara Marx. As the shutters clicked, the procession continued: Freeman Gosden, Amos of *Amos and Andy* and his wife, Jane; Leonard Firestone, the U.S. ambassador to Belgium, and his wife, Barbara; John Swearingen, the chairman of Standard Oil of Indiana, and his wife, Bonnie; automobile dealer Holmes Tuttle, the fattest of the California fat cats; John Mulcahy, the former ambassador to Ireland; Willard Keith, the Los Angeles insurance executive and his wife, Adeline. Spiro Agnew, who was now a houseguest in Sinatra's neighboring estate, did not attend. Nor was the press invited. It was, explained the host, "just a very quiet, private dinner for a few old friends."

The guest of honor, accompanied by his wife, chief of staff, medical corpsman and six Secret Service agents, had arrived several days before, roughly at the same time that several of his former aides were being sentenced in Washington. Richard Nixon had made no comment about the terms Sirica had handed down, nor would he the rest of that sunny weekend. On this, his first public outing since the conclusion of the official transition two weeks before, he had come to relax.

That afternoon, at Annenberg's urging, he'd tried his hand at a round of golf. He had shown good form, considering the rustiness of his play. But after two holes he had tired, and, limping noticeably, retreated to the house for a nap. By cocktail time, however, he was fully refreshed, and as the party sat down for dinner, he was even managing a few jokes. Turning to Kahn, who was seated on his left, Nixon cracked, "You know, the last guy who sat there was assassinated last week." Kahn smiled politely. He had no idea to whom Nixon was referring.

The banter continued over dinner. The governor of California described the adobe ranch house he and his wife were in the midst of restoring outside Santa Barbara, which touched off a colloquy on the virtues of the Old West. Finally, Nixon noted that it had been Tricia's birthday the day before. She was doing well, he reported, enjoying life in New York with Eddie. David and Julie, who were still in Washington, were doing fine, too, though he missed them, and hoped that they would soon move to California. He was doing fine himself, Nixon added, working on his memoirs and looking forward to the next political season. He wouldn't be involved personally, of course, but perhaps there would be a role for him someday. Pat, looking resplendent in a long red gown and looking all the better, thanks to a recent gain in weight, merely smiled.

Toward eleven, Annenberg delivered a toast. He thanked Nixon for having appointed him ambassador to the Court of St. James's and expressed appreciation for the support he had given him during his diplomatic tour. "Not," he added, "that it was always easy." There were knowing smiles. Walter had had a difficult time of it in London.

Lifting a glass of Dom Perignon, Nixon got up to reply. He praised Annenberg and his "beautiful, gracious wife Lenore," then began extolling the wonders of their house. He too had once lived in a big house with many rooms, Nixon said. "When you are on top," he went on, "it is filled with all your friends." He paused and smiled self-consciously. "Afterward, you don't need a house so large." Some of the dinner guests began dabbing at their eyes with napkins. Nixon smiled again. Like Lenore and Walter, all those present were true friends. They had remained loyal through the years, been by his side when he was up, and stayed with him now, when he was down. The word "down" hung in the air. Nixon gazed about the room. "But let me assure you—I'm not out."

Nixon, who returned to San Clemente the next morning, had been telling the truth. He was down—there was no doubt about that—as low and troubled as he had been since the surgery. But for all his woes, legal, financial, physical, emotional, he was not out—not by any measure. And, ever so slowly, he was beginning to climb back.

His most immediate concern continued to be money. Despite Abplanalp's budget tinkering and Korff's fund-raising, he was still short of cash, and at a rate of $225 an hour his legal bills were mounting. Haldeman, who was in the midst of an equally expensive appeals process, had recently devised a solution: for $100,000, he had sold two hours of televised conversation to CBS. The interview itself had been unremarkable, Haldeman dodging Mike Wallace's questions, particularly those on Watergate ("I don't know what happened") every step of the way. But it had paid off handsomely, and it had given Nixon an idea: if Haldeman could be paid for talking, why not he?

In early March, over dinner with Johnny Grant and Paul Presley, Nixon casually remarked how extraordinary it was that Haldeman had been paid all that money for doing so little. Not that he begrudged Bob, Nixon hastened to add. God knew, he had bills to pay—$400,000 to his lawyer alone he had heard. So why shouldn't he sell his recollections to television? Publishers paid for books; it was only fair that television paid for interviews. CBS had paid Lyndon Johnson, and Eisenhower, too, and there had been no complaint then. The only reason Bob was getting so much flack now was because he had worked for him. Yes, he concluded, Bob was on to something.

Nixon did not say explicitly that he was interested in following the same course, but Grant and Presley took the hint. They alerted Korff, and within weeks the trio began what Nixon's office described as "un-authorized, exploratory talks" with the networks. Their asking price, however, was stiff—$250,000—and the networks, stung by the publicity that had followed disclosure of the payments to Haldeman, were leery. Nor was Nixon's staff enthusiastic. Ziegler opposed the idea, warning no good could come of it. Lungren didn't like the notion for health reasons, no more than Nixon's attorneys did for legal ones. Even Halde-man ventured that perhaps the public might not yet be "in a mood of acceptance for what [Nixon] would have to say." In any case, the negotiations were going nowhere, and finally Nixon called them off.

With television plans abandoned at least for the moment, Nixon turned to his book, and as his body strengthened, dictated increasingly long recollections of his family, Whittier, California, childhood and adolescence. How, if at all, the material would fit into the final manu-script had not yet been decided. Some members of the now-shrunken staff favored deleting it entirely, concentrating solely on the events of the Nixon presidency. As with nearly everything else connected with the book, including possession of the papers that were to provide the bulk of the research material, the question was still hanging. One of the few matters that had been resolved, however the book ultimately emerged, was that Rose Mary Woods would play a part in its shaping.

Her nominal title, personal secretary to the President, had never given her justice. "Aunt Rose" was more like family. She was "the fifth Nixon," friends said, the one who could talk back to him and argue with him, the one whose political judgment he respected, the one, perhaps, who knew him best. A White House aide, who, like everyone who worked for Nixon was both baffled by the relationship and not a little awed by it, tried once to describe her. "She's a little like the choir member in the Baptist Church who falls in love with the minister," he mused. "It's the classic Christian fantasy of the virgin and God—and obviously part of the fantasy is that nothing ever happens. It just remains a kind of worship." Nixon's mother, Hannah, put it more simply. "Rose," she told her son, "is our kind of people."

Born in a small town in Ohio, she had come to Washington in 1943, after her high-school sweetheart had died of spinal meningitis, and there quickly found a job in the wartime bureaucracy, working as a secretary in the Office of Censorship. After the war, she moved to Capitol Hill to take another secretarial post on a House committee studying the Marshall Plan. It was here that she met a freshman congressman named Richard Nixon. She liked him—Nixon, she later recalled, was the only member of the committee who submitted expense accounts "titled, totalled, signed, and all properly done"—and he, her—"One of my most honest critics," he wrote of her in *Six Crises*; "always at her best when the pressures are greatest"—and, when Nixon went on to the Senate, she came with him.

Her duties had little to do with stenography or typing. Rose Woods more often took names than dictation. She knew who the friends were, and who were the enemies, who had helped—how often and when—and who hadn't, who was owed, and who wasn't. She was the gatekeeper, guardian and mother protector, and her loyalty was fierce and absolute. When, after Nixon won the Republican presidential nomination in 1968, and Len Hall, who had been his campaign chairman in 1960, but had since defected to George Romney and Nelson Rockefeller, phoned to offer his congratulations, Woods cut him off with one sentence: "Don't call us, we'll call you."

Ironically, it was Nixon's triumph that year that had been the source of most of her problems. The system Haldeman had devised for regulating traffic in and out of the Oval Office allowed for only one gatekeeper. Rose was to be shunted aside, put in charge of such chores as maintaining the Nixon family Christmas-card list.

Though her demotion had come at Nixon's instruction, Woods focused her anger on Haldeman, and he, in turn, began carrying tales to Nixon of Rose's supposed drinking. As a result, she came to detest Haldeman—and those who worked for him, including Ziegler—all the more. When Watergate broke, Woods blamed Haldeman, even as she continued to defend Nixon. After Alexander Butterfield disclosed the existence of the White House taping system to the Ervin Committee, Woods swore at him, "You dirty bastard. You have contributed to the downfall of the greatest President this country ever had. You are on the other side."

But Woods was soon swept up in Watergate herself. On September 28, 1973, Nixon asked her to go to Camp David for the weekend to transcribe some tapes, including one of a conversation between him and Haldeman on June 20, 1972, three days after the Watergate break-in. The tape was of poor quality, and she had trouble picking up the voices. At one point, Nixon came into her cabin, jiggled the tape back and forth a few times, then expressed wonderment that she could hear anything.

But Woods pressed on, finally halting at 3:00 A.M. Three hours later, she rose to continue the transcribing. But it was not until approximately two the next afternoon, back at her office in the White House, that she finally reached the relevant section on the June 20 tape.

She had just begun to listen to it, she later recalled, when the telephone behind her rang. Turning to pick up the receiver, Woods inadvertently pushed down the record button. When she got off the phone, four or five minutes later, she realized her mistake. Part of the tape had been recorded over, and now played only as a hissing buzz. Immediately, she informed Nixon what had happened. He told her not to worry; the tape had not been subpoenaed.

But the tape had been subpoenaed, and when Nixon's lawyers went into Sirica's chambers to explain what had happened, there was consternation. Not only was the five minutes Woods had admitted erasing missing, but thirteen and a half additional minutes as well. "Maybe I'm out of line for saying this," Special White House Counsel Fred Buzhardt told Sirica, "but quite frankly, I think that Miss Woods ought to have time to reflect on this and she ought to have time to secure counsel."

Rose Mary Woods had reflected, and she was positive she was not responsible for the additional erasures. But that did not change the White House position: she was guilty until proved otherwise, and the President's lawyers would not defend her. With Nixon's approval, what the White House did do was have her pose for a series of awkward-looking press photos to demonstrate how she had erased the tape. The pictures wound up on front pages and the cover of Newsweek, and Aunt Rose, who had worked for Richard Nixon seventeen hours a day, seven days a week, who had baby-sat for his children and exchanged clothes with his wife, became a national joke.

Since the resignation, she had remained in Washington, overseeing the packing of Nixon's personal belongings. Ford's staff, Buchen in particular, had done their best to make her life miserable. Guards had been posted at the door of her office—Nixon's former EOB "hideaway"—to ensure that she removed nothing from the premises. All of Nixon's possessions—and many of her own—were frozen by congressional order. Until February, and the end of the official transition, she had been forbidden even to read her own mail. She also had been prohibited from sending anything to San Clemente, including Nixon's family photographs or his treasured collection of gavels and elephants. The files that Nixon had wanted her to sort through and categorize were closed and locked. When she protested to Buchen, he was contemptuous and hostile, and several times after talking to him she had been left in tears.

Cut off and alone, unable to visit Nixon in California because of the cutback in staff funds, she had converted his former office into a kind of shrine. For six months she kept his half-smoked cigar in his ashtray, his glasses on his desk and his wastebasket half-filled, everything preserved, just as he had left them. She refused even to let the office be dusted for fear that the items might be moved around. She was keeping it, she explained, for historical reasons. One day years from now a Nixon library would be built. Then, perhaps, people would understand.

But with the end of the transition even that wish was frustrated. On Buchen's order, the office had been shuttered, and Nixon's personal items packed for shipment to California. Woods herself had been transferred to a white brick house overlooking Lafayette Square, where Spiro Agnew had culled through his possessions after resigning the vice presidency.

Lately the climate had improved. Though the bulk of Nixon's belongings remained under federal seal, 141 crates full of others had been sent to California, and soon Woods herself would be going as well. Nixon, with whom she had talked every day on the phone, was cheered by the prospect of her return. It was one of the few pieces of good news he'd received recently.

Apart from the acquittal of former Treasury Secretary John Connally on charges of having received a $10,000 bribe from a dairy industry lobbyist, nearly everything else that occurred lately had been bad, from the conviction for lying of an appraiser who had been charged with helping Nixon take an illegal tax deduction, to a consortium of reporters and editors bringing suit to block the release of his papers and tapes.* Even Korff was acting up again. The rabbi said he was "physically tired" and "mentally exhausted," and his public statements showed it. At one point he claimed that Nixon had been "set up during Watergate" by unnamed intelligence agencies. At another, he charged that his

---

* The reporters in question were columnist Jack Anderson, who had been trying to obtain access to Nixon's papers and tapes since 1974, and a group of Washington journalists called "The Reporters Committee for Freedom of the Press."

The deposition took place at Casa Pacifica on July 25, 1975. During the six hours of questioning, Nixon was frequently testy, especially in response to queries put to him by Anderson's lawyer, William Dobrovir, a former Watergate assistant prosecutor who had won notoriety by playing a portion of a subpoenaed Nixon tape at a Georgetown cocktail party in December 1973.

At one point, Dobrovir asked Nixon if he thought the public had a right to know the full story of Watergate. Before Nixon could answer, one of his attorneys cut in, saying, "What do you mean by Watergate? The building?" When Dobrovir asked again, Nixon replied, "If my counsel doesn't know, I would never put my wisdom above his."

Later in the session, Dobrovir asked Nixon for his definition of "wrongdoing." Nixon threw the question back at him: "I am asking you, what do you say is wrongdoing? I don't know."

Finally, as the questioning was coming to an end, there was this exchange:

DOBROVIR: Let me ask the question, then, Mr. Nixon. Do you have a time period that you expect, within which to make full disclosure of all Watergate matters?

NIXON: No.

DOBROVIR: Do you expect it to be longer than five years?

NIXON: I can't tell you until I see how big the task is. Most of the tapes are not as audible as the one you played at that cocktail party.

office had been broken into and tape recordings of his conversations with reporters stolen. Finally, in late May, at a Washington press conference, he announced that he was resigning as head of the Justice Fund for what he would only describe as "personal reasons." Afterward, Nixon had been able to convince him to stay on an additional two months to raise the $155,000 that was currently owed to the lawyers. What would happen after the period was over was one of many things Nixon did not know.

The ongoing uncertainty—over money, over his legal problems, over what he would do with himself in the future—affected Nixon's mood, which, though considerably improved since the fall, continued to swing. Some days he seemed almost euphoric, telling visitors that next year, when his book was finished, he would be off to Europe for a round of talks with political leaders—"doing what I can," as he put it, "to help solidify the cause of peace." In his more expansive moments he even predicted that the distaste for him would soon pass away. A year, maybe two, and then the record of his achievements would be apparent. "Our day," Nixon assured an old friend, "will come again."

At other times he was just as gloomy, worrying over his book (and telling friends he would be fortunate to finish it in five years, much less one or two), blaming himself for the recent fall of Saigon ("South Vietnam would not have gone down the drain, if I hadn't had my problem," he told Harry S. Dent, a former political aide), despairing over criticisms from former Republican friends ("If they want me, fine; if they don't, fine. I just wish they'd keep quiet about it. They don't have to go around talking about it all the time."), anguishing whether he would forever remain imprisoned behind the walls of his estate.

Depending on his temperament, he welcomed visitors (even unlikely ones, like Charles Evers, the black mayor of Fayette, Mississippi, who had a long talk with him in March), or shooed them away (including the closest of friends). Sometimes he could talk nonstop for hours, discoursing on the state of the economy ("Things may be heating up too quickly; I was for a slower recovery."), assessing the performance of his successor ("Okay . . . but he's too accessible; you can't get caught up in absurdities."), detailing what he would do to mark the American bicentennial were he still President ("I would ask five or six of the best brains around me to go off on a retreat for several weeks to ponder some things—how we could make our people feel more pride, not be so concerned with Arab wealth. . . . I'd work on a major television presentation . . . remind them that in 1776 we only had spiritual growth and look where it took us.") But if he was feeling low he barely uttered a word.

His feelings about Watergate were as divided as his moods. On his better days he could joke about it. "You ought to write about Watergate," he teased a former aide, who was thinking of embarking on a career as a novelist. "There's a lot more money in it." At other moments he could not bring himself even to mention the word. Whatever responsibility he felt varied from day to day, visitor to visitor. When the Reverend T. Eugene Coffin, the pastor of his Whittier church, paid him a call in late April, Nixon was feeling contrite. "There was some wrong in what I did," he admitted. "I made a big mistake." A few weeks later, when Los Angeles television producer Wally George stopped by, Nixon was brimming with defiance, denying culpability, ascribing his problems to Haldeman, claiming that whatever he had done, other Presidents had done worse. "This Watergate thing was ridiculous," Nixon snorted to George. "Nothing like the press made it out to be." Korff, who at various times had heard Nixon express contrition and defiance both, eventually became convinced that Nixon didn't know what to believe, if only because he remained puzzled by Watergate itself. "To this day," Korff reported to the press after one of his meetings with Nixon, "he does not know the full story."

So it frequently appeared. In conversation with friends, Nixon continually expressed bewilderment that Mitchell could have become involved with anyone so "nutty," as Nixon put it, as Watergate burglar Gordon Liddy. He was equally baffled by the criminal involvement of Jeb Stuart Magruder. The Williams-educated deputy director of CREEP was as polished as he was buttoned-down, and not at all the sort, in Nixon's estimation, who would be, as Magruder had been, at the very center of the break-in conspiracy. Indeed, at times Nixon had difficulty keeping track of who was guilty and who was not. At one point during a meeting with a former junior aide, Nixon complimented the man on his evident good health. Apart from seeming a trifle pale, Nixon went on, he seemed remarkably well, considering all the rigors of prison. Ruefully amused, the aide told Nixon he was mistaken; he had never been to prison.

The Watergate Special Prosecution Force, whose work was finally winding down, was mystified itself by certain aspects of the scandal. Despite nearly three years of investigation, the prosecutors had yet to unravel the mystery of the eighteen-and-a-half-minute tape gap, or, with certainty, the motive behind the Watergate break-in itself. Nor had they been able to pin specific responsibility for the illegal wiretapping of a number of reporters and national security aides, or the subsequent transfer of the tapes' logs from the FBI to the White House in 1972, an event that ultimately led to the dismissal of charges against Daniel Ellsberg. Taken together, there were perhaps half a dozen matters, large and small, that continued to tantalize. But the one that touched Nixon most intimately was the case of his best friend, Charles G. ("Bebe") Rebozo.

.   .   .

Bebe—the name was given to him as an infant by a brother who could not pronounce "baby" in Spanish—was not a presidential pal, as Dave Powers had been to John Kennedy; a golfing buddy, as Charlie Allen had been to Dwight Eisenhower; or an intellectual valet, as Harry Hopkins had been to FDR. Bebe Rebozo was simply there whenever Richard Nixon needed him, which turned out to be much of the time.

They had first met in 1950, when Nixon, weary from the rigors of his just-completed senatorial campaign, came to Miami for a brief vacation. George Smathers, Florida's junior senator, and a friend of Rebozo's since boyhood, asked Bebe to "show him a good time." Rebozo, who frequently entertained Smathers' Democratic friends, among them Lyndon Johnson and Louisiana Senator Russell Long, was happy to oblige, and invited Nixon for a cruise on his houseboat. Nixon brought along his briefcase, and as Rebozo subsequently recalled, "I doubt if I exchanged a dozen words with the guy."

A few days later, however, Rebozo received a note from Nixon, thanking him for the cruise, and expressing the hope they'd see each other again. More trips followed, and soon the two of them were the fastest of friends.

Warm, gregarious, good-humored, a legendary ladies' man and master martini maker, Rebozo, said William Safire, who knew him well, became for Nixon "the operative brother, the man who could be 'there' without having to be addressed, noticed or otherwise attended to." They golfed, fished together, lazed in the sun. They played sophomoric pranks and swapped ribald jokes. But mostly they were simply alone. Long moments, hours even, would pass with the two of them together, neither man saying anything. When finally the moment came to speak, it would be Nixon who would do the talking, Bebe the devoted, endlessly patient listener.

Such men were rare in politics, and Bebe became a valued companion. The night Nixon lost the presidency to John Kennedy, Bebe was the lone outsider who commiserated with him in his suite. When Nixon made the decision to run in 1968, he was a guest at Bebe's house. He was there again five years later, when he learned of the Watergate break-in. From then until the resignation, when Nixon looked for advice, when he needed solace from the pressures, or sustenance in his trials, it was to Bebe that he turned. They walked the beach together and cruised the Potomac. At Key Biscayne, where Bebe's was the only private house within the presidential compound, they listened to music, drank—Nixon mixing the martinis, Bebe whipping up the *picadillos*—and tried to find cheer in the ball games. Like Rose, he was family, an uncle to the girls, a companion to Pat, the only non-Nixon, save for Rose, present at the Nixons' table every Thanksgiving, Christmas and Easter.

Since the resignation, Rebozo had remained in constant touch, flying to San Clemente for long weekends, several times per month. Even when close friends were being kept away from Casa Pacifica, Rebozo was always the exception. He was loyal and could be trusted. His advice was valued, especially about Nixon's money.

Making money—for himself and for Nixon—was Bebe Rebozo's principal talent. Poor as a child (his father was a Cuban immigrant cigar maker), Rebozo hustled through a score of menial jobs, before taking a modest plunge in the postwar Florida real-estate market. He bought low, sold high, then bought again. By the time he met Nixon, Rebozo was president of two personal finance companies and controlled a string of holdings ranging from coin-operated laundries to office buildings. He was also heavily invested in real estate, and with his guidance Nixon invested as well and profited substantially. Eventually, Rebozo sold his finance companies to go into the banking business, as board chairman, president and principal stockholder of the Key Biscayne Bank. His friendship with Nixon did not hurt him. During the five and a half years of Nixon's presidency, Rebozo was the recipient of various forms of federal largesse, and partly as a result his wealth increased sevenfold.

How Rebozo came by all his money was a source of continuing interest to the Watergate prosecutors, who had been pursuing his financial connections to Nixon since the beginning of the Watergate investigation. They had checked out rumors (later proven to be false) that Rebozo had served as the conduit to Nixon for a $1 million campaign contribution from Arab oilmen. They had followed up allegations (also false) that Rebozo and Nixon maintained a multimillion slush fund in a secret bank account in the Bahamas. In all they had served 200 subpoenas, questioned 123 people (among them Nixon's gardener at Key Biscayne), hauled 28 witnesses before grand juries, and thus far their efforts had led nowhere.

Nonetheless, the suspicions persisted, and Rebozo remained under investigation for possible perjury, bribery and violation of income tax and campaign contribution statutes. But what intrigued the prosecutors most was the $100,000 Rebozo had received from Howard Hughes.

The money—two installments of $50,000, all in cash—had been delivered in 1970 by Richard Danner, a former FBI agent and Nixon friend, who had gone to work for Hughes in the late 1960s. Though the White House later claimed the money was a campaign contribution, the cash was not put in any political account. Instead, Rebozo placed it in a safety-deposit box in his own bank. There, according to Rebozo, it remained secure and untouched until 1973, when, in the wake of investigations by *Newsday*, the IRS and the Senate Watergate Committee, he returned it to Danner.

Rebozo later explained that he had initially retained the cash because there was "no campaign manager or no finance director at the time and I was waiting to be named." After the former secretary of commerce, Maurice Stans, was named head of Nixon's fund-raising efforts in February 1972, Rebozo continued to keep the cash, because "I didn't want to risk even the remotest embarrassment of Hughes' connection with Nixon."

Others had a different story. According to Herbert Kalmbach, the Nixon personal attorney who was convicted for dispensing hush money to the Watergate burglars, Rebozo told him that he had given part of the cash to Nixon's brothers, Donald and Edward, as well as to Rose Mary Woods (all of whom later denied receiving anything), along with "unnamed others." When Kalmbach suggested that Rebozo explain everything to the IRS, Rebozo replied, "This touches the President and the President's family, and I just can't do anything to add to his problems at this time, Herb."

Clearly the money had gone somewhere during the three years it was supposedly in Rebozo's safety-deposit box, for when government investigators opened the box, they discovered that the original paper wrappings had been replaced by rubber bands, that a number of the bills had been shuffled and that five pieces of currency bore serial numbers showing they had been printed after Danner had given Rebozo the cash. In their haste to replenish the horde, someone had also added an extra $100 bill.

The most likely explanation is that the original $100,000 went into a slush fund created for Nixon's personal use by Danner, Rebozo and Nixon in 1967. The fund, which by some estimates contained as much as $790,000, was maintained by Rebozo in several different accounts and consisted of leftover contributions to the 1968 presidential campaign as well as donations from more recent political givers. In 1972, Rebozo's attorney drew $4562.38 out of the fund to buy Mrs. Nixon a set of platinum and diamond earrings. Rebozo himself spent another $45,621 for improvements and furnishings for Nixon's Key Biscayne homes. "I'm not going to nit-pick with the President," Rebozo told Senate investigators, when they asked him about the expenditures. "If there's something I think he should have, I might just go ahead and do it without him even knowing about it. He just doesn't concern himself at all with financial problems; never has."

But the fund had another purpose: buying silence. Nixon himself alluded to it in a conversation with Haldeman and Ehrlichman twelve days before he fired them. "Let me ask you this," he said, "legal fees will be substantial. But there's a way we can get it to you and, uh—two or three hundred thousand dollars, huh? . . . No strain. Doesn't come out'a me. I didn't, I never intended to use the money at all. As a matter of fact, I told Bebe, basically be sure that people like, uh—who have contributed money over the contributing years are, uh, favored and so forth in general. And he's used it for the purpose of getting things out, paid for in check, and all that sort of thing." In a conversation with John Dean in March 1973, Nixon apparently referred to the fund again, this time as a source for buying off E. Howard Hunt. "We could get a million dollars," he boasted. "We could get it in cash. I know where it could be gotten . . . the question is who the hell would handle it."*

Thus far, however, neither the tapes nor the other evidence that had been gathered was sufficient to charge Rebozo with a crime. To do that, the prosecutors required a firmer link. What they needed was the testimony of Bebe's best friend.

Early that spring, Henry Ruth, who had succeeded Jaworski as Watergate prosecutor, called Miller to tell him that, despite the conclusion of the trial of Haldeman, Ehrlichman and Mitchell, Nixon's testimony was still necessary to complete several investigations. Ruth didn't specify what the investigations were, but Miller assumed that Rebozo and the Hughes money were one of them. Miller told Ruth he would talk to his client and get back to him.

The negotiations between Ruth and Miller continued the next several weeks. Nixon, Miller made it clear, was not anxious to testify at all and regarded the request that he do so now as harassment. In response, Ruth warned Miller that if Nixon refused to testify voluntarily, he would go into court to secure a subpoena. In that event, Ruth added, he would have no choice but to require Nixon to come to Washington, where the press would be gathered in droves. It would be, said Ruth, "a legal circus."

After a number of phone calls and meetings, a compromise was arrived at: Nixon would agree to testify "voluntarily" in California; in return, no subpoena would be issued, and the proceedings would take the form of a "prosecutional ancillary." A somewhat unusual legal device, similar to a civil suit deposition, the ancillary, unlike testimony given before a grand jury, allowed a witness's lawyer to be present during the testimony. Nor did the grand jury have to be present, though in this

---

* During a visit to San Clemente in 1976, Haldeman, who, like Ehrlichman, never accepted money from Nixon for his legal fees, asked Nixon where the money would have come from if he had accepted. Nixon answered: "Bebe had it."

A year later, in the fourth part of his televised interview with David Frost, Nixon, in answer to a question about the source of legal fees for Haldeman and Ehrlichman, replied, "Well, as a matter of fact, I had in mind the campaign contribution that he [Rebozo] received from Hughes."

It was not until February 1978, however, that Rebozo himself confirmed that one of the purposes of the fund was to buy silence. In a court deposition released that month, Rebozo said: "I may have told him [Nixon] that between us, we could raise it [Haldeman's and Ehrlichman's legal fees], but I don't recall specifically the details nor do I think that he seeked [sic] additional assurances. I think just the statement that it could be handled was enough."

instance Ruth had decided to bring two grand jurors with him to report to their fellow jurors on Nixon's mood and demeanor. Most important for Nixon, testimony taken during an ancillary was secret. Most important for Ruth, it was also under oath. If Nixon lied, he could be charged with perjury.

Monday morning, June 23, a small cavalcade of federal vehicles set out from San Diego, heading north toward San Clemente, fifty freeway minutes away. In the lead car, Ruth and the two deputies who would assist him in the questioning were discussing the significance of what was about to occur. Never before had a President or former President been put under oath to testify in a criminal case, and Ruth was moved by it. "This is history, you know," he said to his companions. "Yeah," one of them agreed, "only in America." A few miles slipped by. Ruth, who had been silent, repeated the words to himself: Only in America.

Nixon and Miller were waiting for them in what had been the national security conference room of the neighboring Coast Guard station. When the prosecutors, accompanied by the grand jurors, court stenographer and Chief U.S. District Judge Edward J. Schwartz, who was to administer the oath, entered the room, Nixon sat upright and quickly rose from his chair. Flashing a large, if somewhat nervous smile, he walked over and shook hands. To Schwartz, who departed as soon as the oath had been administered, the former President seemed in excellent spirits: pleasant, affable, courteous, as if anxious to please.

His good humor continued the rest of the day. Not until the next morning, when Ruth began to question him about the eighteen-and-a-half-minute tape gap and Rebozo's handling of the Hughes money did Nixon's composure begin to falter. As Ruth pressed for explanations, Nixon grew increasingly testy. When the interrogation finished late that afternoon, Nixon, who had been under oath a total of eleven hours, struggled to his feet. He appeared pale and shaken.

His testimony, however, had achieved its purpose. Nixon had admitted to nothing criminal. He had protected Bebe. He had denied responsibility for erasing the eighteen and a half minutes of tape. And Ruth, for all his persistence, had little to show for his efforts.*

---

* The investigation of Rebozo dragged on a few months more, but for all intents and purposes Nixon's testimony brought any thought of indicting him to an end. In its final report, dated October 1975, the Watergate Special Prosecution Force said of the Rebozo affair: "After all investigation was completed, and the evidence had been evaluated by the prosecutors who ran the investigation and by the General Counsel's office of the Internal Revenue Service, it was concluded by the prosecutors that the evidence would not support an indictment."

8

End of a Year

The interrogation by Ruth had added to Nixon's legal bills, which now stood at $500,000—more than twice what Korff's fund-raising efforts had thus far brought in—and soon Nixon was facing another cash-flow crunch. Once again he began thinking about television.

Despite the collapse of the first negotiations with the networks, and the continuing opposition of his doctors, lawyers and staff, Nixon had not abandoned the idea of selling his reminiscences to TV. What had altered was his approach. Rather than leave the negotiating to well-intentioned amateurs like Presley and Grant, he had decided to enlist Swifty Lazar.

In early July, Lazar approached the major networks and found each of them leery. CBS, still smarting from the Haldeman debacle, refused even to talk to him. ABC did talk, then, after thinking it over, decided to pass on grounds that it didn't want to pay for news. NBC was willing to pay, but balked at Lazar's asking price of $750,000. Instead, NBC offered $300,000 for two hours of televised talk. If Lazar were to force the bidding higher, he needed another contender. He found one in the son of an English parson turned talk-show host named David Frost.

"Showman" was the term usually applied to David Frost, and it fit. Host and creator of the BBC's spectacularly successful *That Was the Week That Was* at the age of twenty-three, multimillionaire by the time he was twenty-five, American television celebrity a year later, David Paradine Frost was an entertainment presence to be reckoned with. Nixon had reckoned with him already, and been pleased with the results. In 1968, the then presidential candidate had granted Frost a ninety-minute-long televised interview, which, if hardly searching ("This is a vast question, I know," Frost had asked him, "but, at root, what would you say that people are on earth for?"), had served Nixon well. Impressed, Nixon had invited Frost to the White House a year later to produce a show on

112

American Christmas, and afterward presented him with an inscribed presidential portrait that took up a place of honor in the Frost family's Suffolk cottage.

The day of the resignation, Frost had watched Nixon's farewell over a black-and-white set in a hotel room in Sydney, Australia. Despite the distance, and the graininess of the reception, Frost was captivated, and afterward announced to a colleague that as soon as Nixon was ready he would interview him. His friend scoffed; Frost had neither network connections nor the funds to mount such a project on his own. But Frost was confident. "In the words of David Schoenbrun during World War II," he sniffed, "let de Gaulle say no."

At first Nixon did say no; Frost's calls to San Clemente were not returned. Frost, however, was not easily put off. In January, with Nixon still recuperating from surgery, Frost contacted Herb Klein, laid out the broad outlines of his proposal and asked Klein to intercede with Nixon. A few weeks later Klein called Frost to report that while Nixon had not said yes, neither had he said no. Rather, according to Klein, he was seriously thinking about it.

The months passed; from San Clemente there was only silence. Then in May Frost's Los Angeles business partner, Marvin Minoff, had breakfast with Klein. Klein was encouraging but vague; Nixon, he said, was still thinking about it.

The breakthrough finally came in June, with a phone call from Clay Felker, editor of *Esquire* and an old acquaintance of Frost's. Over the weekend, Felker said, he had bumped into Lazar at a party in the Hamptons on Long Island, New York, and, from what he had been able to gather, the agent was actively seeking a television outlet for a major Nixon interview. Frost thanked Felker for the intelligence and immediately called Lazar, who, unknown to Frost, was negotiating not only with NBC, but in recent days Merv Griffin as well.

"Swifty believed in coming right to the point," Frost later recounted in a memoir of the interviews. "He wanted $750,000 for his client for a maximum of four one-hour shows. The main competitors—later revealed to be NBC—were currently at $300,000 and on their way to $400,000 for two hours, and would not guarantee more than two hours. That seemed to me to be a heavy rate per hour—and an underestimate of how much Nixon had to offer, both in terms of information and public interest. Others might not agree, but I was sure there was more—much more—of potentially riveting television in Richard Nixon. I said I was thinking of a maximum of $500,000 for a minimum of four hours."

Frost also had a number of conditions, including complete editorial control, and a "cast-iron contractual assurance" that Watergate would be one of the four shows. In addition, Frost insisted on sufficient time for interviewing, as much as sixteen hours, and written assurances that Nixon's memoirs would be published no earlier than three months after the airing of the interviews. Finally, Frost demanded exclusivity: until the interviews, Nixon could talk to no one else.

There followed several days of dickering, as Lazar shuttled between NBC and Frost, attempting to play one off against the other. Eventually, NBC raised the ante to $400,000. Frost told Lazar he would go higher, but only if the agent Lazar could provide him with all of his contractual guarantees. Lazar, who by then had consulted with Nixon, said there was no problem, and with that the deal was reached. In return for $600,000, plus 20 percent of any profits, Frost would get twelve two-hour sessions with Nixon, enough material for four ninety-minute shows. The question of Frost's lack of journalistic credentials was never discussed.

On August 9, the first anniversary of Nixon's resignation, Lazar, Frost, his lawyers and business partners traveled by limousine to San Clemente to conclude the final arrangements. Nixon, who was waiting for them in his office, looked better than he had in months. Under his wife's dietary supervision, he had gained weight. His face was tan, his gaze steady, his voice relaxed and confident. The only sign of aging was a noticeable graying of his hair.

As the men shook hands, Nixon teased Frost's lawyer, Paul Ziffren, a Los Angeles Democratic activist who had been Helen Gahagan Douglas' campaign manager, about political wars past. "You better watch out for him," Nixon kidded Frost. "He's written speeches for George McGovern." Ziffren laughed. "Mr. President, that's one charge to which I'll not plead guilty."

They went over the lengthy contract line by line, page by page. Nixon did his own lawyering, discussing the terms with Lazar and quibbling over fine points. The session lasted all morning and, after a lunch break, continued the rest of the afternoon. At one point, Frost mentioned the guarantee of complete editorial control. Nixon seemed untroubled. "No holds barred," he muttered. "No holds barred." He looked up at Frost and smiled, as if pleased that his adversary had stood his ground. "You know," Nixon said, "I'm a pretty fair poker player myself. During the war, I won a helluva pot with less of a hand than you're holding."

"Oh," said Frost, "what was that?"

Nixon grinned. "Two deuces."

By five, the final details had been completed. Frost, who had had to scramble to borrow the money for Nixon's first payment, quivered as he wrote out the check. He filled in one blank—"Richard M. Nixon"—then another—"Two hundred thousand dollars." As he was signing his name, Nixon reached for his wallet.

"Can I have the check please?" Lazar interrupted.

"It's made out to me," Nixon protested. "I'll deposit it."

"No, no, give it to me," Lazar replied. "That is the customary procedure."

"But what about the bank?"

"I'll take care of it."

"But, but—"

"Will you give it to me . . . *please?*" said Lazar, this time in a scolding tone.

Forlornly, Nixon handed over the check. His face, Frost wrote later, had the look "of a little boy not allowed to consume the cookie he has swiped from the jar before dinner."

Afterward, Nixon conducted them on a tour of the house, describing each of the rooms and the history that had occurred within them in detail.

"This is where Brezhnev and I met," he announced, when they came to his turret-shaped den on the second floor. "It was 10:30. We had already retired when the word came that he wanted to see me. And for three hours we talked. He said we had to lean on Israel for a settlement. I told him we would reason with Israel, but we could not dictate the terms of a settlement."

Nixon pointed to the armchairs. "Brezhnev sat there, Dobrynin there, Kissinger there." He paused. "He didn't say much," he added finally. Nixon's voice sounded wistful. It had all happened so very long ago.

The rest of the summer passed quietly. Slowly, painstakingly, Nixon was beginning to adjust. His weight was still ten pounds lower than it had been in the White House, making his jowls seem flabby, and he complained about sleeping entirely too much, but his former vigor had started to return. He now walked the three hundred yards to his office rather than ride in his golf cart as he had only a few months before. The time he spent there was longer, the work more concentrated. Besides the book and the lengthening stream of visitors, he was also involving himself in affairs of state in low-keyed fashion. He was in regular contact with a number of foreign ambassadors and by mail with a few foreign heads of state, including Mao, Brezhnev and the shah. Several times during the last few months he had also called Ford, most recently to congratulate him for his handling of the *Mayaguez* affair. However bloody the outcome, the toughness Ford had shown—dispatching the marines to rescue the crew of a U.S. container ship, which had been impounded by the Cambodian Communists—was a virtue Nixon appreciated.

Nixon had also maintained his links with Kissinger, whom he telephoned regularly, and who, in turn, consulted him frequently. During one such call, placed by the Secretary of State from an airplane flying between Jerusalem and Cairo, a visitor from Washington was in Nixon's office. It was apparent to the visitor that Kissinger was threatening to resign and that Nixon was doing his best to talk him out of it.

"Now, now, Henry," he heard Nixon saying. "You can't do that. The President needs you. The country needs you. The *world* needs you."

Nixon rolled his eyes up to the ceiling and smiled at his watching guest as Kissinger replied. Finally, after some minutes, Kissinger was mollified. When Nixon put down the receiver, he said to his guest, "When you get back to Washington, you've got to tell Ford. There are two ways of handling Henry. Sometimes you've got to pat him on the head. Make him feel like he's the star pupil in the class. And sometimes you've got to kick him right in the nuts."

Between such dealings, Nixon tried to relax. He swam in his pool, watched TV by the fire with Pat, chatted idly with old friends like Hillings and Hitt. Occasionally he also invited in the staff for an impromptu round of drinks, Nixon providing the entertainment by playing show tunes on the piano and leading them in hoarse renditions of the U.S.C. football cheer. Though anxious to get out more, he was still reluctant to leave the confines of his estate. He remained wary of outsiders, and once, after a photographer with a telephoto lens had captured him in conversation with Mitchell and Rebozo, Nixon asked the White House to provide him with more Secret Service protection. As there were already thirty-three Secret Service men guarding him, the request had been turned down. Furious, Nixon had altered his route to the office, lest he be photographed again. "If they can get me with a telephoto lens," he explained, "they can get me with a scope on a rifle." Later, he reflected to a friend, "It puzzles me a bit, and I suppose it is a natural thing, but I think I would get a good reception abroad—perhaps even as good a reception in the Middle East today as when I was President. But not here. Not here in the United States."

The few times Nixon did venture out, it was usually not very far. Shortly after the first anniversary of his resignation, he attended a staff party at a deserted beach house on the far end of the compound. "Ah," he said, spotting Ann Grier, who had been appointed chef for the party, "The Secretary of Nutrition." Ziegler, who would shortly depart to take a job with an electrical engineering firm in New York, flashed a grin. "I see the Ambassador Without Portfolio is happy," Nixon joshed.

A few weeks later Nixon showed up at another party organized by his barber, Ken Allan, at a private home in nearby Corona Del Mar. "My God, Ken, I can't go in there," Nixon gasped, when he saw the hundred guests who had gathered. "Not with all those people."

Allan was reassuring him when John Wayne came up behind Nixon and grasped him in a bear hug. Later, Wayne presented Nixon with a Boehm sculpture of a horse. "You know, Mr. President," the actor drawled, "it's kind of ironic I'm giving this horse to you, especially after that rough ride you've had in Washington the past couple of years." Nixon laughed, and holding up the horse, announced to the guests, "You never know, one day this horse may gallop again."

Such outings, however, were rare, the guests carefully selected, the circumstances tightly controlled. When, as he had a few times, Nixon wanted to walk the beach, he drove thirteen miles to Camp Pendleton's Red Beach, where access was to military families only. Similarly, when he played golf, Nixon usually did it on the Marine base's course, where his errant drives would be hidden from public view.

Golf, in fact, was becoming something of a passion for Nixon. A duffer during his White House years, seldom if ever breaking 100, he had vowed to break 90, and, with the help of Brennan, who had resigned from the marines in August to return as Nixon's chief of staff, had been working hard at it. To help Nixon's game, Brennan had enlisted a cadre of volunteers, who, for regular cases of beer, restored and maintained the formerly overgrown three-hole putting course on Casa Pacifica's grounds. The greens were now in excellent condition, much to the wonderment of Mrs. Nixon. Appalled at the $100 monthly cost of watering them, she had ordered the sprinklers shut off. Brennan had dutifully complied, and just as dutifully installed a timer to turn them on every night at 1:00 A.M., long after Pat had gone to bed.

By October, Nixon's game was sufficiently accomplished that he was ready to show it off. He chose a provocative locale in which to do it.

There was nothing wrong with the golf course. The La Costa Country Club of Carlsbad, California, featured one of the finest layouts in the country. Moreover, the tournament in which Nixon was playing was for a good cause: a retarded children's home in Palatine, Illinois. Everything was sparkling except the reputation of Nixon's hosts and playing companions: Frank E. Fitzsimmons and members of the International Brotherhood of Teamsters.*

---

* The Teamsters and Nixon had a long history. During the 1960 election, Teamster president Jimmy Hoffa, then under assault by John and Robert Kennedy, had thrown the support of the two-million-member union to Nixon. Despite Nixon's loss, and Hoffa's subsequent imprisonment for jury tampering and looting the largest of the Teamsters' pension funds (the same fund, as it happened, that had financed the construction of La Costa), the bond between Nixon and the Teamsters remained intact. In 1968 and 1972, Hoffa's successor, Fitzsimmons, again supported Nixon, and Nixon, in turn, appointed Fitzsimmons to several honorific government posts. During the Nixon presidency, senior Teamsters officials, including those under federal investigation, had ready access to the White House, Justice and Labor departments, and the formerly aggressive federal pursuit of Teamster corruption ground to a virtual halt. The relationship between Nixon and the Teamsters was climaxed, when, on December 23, 1971, Nixon commuted Hoffa's sentence to time served. Hoffa was released, but he did

The skies above La Costa were gloomy and leaden the afternoon of October 9, as the guest of honor, making his first public appearance since resigning the presidency, strode to the first tee. Declining the offer of a tournament cap ("I don't wear hats"), Nixon handed Fitzsimmons a box of six presidential golf balls inscribed with his signature.

"Give these to the poorest golfers in the tournament," he instructed. "Somebody might want one."

A crowd of reporters, drawn as much by Nixon as by the fact that Fitzsimmons was a prime suspect in the disappearance and presumed murder of Jimmy Hoffa ten weeks before, stood to one side, taking notes. One of them approached and asked Nixon how he felt. Momentarily, Nixon shrunk back. "I'm just fine," he answered finally, "and I'm going to play good golf today, too."

The former President hit his first drive. It sailed down the fairway, then veered to the right. He teed up another. It careened to the left. He smacked a third ball, studied its arc, then, apparently satisfied, stepped back to allow Fitzsimmons his turn. Fitzsimmons, too, hit several shots before finding one to his liking. Nixon stepped to the tee again. "Those others were for practice," he announced. "This is for real." The ball zoomed out in the direction of the hole. Mounting his golf cart, Nixon followed after it.

He ended up shooting 92 on the par 72 course, a credible performance that Fitzsimmons rewarded with a small trophy. "This is nice," said Nixon, examining his prize. "Where is the union bug on it?" Fitzsimmons looked embarrassed; there was none.

Afterward, Nixon and a number of Teamsters officials retired to the clubhouse for drinks and forty-five minutes of talk. Present, besides Fitzsimmons, who would later come under investigation for misappropriation of union funds, were Allen Dorfman, a convicted felon, who would later be executed gangland-style, following a 1982 conviction for bribery; Anthony ("Tony Pro") Provenzano, a New Jersey Teamster leader and suspect in the Hoffa disappearance, who would later be convicted of murder; Jack A. Sheetz, a Chicago area businessman, who had been indicted but not convicted of misusing Teamster pension funds; Allen Roen, one of La Costa's developers, and the possessor of a criminal record for stock fraud, and Teamsters executive secretary, Murray W. ("Dusty") Miller, a frequently investigated union official whom Jack Ruby, the slayer of Lee Harvey Oswald, called several days before the assassination of John F. Kennedy.

---

not return to the Teamsters' presidency. As part of a deal worked out between Fitzsimmons and John Mitchell, the former Teamster boss was barred from participating in union affairs until 1980.

Nixon's golf outing received wide and unflattering coverage. By rubbing shoulders with Fitzsimmons and his "mobster associates," *The New York Times* editorialized, Nixon "seemed deliberately . . . to raise anew all the unanswered questions about his relations with Frank E. Fitzsimmons and the scandal-stained International Brotherhood of Teamsters."

Startled by the reaction, Nixon retreated behind Casa Pacifica's walls for the rest of the year. He was not to be seen again by an outsider until the middle of January.

The occasion then was the taking of a deposition in a civil lawsuit filed by Morton Halperin, a former Kissinger aide, whose phone had been wiretapped on Nixon's order after Halperin had come under suspicion for leaking information to reporters. Nixon's testimony, like that to Ruth, revealed little of substance. It did, however, say much about Nixon's mood.

As usual, he had been anxious to please, opening the session by leading his interrogators through a twenty-minute, quarter by quarter replay of the recently completed Super Bowl. At one point during the questioning, referring to the Cambodian bombing program by its code name, "Menu," Nixon had tried to make a joke.

"Did you say 'Menu'?" one of the lawyers asked him.

"Yes," Nixon smiled, "Menu, like the one you get at Sans Souci, but it doesn't cost that much."

Afterward Nixon had pulled Halperin aside and attempted to apologize for the tap that had been on his home phone for nineteen months. "Listen," Nixon said, "I understand why you are upset. But, believe me, I didn't know you were being wiretapped. It was Henry's doing." Halperin, who was suing Nixon for $1 million, did not reply. Still hoping to ingratiate himself, Nixon continued: "Say, you must be hungry. You like Mexican food? I'll tell you about a great place. The El Adobe. Try the President's Special—and tell them I sent you. They'll take good care of you."*

But the majority of Nixon's days passed uneventfully. He worked

* The Halperin lawsuit, one of three filed against Nixon in connection with the Kissinger wiretaps, was to drag out five and a half more years before the question of Nixon's culpability was even partially settled. In the process it was to create a pair of odd political bedfellows.

The skirmishing began on August 7, 1977, when U.S. District Court Judge John Lewis Smith, Jr., dismissing Nixon's assertion of presidential immunity from civil lawsuits, awarded Halperin nominal damages of $1. Halperin appealed, and, in a surprise development, so did the Carter Justice Department on Nixon's behalf. The case went next to a three-member panel of the U.S. Court of Appeals. There, by unanimous vote, the judges affirmed the lower court decision on presidential immunity, declaring, "Presidents are scarcely immune from the judicial process. The President is the elected on his memoirs and talked of the old days with friends. Often, he would seem lost in his own reverie, referring to himself as "The President," as if the title that had once been his belonged to someone else entirely. Julie, who called him nearly every day, tried to cheer him. "Daddy," she exclaimed once, after she had completed a successful speaking tour in South Carolina, "there are still people out there who love us!" Heartened, Nixon wrote a thank-you letter to the governor of South Carolina, addressing it to John West, a Democrat. A former political aide who happened to be in his office advised him to call the letter back.

"Didn't you hear?" the aide asked. "The last election—we elected a Republican down there. John Edwards."

"Oh," Nixon answered, embarrassed. "That one must have gotten by me."

Before, nothing would have gotten by him. He would have known not

---

Chief Executive of our Government, not an omniscient leader cloaked in mystical powers."

Again, the Justice Department appealed, this time to the Supreme Court. On June 22, 1981, by a 4 to 4 tie vote (Nixon appointee William H. Rehnquist, a senior Justice Department official at the time of the wiretaps, did not take part in the decision), the High Court affirmed the Court of Appeals ruling, clearing the way for Halperin to seek monetary damages. The Supreme Court, however, did not issue a formal opinion, and, because of the split vote, the decision was not precedent setting. As a result, the civil claims against Nixon continued to pile up.

It was not until 1982, and a different case altogether, that the Court finally settled the larger question of presidential immunity from civil lawsuits. At issue was a $3.5 million lawsuit filed against Nixon by Air Force budget analyst A. Ernest Fitzgerald, who in 1968 had testified before Congress on cost overruns incurred in the development of the C-5A transport plane. Fitzgerald's revelations infuriated Nixon— "Get rid of that son of a bitch," he ordered Colson—and in 1970, in what the Air Force claimed was a "reorganization," Fitzgerald lost his job. The Civil Service Commission found the dismissal improper and ordered Fitzgerald reemployed with back pay. Fitzgerald, however, claimed that his new position was not equivalent to his old one, and eventually sued, charging that Nixon had conspired to deprive him of his job and prevent his future employment. Nixon admitted he had ordered Fitzgerald terminated—"It was a decision that was submitted to me; I made it and I stick by it"— but, as he had in the Halperin case, claimed presidential immunity for his actions. After two lower courts had found for Fitzgerald, Nixon appealed to the Supreme Court.

In a 5 to 4 decision, the High Court agreed with him, ruling that Presidents retain absolute immunity as long as they are acting within the "outer perimeter" of their duties. As Associate Justice Lewis Powell put it for the majority: "The President's unique status under the Constitution distinguishes him from other executive officials. Because of the singular importance of the President's duties, diversion of his energies by concern with private lawsuits would raise unique risks to the effective functioning of government."

Gratifying as the decision was for Nixon, he had not waited for the Court to reach it, and, hedging his bets, had made his own private settlement with Fitzgerald nearly two years before. Under the terms of that agreement, Nixon paid Fitzgerald $144,000, and, in return, Fitzgerald promised not to pursue him further in the courts no matter how the Supreme Court ruled. The agreement also contained one "side bet." If, as turned out to be the case, Nixon prevailed before the Supreme Court, he owed Fitzgerald no additional money. If he lost, Nixon, the old poker-player, agreed to pay Fitzgerald an extra $28,000.

only the identity of the governor and his political affiliation, but the margin of his victory, the names of his wife and children and what skeletons, if any, rattled in his closet. But Nixon's life had changed. He was out of the mainstream, and a part of him still hadn't figured out why. "Tell me," Richard Nixon asked Vernon Walters, when the former deputy director of the CIA dropped by. "What did I do wrong?"

9
China Passage

There was never any doubt that the President who had "opened China" would one day return to the scene of his greatest foreign policy triumph. The only questions had been how and when.

Emotionally, Nixon had been preparing himself for the trip almost from the moment of his resignation. Giant-sized pictures of himself in the company of Mao and Chou En-lai hung on the walls of his office, which, under Pat's direction, had taken on an increasingly Oriental motif. He had begun reading Chinese history and had spent long hours schooling himself about the country's culture and traditions. He spent even longer hours worrying over the course of Sino-American relations, which had stagnated since Nixon's visit in 1972.

"The roots are so shallow," he remarked one day to a visitor, as the two of them stood on the bluff overlooking the Pacific. "There was so much more to be done." Nixon gazed out in the direction of China. "There wasn't the time," he said quietly. "I didn't have the time."

No one was more acutely aware of that than the Chinese themselves, who had lost none of their affection for him. Within days of Nixon's arrival in California, a message had arrived from Chou En-lai, expressing continued good wishes, along with the hope that Nixon would one day visit again. Two months later, when Nixon was hospitalized for phlebitis, Mao himself called and through an interpreter told Nixon he considered him one of the greatest statesmen in history. He added that Nixon was welcome in China whenever he wanted to come.

Since then, Nixon had stayed in regular contact with both leaders, sometimes by mail, but more often through personal messages conveyed by Huang Chen, the head of China's Washington liaison office, and a frequent San Clemente visitor. The previous July, as Ford—much to the distress of the Chinese—was flying to Finland to sign the Helsinki Accords, Huang brought a second invitation from Mao, more urgent than the first. There were important matters the Chinese needed to discuss. He wanted to see Nixon just as soon as his health permitted him to travel.

It was the message Nixon had been waiting for. He called Kissinger and said that if Ford did not object he would like to depart as early as September. Kissinger was discouraging. Ford had yet to make a China pilgrimage himself, and should Nixon now make a second one, hardly a year since the resignation, it would embarrass the new administration. Disappointed, Nixon nonetheless agreed to wait and consult with Kissinger again before setting any plans. He implied, however, that he would not wait long. Kissinger guessed as much and quickly prevailed on the Chinese to extend Ford an invitation of his own, and on November 29, Ford set off for Peking for a week of sight-seeing and talks.

This trip did not make history. Miffed at Ford's recent bear hugs of Leonid Brezhnev and irritated at the administration's slowness in establishing full diplomatic ties, Ford's hosts were decidedly cool. Teng Hsiao-ping, the moderate, new vice-premier, hectored him about trusting the Soviets ("Rhetoric about détente cannot cover up the stark reality of the growing danger of war"), and in private conversations with American reporters, other Chinese officials made no secret of their preference for the hard-line policies of Ronald Reagan. When the trip was over, the best Ford could say about it was that it had resulted in "no minuses and a lot of pluses."

The Chinese, meanwhile, were continuing to work the Nixon connection, this time with Julie and David. With Nixon's blessing, the couple had been planning a China trip of their own since early September. Nixon had seen to their visas, and departure was scheduled for late December. Their itinerary, however, had not been finalized. Then, a few days after Ford's return to the United States, the Chinese called to inquire whether Julie and David would have any objections to "meeting our leaders alone," namely, without officials of the Ford administration present. It was a portent of an extraordinary reception, and Julie and David quickly agreed.

They arrived in Peking in the early morning hours of December 29, carrying with them letters Nixon had written to Mao and Chou, who then lay dying of cancer in a hospital. Forty-six hours later, less than an hour before the turn of the New Year, they were summoned to Mao's book-lined apartment in the Forbidden City. The chairman greeted them cordially and inquired after Nixon's health. David's detailed description of Nixon's condition seemed to bore him, perhaps because his own at the moment was none too good. Two aides had had to assist him to his feet when Julie and David came in, and, as he stood there, he seemed to totter. To Julie, he seemed like a frail old man. "His jaw hanging down— obviously the result of a stroke—gave him a vacant look," she later recounted. "His yellow skin seemed almost translucent. It had a waxlike texture and was almost totally unlined. His immaculate Mao suit, gray just like those of his attendants, hung loosely on his body. His long arms and large hands seemed dead weights dangling at his sides. And when he spoke, the sound emerged as grunts—harsh, primitive, labored." Mentally, however, Mao seemed in complete control. He nodded approvingly as Nixon's letter was translated for him, and, when the reading was finished, said emphatically, "Mr. Nixon is welcome in China."

Mao and his young American guests talked for nearly an hour. Despite his infirmities it was apparent that the chairman had lost none of his revolutionary vigor. "Young people are soft," he rumbled. "They have to be reminded of the need for struggle. There will be struggle in the Party. There will be struggle between the classes. Nothing is certain except struggle." Then, as if mimicking Nixon, Mao suddenly leaned forward and asked, "What do you think?"

As the Eisenhowers got up to go, Mao repeated his invitation to Nixon, bringing his arms down heavily on the sides of his chair for emphasis. "When your father comes," he declared, "I will be waiting for him."

For the remainder of their stay, David and Julie were accorded, as one local account put it, "astonishing treatment . . . unprecedented for people without high rank." Teng, who hosted a New Year's Day lunch in their honor, informed them, "We have never attached much importance to the Watergate affair." Huang Chen, who presided over their farewell banquet, quoted Nixon's words on his return to San Clemente in a toast: "When I left office, I discovered who my friends really are." Huang added, "The Chinese do not forget *their* friends." The going-away present the Chinese gave them underscored the point. Inside an elaborate silken box was a birthday cake for Nixon.

The cake was stale by the time it reached San Clemente, but the recipient barely seemed to notice. Nixon was euphoric. All the obstacles that had kept him from returning to China were now gone. He had his invitation—his fourth in a year—and Ford had made his trip. There was no need for further delay.

Still, Nixon was cautious about revealing his plans. The timing of the trip would put him in Peking—and back in the headlines—in the middle of Ford's campaign for reelection, and there was bound to be a stir. He decided to say nothing about the trip until the last possible moment, and then only after the Chinese had made the formal announcement.

The one exception he made was with Gulley, with whom he was developing an increasingly warm relationship. When "the general," as Nixon had taken to calling him, brought him his next security briefing in mid-January, Nixon, who was weekending with Pat at Annenberg's estate, invited him into the guesthouse for a drink. They gossiped about events in Washington for a few moments, then Nixon announced, "I'm going to China. It's all set. The Chinese are sending a plane to pick me up. But don't breathe a word to a soul."

Gulley was stupefied. He had heard rumors that Nixon might be planning a trip either to China or the Soviet Union sometime during the next year, but, like everyone in the White House, he had assumed that Nixon would defer any travel plans until the presidential election was safely over. Nixon greeted his questioning look with a shrug. The trip, he insisted, would actually do Ford some good. "Besides," Nixon added, "Jerry's got New Hampshire anyway. This won't hurt him. And it's better if I go now than closer to the election."

Afterward, Gulley phoned the White House to alert Scowcroft.

"You won't believe this, and you can't tell anybody, but guess where the old man is going? China."

"He's *what*?" Scowcroft exclaimed.

"Going to China," Gulley repeated. "And that's no shit."

Still professing astonishment, Scowcroft promised to keep the news secret, and word of it had not leaked when Kissinger visited Nixon at Casa Pacifica on February 2. Over dinner, the two men discussed foreign policy, and Nixon mentioned vaguely that someday he would like to return to China. Kissinger attached no importance to the remark; Nixon had been talking about going to China for months, and there was nothing in his tone to suggest that any trip was imminent. When Kissinger returned to Washington, he was under the impression that the trip Nixon was planning would occur sometime in 1977 at the earliest, well after the elections were over.

Three days later, on the afternoon of February 5, Han Hsu, the deputy chief of the Chinese Liaison Office, kept an appointment with Scowcroft in the general's White House office. After exchanging pleasantries, Hsu reached into his briefcase and pulled out a copy of a statement the Chinese were about to release in Peking, announcing that Mao had invited Nixon to China, and that Nixon had accepted "with pleasure." According to the statement, Nixon would arrive in Peking aboard a special Chinese airliner on February 21, the fourth anniversary of his first visit to China, and, though the statement did not mention it, exactly three days before New Hampshire Republicans went to the polls.

As soon as Hsu departed, Scowcroft alerted Cheney, the chief of staff, and a few minutes later they went in to see Ford. The President listened to the news in disbelief. Nixon had called him less than two weeks before for the express purpose of promising that he would do nothing during the coming campaign to hurt his electoral chances. Now he was doing exactly that. Ford reached for the phone to call Nixon in San Clemente.

Feigning cordiality, Ford congratulated him on his apparent good health, wished him well on his upcoming trip and asked that Nixon convey his respects to Mao. The conversation lasted sixteen minutes, and, when it was over, Ford was furious. Nixon, as usual, had patronized him, lecturing him on the importance of good relations with the Chinese. What was more galling still was Nixon's apparent unconcern for the timing of the trip or the political consequences it was certain to have. For Ford, already trailing Reagan in the New Hampshire polls, in no small part because of his pardon of Nixon, the publicity fallout was potentially ruinous.

Kissinger, who had hurried over from the State Department, was even angrier than Ford. While Nixon had called him as soon as he had gotten off the phone with Ford, his explanation—that the Chinese had given him only thirty-six hours advance notice—was not convincing. The Chinese, Kissinger informed Ford, simply did not do business that way. Nixon was lying. He had staged this stunt to humiliate them. Scowcroft concurred, and proceeded to let loose with a string of expletives. Ford tried to calm them. There was nothing any of them could do now; perhaps they were overestimating the political consequences. In any case they would soon have a chance to find out; the next morning he and Betty were going to New Hampshire for a weekend of campaign appearances.

That night a group of Ford's advisers gathered in the White House office of chief scheduler Terry O'Donnell to assess the damage. Various notions for striking back at Nixon were discussed. One idea was to inform the Chinese that the plane they were sending for Nixon might be seized by federal marshals, acting on behalf of American citizens whose property had been expropriated in China.* It was still being considered when David Kennerly, the President's young photographer, burst into the room. "That bastard! That fucker!" Kennerly shouted. "He's determined to ruin the President."

As it turned out, Kennerly's fears were overstated. Ford's New Hampshire trip went well, and the only mention of Nixon and China came from the traveling press. Ford tried to deflect them. Nixon was a private citizen now; his travel schedule was his own concern. There were no plans to have Nixon brief him on his return. Would the Nixon trip hurt him? a reporter asked. Ford smiled thinly: "Probably."

Others were not as restrained. Barry Goldwater took to the Senate floor to suggest that the Justice Department should consider prosecuting Nixon under the provisions of the Logan Act, which barred private citi-

---

* The Chinese were not easily bluffed. Told that the airliner they were sending for Nixon might be impounded, they informed the State Department that, if it were, its crew would refuse to return to China. The White House thereupon backed off.

But by then the idea of seizing the aircraft had spread to several of the Chinese creditors, who in turn secured state court orders for the aircraft's impounding. When the plane arrived at Los Angeles, sheriff's deputies were there to meet it. A potential diplomatic incident was avoided only by the intervention of Nixon's Secret Service agents, who physically prevented the deputies from serving the seizure order.

zens from negotiating with foreign countries. "If he wants to do this country a favor," Goldwater snapped, "he might stay over there." The Nixon visit was also denounced by the press. "A sleazy act," columnist Joseph Kraft called it, "thoroughly typical of the qualities which earned him the sobriquet Tricky Dick." Mary McGrory wrote in the *Washington Star*: "Any other man might have delayed the many-squalored thing until Gerald Ford, under strong challenge from Ronald Reagan, could have had a clear run in the New England primary. But it was a question of disappointing the Chinese or disappointing Gerald Ford. Richard Nixon unerringly opted for the Chinese. They could do more for him. Sure, Gerald Ford spared him indictment, trial, possible prison and even admission of anything graver than 'errors in judgment.' But what has he done for him lately?" Even so mild-mannered a soul as political commentator David S. Broder broke a promise to himself never again to write about Nixon by commenting in the *Washington Post*: "The utter shamelessness of the man—his willingness to exploit and corrupt every institution and relationship of which he has ever been a part—has become so blatant that one would think that it would not require comment. But Nixon goes blithely on his way, demonstrating again in his incredible journey to Peking that there is nothing, absolutely nothing he will not do in order to salvage for himself whatever scrap of significance he can find in the shambles of his life." Nor was it only liberals like Kraft, McGrory and Broder who were upset. Some of the most withering criticism came from William F. Buckley in *The National Review*. "The Chinese," wrote Buckley, "apparently do not know that Richard Nixon is not the leader of anything at all these days. He has less influence on the Republican Party than Howard Cosell. . . . He has to offer: only sycophancy."

Nixon finally felt compelled to defend himself. In a letter to *Times* columnist William Safire, he stated, "In 1972, I went to the People's Republic of China because I concluded that a new and constructive relationship between the U.S. and the P.R.C. is indispensable if we are to have lasting peace in the Pacific and the world. I believe that this relationship is, if anything, more important today than it was four years ago. I look forward to the opportunity of seeing again the leaders and the people of the P.R.C." Then, in a clear signal that the China visitation would be his last intrusion on the presidential election, Nixon added: "When I return, I will be spending my time in San Clemente working on my memoirs."

Thirteen days later, without further contact from the White House, Nixon, accompanied by Pat, Brennan, two communications specialists, a fifteen-member Secret Service contingent, and Robert Dunn, his Navy medical corpsman, made the fifty-mile drive from San Clemente to LAX. Outside the Pan Am service facility, a crowd of a hundred reporters and cameramen were waiting for him. As Nixon's black limousine pulled onto the tarmac, they began shouting questions. Ignoring them, Nixon stepped from the car, shook hands with several Mao-suited Chinese officials, then, taking Pat's arm, walked hunch-shouldered and deliberately up the steps to the blue-and-white 707 the Chinese had sent to ferry him to Peking. He paused while Brennan struggled with the luggage, posed again with the Chinese, then ducked inside.

The flight took eighteen hours, with refueling stopovers in Anchorage and Tokyo. During the trip, Nixon slept only fitfully, and by the time the jet put down in Peking at 10:16 P.M., local time, his eyes were red-rimmed with exhaustion. Landing, however, seemed to revivify him. When the hatchway swung open, he stood waiting with a smile and a wave, apparently oblivious to the fine, freezing mist that bathed the airport floodlights in an eerie glow.

There were no bands waiting to greet him, as there had been four years to the day before, no banners or military color guards, only three hundred "representatives of the masses" waving bouquets of plastic flowers. But the red carpet had been unrolled, and standing at the foot of it were a host of dignitaries, including Huang Chen and foreign minister Chiao Kuan-hua. Chou En-lai was not there to meet him; he had succumbed to cancer January 9. Nor was Teng standing at the ramp. In the upheaval after Chou's death, he had been denounced as a "capitalist-roader" and at that moment was under house arrest. Instead, there stood on the tarmac the bland, portly outline of Hua Kuo-feng, the newly appointed acting premier and Mao's heir apparent. The China watchers murmured among themselves; it was Hua's first major public appearance.

In deference to the hour, the welcoming ceremonies were kept brief, and soon the cavalcade of "Red Flag" limousines was heading off to State Guest House No. 18 where then-President Nixon had stayed in 1972. "Wow," said Nixon when he walked through the door, "what memories this brings back." He roamed the rooms, reminiscing, as Hua tried to shoo him to bed. "You must be tired after your long journey," the premier urged. Finally, still talking about his first trip and complimenting the Chinese for their pilot's proficiency on the second, Nixon took the hint.

The schedule the Chinese had laid on, however, allowed little time for rest. Early the next morning, Nixon, limping slightly from the effects of phlebitis, paid a condolence call on the widow of Chou En-lai. Then at noon the Chinese chief of protocol arrived at the guest house to inform Nixon that Mao would be pleased to receive him the next day. Following lunch and a brief nap, Nixon conferred with Hua for an hour and a half. Another brief rest, and it was on to the Great Hall of the People, where Hua was hosting a state dinner.

The mood that evening was one of disconnected déjà vu. There Nixon was, just as he had been as President: the same setting, the same deference, the same elaborate courtesies, even the identical ten courses of food. The Red Army band played "Turkey in the Straw" and "America the Beautiful" no better than it had in 1972. The *mao-tai* was just as fiery, the toasts to Sino-American friendship as fulsome. When toward the end of the meal Nixon rose to deliver a short speech, he spoke as if he were still President, as if Watergate and the resignation had never happened. "The future of all the people in this world depends on the reliability and the capability and the determination of our two nations to work together for the cause of peace with security for all nations," he intoned. Then, in apparent reference to the 1972 Shanghai Communiqué, Nixon added, "There are, of course, some who believe that the mere act of signing a statement of principles or a diplomatic conference will bring lasting peace. This is naive."

By the next morning Nixon's pronouncement was already causing trouble. Whatever Nixon had meant (later, through Brennan, he insisted he had meant nothing: "My God, I've used that statement a dozen times. . . . It could also apply to the United Nations Charter."), the White House was construing it as criticism, and at his regular press briefing later that day, Nessen announced that Nixon was merely a "private citizen," off on a personal visit, and that his statement carried no more weight than any other's. Ford, in the midst of another swing through New Hampshire, was immediately hoist on his press secretary's petard. During an appearance in a high-school gymnasium, a student got up to ask, why, if Nixon truly were a private citizen, Ford "didn't treat him as any other American and have him face criminal charges as any other American would instead of pardoning him?"

Ford reddened. "The former President obviously resigned in disgrace," he replied icily. "That is a pretty severe penalty."

Meanwhile, Nixon continued on his rounds. The morning after the banquet he paid a quick visit to an agricultural exhibit, where he patted stuffed pigs, admired models of terraced fields and joked to his hosts, "We'll make an even trade. We'll send you technology if you send us the pretty girls who showed us around today." From there, Nixon went to visit Mao. They conferred for an hour and forty minutes about what the Chinese would only describe as "a wide range of matters on the international scene as well as our bilateral relations." At the conclusion of the meeting, Nixon presented Mao with a Boehm porcelain panda, and Mao, looking frail and thin, toasted him with green tea. Afterward, Nixon invited half a dozen of the reporters who were covering him to his room overlooking the Jade Abyss Pool for an off-the-record chat.

He apologized that they had not been able to photograph the session with Mao ("I wanted you to, but the Chinese would not permit it. I guess that's their custom."), then casually started talking about Japan. He asked one photographer, "Have you been down to that place where they have 15,000 bars? Do you know the famous one, called Gordon's? Have you been there?" Before the photographer could answer, Nixon advised: "Don't go." It was obvious, however, that Nixon had gone, for a moment later he added, "We would go to places where they have geisha. You sit down and play games—not the games you guys play." He laughed at his own joke. "You don't ever want to bring your wife there," he smiled. "That's like bringing hamburger to a feast." Nixon talked on, more wistfully, about wanting to return to Japan one day. "I have many friends who say, 'Come back.'" He sighed. "All my friends were in the government. Is Kishi, for example, still around?" Told that the former Japanese prime minister was now president of the Japan-America Friendship Society, Nixon cracked: "I hope he doesn't have any Lockheed stock."

That night, after more talks with Hua, the Nixons attended a cultural program at the Great Hall of the People. With them, togged out in a brown Mao suit, was Mao's wife, Chiang Ching, making a rare public appearance. Before the program of songs and dances commenced, Chiang, who would later gain infamy as the leader of "The Gang of Four," presented Nixon with an English-language translation of the evening's performance, and Nixon, putting on his reading glasses, scanned through it. It was well that he did. For as the program commenced, one of the singers began belting out a political ballad in a shrieking tenor. "*People of Taiwan*," one of the verses went,

> "*Our own brothers*
> *Day and night you are in our hearts*
> *We are determined to liberate Taiwan Province*
> *And let the light and sun shine on the island.*"

When the song ended, Chiang Ching leaped to her feet, applauding wildly. Mrs. Nixon, without benefit of a program, followed suit, while her husband clapped politely, then rose to a reluctant half-crouch. When the program was over, Nixon went up to congratulate the musicians, and, losing his footing, nearly tumbled into the orchestra pit.

The next two days were given over to more talks with Hua, who, like the rest of the Chinese leadership, was less than pleased with the slow course of normalization. Between conferences there were more rounds of sight-seeing. Nixon toured one of the bomb shelters that honeycomb Peking, inspected firsthand the "large character" wall posters denouncing "capitalist-roaders" like the recently fallen Teng Hsiao-ping, and visited Tshinghua University, a center of Leftist ferment. Later, during a stop at a historical museum, he was shown some Chinese characters dating back five thousand years. "You will notice," his guide pointed out, "some of them look like letters in your alphabet."

"Yes," said Nixon. "I see. There's an 'O,' 'A,' 'C' and 'S.'"

"There's also a 'K,'" the guide noted, pointing to the largest and most prominent of the characters. Nixon joked: "That's how far Kissinger goes back." Chiao Kuan-hua, the foreign minister, roared with laughter. The banter continued at an exhibit of ancient weapons, which, Nixon was informed, had been used against invaders from the north during early border wars.

"Did you use those against the Russians?" Nixon teased.

Chiao laughed. "You mean in 1969?"

"Who started it?" Nixon went on.

"Of course, they started it," Chiao replied.

"Who won it?" Nixon pressed.

Chiao's smile disappeared. "We just drove them out."

There was more ideological back and forth when Nixon walked across Tien An Men Square. As hundreds of Chinese crowded round, pointing and grabbing his hand, Nixon asked one man, holding a young boy in his arms, if he wanted to have more children.

"Only one more," the man replied. "We must answer the call of our government to practice birth control."

"What do you want him to be when he grows up?" Nixon asked.

"Whatever the party decides," the father replied. "To answer the call of Chairman Mao."

"Oh," said Nixon, uncomfortably. "You mean whatever the party decides." The man nodded solemnly.

It was all gaiety again, Nixon's last night in Peking. Following Chinese custom, Nixon staged a reciprocal banquet for his hosts, and, over courses of such delicacies as "eight-jeweled pigeon," lotus root and fried mandarin fish, talked politics, American and Chinese. Then he delivered a toast. "We have not finished the bridge," he said, referring to the process of diplomatic normalization. "There is much work to be done. But we are determined to complete it. We must complete it and we must not fail, because of the young people we saw at the university today and young people like that in America and all over the world." The Chinese were delighted. "This," said one diplomat, gesturing at Nixon, "is a slap in the belly of Kissinger with a big wet fish."

Kissinger apparently had reached the same conclusion. Still bristling over the visit, he had ensured that press statements issuing from the White House and State emphasized Nixon's private role, and that whatever developed in Peking, Nixon would not be briefing the administration on his return. During a trip to Brasília, however, Kissinger began to have second thoughts. They became more pronounced after Hua, whom no other American had yet to meet, greeted Nixon at the airport and then spent nearly nine hours with him in talks. Finally Kissinger told a news conference, "We will, of course, wish to learn about the nature and result" of Nixon's trip, and with that contradicted everything he and Ford had been saying the previous two weeks. Ford himself was in a mellower mood, having scored an unexpected triumph in the New Hampshire primary. The victory over Reagan was narrow—less than 1400 votes— but it was a victory, nonetheless, and in the afterglow he, too, began talking more fondly about Nixon.

Nixon, meanwhile, was beginning to tire. The weather in the tourist city of Kweilin, next stop on his tour, was only a slight improvement over that in Peking and, while the political talks were over, the sight-seeing schedule was just as demanding. Particularly grueling was a three-hundred-yard ascent up stone steps to The Cave of the Reed Flute, famed for its spectacular formations of stalagmites and stalactites. Nixon was puffing and limping by the time he reached the top, and seemed distracted as his guide pointed out the sights. As the day wore on, Nixon's limp grew worse. The Chinese, who had already taken the precaution of sending along a cardiovascular specialist to accompany him, were worried. When the Nixon procession moved on, an ambulance trailed in its wake.

The next day was no better than the one that had preceded it. On a boat trip up the Li River, Nixon huddled in a heavy topcoat, making small talk with the accompanying Chinese (and betting a bottle of *maotai* on an upcoming table tennis match between two of them), while shooting occasional dark glances at his Navy corpsman. When the corpsman pulled a bottle of anticoagulant medication from his bag, Nixon snatched the bottle away, and, stiff-fingered from the cold, tried to extract a pill. Eventually he succeeded, only to have the pill slip out of his hand and go rolling onto the deck.

By the next morning, when Nixon's jet departed for Canton and the last leg of the tour, Nixon was in a foul temper. Settling into his seat, he looked across the aisle to see John Lindsay of *Newsweek*, staring at him. "It must be easy to be a reporter," Nixon scowled. "All you have to do is ask the questions. You don't have to answer." Before Lindsay could reply, Nixon turned away and remained silent the rest of the flight.

Nixon's spirits brightened when they reached Canton. As he toured the city, thousands of Chinese spilled into the streets to greet him, calling, "Neek-son, Neek-son!" It was an unprecedented reception for a foreigner, and Nixon's limp seemed to disappear. The color returned to his cheeks, the bounce to his step, as for more than an hour he worked the crowd. His good humor extended even to the press, with whom he insisted on posing at the airport for a farewell group picture. The reporters milled around, uncertain what to do, until Nixon, taking command, arranged them in a line and ordered "smile." They did, though none more easily or widely than the man they had been assigned to cover.

Several days after Nixon returned to San Clemente, he received a phone call from Kissinger who was staying in Palm Springs where his wife, Nancy, had gone to recuperate following stomach surgery. Apologetically, Kissinger told Nixon that he would like to have called on him in person, but to have done so with the campaign season still on would have embarrassed Ford. Nixon listened without comment. Finally, Kissinger came to his point. The White House would like a complete accounting of Nixon's trip, a briefing, as it were, from an old China hand. And so the President would like to send Lieutenant General Vernon Walters to San Clemente to take some notes.

"That won't do, Henry," Nixon cut in. He would provide the White House with its report, and gladly so, but not through Walters nor through the State Department bureaucracy. He would talk only to Brent Scowcroft, Ford's national security adviser. That was the proper, dignified channel. A former President deserved no less. Henry Kissinger could only agree.

10
Interval

Going to China had been a tonic. On his return, Nixon plunged back into his work, alert and refreshed, as if injected with new life. He needed a lift just then, for there was no lack of things to be done.

The overriding concern remained the memoirs, whose publication date repeatedly had been postponed. Work on the book was progressing steadily, but it was slow going, in part because custody of the prime research material—Nixon's papers and tapes—was still at issue. Miller had filed a brief, challenging the Court of Appeals' decision, but it would be months before the Supreme Court heard the case, and months more before the Court rendered final judgment. In the meantime there were other problems from an old source. In Washington, Bob Woodward and Carl Bernstein were about to publish another book.

In their account of Nixon's last months in the White House, the reporters portrayed him as emotionally unstable, potentially suicidal and frequently drunk. "Our meatball President," they had quoted Kissinger as calling him. In *The Final Days*, Nixon was every bit of that and more. There were scenes of him soliloquizing to the portraits of past Presidents, pounding his fists on the floor in preresignation frustration, tearfully falling to his knees in the Oval Office, while beseeching Kissinger to join him in prayer. Nothing had been spared, including his relationship with his wife, with whom, Woodward and Bernstein claimed, he had not slept in the last sixteen years.

Nixon had not read the book, but he had seen the excerpts in *Newsweek*, and he was furious. For a time he considered bringing suit for libel and went so far as to consult several lawyers, dropping the notion only after Bob Finch convinced him that suing would be, as Finch termed it, "a lousy game." Still, Nixon was upset. "Hell," he complained to Gulley, "Quakers don't get down on their knees and pray like Baptists. I might very well have said a silent prayer with Kissinger, but I certainly wasn't hanging on to Kissinger and saying, 'Let's pray.' And how the hell would they know? Who could tell them except me or Kissinger?"*

Gulley, who wondered whether Nixon was asking him if the source had been Kissinger, said nothing. "It doesn't bother me," Nixon went on. "I just hope it doesn't bother Mrs. Nixon. That's my concern. The bastards have got no reason to talk about her . . . [She] never did anything to anybody."

But Nixon was bothered, and not only about the book's impact on his wife. Its appearance had come at a delicate time. Haldeman, Ehrlichman and Mitchell were still in the midst of their appeals, a process that might involve him at any moment. Korff was also gearing up another fund-raising campaign, and first reports of its progress were discouraging, in part because of the publicity from the book. Finally, *The Final Days* would provide additional grist for David Frost, just as Frost was readying his own interrogation.

It was now eight months since the contract for the Frost interviews had been signed and four months since Nixon had seen Frost last. That had been in January, when Frost, in California to see his latest girlfriend, socialite model Caroline Cushing, had dropped by to pay a social call. While Frost had little of substance to report, Nixon had been charmed by Cushing, with whom he insisted on posing for a photograph.

"There," he said, when the picture-taking session was complete. "You can put that in your apartment in New York and all your liberal friends can use it as a dart board."

Laughing, Cushing confessed that she actually lived in Monte Carlo, which seemed to charm Nixon all the more. As he was making his good-byes, he pulled Frost aside and whispered conspiratorially, "Marry that girl. She's a resident of Monaco. She lives tax-free."

With his Monte Carlo girlfriend and his trademark blue suede shoes, it was easy to underestimate David Frost, and Richard Nixon was not the first. "Not since Ed Sullivan," commented one American critic, "has anyone on television backpatted, hugged and smooched so rapturously. His wide-eyed, basset-unctuous, hand-kneading style reminds some viewers of Uriah Heep. 'It's been a joy having you here,' he tells the dullest talk show guest."

But for all Frost's liabilities, including a fondness for water-closet jokes and a habit of doing his interview research aboard the Concorde, he could, when the moment moved him, be a startlingly effective interviewer. He did not overwhelm his subjects in the manner of a Mike

---

* Despite his protestations to Gulley, Nixon had fallen to his knees to pray with Kissinger, and he admitted so later, both during the Frost interviews and in his own memoirs.

Wallace, but seduced them in the manner of, say, a Charles Boyer. Long moments would pass in the most boring of banalities as Frost, the lover, lulled his prey. Then, at the very brink of somnambulence, there would come a turn, a slight lifting of the eyebrow, a nearly imperceptible pursing of the lips. And then all at once the mood would shift.

It was a delicate process, one that required timing and tact, and Frost had honed it to an art. He knew the value of silences, of letting his victim sit there, watched by the electronic, all-seeing eye. He had a knack for asking the right question—including some that others might be too embarrassed to pose—at just the right time. At his very best, when he was not staging stunts like underwater kissing contests, or asking Zsa Zsa Gabor for her definition of love, Frost could elicit from his subjects not only data and drivel, but that rarest of televised commodities, soul. "The aim of everything I do," he said of his technique, "is to leave the audience a little more alert, a little more aware, a little more alive."

That he was a superb organizer in addition to everything else was already apparent. Within months of Nixon's return from China, Frost had not only managed to erect an ad hoc "network" of more than a hundred independent stations to carry the program, but had found backers to finance it in Europe and California, and, from even more disparate sources, an editorial team to produce it. The last consisted of producer John Birt, a prickly British television wunderkind, who at the age of thirty-one was already a veteran of ten years' documentary experience, and three reporters: Robert Zelnick, a lawyer and former chief of National Public Radio's Washington Bureau; his assistant, Phillip Stanford, a free-lance writer; and James Reston, Jr., son of *The New York Times* columnist, author, with Frank Mankiewicz, of *Perfectly Clear Nixon: From Whittier to Watergate*, and, until syndicated columnist Joseph Kraft recommended his employment to Frost, assistant professor of English at the University of North Carolina.

In July, as Nixon continued to work on his memoirs, Frost met with his team in Washington, and almost immediately there were problems. Reston, who had been charged with gathering material on Watergate, came to the session armed with hours of tape recordings of conversations he had conducted with his fellow academics. Rather than subject Nixon to a traditional journalistic interrogation, the professors had favored a more analytical inquiry, one that would plumb the depths of the Nixon character, including his supposed "survivor guilt" from the deaths of his two brothers and a rumored though never substantiated homosexual relationship with Bebe Rebozo. Reston, a confirmed Nixon-hater, had emphatically concurred, and the discussion with Frost and Birt grew heated, particularly after Reston suggested that Frost wasn't up to the rigors of being a journalist in any case. Birt wanted to fire him on the spot, and Frost was tempted to take the advice. Finally, though, the atmosphere calmed, and Reston stayed on, although his relations with Birt and Frost remained strained.

Two days after the meeting in Washington, Brennan called from California with more bad news. Nixon, Brennan informed Frost, would be unable to discuss Watergate until after the conclusion of Haldeman's, Ehrlichman's and Mitchell's appeals. That much Frost already knew and had made provision for in his contract. What he did not know until Brennan's phone call was that by "Watergate" Nixon meant not only the break-in and the cover-up, but Nixon's resignation, pardon and final days. Gannon, who was also on the line, expanded the definition further, ruling as out of bounds anything that had occurred during the Nixon presidency from June 1972 onward. As a result, Nixon was now proposing to defer taping until as late as June of 1977, which would push the earliest possible air date back to August, the very depths of the summer television doldrums. Frost was too stunned to make anything but a noncommittal reply; and, with the question of scheduling still unresolved, departed a few days later for Iran, where with the financial backing of the shah he was producing a $2.5 million epic on the history of the Persian Empire.

Meanwhile, Reston continued with his research. Having digested the 47 volumes of the House Judiciary Committee's impeachment hearings, as well as the 12,000-page proceedings of the Haldeman, Ehrlichman and Mitchell trial, he was in the U.S. Court of Appeals' clerk's office the morning of July 6 inquiring whether there was anything else to read. The clerk thought for a moment, pawed through a box of index cards, then said, "Well, there are the appendices, if you're really interested." Reston replied that he was, and the clerk disappeared into a back room. Some moments later he came back lugging a number of battered boxes. Within were the exhibits that had been entered into evidence, but had not been used during the course of the actual trial. Reston began scanning them, and before long came across a transcript of a conversation between Nixon and former special counsel Charles Colson, dated June 20, 1972, three days before the Nixon-Haldeman smoking gun.

The existence of the conversation was no surprise. Some days earlier, Reston and Stanford had visited Colson, a former marine who had once boasted he would "walk over my grandmother if Richard Nixon asked me to." Colson, who claimed to have become a born-again Christian during a stay in prison for Watergate crimes, had admitted discussing Watergate with Nixon on a number of occasions. Indeed, according to Colson, who was now working as a lay minister in Washington-area prisons, he had transcripts of the talks.

"Well," said Reston, "given the fact that you've made a full breast of your involvements, you wouldn't mind letting me see the transcripts of those Nixon conversations?"

"Sure," Colson had smiled, "come back in a week."

Reston returned as requested. But in the meantime Colson had been on the phone to San Clemente, and as a result the transcripts he handed over had been highly sanitized. The document Reston now held in his hands was not.

Early in the exchange, Nixon, referring to the break-in, tells Colson: "If we didn't know better, we would have thought it was deliberately botched." Colson agrees, but reassuringly adds, "Bob is pulling it all together. Thus far I think we've done the right things to date." Reston quickly read on, until his eyes rested on the following passage:

NIXON: Basically, they are pretty hard-line guys.

COLSON: You mean, Hunt?

NIXON: Of course, we are just going to leave this where it is, with the Cubans . . . at times I just stonewall it.

Later, Nixon adds: "We've got to have lawyers smart enough to have our people delay, avoiding depositions. . . . that's one possibility."

The conversation, Reston thought, was damning in itself. But there was more, two other transcripts in particular, both of earlier conversations between Nixon and Colson. On February 13, 1973, more than a month before Nixon claimed he had learned of the cover-up plot, when John Dean informed him there was "a cancer on the Presidency," Nixon said to Colson: "When I'm speaking about Watergate, that's the whole point of . . . of the election; this tremendous investigation rests unless one of the seven begins to talk; that's the problem." The next day, again with Colson, Nixon was even more specific:

NIXON: Hiss was a traitor. It was a cover-up.

COLSON: Yeah.

NIXON: A cover-up is the main ingredient.

COLSON: That's the problem . . .

NIXON: That's where we gotta cut our losses. My losses are to be cut. The President's losses gotta be cut on the cover-up deal.

Reston could scarcely believe what he was reading. Two hundred reporters had preceded him, and none had come across the Nixon-Colson transcripts. This is it, he whispered to himself. Conspirator with a capital C.

As Reston was making an appointment to discuss his discovery with the special prosecutor's office, the Nixons were recuperating from a round of holiday parties in San Clemente.

It had been a long, festive—and, for Mrs. Nixon, tiring—weekend. Friday, the second, they had dined with friends at the El Adobe and had not returned to the residence until well after their usual bedtime. The next night they were out even later, attending a $76-a-couple bicentennial dinner-dance hosted by Ken Allan for 376 Nixon friends in the Grand

Ballroom of the Newport Beach Marriott. Then, after a brief respite on the Fourth, they had driven to Palos Verdes for a small party in honor of Julie's twenty-eighth birthday at the home of Jack and Helene Drown. Pat was uncommonly quiet, and Julie, still recovering from an upset stomach, the result of having eaten some unripe fruit that morning in San Clemente, went into another room to lie down. Nixon, however, was in an expansive mood. Settling into an easy chair with a light Chivas Regal and soda water, he began to ruminate about the weekend's happenings, which had included a coast-to-coast barnstorming tour by Ford and a successful raid on Entebbe by Israeli commandos. His hosts, son-in-law David Eisenhower and Benjamin Stein, who had been a young speech-writer in the administration, provided a rapt audience.

"Ford missed a good chance," Nixon said, "a really good chance. How many speeches did he give? Seven? Ten?" He looked out over the room. "However many it was, it was too many. He just flew all over giving speeches and putting wreaths on things. Now does anyone re-member anything that Ford said?"

Nixon paused, waiting for an answer. When none was forthcoming, he beamed. "That's exactly the point. He had a chance to make a speech that everyone in the country would watch and remember. He should have said, a week before July Fourth, 'Look, I'm going up to Camp David to work on this speech.' He didn't actually have to work on it. He could go swimming or do anything. But people would have thought he was work-ing on it. Then he could have given it and he could have locked up the nomination right then and there. Or am I wrong?"

David told him he was right, and Nixon, seemingly satisfied, con-tinued: "Then why didn't Ford do it? Didn't he have anyone telling him he should do it? Jerry's a smart fellow, but even smart fellows need to get good advice. Why didn't someone suggest that to him?"

No one, including Nixon, had any explanation, and Nixon, as if bored analyzing his successor's flaws, turned to Ford's opponents. The Democrats were about to name their presidential nominee, and Nixon, despite Carter's overwhelming lead in the delegate count, was certain it would be Minnesota Senator Walter Mondale.

"It has to be Mondale. It has to be," he insisted. "He's a liberal. He's from the Midwest. He looks good on the tube."

Nixon paused. "The tube," he repeated. "That's what it's all about. How you come across on the tube. . . . I know that, and you know that, but a lot of people don't know it yet."

Someone mentioned that Senator John Glenn of Ohio came across well on camera. "Well," Nixon replied, "some people think Glenn isn't very smart. I'm not saying I think that. I'm not saying that at all. But some people think that. On the other hand, Glenn would be awfully good on defense, and that's important. You know how fast the Russians would be in there if we started cutting back on our defense? You know how fast they'd be all over the place?"

Then Nixon asked, "What about Muskie?" A moment later he answered his own question. "No, no—he's too old."

Which brought him to Carter. "He was in the Navy," Nixon mused. "He might be good on that. That's important."

Nixon recalled a recent conversation with Kissinger about Zbigniew Brzezinski, Carter's chief foreign policy adviser. Mimicking Kissinger's Germanic accent, Nixon quoted him as saying, "Brzezinski knows a lot, yes, and his opinions are sound, but, Mr. President, he is an o-por-too-nist." Nixon smiled, then, mock accent even thicker, he repeated the remark, "Mr. President, he is an o-por-too-nist."

The group moved out onto the patio, and there Nixon began evaluating the Israeli raid on Entebbe. "The Israelis still have guts," he enthused. "If we had the guts the Israelis have, we'd be in good shape. Or am I wrong?"

No one disagreed, and the talk turned to Ugandan dictator Idi Amin. "Amin?" said Nixon loudly. "Amin? He's just a goddam cannibal. A goddam cannibal asshole. He'd eat his own mother. Christ, he'd eat his own grandmother."

Warming to his topic, Nixon began to evaluate other African leaders. "Give them the edge because they're black," he observed. "Always. They deserve it for the way they've been treated. Absolutely. But for Christ's sake, when they start acting like god-awful idiots, you don't coddle them and tell them they're doing great. That's what those jackasses at the State Department do. But that's just more insulting. . . . You've got to treat them like adults. You can't just say, 'Oh, let them act like assholes like Amin because they're black."

"That's right," David cut in, "but what can you do about it?"

"You can do what Israel did," Nixon replied.

At that, one of the guests noted that UN Secretary General Kurt Waldheim had said that in raiding Entebbe to free the hostages Israel had violated international law. Nixon was dumbfounded. Then, assured the report was true, he said, "I'll tell you why he did it. He did it because the whole U.N. is a bunch of goddam jackasses. That's why he did it."

Nixon's tone turned gentler over dinner, and, by the end of the meal, the bile had gone out of him. He proposed a birthday toast to his daughter.

"I remember the day Julie was born," he reminisced. "It was the hottest day of the year. I had just come back from the Republican convention in Philadelphia and Earl Warren had gotten the Vice-Presidential spot. I rode down in an elevator with Charlie Halleck and he grabbed my arm and said, 'Dick, how could Tom [Dewey] do that? He promised it to me.' And I just said to him, 'Well, Charlie, people promise a lot of things.' So I get back to Washington and it was hot as hell. There was no air conditioning then. So I got home, and they said that Pat was in the hospital already. She was over there at Columbia Hospital and, you know, of course, most of the doctors there were Communists or incompetents or worse, but we had gotten Pat a good Republican doctor.

"So I went up to the hospital room, and Pat was asleep and the doctor came out and he was wiping off the sweat and I asked, 'Well, is it a boy or a girl?' And the doctor said, 'Dick, you've got a great big beautiful baby girl.' And I went in to see her, and there she was: My great big beautiful baby girl." He paused, looked down the table at Julie, then winked. "And she's still my great big beautiful baby girl."

A few minutes later, the party broke up. As he walked Nixon to his waiting limousine, Stein took his hand.

"You know, Mr. President, you have had some very bad things happen to you. But you have about the best daughter in the whole world, and that's an awfully good thing."

"I know," Nixon mumbled. "Of course, I know. Tricia's a great girl, too. They're wonderful girls." Nixon's face clouded, and, for a moment, it appeared that he might cry. Then Julie appeared to hug and kiss him good-bye. Standing alongside the car, Stein could hear Nixon tell her quietly, "You're still my great big beautiful baby girl."

Two days later, late the afternoon of the seventh, Pat Nixon was reading on the patio of Casa Pacifica. Ordinarily, she tended to historical fiction, works like Morris West's *The Ambassador,* or sprawling biographies such as Antonia Fraser's *Mary Queen of Scots.* On this particular afternoon, however, she was delving into something more recent and decidedly more intimate. She was reading *The Final Days.*

Suddenly she felt weak. Saying nothing, either to her husband or to David and Julie, who were spending the long holiday weekend at the estate, Pat went inside and went to bed.

The next morning at breakfast, however, Nixon noticed she was having trouble unscrewing the top from the jar of instant coffee. Her speech was also slurred, and she was having difficulty moving the left side of her body. Alarmed, Nixon called Lungren, and, a few hours later, still conscious and alert—"I can't believe this is happening to me," she said —Pat was being rushed by ambulance to Long Beach Memorial. What she had suffered was a stroke.

Fortunately it was a relatively mild one, "a dinky lesion . . . the size of a pea," as her neurologist described it, on the right side of the brain. Though listed in serious condition and confined to the hospital's intensive care unit, she was said to be responding to treatment, and all the statements about her health, including her husband's, were optimistic.

"My wife is one who has been through a great many difficult experiences over many years and one characteristic she has is self-reliance and strength of spirits," Nixon told reporters, when he emerged from the hospital. "Her spirit is great, and because her spirit is good, she is going to see this thing through and she is going to beat it. She is a fighter. She is not giving up."

11
The Wizard

It would be two weeks before Pat was sufficiently well to return to San Clemente, and months of painful therapy before she was completely recovered. For Frost, it promised additional delay. And, for that, Nixon was grateful.

Even without the strain of his wife's illness, Nixon at that moment had all that he could handle, including—though the fact was known only to a few—a major role in seeking the reelection of Gerald Ford.

It was an odd coupling, given the history since the pardon, and odder still, considering the personalities involved. Nixon had lost none of his reservations about Ford's abilities, and Ford, for his part, had yet to forgive him for the China trip. The two men seldom spoke; relations between their staffs remained icy. Yet, for all the sights and wounded egos, when it came to politics there was an overarching mutuality of interests. His popularity at low ebb, challenged by Ronald Reagan for the nomination of his own party, Gerald Ford, the genial stumblebum, was in trouble, and Richard Nixon, the consummate pol eager to make a comeback, was in a position to help.

The process had started the previous March, with a chance conversation between Nixon and Gulley over the St. Patrick's Day weekend. Gulley, who had been having drinks with Nixon and Pat in Casa Pacifica's living room, was about to go when Nixon suddenly asked, "Who do you think will be the Democratic nominee?"

Gulley was surprised; Nixon had never discussed politics with him. Finally he offered, "Well, there's a lot of talk about Glenn."

"Glenn!" Nixon scoffed. "Not Glenn. He's dumb."

They talked on a few minutes about both Democratic and Republican possibilities. Finally the meeting broke up.

When Gulley got back to the White House, he repeated what Nixon had told him to Donald Rumsfeld, who had returned from his post as NATO ambassador to become Ford's chief of staff. Rumsfeld was intrigued. "The next time you see him, tell him that we would be pleased to see any advice he has to pass along."

Two weeks later Gulley returned to San Clemente and told Nixon what Rumsfeld had said. Nixon, who was sitting behind his desk, sat bolt upright. His eyes sparked with excitement.

"What does that mean?" he demanded. "Did Ford ask for this? What kind of advice?"

The next morning, when Gulley went in to see him again, Nixon's enthusiasm had been tempered. Since their first meeting, Nixon revealed, he had been on the phone with a number of friends in Congress, and they had urged him to get specific commitments.

"The little stuff doesn't matter to me," Nixon said, "but the big stuff does. I want to be sure that anything I send back goes only to Ford." He paused. "There's one other thing you have to know. If Reagan's people ask me for advice, I'm going to have to give it to them."

Gulley said he would check with the White House and get back to him. A few days later, having conferred with Rumsfeld and Cheney, Gulley called from Washington to report that, with one proviso, the White House had accepted the deal. Rumsfeld had asked Gulley to see if Nixon would allow him to see the material as well. Nixon, who was in the habit of staking out apparently nonnegotiable positions and just as abruptly changing them at the first sign of pressure, said the arrangement would be fine. Thereafter, with Gulley serving as the conduit, the counsel came in reams.

"The Wizard," as Nixon was code-named within the White House, had opinions on nearly everything, from keeping the Secret Service at arm's length ("The minute you start getting familiar with people, they start taking advantage.") to tightening up the White House staff ("One of Jerry's biggest problems is that he doesn't have the balls to take them on head-to-head and get rid of the people he should. He doesn't run a taut enough ship.") to relations between the candidates' wives. When Betty Ford took a mild public swipe at Nancy Reagan, Nixon was flabbergasted.

"Nancy Reagan runs Ronald Reagan," he lectured Gulley. "She's a very strong woman, and, if you make her angry, you're never going to pull this guy into camp, and Ford's really going to need Reagan after the convention. In fact, if he doesn't change his ways, he's not even going to win the nomination, Reagan's going to get it. He just cannot afford to alienate Nancy Reagan, because she's the guy's chief adviser. I'm telling you, Nancy Reagan's a bitch, a demanding one, and he listens to her."

Nixon's feelings about Reagan himself were rather more complicated. During Reagan's first term as California governor, the two of them had not been close. Partly it was the natural rivalry of two outsized personalities sharing the same geographical stage. But partly, too, it was plain envy. Reagan possessed a self-assurance and social grace that Nixon lacked; he was a member of the Hollywood establishment, a community to which Nixon, save for an old friendship with the late actor, Dick Powell, had never been granted access; and he had been elected governor, while Nixon had not. Deepening the resentment was Reagan's short-lived try for the 1968 Republican nomination which Nixon had regarded his by right.

Matters improved during Nixon's presidency. Reagan had been supportive throughout, and, unlike many other conservative stalwarts, his loyalty had not flagged once Watergate began to boil. The result was that Nixon's regard for his talents soared. It climbed even higher during Nixon's hospitalization when Reagan, on being informed that Nixon had slipped into shock, had snapped, "Maybe that will satisfy the lynch mob." Soon after Nixon's discharge, a dinner invitation was dispatched to Sacramento, and relations were cordial thereafter.

Meanwhile, unknown to either Reagan or Ford, Nixon was trying to boost the chances of yet a third presidential contender, his former treasury secretary and three-term governor of Texas, John Connally.

Connally had caught Nixon's eye in 1969 during his service on the Ash Council on Government Reorganization. Headed by Litton Industries president Roy Ash, the council came up with a number of recommendations for improving the workings of the executive branch, largely by transferring to the White House much of the policy-making authority that had formerly resided in Congress and the various cabinet departments. The changes were sweeping, and fierce opposition was expected. Thanks to Connally's lobbying, however, the bulk of the reforms, including the creation of the Office of Management and Budget, became law. Nixon paid him the ultimate compliment. "John Connally," he told Ehrlichman, "is a gut-fighter and total politician." A year later, when Nixon was looking for a "presidential-caliber" replacement for David Kennedy as secretary of treasury, the "gut-fighter" was the man he tapped.

Silver of hair, ruddy of cheek, a man seemingly unacquainted with self-doubt, Connally quickly became the dominant member of Nixon's cabinet, taking the lead not only on the economy, but pressing his views on political and foreign policy matters as well. With the exception of Mitchell, whose influence by then was on the wane, he was also the only cabinet member able to penetrate the Haldeman-Ehrlichman "Berlin Wall," and he and Nixon spent hours together in the Oval Office, talking politics and planning Connally's future. That Connally was a Democrat, protégé of Lyndon Johnson and in 1968 virtually single-handedly had seen to it that Texas was the only Southern state to go for Hubert Humphrey, troubled Nixon only slightly. What mattered to him far more was that Connally, like himself, was a high-stakes, go-for-broke risk-taker with an eye firmly fastened on the political bottom line. "I brought him up from the Texas League," Nixon boasted of him. "Sometimes he singles, sometimes he doubles, and he often gets a home run. Furthermore, when a ball comes at his head, he knows when to duck."

So taken was Nixon with Connally's abilities that he decided not only that Connally would be his successor in 1976, but that the Republican party would be abolished four years later. In its place he envisioned a grand alliance of conservatives and moderates from both political camps, an umbrella that would encompass, as he put it to Ehrlichman, "everyone except the damn liberals." The new party would be formed along British political lines, perhaps, Nixon speculated, even borrow for its title the name of a British grouping like "Liberal" or "Conservative." Though Connally, as President, would be the party's titular head, Nixon planned a major role for himself in its shaping and running. From his operatives in every state would come the party nucleus; from him personally would come its guiding principles. He also would direct the process of the party's creation, the assembly of its first convention, the mode and manner of its operation, and, he was certain, its eventual dominance of the American political scene.

For the plan to work, Connally, who had yet to change party labels, had to be put center stage as Nixon's vice presidential running mate in 1972. Unwilling to wait for the GOP to nominate him, Nixon at one point had decided to appoint Connally as vice president under the provisions of the Twenty-fifth Amendment, ridding himself of Agnew by naming him to a vacant spot on the Supreme Court. When Mitchell, among others, counseled against that move, noting that both Agnew and Connally would have difficulty being confirmed, Nixon retreated, but not by much. Connally would be his vice president, but he would have to wait until 1972. When that, too, was ruled out for political considerations, Nixon reluctantly settled for having Connally stay on in the cabinet, leavening his disappointment by appointing him secretary of state. Ultimately, that intention went awry as well, and Connally, who became a Republican in 1973, left the cabinet altogether in 1974.

Since then, Connally's fortunes had plummeted. The most serious setback was being indicted by the Watergate grand jury in the milk-fund case. Though he had been acquitted after a lengthy trial, the incident further enhanced Connally's wheeler-dealer reputation and made all the more unlikely his prospects of unseating Gerald Ford.

Nixon, however, had not given up on him. He had talked to Connally frequently since the resignation, bolstering his morale and urging him to keep his election options open. More concretely, Nixon also tried to enlist allies on Connally's behalf, notably Harry S. Dent, a South Carolina political operative, who during his tenure in the Nixon White House had played a key role in devising the so-called "Southern Strategy." Under Nixon, Dent had also been a leading Connally partisan, and after the 1972 election Nixon had sent him to Camp David to draw up a blueprint for Connally's succession to the White House. Dent had performed admirably, just as he had later for Gerald Ford. And it was to Gerald Ford that Dent was still committed. Three times in 1976, Nixon called Dent, pleading with him to defect to Connally's cause. Each time the answer was no.

With all the advice Nixon was dispensing to the various Republican contenders, it was difficult even for his closest friends to guess which of them he actually preferred. To some visitors, Nixon intimated that he was thinking of voting for Reagan in the California primary; to others, that he would, of course, vote for Ford, though keeping his preference secret, lest any endorsement hurt Ford's already perilous chances. Still others, like Pepsico chairman Donald Kendall, came away from San Clemente just as convinced that Nixon was still pining for Connally, who as the political season wore on had concluded that the nomination was out of reach, endorsed Ford and currently was angling for nothing more exalted than the vice presidential nod. While keeping his own preference secret, Nixon was quite eager to learn the choice of others. He asked a number of his friends whom they were going to vote for and listened intently as they explained their reasons. One of those he questioned was Bob Haldeman, who was then appealing his Watergate conviction. When Nixon asked Haldeman whom he was going to vote for in the California primary, Haldeman replied, "In case you've forgotten, in California convicted felons can't vote." After a moment of uneasy silence, Nixon laughed, "Well, in that case, I'll vote twice." Haldeman, who would shortly begin serving an eighteen-month sentence at the Federal Prison Camp at Lompoc, California, laughed as well.

Nixon's party did not seem to care who he was backing. He was conspicuously absent from the list of dignitaries invited to the Kansas City convention, and during the proceedings his name was not uttered from the podium. Vainly, Korff patrolled the hotel corridors, enlisting delegate signatures on a petition condemning the Ford-dominated platform committee for, as Korff put it, "a cover-up of virtue."

"People speak of events like the open door to China as if they were done by a phantom," Korff protested. "They deny the man who was responsible." The committee was unmoved; with Ford's blessing, the single reference to Nixon—that, in a brief bow to his China policy—was deleted from the party platform.

Meanwhile, Nixon continued to work behind the scenes in a last-ditch attempt to win Connally the vice presidential nomination. He made a number of calls to Republican leaders urging Connally's selection and for a time his game plan seemed to be succeeding. On the convention floor, where Ford's handlers were battling with Reagan's for control of the pivotal Mississippi delegation, promises were being made that if Mississippi went for Ford, Ford in turn would go for Connally. In fact, Ford had already settled on Kansas Senator Robert Dole as his running mate. Worried that the Connally nomination was slipping away, Nixon frantically phoned Ford's suite, trying to learn from Gulley the latest vice presidential intelligence. At Cheney's instruction, Gulley pleaded ignorance, and though the phone calls from Nixon kept coming until two hours before the vice presidential announcement, the secrecy held.

Dole's selection worried Nixon. "They're going to have trouble with that guy," he predicted to an aide; "he's able, but his personality's abrasive as hell, and he's going to cause a helluva lot of problems with the press. They better get somebody good to handle him, someone who can control him, limit his appearances to select audiences, or this guy's going to alienate a helluva lot of people."

He was far more concerned, however, about the Democrats who, confounding his earlier predictions, had designated Jimmy Carter as the party's standard-bearer the week before. When Gulley showed up in San Clemente shortly after the Republican convention, Nixon handed him a sheet of yellow legal paper which had been divided into two columns, one listed "Carter," the other "Ford." Beneath each heading, Nixon had listed the states each candidate would win in November. The tally showed Carter eking out a narrow victory.

"We know who our guy is," Nixon said. "Now let's get to work."

From then until the election, Gulley transported a steady stream of advice back to Washington. One piece detailed the key political contacts in every major city and state; another advised keeping Hartmann out of California "because the Republicans [there] hate him"; a third recommended covertly employing John Mitchell in New Jersey and Missouri because, "He knows more about those two states than anybody around."

At one point, Nixon worried to Gulley that, "Kissinger's talking too much about black Africa. It's pissing off the rednecks. The Negro vote's lost; don't let it lose you white votes. The Democrats have Negroes and the Jews—I don't give a shit what Max Fischer is telling Ford about the Jews, they have them—and let them have them. In fact, tie them around their necks."

He was similarly insistent about how Ford should conduct himself during the televised debates. His advice filled up a number of handwritten pages and ranged from how Ford should react if Carter turned mean (saddened, rather than angry) to what to wear and where to stand and how the content of the programs should be structured. Nixon also reminded Ford to be sure to deliver a couple of "spontaneously" funny lines and to have one of his own TV advisers in the control truck lest a Democratic director sabotage the choice of shots. One bit of counsel was unexpected. "Don't worry about what you say about Nixon. Murder me. I understand."

The trick was getting Ford to understand. Ford had never campaigned in an arena larger than a congressional district, and his inexperience was beginning to tell. He fumbled, bumbled and in one remarkable pronouncement made during the nationally televised debates with Carter, proclaimed, "There is no Soviet domination of Eastern Europe." Worse from Nixon's standpoint was that Ford was ignoring key elements of the San Clemente strategy.

Repeatedly, Nixon demanded to know whether Ford had followed up on the contacts he had provided him in various cities and states. When Gulley would tell him that to the best of his knowledge he had, Nixon would explode, "Well, goddam it, I checked, and he hasn't, and the guy is getting pissed." Nixon was even more upset when, during the latter stages of the campaign, Ford ignored his counsel to spend more time in California and Texas, both of which Nixon deemed to be winnable, and instead scheduled a number of appearances in New York which, with benefit of Senator Patrick Moynihan's coattails, Nixon was sure Carter was bound to take.

"Jerry's running for President of the United States now," Nixon complained to Gulley, "not just a seat in the House." He was even blunter in his next memo to Ford. "Remember," Nixon wrote, "Carter scares the hell out of me. Scare the hell out of the American people about Carter's foreign policies; bear down on it. He'll come close to making us a number two power."

As Election Day approached, Nixon continued to pound away at the foreign policy theme. "An international incident could be useful to Ford," he mused to Gulley. "But be careful how you use it. If an international situation blows up, dramatize it. . . . Of course, if it comes out that I suggested it, they'll say, 'Nixon says "start a war." ' "

The election, however, was not turning on foreign policy, but on the record of what Carter had taken to calling "the Nixon-Ford Administration." Considering the continued high public esteem for Ford's personal integrity, it was a politically dubious tactic. Nonetheless, Carter continued to press it and, partially as a result, his standing in the polls started to slide. Nixon was momentarily hopeful. He understood better than Carter the antipathy toward him and that however profound, it was not easily transferable. "The American people wouldn't accept it if Jimmy Carter went after Jerry Ford with a knife," he told Gulley. "They'd accept it all right if it was Dick Nixon, but not Jerry Ford."

Unfortunately, even as Carter unsheathed his knife, so did Ford his, accusing Carter of all manner of sins, from planning to denude the United States of its defenses to emulating Bella Abzug. As the campaign degenerated into a welter of charges and countercharges, memories of Watergate were stirred afresh. On September 21, *The Wall Street Journal* reported that Charles Ruff, the latest Watergate special prosecutor, was investigating whether Ford had diverted campaign contributions he had received as a congressman to his personal use. Meanwhile, John Dean was charging in an about-to-be-published book, *Blind Ambition*, that Ford, contrary to previously sworn testimony, had discussed with the White House ways to block plans for hearings into Watergate before the 1972 election. The transcript of one of the Nixon tapes was resurrected, on which Nixon, Haldeman and Dean discussed how best to employ Ford, with Nixon issuing instructions how Ford was to be threatened.

All at once, Richard Nixon, his crimes and his pardon were again the issue, and Carter pounced. In a final campaign rally in Boston, Carter, his voice nearly gone, rasped, "The spirit of this country has been damaged by Richard Nixon and Gerald Ford. We don't like their betrayal of what our country is, and we don't like their vision of what this country ought to be."

The night before the election, with many surveys deeming the race too close to call, Bob Teeter, Ford's pollster, went to bed with one nagging worry. "I could just see myself waking up in the morning, turning on my television set, and there would be Nixon voting early in San Clemente," he later recalled to journalist Jules Witcover. "And some network reporter would go up to him, stick a microphone in his face, and ask him who he voted for. And Nixon would say: 'Who do you think? I put him in, didn't I?' "

But Nixon had voted by absentee ballot weeks earlier. It didn't matter. By a margin of only 2 percent—the turn, electorally, of one key state—Gerald Ford had lost the presidency. In the exit polling conducted by the Republicans, 7 percent of those who voted against him gave as their reason his pardon of Richard Nixon. Would he have done it again? someone asked Ford later. Gerald Ford thought a moment, then replied, "I think I still would have."

Richard Nixon had no comment on the outcome, then or later. He had made his predictions months before on the sheet of yellow legal paper he had given Gulley. Without exception, they had been correct.

12
The Frost Interviews

While Nixon was seeing to his wife's recuperation and the reelection of his successor, David Frost had not been idle. In early September of 1976 Frost had flown to San Clemente to discuss the scheduling problem with Nixon. He found him in a wisecracking mood. Hearing that Frost would shortly deliver a paid lecture at Northern Illinois University, Nixon gibed: "Be sure you pay your taxes. Otherwise you can get in trouble." Frost chuckled, then came to the point: delaying the telecast until August, the traditional television doldrums, would mean a ratings disaster.

"I don't know about that," Nixon shot back. "As I recall, we got a helluva rating August 9, 1974."

"Yes," Frost replied, "but what do you do for an encore?"

Nixon smiled. A few weeks later he agreed to moving the taping up to March and to provide Frost with four additional hours of interview time.

The warmth, however, soon cooled. When next Frost appeared in San Clemente the following February, Nixon, whose staff had begun investigating his background, regarded him cautiously.

"Ah," Nixon greeted him, "the grand inquisitor."

"No, no," Frost protested, "just your friendly neighborhood confidant."

Nixon did not seem wholly convinced. After some back and forth about makeup and lighting, he said to Frost, "It's the way you look that I'm really worried about. After all, you've got your whole career ahead of you."

A month later, Brennan, who along with the rest of the senior staff was suffering doubts about doing the interview at all, challenged Frost directly. "How do we know," Brennan asked, "that you aren't going to screw us in the editing?"

151

"And how do we know," Frost retorted, "that you aren't going to screw us with the stonewalling?"

The exchange grew more heated and one of Frost's companions wondered whether Brennan might throw a punch. As it was, Brennan left little doubt about his feelings. "You know," he told Frost, "60 percent of what this guy did in office was right. And 30 percent may have been wrong, but he thought it was right at the time."

Frost concluded that what Brennan was telling him was that 10 percent of the time Nixon did things he knew were wrong. There was a pause, then Brennan added, "If you screw us on the 60 percent, I'm going to ruin you if it takes the rest of my life."

"And if you screw us on the ten percent," Frost replied, "I'm going to ruin you if it takes the rest of my life."

Brennan's testiness was understandable. The last ten months had been rough ones on everyone at Casa Pacifica. In addition to the strain imposed by Mrs. Nixon's stroke, whose aftereffects were proving more serious than originally thought, there had been a series of troubles. They had begun the previous spring with the sale of the Key Biscayne property, an event that dredged up Nixon's finances and that he had reneged on a promise to repay the IRS the $148,000 owed in taxes on which the statute of limitations had run out.

Then, in New York, literary agent Scott Meredith announced that he had obtained copies of twenty-two "love letters" purportedly written by Nixon to an unnamed married woman—allegedly a Spanish contessa —during the last months of his administration. Handwriting analysis eventually would put an end to Meredith's claims, though not before the letters fell into the hands of *The National Enquirer*, which enlisted John Dean to attest to their authenticity.

Meanwhile, it was disclosed that during the late sixties, the FBI had investigated another supposed Nixon liaison, this one with a Hong Kong tour guide named Marianna Liu, whom Nixon had come to know while lawyering for Pepsico in the Far East. It was not merely the suggestion of intimacy that titillated, but the allegation that Liu was a foreign agent, presumably for the Chinese Communists. Once again the tabloids had a field day which halted only when Liu, backed by an offer of cooperation from Nixon, filed a $5 million lawsuit for libel.

Always, it appeared, there was something, from the serious—the New York Supreme Court disbarring Nixon—to the frivolous—the Washington Social Register dropping from its listings those who had been involved in Watergate—to the merely irritating—the soaking of 180 boxes of Nixon's papers, when an air-conditioning vent clogged in a government warehouse. And now, incredibly, the pinprick that was worrying Richard Nixon in the spring of 1977 was an English entertainer named David Frost.

No one could have been more pleased than Frost himself. He was enjoying the worry he was causing Nixon, enjoying even more the attention and publicity that was coming his way. It was one thing to be a mere celebrity. It was quite another to have a camera crew from 60 *Minutes* trailing in your wake ("It is like he is in training for a heavyweight fight," said the admiring producer), to be compared flatteringly to the Watergate special prosecutor by columnist Jack Anderson, to have waiters at Rive Gauche whisper words of encouragement in your ear. And if inevitably some of the notices were not so nice (TV columnist Gary Deeb wrote in the *Chicago Tribune*: "The Frost-Nixon sessions represent another typical Nixon deal. The deck is stacked and the cards are marked."), that was the price of going after the Big One.

"I hope the approach he takes will be one of a cascade of candor," Frost told Mike Wallace a few weeks before the first cross-examination.

Wallace screwed up his face. "A cascade of candor from Richard Nixon? Is this what you expect?"

Frost smiled. "No, it was just a phrase I thought would appeal to you."

With what he had taken to calling "N-Day" only two weeks off, Frost and his staff encamped in the Beverly Hilton, where he had bartered free lodging for advertising space and prepared, as the interviewer put it, "to take television by storm." Financially, at least, he had already succeeded. Lured by a rare chance to best the networks in prime time, a total of 145 independent stations in the U.S. and fourteen other nations overseas had agreed to carry the interviews. When all the revenues were totaled, Frost could expect to realize a profit of well over $1 million.

Editorially, preparations seemed at least as complete. Reston and Zelnick had interviewed scores of sources and combed through thousands of pages of clips and data. The Watergate prosecutors had opened their files and spent hours schooling them in cross-examination techniques. Lists of scripted questions had been prepared, covering every conceivable topic, from Nixon's taxes to his sex life. There had been hours of elaborate dress rehearsals, with Zelnick playing Nixon, aping not only his expected answers, but his speech patterns and mannerisms as well. Particular attention had been paid to the Colson transcripts which, for all Reston's anxiety, had remained secret.

"Assuming the worst," Reston advised in an accompanying memo, "that Richard offers no explanation for the 18½ minutes, and that further he maintains that he had no interest this early in a cover-up, David will keep the following as a final back-up: his excerpts from another conversation on June 20, this time with Charles Colson, and these comments have never been made public. It shows Nixon talking about 'stonewalling' for the first time and about 'leaving this where it is:

with the Cubans.' This is a trap for Nixon and should be sprung deftly."
The memo was now part of four thick briefing binders that had been
prepared for Frost. The question was whether Frost had read them.

He had, though only in cursory fashion and, even then, the great
bulk of his education had come at the eleventh hour. Since signing the
contract, Frost had been distracted by other projects, including the staging of a pop concert in Australia from which he had only recently returned. As a result, he was woefully uninformed in many key areas, nor
was his knowledge notably increased by such stabs at original research as
having drinks with Tony Ulasewicz in a dark corner of Nixon's favorite
restaurant, Trader Vic's.

"Don't worry," Birt assured Reston, who was becoming increasingly
nervous, "David doesn't like to be overprepared. He may seem like Clark
Kent for a long time, but then, just when the villains are about to take
over Gotham, off comes the shirt, and there is a Superman with the
knockout punch."

"Yeah," said Reston, "and I'm Lois Lane."

Nixon, by contrast, appeared the model of composure. When Jörn
Winther, Frost's Danish director, came to Casa Pacifica to check lighting
and camera angles, the former President not only welcomed him but took
time out to provide a history lesson. Standing in his office as Winther and
the technical crew looked on, Nixon spun a large globe, and pointed to
Denmark as if to reacquaint Winther with his birthplace. Then he spun
the globe again, this time bringing it to rest halfway around the world.

"This is China," Nixon intoned. "There are seven hundred million
people living here, as opposed to one hundred million in the Middle
East."

He twirled the globe a quarter turn. "And two hundred fifty million
in Russia. Where do you suppose most of the troubles our world has
have come from?"

"Not Denmark," Winther replied.

Like Frost, Nixon had been cramming and rehearsing with Ken
Khachigian, a former White House speechwriter who had come to San
Clemente to work on the memoirs, and Sawyer acting as interrogator. He
had gone over lists of likely questions, practicing not only his answers
but—or so Frost later suspected—the gestures that would go with them.
The senior staff had worked with him many hours, and Nixon himself
had made a number of phone calls to Kissinger to refresh his memory on
foreign policy.

The one area where his preparation was incomplete was Watergate.
He had yet to deal with the scandal in his memoirs, and though the staff
had prepared exhaustive briefing materials, including copies of the twenty-
three most crucial Watergate tapes, Nixon had perused them only halfheartedly. He was sure, he told his aides, that the battle he would wage

with Frost over Watergate would be strategic, involving the "big-picture" questions on which he was already well versed. That sort of combat he could win easily; he had already been through it with the White House press.

But his aides were less confident. Khachigian in particular had had extensive dealings with Frost's staff, and though Zelnick and Reston had been guarded, they had left him with the impression that at least on Watergate Frost had done his homework. Khachigian was equally sure that the adversary proceeding would not be as Nixon imagined it. Frost would be hard and tough; the questions would be detailed and, unlike a White House press conference, the questioner would have ample opportunity for follow-up. David Frost was a guerrilla fighter. He wasn't going to play by strategic rules.

"N-Day," March 23, dawned clear and sunny, the temperatures in the upper seventies. By 8:00 A.M. Frost and his team were heading south down the San Diego Freeway in a rented blue Mercedes, towards Monarch Bay, an exclusive suburban enclave six miles north of San Clemente. Casa Pacifica, where Frost had wanted to tape the interviews, had been ruled out because of electronic interference from the radar of the nearby Coast Guard station. So the site for the tapings had been switched to Monarch Bay and the home of H. L. Smith, a millionaire industrialist and old Nixon loyalist, who had been paid $6000 to vacate the premises temporarily.

Frost, who had been up long past midnight going over the research material, was only mildly disappointed. Sitting in the back seat of the Mercedes, jotting notes on blue question sheets, he had other things on his mind. For one, he had still not decided how to start the interviews.

"Why don't we begin with the question everybody talks about?" he asked Zelnick. "Why didn't he burn the tapes?"

Zelnick was not enthusiastic. "It could open up the entire Watergate matter long before we are ready to delve into it. It's likely to set exactly the sort of negative tone you're worried about."

The ensuing discussion resolved nothing, and Frost went back to his notes.

At 9:35 the Mercedes swung onto the grounds of the Smith estate. The waiting press surged forward as Frost waved and called out a greeting. Ten minutes later, precisely on schedule, Nixon's white Lincoln Continental pulled to the curb.

In the Smith family living room where the taping sessions would take place, two beige-colored easy chairs faced one another. On the surrounding bookshelves, Nixon's collection of model elephants peered out; they had been imported from Casa Pacifica for the occasion, and, like everything else in the room, including the volumes of presidential papers from the Nixon, Kennedy and Johnson years, their placement had been approved by Nixon.

At 10:30 the two protagonists walked onto the set. Nixon, wearing a blue suit with a blue-patterned tie, gazed steadily into Frost's eyes and tried to make small talk. He mentioned the 100,000 cards and letters, mostly from schoolchildren, that Pat had received since her stroke. Frost joked that the cameramen spoke only Turkish, the better to keep the contents of the program secret. The assistant director called off the seconds . . . three . . . two . . . one.

"Mr. President," Frost began, "we are going to be covering a lot of subjects in a great deal of detail over the next six hours, but I must begin completely out of context by asking you one question, more than any other, almost every American and people all over the world want me to ask. They all have their questions, but one of them in every case is, 'Why didn't you burn the tapes?' "

Nixon appeared startled. He paused, then began to ramble about the taping system Lyndon Johnson had installed in the White House, saying how its existence had become known to the Nixon staff during a visit to the Johnson library, and that Haldeman had decided, in the interests of "history," that Nixon should have one of his own. Twenty minutes later he was still talking, asserting that he never watched himself on television, then disconnectedly describing some of his personal quirks.

"It is true," he admitted, "I have a tendency to look down when I am thinking, with my heavy eyebrows—I had them trimmed this morning —because they tell me you should keep them trimmed and then the audience can see your eyes. Or you shouldn't gesture so much because your hands get in front of your face. Well, maybe that's good. Maybe that the hands are better looking than the face."

In one of the outer bedrooms, where the Frost team had assembled, Zelnick yelled into a monitor, "Move in, tear the son of a bitch to pieces." Finally, Nixon's recitation came to an end. Frost probed more, and once again Nixon was off and running, this time about Dean, Haig and George Wallace. Barely missing a beat, he began reminiscing—about Eisenhower, Kissinger and Truman, about China and the Soviet Union, even about his former football coach, Chief Newman.

The reverie was broken only when Frost asked him about his resignation. Briefly, Nixon seemed to falter as he recounted his final days in the White House. He talked of Tricia coming into his office, throwing her arms around him, kissing him and crying—"She so seldom cries. And I said, 'Don't cry, honey.' She said, 'Daddy, I know I shouldn't, but you know except for Eddie, I just want you to know you're the finest man I know.' "—then later the same day discovering a note Julie had pinned to his pillow—"Dear Daddy, whatever you do, I will support you, but wait a week or ten days. Just go through the fire a little longer. I love you. Julie." He talked on about his mother, "the Quaker saint," about his wife, who "with her rare sense of intuition" had started to pack on Tuesday morning, even about the prayer scene with Kissinger in the Lincoln sitting room. And finally he came to himself—what the resignation had meant to him.

"I never think in . . . suicidal terms, death wish and all that. That's all just . . . just bunk. But on the other hand, I feel myself that life without purpose, ah, I feel that life in which an individual has to . . . is forced to go against his intuitions about what he ought to do, that life then becomes almost unbearable. And so resignation meant life without purpose so far as I was concerned.

"I had nothing more to contribute to the causes I so deeply believed in. And also, I felt that resignation meant that I would be in a position of, of not having really anything to live for, and related to the fact that it is life without purpose, not having anything to live for, that it could be a very, very shattering experience, which it has been. And it, to a certain extent, still is.

"I mean, you see, people . . . the average person, and I understand this, I'm . . . I do not consider myself to be other than an average person, and none of us should really. We all think we're a little smarter than we are, but you feel that, 'Well, gee, isn't it just great to, you know, to have enough money to afford to live in a very nice house and to be able to play golf and to have nice parties and to wear good clothes, and shoes, and suits, *et cetera, et cetera, et cetera,* or travel if you want to.

"And the answer is, if you don't have those things, then they can mean a great deal to you. When you do have them, they mean nothing to you. . . .

"I know a lot of people, and I can understand it, say, 'Gee whiz, it just isn't fair, you know, for an individual to be, ah, get off with a pardon simply because he happens to have been President, and when another individual goes on trial, and maybe has to serve a prison sentence for it.' I can understand how they feel.

"I can only say that no one in the world, and no one in our history could know how I felt. No one can know how it feels to resign the Presidency of the United States. Is that punishment enough? Oh, probably not. But whether it is or isn't . . . we have to live with not only the past, but for the future, and I don't know what the future brings, but whatever it brings, I'll still be fighting."

The answer was tendentious, discursive, syntactically nightmarish. But at least it was something. The same could not be said of most of Nixon's other replies. In two hours and fifteen minutes of questioning, Frost had not rocked him and on such key matters as the tapes and his own culpability, had barely budged him. The worst Nixon was willing to concede for his administration was that it had engaged in "political activities which led to the resignation." Moreover, Nixon had quickly noted, other Presidents had done the same. There had been Eisenhower's "barracks-room talk," Johnson's taping system, and the decision by Harry Truman—who, as Nixon smilingly put it, "is deservedly getting higher marks now than he did then"—to pardon fifteen members of the Pendergast machine who had been convicted of vote stealing. That they had survived while he had not, was, according to Nixon, attributable to one thing: "a double standard." If Frost thought differently, Nixon concluded with a defiant flourish, he would be happy to "demolish" any charges he might wish to make.

Frost walked off the set downcast. It was, he told his staff, "a mitigated disaster."

The next day had been set aside for rest, and Frost used the break to show the first day's taping to columnist Joseph Kraft, an old friend whom Frost had invited to California.

"Well," Kraft shrugged when the screening was over, "he's tough." He thumbed through the interview transcript. "You've got to take control," he urged. "Look, you've got a line or two of Frost and then four or five pages of Nixon. A paragraph by Frost and a three-page response. There has to be more give and take. And, remember, you weren't even dealing with particularly controversial material. When you get into the tough areas, you're certain to see a real full-blooded filibuster."

Kraft's prediction proved correct. The next four taping sessions, devoted in the main to Nixon's foreign policy record, were like the first. Nixon was in control, whether it was talking about his relations with the Soviets ("Brezhnev was something of a fashion plate. He liked beautiful cars, he liked beautiful women. . . . His yacht makes that old *Sequoia*, that President Carter's now put in mothballs, look like a rowboat."); his calming of Kissinger after the Cambodian invasion (" 'Henry,' I said, 'we've done it.' I said, 'Remember Lot's wife. Never look back.' I don't know whether Henry had read the Old Testament or not, but I had, and he got the point."); or his agonizing over the war in Vietnam ("I hated every minute of it. . . . Believe me, it was a sore temptation not just to end it and blame it on Kennedy and Johnson. They got us in, I didn't. They sent the men over there, I didn't."). Nixon handled Frost's few jabs with ease, often as not turning them back on him. When Frost asked whether having seen the movie *Patton* twice played any role in his decision a few days later to invade Cambodia, Nixon smiled. "Well, I've seen *The Sound of Music* twice, and it hasn't made me a writer, either."

And so as the hours slipped by it continued to go. Nothing seemed to rattle Nixon, not even Frost's repetition of a loose Kissinger remark, made in front of an open microphone during a state dinner in Ottawa.

"What we have to understand," Nixon said, "is that Henry likes to say outrageous things. . . . Henry . . . [is] fascinated first by the celebrity set, and second, he like[s] being one himself. . . . Well, anyway, that's Henry. . . . He likes parties (I despise them, because I've been to so many . . . but Henry will learn to despise them too after he's been through a few more) . . . and I can see exactly what happened in Canada. He runs into a lady who has a very low opinion of me, so Henry feels that he's really defending me, and that the way to defend me is to concede that, 'He's sort of an odd person. He's an artificial person.' The only problem was he didn't turn his microphone off. But, on the other hand, I didn't turn it off either in the Oval Office on occasions, so I never held him for that."

The performance was vintage Nixon, including an off-camera comment made to Frost one Monday morning as they walked through the Smiths' kitchen onto the set. "Well," he said, "did you do any fornicating this weekend?"

Frost had been too taken aback to make more than a stumbling reply and that, in the opinion of his staff, was the trouble with the whole interrogation. After a lackluster performance by Frost during a taping session on Vietnam, Reston, who had begun leaking interview transcripts to Nixon psychohistorian Fawn Brodie in hopes that she would provide some insights, hissed at Frost, "This program does the one thing that I warned all along that this series should never do, and that is make Nixon look Presidential. You may win a point or two along the way, or even the debate viewed as a whole. But it will seem like two rational, reasonable men discussing a policy which in my view amounted to murder."

Frost, who had come to regard Reston as something of a crank, ignored him. But Reston was not the only critic. Minoff, who had been struggling with only partial success to keep Frost away from the Hollywood party circuit, was becoming increasingly worried about sponsor and network reaction. His worries were heightened when Frost showed Clay Felker one of the tapes. Halfway into it, Felker fell asleep. Something had to be done, Minoff warned Frost. The interviews to date were entirely "too PBS." If a harder line wasn't taken, and quickly, they would face a critical and financial catastrophe. What Minoff did not tell Frost was that the members of the editorial team had come to him one by one, threatening to quit unless Frost immediately got tougher with Nixon.

Matters finally came to a head following the taping session Wednesday, April 6. Frost's questioning that morning had dwelt on the so-called "Huston Plan" which, though never approved, set the stage for subsequent White House "dirty tricks." To Frost's astonishment, Nixon was aggressively uncontrite.

"When the President does it," Nixon declared, "that means that it is not illegal."

The answer startled even Nixon's staff. Frost, however, let it slide, and, during a break in the taping, Zelnick tore into him. "You sound like two old chums, sitting around a pork barrel, talking about a bowling game rather than about the incredible divisiveness Nixon caused by design."

"But he's admitted what we wanted him to," Frost protested.

"Yes," Zelnick replied sarcastically, "but how do you expect your audience to know?"

When the taping resumed that afternoon, Nixon's tone had not changed. By turns he was bathetic and bombastic, especially in his comments about the press. "It hasn't been easy," he said at one point, alluding to Woodward and Bernstein. "Particularly let me say, I've mentioned the stories that have been written, and some written by, ah, some book authors." Nixon paused, pretending not to remember Woodward's and Bernstein's names. ". . . I respect some, but [for] those who write history as fiction on third-hand knowledge, I have nothing but utter contempt. And I will never forgive them. Never!"

The performance delighted Nixon's staff, and Brennan bounded into the room to pump Frost's hand. Frost, who was celebrating his birthday, seemed equally pleased, though no more so than Nixon. For the first time since the taping sessions began, he paused to sign autographs and exchange quips. "If that guy runs for President again," said one of the watching cameramen, "I'm going to vote for him."

That evening there was a birthday party in Frost's honor at Ma Maison. It was a lavish, celebrity-studded affair and, after the plates had been cleared away, the songwriter Sammy Cahn rose to sing several compositions he had adapted specially for Frost. One of them, to the tune of "Love and Marriage," had an immediately sobering effect.

"Frost and Nixon, Frost and Nixon," Cahn crooned in a gravelly voice. "Now there's an act that's gonna take some fixin'."

The next morning during a staff meeting in Frost's suite, the good humor of the previous evening was put aside.

"Look at this answer," Zelnick sneered, gesturing at a spot on the transcript. "Ten goddam minutes of bullshit and you didn't say so once. Who cares about whether he brought the White House bed to Europe when he traveled? Jesus, David, look what you are letting him get away with."

Frost tried to defend himself, but Zelnick continued to bore in. "You hardly laid a glove on him. You let him carry the day. He's set up perfectly now for kicking your tail from one end of Monarch Bay to the other. Don't you know what you are up against? By next Wednesday he will have committed every word on every Watergate tape to memory. He'll know every statute cold. He'll call you every time you put a comma in the wrong place. You're in against a master, man, a master."

Birt picked up the attack. "You can't back down with Richard Nixon, because he takes it as a sign of weakness. There's no mercy in the man, not as a warrior and not as an antagonist in this setting. He takes what he gets. You've got to stop him on the spot when he misrepresents the record and say, 'No, Mr. President, I know this better than you do, and I'm not going to let you rewrite the record.' You have to declare your points. You have to stand with them. And you have got to destroy his points. Otherwise, we will fail. You will fail."

"And right now," Zelnick added glumly, "that's where we are heading."

The next few days, which had been set aside as an Easter break, Frost closed the door of his suite, put away the customary bottles of white wine and, working eighteen hours at a stretch, immersed himself in the research. By Wednesday, when the first of the Watergate taping sessions was scheduled to begin, he felt prepared. The staff, however, did not share his optimism, and the ride to Monarch Bay that morning passed largely in silence. As they neared the Smith estate, Frost had a sudden thought.

"Does anyone have the conspiracy to obstruct justice statute?"

Reston flipped through one of the Judiciary Committee volumes and passed it back. Frost began reading aloud: "Whoever corruptly endeavors to prevent, obstruct or impede the administration of justice . . . A corrupt endeavor to prevent, obstruct or impede," he repeated. "Thank you, Jim, it may come in handy."

Nixon had been preparing that morning as well. Instead of reading through federal statute books, he had gotten a haircut. "Well, Ken," he said to his barber, "what am I going to say when he asks me why I did it?"

"Don't be a Philadelphia lawyer about it, Mr. President," Allan advised. "Just say you screwed up."

On the set, Nixon and Frost shook hands and while waiting for the tape to roll chatted about which of them perspired more. The moments dragged by as Winther struggled with an audio problem. Nixon began to hum. The sound of a plane drifted in from overhead. Nixon joked that it was CBS. In the bedroom command post, Nixon's staff, all present for the first time since the beginning of the tapings, watched the monitor expectantly. Finally, the camera lights blinked on.

"Mr. President," Frost began, "to try to review your account of Watergate in one program is a daunting task. But we'll press first of all through the sort of factual record and the sequence of events as concisely as we can to begin with. But just one brief preliminary question. Reviewing now your conduct over the whole of the Watergate period, with additional perspective now, three years out of office and so on, do you feel that you ever obstructed justice or were part of a conspiracy to obstruct justice?"

Nixon feinted. He would answer the question but, since Frost had volunteered to go through the record, he would let him do exactly that first, explaining the circumstances and his motives as he went along. Slowly, but with growing self-assurance, Frost started in, walking Nixon through the break-in, the briefings by Haldeman, Ehrlichman and Dean, the attempt to lay responsibility on the CIA, and finally, the eighteen-and-a-half-minute tape gap.

At every step Nixon deflected blame. "My motive was not criminal," he insisted. "I didn't believe we were covering up any criminal activities. I didn't believe that John Mitchell was involved. I didn't believe that, for that matter, anybody else was. I was trying to contain it politically. And that's a very different motive from the motive of attempting to cover up criminal activities of an individual. And so, there was no cover-up of any criminal activities; that was not my motive."

Nixon settled back into his seat and half-smiled. Frost did not smile back.

". . . And so you knew, in terms of intent, and you knew, in terms of foreseeable consequences, that the result would be that in fact criminals would be protected. Hunt and Liddy, who were criminally liable, would be protected . . . So that's obstruction of justice."

"Now just a moment . . ." Nixon cut in.

"Period," said Frost.

Like a lawyer reviewing his case, Nixon began reciting facts. True, he admitted, on June 23 he had instructed Haldeman to use the CIA to turn off the FBI's investigation. But when the CIA refused, he had gone ahead and on July 7 told acting FBI Director L. Patrick Gray to "conduct your thorough and aggressive investigation." Whatever he might have been doing in June, Nixon concluded, by July he was certainly not obstructing justice.

"An obstruction of justice is an obstruction of justice," Frost retorted, "if it's a minute or five minutes, much less the period June 23rd to July the fifth."

Nixon seemed shaken, but only for a moment. Then he started to lecture Frost, telling him that since he had probably not read the statute, he didn't know that "criminal intent" was the decisive factor. Without intent, Nixon insisted, there was no crime, and he had had no intent.

Frost's rejoinder was unequivocal: "The law states that when intent and foreseeable consequences are sufficient, motive is completely irrelevant."

The sparring continued as gradually Frost maneuvered Nixon toward the snare Reston had constructed.

"And so March 21st was the first time you really knew about the cover-up?"

"March the 21st was the date in which the full import, the full impact of the cover-up came to me. . . ."

"But in that case," Frost continued, ". . . why did you say in such strong terms to Colson on February the 14th—which is more than a month before—. . . 'The cover-up is the main ingredient. That's where we gotta cut our losses; my losses are to be cut. The President's losses gotta be cut on the cover-up deal'?"

Nixon looked stunned. A moment later, Frost began quoting from the Colson transcript of February 13.

"It hasn't been published yet, you say?" Nixon interrupted.

"No," Frost answered, "I think it's available to anyone who consults the record."

A nervous smile traced across Nixon's face. "Oh," he said, "I just wondered if we'd seen it."

Frost continued reading from the transcript slowly, as if savoring every word. " 'When I'm speaking about Watergate, that's the whole point of the election. This tremendous investigation rests, unless one of the seven begins to talk. That's the problem.' "

"How many times do I have to tell you?" Nixon replied, ". . . I didn't know if anybody at that point—nobody on the White House staff, not John Mitchell, anybody else that I believed was involved, ah, criminally."

Frost pressed on, concluding with a litany of Nixon quotes from a March 21 conversation with Haldeman, discussing payment of hush money to Watergate burglar E. Howard Hunt.

"You could get a million dollars and you could get it in cash. I know where it could be gotten. . . ."

"Get the million bucks, it would seem to me to be worthwhile. . . ."

"That's worth it, and that's buying time. . . ."

"First, you've got the Hunt problem, that ought to be handled. . . ."

"The money can be provided. Mitchell would provide the way to deliver it. That could be done. See what I mean? . . ."

"Would you agree that this is a buy-time thing? You better damn well get this done, but fast. . . ."

"We have no choice. . . ."

"Let me stop you right there. Right there," Nixon commanded. Frost could not suppress a smile.

"You're doing something here which I am not doing and I will not do throughout these broadcasts," Nixon said. "You have every right to, ah, you were reading there, out of context, out of order, because I have read these and I know."

"I'm sure you do," Frost replied.

When the session was over, Zelnick bolted from the production trailer to embrace Frost. "Super, first-rate, sensational," he exalted. Off to one side, Brennan was shaking his head. "What a mistake," he muttered. "What a mistake."

Khachigian was mournful. "The President of the United States made himself look like a criminal defendant with David as prosecutor."

"We didn't want him to go that route," Brennan agreed.

"But this was one subject that we simply could not discuss with him," Khachigian said. "It was just too personal."

"That's right," said Sawyer. "He hasn't written the Watergate part of his book yet. So none of us knew what he was going to say . . ."

The next taping was scheduled for Friday. That morning Nixon, breaking his pattern, showed up late. Frost, who had worried whether he would appear at all, was appalled by his appearance. Almost overnight he seemed to have aged five years. His face was drawn, his voice was husky with fatigue, his eyes were bloodshot and weary. Though Frost did not know it, he had been up most of the night, replaying with his staff his performance of the day before. The Colson tapes had jolted him. He was alarmed not so much by their contents as by the fact that Frost had managed to come by them and in so doing shifted the battle to tactical grounds. That, Nixon hadn't expected. Frost, he had told a member of his staff, had made him look foolish and unprepared. He worried over what Frost would spring next.

The cameras revived him only slightly. When Frost, picking up from where he had left off, began to move in, Nixon made only a pretense of fending him off. He seemed distracted, unable to comprehend Frost's line of attack, as if uncaring where it led. Then as Frost was recounting Nixon's instructions to the CIA, an overhead light exploded like a gunshot. Frost ducked in panic. Nixon, however, remained motionless and, as Frost collected himself, made a vague comment about assassins.

"Let the bad come out," Nixon told Frost when the questioning resumed. ". . . There's plenty of bad. I'm not proud of this period. Ah . . . I didn't handle it well. I messed up. . . . It was a disaster. Ah . . . and I recognize that it was a mistake. I made plenty of them. Ah, but . . . ah . . . I also insist that as my mistakes were concerned, ah . . . they were mistakes frankly of the head and they weren't mistakes of the heart. They were not mistakes that had what I call an improper, illegal motive, ah . . . in terms of obstructing justice. Ah . . . that's all I am trying to say."

As if strained by the admission, Nixon's concentration seemed to fragment, and he began to reminisce about Eisenhower and the difficulties he had gone through firing his aide, Sherman Adams, difficulties, Nixon said, not unlike his own in dismissing Haldeman and Ehrlichman.

"I knew their families. . . . I'd known them since they were just kids.

. . . We weren't close personal friends, but boy they had worked their butts . . . for good causes, and I appreciated that. . . . I remember the day at Camp David when they came up. Haldeman came in first, he's standing as he usually does, not a Germanic Nazi storm-trooper, but just a decent, respected crew-cut guy; splendid man . . .

"Ehrlichman then came in. . . . I took [him] out on the porch at Aspen—you've never been to Aspen, I suppose. That's the Presidential Cabin at Camp David, and it was springtime. The tulips had just come out. I'll never forget, we looked out across—it was one of those gorgeous days when, you know, no clouds were on the mountain. And I was pretty emotionally wrought-up, and I remember I . . . said, 'You know, John, when I went to bed last night, I hoped, I almost prayed, I wouldn't wake up this morning.' "

His voice thickened. "I cut off one arm and then I cut off the other. Now I can be faulted. I recognize it. Maybe I defended them too long. Maybe I tried to help them too much. But I was concerned about them. I was concerned about their families. . . .

"I suppose you could sum it all up the way one of your British prime ministers summed it up, Gladstone, when he said that the first requirement for a Prime Minister is to be a good butcher. Well, I think that the great story, as far as the summary of Watergate is concerned, and, I, ah, did some of the big things rather well, I screwed up terribly in what was the little thing and became the big thing. But I have to admit, I was not a good butcher."

"Would you go further than 'mistakes'?" Frost coaxed. ". . . The word, it seems, is not enough for people to understand."

Suddenly Nixon was alert. "Well," he challenged, "what would you express?"

"My goodness," Frost fumbled, "that's a, I think there are three things, since you asked me, I would like to hear you say—I think the American people would like to hear you say. One is: 'There was probably more than mistakes, there was wrongdoing. Whether it was a crime or not. Yes, it may have been a crime, too.' Secondly, 'I did—' and I'm saying this without questioning the motives, right?—'I did abuse the power I had as President, or, ah, not fulfill the totality of that oath of office.' . . . And thirdly, 'I put the American people through two years of needless agony, and I apologize for that.' "

Nixon once again became defensive, talking about the "good" he had done for the country, the summits, the opening to China, the Vietnam peace. In spite of that, he went on, he was faced with an "enormous political attack" from a "partisan Senate Committee staff," a "partisan Special Prosecutor staff," a "partisan media."

Behind one of the cameras, Brennan suddenly appeared, holding a handwritten sign. "Let him talk," it read. Frost mistook it for "Let's talk" and quickly called for a break. He walked over to Brennan; the colonel's face was flushed. Nixon, he told Frost, had reached a critical moment. He would go further, make a complete accounting, but Frost had to stop playing prosecutor. Brennan reached out for Frost's arm. "You've gotta let him do it his own way."

Birt, who had come out of the production trailer to join the conversation, piped up, "What do you mean by full accounting? That he was guilty of a crime?"

"I don't know if he'll say that," Brennan replied.

"That he committed an impeachable offense?"

"I don't know if he'll say that, either."

"Then David's cross-examination will continue."

"Just a minute," Brennan said. "Let me talk to him." He walked into the bedroom where Nixon was waiting. A few minutes later he returned.

"He knows he has to go further," Brennan reported. "I don't know what he'll say, and I'm not sure he does. But ask him. Just ask him. He's got more to volunteer."

"Look, Jack," said Birt, "we can't plea-bargain with you. . . . The interrogation will have to restart. That's all we can tell you."

"I'll go and tell him," Brennan replied. "And, if it doesn't happen now, we can always try again on Monday."

Minoff, meanwhile, had gone to the kitchen for a drink of water. He was standing in front of the sink when Nixon appeared beside him. Minoff didn't know what to say; neither, apparently, did Nixon, and the two men stood side by side in silence. Finally Nixon said, "Sand dabs."

Minoff looked at him questioningly.

"Sand dabs," Nixon repeated. "You ever have them? They're very healthy and very good for you. Very expensive, but you have to have them."

Then he walked out of the room.

When the cameras came back on, Frost's tone was gentler.

"You got caught up in something . . ."

"Yeah," Nixon answered.

"And then it snowballed."

"It snowballed," Nixon agreed. "And it was my fault. I'm not blaming anybody else. I'm simply saying to you that, as far as I'm concerned, I not only regret it—I indicated my own beliefs in this matter when I resigned. People don't think it was enough to admit mistakes, fine. If they want me to get down and grovel on the floor, no. Never, because I don't believe I should."

He continued with increasing emotion. "I brought myself down," he admitted. "I gave them a sword. And they stuck it in. And they twisted it with relish. And, I guess, if I had been in their position, I'd have done the same thing."

A moment later the defiance returned. "No, I . . . I did not . . . commit a . . . the crime of obstruction of justice. Because I did not have the motive required for the commission of that crime. . . . I did not commit, in my view, an impeachable offense. Now, the House has ruled overwhelmingly that I did; of course, that was only an indictment and would have to be tried in the Senate. I might have won, I might have lost. But, even if I'd won in the Senate by a vote or two, I would have been crippled and the . . . for six months the country couldn't afford having the President in the dock of the United States Senate. . . . I have impeached myself. That speaks for itself."

"How do you mean, 'I have impeached myself'?" Frost asked.

"By resigning. That was voluntary impeachment," Nixon answered.

The concession seemed to shred Nixon's remaining resistance. "I will admit," he went on, "that, acting as a lawyer for their defense, I was not prosecuting the case. I will admit that, during that period, rather than acting primarily in my role as the chief law enforcement officer in the United States of America . . . as the one with the chief responsibility for seeing that the laws of the United States are enforced, I did not meet that responsibility . . . and, under those circumstances, I would have to say that a reasonable person could call it a cover-up.

"I didn't think of it as a cover-up. I didn't intend it to cover up. Let me say, if I intended to cover up, believe me, I'd have done it. You know how I could have done it? So easily? I could have done it immediately after the election, simply by giving clemency to everybody, and the whole thing would have gone away. . . . But now we come to the key point— and let me answer it in my own way—about 'How do I feel about the American people?' "

Frost barely breathed. He knew they had come to the crucial moment. Nixon recalled his last meeting with congressional supporters the night before his resignation.

". . . Half the people around the table were crying. . . . I get . . . just can't stand seeing somebody else cry, and that ended it for me. And I just, well, I must say, I sort of choked up, started to cry . . . then just blurted it out . . . 'I'm sorry. I just hope I haven't left you . . . let you down.' "

Nixon closed his eyes. "I had. I let down my friends. I let down the country. I let down our system of government and the dreams of all those young people that ought to get into government, but think it's all too corrupt and the rest. . . . I, I let the American people down. And I have to carry that burden with me for the rest of my life.

"My political life is over," he went on. "I will never yet, and never again, have the opportunity to serve in any official position. Maybe I can give a little advice from time to time. I can only say in answer to your questions, that while technically, I did not commit a crime, an impeachable offense . . . these are legalisms. As far as the handling of the matter is concerned, it was so botched up. I made so many bad judgments, the worst ones, mistakes of the heart rather than the head, as I pointed out. But let me say, a man in that top judge . . . top job, he's gotta have a heart. But his head must always rule his heart."

There was a momentary silence. Frost started, "This has . . . this has been more—"

"Tough on you?" Nixon interjected, managing a laugh.

"Well, no," Frost answered, searching for the right words. "But I was going to say that I feel we've . . ."

"Covered a lot of ground?"

"Been through a life, almost, rather than an interview, and we thank you."

Watching over a monitor in one of the outer bedrooms, Minoff felt as if some great weight had been lifted. "This is gold," he whispered to himself. "Pure gold." He turned to Reston and grinned. "Maybe we're going to get out of this with our skins after all."

On the set, Nixon's aides were crowding around him protectively. One of them appeared close to tears. Nixon, however, seemed relieved. He pulled a handkerchief from his pocket and mopped the sweat from his face. Though the hot television lights had been switched off, perspiration was still streaming down his brow. He looked at Frost, frowned slightly, then, as if thinking better of it, brightened into a half-smile. "Well," he said to his interrogator, "that should make you happy."

According to the national ratings services, an estimated fifty million Americans, an audience equal to that of the top-rated series *Happy Days*, turned on their televisions to watch their former President discuss Watergate the night of May 4, 1977.

Reactions to his performance were mixed. "I am deeply disappointed," said Leon Jaworski. "To say that mistakes were made is not enough. To deny impeachable acts and criminal wrongdoing is untruthful. These are the hard facts. They cannot be diluted by the passage of time. They cannot be erased by the belated efforts of the man who created them."

Carl Bernstein assessed the same old Nixon: "pathetic, outrageous, proud, deceptive, self-pitying, cunning, self-destructive." John Ehrlichman, who listened to the interview over the radio in his Arizona prison cell, thought Nixon's account "smarmy" and "maudlin." "What the series has done," added E. Howard Hunt, free on parole after serving eighteen months in prison, "is provide Nixon with a public forum from which to plead that he did nothing wrong, and anyway whatever wrong he did was not as bad as his detractors in their villainy made out."

Sam Ervin, the chairman of the Senate Watergate Committee, found himself "feeling sorry" for Nixon; Barry Goldwater, viewing the same telecast, had "no sympathy for him at all." "It didn't change my mind," said Jimmy Carter. ". . . I doubt if the American people were enlightened by it."

The Nixon loyalists disagreed. "A much needed act of healing," Ray Price called the interview. Nixon, said syndicated columnist and former presidential speechwriter Pat Buchanan, had "lance[d] a boil."

Overall, the Gallup Poll found that 44 percent of those who watched Nixon came away feeling more sympathetic toward him, while 28 percent felt less. One thing the interview did not do was change the public perception of his guilt. Despite Nixon's denials, 72 percent of those who watched believed he was guilty of obstruction of justice or other impeachable crimes, and 69 percent thought he had lied during the interview itself. An overwhelming majority—some 75 percent—continued to believe there remained no place for him in public life.

As for David Frost, he was in Los Angeles the night of the first telecast, presiding over a party in the Chestnut Room of Chasen's. Joseph Cotten and Deborah Raffin and Hugh Hefner were there, dining on cracked crab and shrimp and snickering as Nixon argued his case on four big color sets. There were cases of Montrachet and Pouilly-Fuissé, Frost's favorites. The host was exultant. The reviews were already in from the East; his performance was being hailed. "One of the best, most interesting interview broadcasts I've ever seen," Dick Salant of CBS was calling it. And so, at least according to the numbers, it was. More Americans were watching Frost that night than had ever watched an interviewer before.

Richard Nixon was not among them.

That afternoon he had played golf with David Eisenhower, then come back to the residence, napped and eaten dinner with his family. By the time the interview aired on the West Coast, he was in his office, alone, going over his papers and taking calls.

He made it a practice never to watch himself on TV, and tonight was no exception. What had occurred with Frost was over. There was no need or purpose in dwelling on it. He thought he had handled himself well, not perfectly, but well. He hadn't groveled; the dramatic requirements of the medium had been met.

Kissinger phoned to congratulate him, then Tricia. "Daddy," she said from New York, "the second part of the program is well worth waiting for." Toward nine, the scheduled air time, Nixon called Khachigian at home to thank him for his help. Khachigian mentioned that the rest of the staff was there to watch the program with him. Some of them were worried. "Don't be swayed by anything you hear or read," Nixon advised. "Wait until you see and hear the interviews."

There was a momentary pause. When Nixon spoke again, his tone was fatalistic. "It is all done," he said, "and it is there, or it isn't."

13

Memoirs

The most immediate casualty of the Frost interviews was Nixon's memoirs, on which work had been suspended for three months. Financially and personally, much was riding on the book for Nixon, and to date, the project had proceeded by fits and starts. There had been delays; there had been problems of format and focus; there had been troubles gaining access to the papers and the tapes—still stored in Washington under federal lock and key.* There was, overarching everything, the still unanswered question: would Nixon, could he, tell the truth?

Publicly, Nixon's publisher remained confident. All the pronouncements coming from Warner Books emphasized the positive, the vast amount of work that had been done. And, it was true: much had been accomplished. Gannon had gone to Washington and brought back thirty

---

* The issue of who owned the papers and the tapes—Nixon or the government—was finally resolved by the Supreme Court in a decision handed down June 29, 1977. By a vote of 7 to 2, with Nixon appointees Burger and Rehnquist dissenting, the Court rejected Nixon's claim that the seizure of the papers violated his rights of privacy and due process. It also dismissed Nixon's contention that by laying claim to the papers and the tapes, Congress had tampered with the principle of separation of powers and placed him in a category uniquely removed from other Presidents. Writing for the majority, Associate Justice William Brennan declared: "We, of course, are not blind to [Nixon's] plea that we recognize the social and political realities of 1974. It was a period of political turbulence unprecedented in our history. But this Court is not free to invalidate acts of Congress based on inferences that we may be asked to draw from our personalized reading of the contemporary scene of recent history. . . . In short, appellant [Nixon] constituted a legitimate class of one."

However, in an earlier decision handed down on April 12, the Court placed limits on the public use to which the tapes could be put. At issue was a suit filed by Nixon, seeking to block Warner Communications (the parent company, ironically, of Nixon's softcover publisher) from releasing a two-record album drawn from the thirty Watergate tapes. In their briefs, Nixon's lawyers argued that, if the Court allowed the tapes to become public, they would be used at "cocktail parties . . . in comedy acts or dramatic productions," causing Nixon acute "embarrassment and anguish." In a 7 to 2 decision, the Court agreed, and ruled that the right of presidential privacy outweighed that of the public's unlimited right to know.

thousand photocopied pages from the files. To these had been added an enormous clipping collection dating to the days of Nixon's first congressional campaign. The staff had conducted dozens of supplementary interviews with figures ranging from Nixon's football coach, Chief Newman, to his secretary of state, Henry Kissinger. Every scrap and reminiscence had been organized, indexed, and set down on a chronological "blueprint" of Nixon's public career, each day carefully cataloged as to personal, national and international happenings. Working from detailed question sheets prepared by the staff, Nixon had dictated a total of 1.5 million words. These, in turn, had been transcribed, shuttled to the staff for editing and then passed back to Nixon for additions and corrections.

Warner's president, Howard Kaminsky, had seen the material and had pronounced it excellent—indeed, startlingly good. "It will be a very important, candid and readable book," he boasted to an interviewer. "And it will include a lot of new information."

Still, Kaminsky was edgy. The deal Warner's had cut with Nixon provided not only a $2.5 million advance, but what was termed "all provable expenses" in excess of $300,000, a figure that had long since been surpassed. Moreover, it was not at all certain when the manuscript would be finished. Some sections of the book had gone through as many as twenty separate drafts, and none had been completely finalized, principally because Nixon kept adding to the manuscript. As it now stood, his unedited words filled forty black binders, and he had yet to deal with a number of important topics. Nor were matters helped any by the fact that Warner's, a paperback reprint house, had little experience editing original manuscripts. As the months wore on, it became apparent that outside help was needed.

In March 1977, as Nixon was sitting down for the first of his encounters with David Frost, Warner's found the help, by selling, for $225,000 against future royalties, the hardcover rights to Grosset & Dunlap, a respected, old-line publishing house. Grosset had no more experience with presidential memoirs than did Warner's, but it did have veteran editorial hands, chief among them its vice-president and editorial director, Robert Markel.

Gregarious, liberal, an irrepressible bon vivant with intellectual interests ranging from Japanese literature to Italian opera, Markel was a member in good standing of the New York literary establishment, and, like his fellows, had cheered at Nixon's resignation. But he was also curious. He had met Nixon once before—in a locker room in Chicago's Soldier Field, following the 1959 College All-Star game—and the then vice president had impressed him by knowing the name and position of every player on the college squad. This, Markel concluded, was a man with total recall; he wondered whether he would use it.

In late February, before concluding the purchase from Warner's,

Markel and Herbert Roth, Grosset's president, flew to San Clemente. During the flight, they discussed the book's commercial possibilities. Roth, recently returned from the annual Frankfurt Book Fair, was guarded. Talk at the fair had been negative; the general prediction was that Nixon's memoirs, like Lyndon Johnson's, would be a sales dud. Even Roth's wife had told him he was "crazy" to become involved with the project. Roth, however, was not so sure. "The man wants to talk," he mused. "After all he's been through, he's got to. He's got a unique story. All it takes is the right prod." He turned to Markel. "That's up to you."

On arrival at San Clemente, Markel immediately began reading the manuscript. It took him five days and nights to get through it. Like Kaminsky, he found the material surprisingly good; far too long and repetitious to be sure, but still better than he had hoped. Nixon's tone was neither defensive nor apologetic, but rather matter of fact. He had an eye for color and anecdote and a way of putting things in simple, declarative sentences. Markel was pleased even more to discover that during his term at the White House, Nixon had kept a diary—10,000 typescript pages in all—and had quoted from it frequently, and, Markel thought, with revealing effect. What troubled Markel was what was not in the manuscript. Even at this late date, with publication tentatively set for the following fall, Nixon had not written a word about Watergate.

When he went to Sawyer and Gannon for an explanation, they were sheepish. Partly, the omission was a matter of strategy. Early on the staff had decided to proceed through the memoirs chronologically, in hopes that by the time they reached Watergate, Nixon would have realized how the scandal had been woven from the other threads of his life. Now they had reached that point; whether the plan would work, they still couldn't say. There was also the matter of the Frost interviews. Nixon had promised—foolishly, in retrospect—to provide Frost with access to anything in his memoirs that dealt with Watergate. Without anything written, Frost had no access; it was as simple as that.

Sawyer, who had been explaining the situation, shot a look at Gannon. Well, she went on, perhaps not that simple. There was also the question of the continuing appeals of Haldeman, Ehrlichman and Mitchell; conceivably, any of the three of them—Ehrlichman especially— might use the existence of Watergate material as an excuse to subpoena the manuscript. That had to be avoided; Nixon could not withstand another Watergate round. Finally, there was the security worry. Nixon was acutely aware of the financial damage that had been done to Haldeman's book when it was leaked to the *Washington Post* before its scheduled serialization in *The New York Times*. That wasn't going to happen with this book; Nixon had taken elaborate security precautions, including locking the manuscript every night in a vault, to prevent it. There would be a Watergate chapter, but later, when David Frost and the other dangers had passed. In the meantime, she would brief Markel on the highlights.

Markel was surprised by what Sawyer told him. While plainly sympathetic to Nixon, she was forthright in describing his misdeeds. Markel liked her all the more, when, later, as the two of them walked through the area where the mail was being sorted, he inquired about the contents of two boxes of letters, one overflowing, the other only partially filled. "The big one," she answered, "are the get-well cards." "And the other?" Markel wondered. Sawyer smiled. "Those are the 'drop-dead letters.'"

Still, Markel continued to worry about the memoirs' length. Drastic cuts had to be made, and Gannon, the book's overall editor, was insistent that the manuscript remain intact. "This is a seamless story. If you are going to know any of it, you have to know all of it." Yes, Markel agreed, "but you also have to be able to lift it."

It was the author, however, who would have the final say, and, two days into Markel's stay, a meeting was arranged with Nixon, his staff and the representatives of both New York publishers. On the way into Nixon's office, the group passed through one of the outer corridors of the Coast Guard station, where the walls were lined with enlarged color photographs of Nixon and foreign leaders. Markel recognized all but one, an African dignitary in full tribal regalia.

"Who's that?" he asked Gannon.

"You don't know?" Gannon replied, deadpan. "That's Don Nixon."

Don's brother, Richard, did not look well. He seemed shrunken into his suit and his greeting was hesitant, almost embarrassed. "You must be weary having read all that material," he apologized to Markel and Roth. "It must be pretty dull."

"No, no, Mr. President," Roth assured him. "It's just fine. You and Gannon are doing a terrific job." Nixon smiled. "Please don't say things like that," he said, winking at Gannon. "I'll have to give him more money."

Awkwardly, Nixon tried to make small talk. He made note of the Super Bowl, and chagrined to find that no one else in the room had paid any attention to it, switched to publishing. He mentioned various houses, describing the quirks and capabilities of each. Doubleday, he thought, was an excellent firm; the job it had done with Six Crises was first-rate. Of course, he went on, Simon and Schuster, which had published Julie (and, though he did not mention it, Woodward and Bernstein, as well), was an outstanding publisher, too. Nodding at Roth, Nixon added, "I hear you're doing good things at Grosset. Maybe Julie should do her next book for you. I have a great idea for a title of a book: 'Women: You Can't Get Along With Them, You Can't Get Along Without Them.'" There was a titter of laughter.

At length Markel brought the conversation to the point: good as the manuscript was, it was unpublishable in its present state. Khachigian and Gannon began arguing. Finally Kaminsky suggested the possibility of publishing a single, trimmed-down version of the memoirs first, to be followed at some point in the future by a multivolume history of the Nixon presidency. Nixon, who had said nothing during the discussion, at last spoke up. "You can cut and cut and cut, and finally all you have left is the bones." His face had a mournful cast, as if the slashing they were contemplating was not on a manuscript, but on himself. "But that's okay with me."

The talk turned to the book's reception. Nixon was sure it would be terrible. He knew the press; there wouldn't be one good word. There had never been any good words for him, not a single favorable review of any of his books. He didn't dwell on it or worry about it; the hatred was a given. "You're a tough guy," he said to Roth. "What do you think?" Roth disagreed. Reviewers could be bastards, but in this case they would bend over backward to be fair. Nixon shook his head. "You don't know this crowd," he said, voice rising. "I know them. There is no way, *no way*. It is all going to be negative."

Markel returned to San Clemente in late April, shortly after the completion of the Frost interviews. He found Nixon's mood and appearance markedly improved. There was color in his cheeks, and he appeared to have gained some weight. One thing that had not changed was his social clumsiness. When Markel, accompanied by his wife and sixteen-year-old daughter, showed up at his office door, Nixon, arms akimbo and head hunkered down, growled facetiously, "Which one is the daughter?"

He ushered them in, and what was to have been a five-minute social call stretched into an hour of Nixon reminiscence. He described each object in the room in detail, including a flip rack containing several hundred pictures, most of them of foreign travels and heads of state. At one point, when Nixon was describing a photograph of former Japanese prime minister Eisaku Sato, Markel cut in: "Sato, you know, is a very common Japanese word. It means sugar." Nixon, with the Lockheed scandal in mind, shot back: "Yes, but it was Tanaka who got the real sugar."

The bantering was interrupted by a Secret Service agent who burst into the room to announce that Markel had the lights on in his car. "That," Nixon laughed, "is the most excitement we've had out here in a year."

When Markel and his family rose to leave, Nixon seemed dejected. He wanted to talk more, about the book, foreign affairs, even La Costa, the nearby Teamster-owned resort where Markel was staying, and which Nixon warned him was "a den of gambling and sin." Finally, after an obligatory group portrait ("I suggest that you open your eyes wide when the photo is taken," Nixon advised. "I've had a lot of pictures taken of me, you know, and when you open your eyes wide, you look more attractive."), Markel made his way to the door. Nixon stood there another ten minutes, chatting about the book, saying that, however the critics judged it, he was determined to make it readable. "That's important," he said, looking down at his shoes. "I want people to read it. I want them to understand."

For either to happen, the size of the manuscript had to be brought down, and when Markel returned to New York, he recruited two copy editors for the task. The first was David Frost, Grosset's forty-one-year-old chief copy editor. A bearded, bespectacled, bachelor Brooklynite, "the good David Frost," as Nixon came to call him, shared Markel's taste for opera, as well as his politics: during the House impeachment hearings, he had written to each of the committee's members, urging Nixon's immediate removal from office. For Frost's partner, Markel selected Nancy Brooks, another veteran copy editor, then running an amateur theater group in Texas. Brooks, too, had no affection for Nixon, particularly his conduct of the Vietnam War. She had participated in a number of antiwar demonstrations, and had been cracked over the head outside the 1968 Democratic Convention in Chicago. The experience helped make her a storehouse of anti-Nixon lore, and she could recite from memory long stretches of the most incriminating Watergate tapes.

In early July, Frost and Brooks flew to Los Angeles. On the drive to San Clemente, Markel gave them their instructions. Their task was to copy-edit and trim the manuscript by two-thirds. If all went well, they would be finished in four to six weeks; in any case, the work had to be finished by September. As Markel put it, "It must not, it cannot, it will not go longer than that."

With the arrival of Frost and Brooks, who were installed in the former National Security Council conference room, the pace on the memoirs quickened. The entire compound was working twelve hours a day, six and often seven days a week. It was numbing, tedious business, the sort on which Nixon thrived. Every morning he was in his office by seven, going over the previous day's revisions, jotting his comments and revisions in the margins. Then, he would begin dictation, not in the broken syntax that had characterized the White House tapes, but in fully finished sentences and paragraphs. After a light lunch, a brief nap and a short swim in the pool with Pat, he returned to his office for two more hours of dictation and revision before breaking for dinner.

Evenings were devoted to reading, usually the memoirs of historical figures. Nixon's appetite for history, especially European history, was enormous, and he devoured virtually the entire corpus of modern European political thought. His favorite works were the writings of

Charles de Gaulle, partly because de Gaulle was one of the few leaders who had befriended him when he was out of office during the middle sixties, but in larger measure because the general's thoughts on the "loneliness of leadership," and the special dispensations provided those who bore it, so closely paralleled his own. A dog-eared, heavily underlined copy of de Gaulle's memoirs rested on Nixon's bedstand, and Nixon read from it obsessively. He quoted the general frequently, likening de Gaulle's "wilderness years" to his own. He was particularly impressed, if only because the words had such relevance to his own situation, by what de Gaulle had said about his retirement at Colombey-les-Deux-Églises. "In the tumult of men and events," the general had written, "solitude was my temptation; now it is my friend. What other satisfaction can be sought once you have confronted history?"

The sole deviation from Nixon's after-dinner reading regimen came on Sunday night, when Nixon (who liked to claim he never watched television and often warned his staff about its mind-softening dangers) lost himself in the adventures of *Kojak*. Around ten, he went to bed. Frequently, however, he would find it hard to sleep, and would rise, go to his upstairs den and work some more.

It was not all toil. At the insistence of his doctor and his wife, Nixon could and did relax. His favorite pastime was taking long walks, usually alone, though sometimes, late at night, with his aging Irish setter King Timahoe on the leash. He also played golf with Brennan two afternoons a week on one or the other of the nearby private courses. According to those who accompanied him on such outings, Nixon played "presidential golf," determining the pairings (and in the process assuring he was teamed with the strongest player) and setting the stakes, since, despite all his counsel against it, Nixon loved to gamble. The presidential prerogatives continued on the course. When Nixon missed a putt, sometimes by as much as three feet, he would say, "Oh, that didn't count." Then he would try it again, and often as not a third time. By the rules of presidential golf, when a ball dropped, the stroke counted.

The remainder of Nixon's sporting enjoyment came vicariously, mainly through watching football on television. Nixon's passion for the game dated to his college days. It was one of two team sports he played at Whittier (the other was a short-lived try at basketball, which ended with the Whittier "Poetlings" losing every game, and Nixon taking an elbow in the mouth that broke his top front teeth in half), and, in his memoirs, he termed it his "favorite sport." "I loved the game," Nixon recorded. "The spirit, the teamwork, the friendship . . . one team's or one man's skill and discipline and brains . . . pitted against another's . . . the most exciting kind of combat imaginable."

As a participant, the 150-pound, 17-year-old freshman had been no better at it than he later was at golf, joking in his memoirs that the only reason he had made the team was that football required eleven players, and that he had been the eleventh and last man to try out. But he had won his letter, and he carried away from his coach, Wallace ("Chief") Newman, a ramrod-straight, copper-skinned American Indian, an enduring lesson.

"*[Chief] inspired in us the idea that if we worked hard enough and played hard enough, we could beat anybody. He had no tolerance for the view that how you played the game counts more than whether you win or lose. He always believed in playing cleanly, but he also believed there is a great difference between winning and losing. He used to say, 'Show me a good loser, and I'll show you a loser.' He also said, 'When you lose, get mad—but get mad at yourself, not at your opponent.' . . . He drilled into me a competitive spirit and determination to come back after you have been knocked down or after you lose.*" [Author's italics]

The staff welcomed Nixon's enthusiasm for the gridiron, if only because they were certain that Nixon would never phone them at home on a football Sunday. However, it did present a problem for Frost and Brooks, neither of whom had the slightest interest in the game, much less the symbolic nuance that Nixon divined in its machinations. The trouble was that every other Monday morning when they arrived for work at the conference room, there would be Nixon having his regular haircut and always eager to chat about the weekend's contests. That they were unable to respond in kind did not seem to bother him. Excitedly, he would recount, big play by big play, whatever game he had watched, analyzing each team's heroics and miscues even as they continued to revise and edit.

The "weeks" Markel had predicted stretched into months, and the months passed. Gradually, the manuscript was being honed to manageable size. Still, there were problems. One was how the book should begin. Frost favored a political opening—"My first memory was of running"—but Gannon, with whom he was waging the battle over cuts, deemed the line psychiatric and instead came up with "I was born in the house my father built."

More serious was Markel's discovery that Nixon, in discussing the abortive raid on the North Vietnamese POW camp at Son Tay, had revealed highly classified intelligence methods. After consultation with Gannon, the material was deleted. Then there was the Jewish question. Several times in the manuscript, Nixon had referred almost offhandedly to "the Jewish press." Markel, a Jew himself, did not take Nixon's comments seriously, but he worried over the public reaction. Gannon agreed; the press lost its religious affiliation.

Finally, there was Watergate.

Despite his "confession" during the Frost interviews, Nixon still shied from dealing with the scandal, and, when friends raised it, he continued to fall back on his White House line defense. He had been preoccupied with the burdens of the presidency. He hadn't realized what was going on. He had trusted his aides too much. "It was like a gnat buzzing in front of my eyes," Nixon told one visitor. "I kept saying, 'Bob, take care of it.' But the gnat kept getting bigger, and one day, the gnat swallowed me."

It was not a rendition that would wash. That much was apparent to everyone, including Gannon and Sawyer, who had responsibility for the Watergate material.

They were a seemingly unlikely pair to be setting down the life story of Richard Nixon. Gannon, for one, had begun in politics as an Adlai Stevenson Democrat, and it was not until after reading William F. Buckley's *Up From Liberalism*, as he jocularly put it to friends, that he was "safely on the road to proto-fascism." The irreverence was typical of Gannon, who, among his other talents, could do wickedly hilarious impersonations of the boss. To Nixon's occasional distress, Gannon was also an accomplished pianist, a fact that Mrs. Nixon, who continually teased her husband about the caliber of his own playing, never forgot. "Oh, Dick," she would say, covering her ears in mock horror when Nixon banged away during staff parties, "you ran the country. Let Frank play the piano."

In 1960, while a freshman at Georgetown, Gannon edited the "Youth for Nixon-Lodge" newsletter, a task that did not prevent him from winning a prize from the New York Democratic club for writing the best essay on why Americans should vote for the Democratic nominee. Eleven years later, following the completion of a Rhodes at Oxford, a spate of teaching at the London School of Economics, and three years editing the memoirs of Randolph Churchill, Gannon returned to Washington as a White House Fellow. His speechwriting skills attracted Ziegler's attention, and Gannon eventually moved to the press office, where he became an increasingly influential Ziegler loyalist. Until the resignation, however, Gannon had had little contact with Nixon. That changed following Nixon's hospitalization. With Nixon's return to San Clemente, and Ziegler's subsequent departure for New York, Gannon, who could discourse with equal facility on Spinoza and New Wave-rocker Patti Smith, became Nixon's most valued intellectual companion.

Mustachioed, approachable, good-humored, he was the perfect, if improbable, foil for Nixon, whose frowning visage Gannon elfishly hung midst a collection of Catholic icons collected during his years in Europe. Yet, though Gannon could poke fun at Nixon, there were few on the staff who were more uncompromising in their devotion to him. He was a Nixonite tried and true, and determined that the memoirs, whose creation he had structured and overseen, would reflect Nixon in the best possible light.

Diane Sawyer had come from a different background entirely. Born in Glasgow, Kentucky, the daughter of a prominent Republican judge, Sawyer, a tall, leggy, blue-eyed blonde, had, as a teenager, won the competition for "America's Junior Miss." A career in modeling was proffered. Instead, she attended Wellesley and majored in English. After a stint as a "weather girl" on Louisville television, Sawyer came to Washington—"like Mary Tyler Moore," she told friends, "looking for adventure." A call to one of her father's friends on the Republican National Committee landed her a job in the White House press office as an assistant to Ziegler. The enlistment was nonideological; she would have been just as happy, Sawyer said later, to work for George McGovern.

Her looks and brains appealed to Nixon, who referred to her as "that smart girl," and since the resignation, Nixon had confided in her nearly as much as he had in Gannon. Like Gannon, Sawyer had a starchy Calvinist streak, and a first-class mind to go with it. She read widely and seriously, and had a habit of quoting Shakespeare and George Eliot in the most casual conversations. Relentlessly intent on self-improvement, she looked on her employment with Nixon as a sort of super post-graduate course in the workings of a psyche not unlike King Lear's. And it was one chapter in the history of that psyche that was worrying her now.

Since the resignation, Sawyer had read literally everything ever written about Watergate, including the transcripts of all the television newscasts. She had also conducted lengthy interviews with many of the principal players, among them Haldeman and Ehrlichman, whom she had visited in prison. Finally she had prepared a detailed "flow-chart," tracing, day by day, the various Watergate events and personalities and establishing the links between them—"the key," Gannon called it, "to *Finnegans Wake*."

In late July 1977, Sawyer brought the document to Nixon and waited apprehensively as he pored over it in silence. A half hour slipped by. At last, Nixon looked up, took off his reading glasses and leaned back in his chair. "You know," he smiled, "this is the first time I've really understood everything that happened."

After that, Nixon started to dictate, not always happily—"For Chrissakes," he complained at one point, "I don't even *know* Donald Segretti"—and continually resentful at the inordinate space—250 pages in all—he was being forced to devote to an episode he'd just as soon forget. But, at the constant prodding of Sawyer, whom the staff had kiddingly begun calling "the Jill Wine Volner of San Clemente," dictate he did. Sometimes, several days would pass with Nixon refusing to see her at all.

Then, temper cooled, Nixon would call her in, compliment her on her dress or hairstyle, and, the previous battles unmentioned, the dictation would begin again.

Much of what he said was predictable. Among others, he blamed the press ("They had a vested interest in my impeachment. After all the months of leaks and accusations and innuendo, the media stood to lose if I were vindicated."), the CIA ("The CIA protects itself, even from Presidents."), the Eastern Establishment ("Establishment types like [former Attorney General Elliot] Richardson simply won't stand with us when the chips are down."), friends of the Kennedys ("It did not take long for my worst fears about the Special Prosecution Force to be realized. Of the eleven senior staff members Cox chose, seven had been associated with John, Bobby or Teddy Kennedy."), even Martha Mitchell ("Without Martha, I am sure that the Watergate thing would not have happened."). His own role in various acts of skullduggery Nixon minimized ("I do not believe I was told of the break-in at the time."), rationalized ("I believed that national security was involved. I still believe it today."), sloughed off to faulty memory ("Today, nine years later, I cannot reconstruct the particular events . . ."), compared to other Presidents ("My decision to approve the recommendations of the Huston Plan, like the decisions of President Roosevelt to incarcerate thousands of Japanese-Americans and of President Lincoln to suspend the constitutional guarantees of habeas corpus, will always be debated."), or, as in the case of the break-in of the office of Daniel Ellsberg's psychiatrist, halfheartedly defended ("I do not accept that it was as wrong and excessive as what Daniel Ellsberg did."). But occasionally there were flashes of concession. "When I was honest with myself . . . I had to admit that I had genuinely contemplated paying blackmail to Hunt. . . . Dean had made me aware of payments that he said constituted an obstruction of justice. . . . Instead of exerting Presidential leadership aimed at uncovering the cover-up, I embarked on an increasingly desperate search for ways to limit the damage to my friends."

Markel read the Watergate rough draft in late October and was reasonably pleased. Still, there were a number of holes in Nixon's account and the most troublesome was his explanation of the eighteen-and-a-half-minute tape gap. Nixon had written little about it, and what he had, Markel judged, was not credible. That alarmed the editor. Nixon could fudge on matters like his taxes and the activities of Donald Segretti, but the tape gap was essential. Somehow, some way, Nixon had to account for it.

Over lunch at the Surf and Sand, Markel revealed his concern to Gannon and Sawyer. The two of them seemed uncomfortable. They had already pressed Nixon on the subject, and he had insisted that he was innocent, and Sawyer, for one, believed him. Still dubious, Markel began to speculate about what actually might have happened. "Of course," he concluded, "Nixon might have erased the tape himself." He looked at Sawyer, trying to gauge her reaction. She gazed out the window. Finally, she said quietly, "That certainly is one of the possibilities."

By the end of the meal, Sawyer and Gannon had agreed that the tape-gap section would not do. Neither of them, however, was prepared to interrogate Nixon further. If Markel wanted a change, he would have to request it himself.

That afternoon, Markel met with Nixon and discussed the problem, framing his suggestion in the context of the book's marketability. "Sure, sure," Nixon mumbled, "no problem." But Nixon's second version was not much better than the first, and Markel, emboldened now, sent it back with a note, telling him to try again.

Nixon summoned Brooks. "Your boss doesn't seem to like my prose. Let's see if we can get it right."

Settling down into his easy chair, Nixon propped his left leg up on the ottoman, and, with Brooks perched over his shoulder, began to write a new version in longhand. The pen scrawled across the page. "Nobody can read my writing," Nixon said. "Can you make it out? I want to be sure there are no misunderstandings. Rose's role has to be clear. She can't be hurt in all of this."

"You're doing fine," Brooks coaxed. "Keep going."

The pen scratched again. "I am aware," Nixon wrote, "that my treatment of the gap will be looked upon as a touchstone for the candor and credibility of whatever else I write about Watergate. I also know that the only explanations that would be readily accepted are that I erased the tape myself, or that Rose Mary Woods deliberately did so, either on her own initiative or at my direct or indirect request. But I know that I did not do it. And I completely believe Rose when she says that she did not do it."

Nixon then enumerated a long list of other suspects, from Steve Bull and Alexander Butterfield to Secret Service agents and White House technicians. He found all of them innocent. He was not so sparing with "the court-appointed panel of experts" who had determined that there had been at least five, and possibly as many as nine, separate, deliberate erasures. Defense attorney Nixon picked apart their case. They had used improper testing methods; they had altered the machine; they had, in effect, tampered with the evidence. "The court paid these six experts $100,000 for their work," he concluded. "It was useless as a legal document, but it produced more than its money's worth of incriminating headlines."

The argument was less than convincing, but it satisfied Markel. He had pushed Nixon as far as he could.

A few days later, Nixon invited him to dinner. "Come at five-thirty," he ordered. "We'll drink for a half hour, eat for a half hour, and then get back to work."

Amused by the precision of Nixon's instructions, Markel arrived to find his author making cocktails for Gannon and Sawyer. A heaping bowl of the shah's caviar had been laid out, and Nixon was in excellent humor; the thirty-minute strictures about drinking and eating were soon forgotten.

Over Alaska king crab and two bottles of '55 Château Margaux, Nixon held forth on foreign affairs, pausing now and again to swap mildly dirty cracks about Barbara Walters with Manolo in Spanish. After dessert, Nixon opened a bottle of *mao-tai* and demonstrated the Chinese manner of toasting. The liquor relaxed him even more. Even so, there were lapses in the conversation, moments when Nixon, having come to a halt in his account of one foreign leader or another, didn't quite seem to know what to say. Markel broke one silence by asking what would happen if one day the nuclear button was actually pushed.

Nixon stirred his coffee. "You want to know what would happen, if the button were actually pushed?" He paused, allowing the solemnity of a former President addressing such a query to sink in. "Let me tell you what would happen if the button were actually pushed.

"If the Soviets pushed the button, we would lose all the major cities in North America." He named them: "New York, New York, Washington, D.C., Chicago, Illinois," on across the country. "Of course," Nixon went on, "it would mean the end of Western Europe, too." He then named all the European capitals.

"Now," Nixon said, "what would happen if *we* pushed the button? Let me tell you what would happen if we pushed the button."

Once again, the litany of the dead rolled forth, this time for the Soviet Union. "So," Nixon concluded, "what you would end up with is Australia, part of South America, and India." He stirred his coffee again, then leaned across the table in Markel's direction.

"And, frankly, who gives a good goddam about India?"

January 9 was Nixon's sixty-sixth birthday. He spent the day at home, receiving congratulatory calls from friends, including one from Hubert Humphrey, then dying of cancer in Minnesota.* Humphrey did

---

* Though they were political rivals and poles apart philosophically, Nixon and Humphrey developed a friendship during the 1950s that continued through Nixon's presidency and resignation. After narrowly defeating Humphrey in the 1968 presidential election, Nixon flew to visit him and later wrote him a note. "Better than most people," it said, "Pat and I know the heartache you and Muriel must be going through —to have come so close, then lost the biggest prize." After Humphrey lost the Democratic presidential nomination to George McGovern in 1972, Nixon wrote him another letter that he later quoted in his memoirs. "I know how deep your disappointment

his best to sound cheerful, but by the end of the fifteen-minute conversation his voice was slurring, and it was obvious he was in considerable pain. When Nixon hung up, he called Brennan into his office. "He's only got a few days," Nixon said. "I don't care what it takes, but I'm going to his funeral. Start working on it."

Humphrey died two days later. A memorial had been planned in Washington, where Humphrey's body was to lie in state in the Capitol Rotunda, before being returned to Minnesota for funeral and burial. After clearing his appearance with Humphrey's widow, who told him she would be "honored" to have him present, Nixon departed for the capital the morning of January 13.

When he arrived late Saturday, Dewey Clower, a former White House advance man, was waiting at the airport to drive him to the suburban Virginia estate of Mrs. Thurmond Clarke, the widow of a California judge, who had been an old Nixon friend. Ordinarily, former Presidents were offered the hospitality of a red-brick town house on Lafayette Square, but Carter, who had snubbed Nixon several times since becoming President, had pointedly refrained from extending an invitation.

The ride into the Virginia countryside passed quietly. Finally Clower asked, "How does it feel to be back?" Nixon stared out the window of the car at the monuments across the Potomac and said nothing.

He spent the next day watching the Super Bowl ("terrible and unprofessional," he judged it), walking through the snow and talking with Tricia and Eddie who had flown down from New York. A number of old friends tried to reach him; their calls went unanswered. Nixon was gloomy, uncertain whether he should have come. He was particularly apprehensive about a reception Howard Baker, the Senate minority leader, had arranged in his office for the next morning. Carter and Mondale would be there, Ford and Kissinger, even Nelson Rockefeller and Lady Bird Johnson, none of whom Nixon was anxious to see. As his worries grew, he instructed Brennan to call Baker to beg off. But Baker was insistent that Nixon come, and reluctantly Nixon finally agreed. The thought of what lay ahead depressed him. He did not sleep well.

The next morning, with Tricia on his arm, Nixon, looking grim, walked into Baker's office. Rockefeller and Kissinger were already there, bantering about New York politics. Across the room, Betty Ford nibbled on a doughnut; her husband's back was turned. Nixon sought out the security of the nearest available corner. He stood there a moment,

---

must be," Nixon said. "You can take comfort in the fact that through the years you have earned the respect of your opponents as well as your supporters for being a gallant warrior. . . . As friendly opponents in the political arena, I hope that we can both serve our parties in a way that will serve the nation."

head down and shoulders hunched. People began glancing in his direction. Someone noticed that his pants were too short. Nixon began shifting from foot to foot. He seemed nervous and morose.

Suddenly, Ford was standing next to him, sticking out his hand: "Good to see you."

Immediately, the mood lightened. Ford and Nixon compared golf games, vying as to whose was worse. Kissinger came over.

"You as mean as ever, Henry?" Nixon teased.

"Yes," Kissinger answered. "But I don't have as much opportunity as before."

They talked about their books; Nixon said his was moving slowly. Carter paid his respects, forced a smile for a photograph then retreated. Lady Bird Johnson asked after Julie and Pat. Nelson Rockefeller mused about the strange fates that had brought them all to the room.

The service afterward was teary and emotional, altogether fitting for the man being remembered. Seated among the front row of mourners, Nixon occasionally let his eyes wander across the room. They rested briefly on Barry Goldwater, a former friend who had come to detest him, swept on to Ford, then Muriel Humphrey, over the ranks of senators and congressmen, until settling on Coretta Scott King. A small bead of perspiration began to form above Nixon's upper lip.

He left quickly when it was over, pausing only to express his condolences to the widow before slipping out a side door. Outside, it was cold and windy. Inaugural weather. Richard Nixon bundled himself against it.

By the time Nixon returned to San Clemente, the manuscript of his memoirs was at the typesetters being set in galleys. However, there remained a number of problems. One was the book's title. The publishers wanted it to be simple and direct: *The Memoirs of Richard M. Nixon.* Nixon, though, had his own ideas. In late February, he called Gannon into his office, took out a yellow legal pad, and, with a broad sweep, wrote "RN." "That's how I want it," he instructed. "Period."

As usual, Nixon proved open to compromise: he had his "RN" in large script at the top of the dust jacket, and, at Markel's suggestion, the publishers had their "Memoirs" in the subhead.

Selecting the appropriate pictures to illustrate the book was more complicated. Nixon had thousands of photographs, and, with Julie's assistance, had culled out several dozen. Notably missing were any of what Nixon had taken to calling "the final days." "Please," Nixon beseeched, after Markel protested. "It's Pat. She can't bear to look at them." Markel did not press. Two days later, Nixon called him back. "You can have the final days," he said. "I'll handle Pat."

Meanwhile, Gannon and Khachigian were studding the manuscript proofs with scores of last-minute revisions. Finally, the galleys had to be reset entirely, an expensive, time-consuming process that brought Markel's patience to an end. Ready or not, he announced, the book was going to press.

Three months later, after an abortive attempt by some of Nixon's critics to mount a national boycott of the book, and a lavish publicity campaign by Grosset & Dunlap, the first 60,000 hardcover copies of *RN: The Memoirs of Richard Nixon* went on national sale at $19.95 a copy. As Nixon had predicted, the reviews were negative, but they did nothing to hurt sales. Within weeks, *RN* had sold out its first printing and had shot toward the top of *The New York Times* best-seller list, where it would remain for months.

With the conclusion of the memoirs, only Brennan and a handful of secretaries would remain with Nixon; the rest of the San Clemente staff either had scattered or soon would be. Rose Mary Woods had already departed, gone back to Washington and retirement on a federal pension. Khachigian had decided to remain in San Clemente, though not in Nixon's employ; with the demands of family, he needed a larger income and was setting up a public relations business. Frost and Brooks had moved on as well. The "six weeks of work" Markel had promised had stretched into nine months, and in that time both of them had changed. Frost, the opera lover, had become a devotee of *Charlie's Angels* and *Starsky and Hutch*; he had also gained forty pounds. Brooks had lost her passion for theater and was returning to publishing in New York. And both had altered their opinions about Richard Nixon. During the first few months at Casa Pacifica, they had joked about their conversations being bugged, how one day at dawn Brennan would take them out to the helipad to have them shot. Now their feelings were different. Politically, they were as opposed to him as ever, but personally, they had become sympathetic and regarded him now almost as a friend.

Sawyer and Gannon had been the last to go, staying on until late March, ensuring that all of the final revisions were complete. The last two and a half years had worn them out, and they were looking forward to the Hawaiian holiday they had planned, after which they would be returning to Washington, Gannon to join the staff of Pennsylvania Senator John Heinz, Sawyer to begin a television career with CBS.

Their last night at San Clemente they had worked in the office late, gathering the manuscript that Gannon was to fly to the typesetter in Chicago the next morning. By the time they were finished it was nearly dawn and both of them were bleary-eyed. As Gannon was stacking pages in a cardboard carton, the conference room door swung open, and Nixon came in, carrying three glasses and a bottle of brandy on a tray. "I guess this calls for a celebration," he smiled.

He opened the bottle and poured. This was very special brandy, he announced. He had sipped it only twice before: the first time, with Kissinger, to mark the conclusion of the secret negotiations for the China trip; the second, his last night in the White House. He raised his glass to offer a toast. Between long pauses he spoke softly and emotionally of all they had done for him, the good work they had accomplished together. "To the book," he said finally. "And to the future."

14
Stirrings

On the evening of June 28, 1978, 18,843 fans turned out at Anaheim Stadium to watch Gene Autry's California Angels play a baseball game against the division-leading Kansas City Royals. Among them was the man who had been the thirty-seventh President of the United States. He enjoyed himself enormously.

"I remember the last time I was here was the 1973 Opening Day," Nixon recounted to sportscaster Dick Enberg during the pregame warm-up, "and I hope it's a good omen. Because that day I remember Nolan Ryan pitched, the Angels won 3 to 2, and Frank Robinson, playing his first game for the Angels, as you may remember, hit one over the left-field wall. And it was against Kansas City with Busby pitching."

With the same facts-at-his-fingertips recall, Nixon analyzed the abilities of the Angels' center fielder Joe Rudi ("Let me say this about Rudi: Despite the fact that he isn't hitting well, he's done exceptionally well in the field and he has saved runs with his ability to throw; there are those who don't score who otherwise would."), recalled the night the Angels came to the White House ("It was one of the finest occasions we ever had in the White House, and there were many fine ones, and will be in the future as well . . . Y'know, it's really great to meet celebrities."), discussed his favorite player ("I've always thought Lou Gehrig was one of the greatest—I guess we all do—because he was great when he played, and he was great in the way he faced up to great adversity."), and, for no apparent reason other than it seemed to be on his mind, provided a presidential assessment of the Angels' radio advertising spots ("As far as the commercials go, I like the one about Continental Airlines, I like the one about Budweiser beer, although I don't much care for beer at a baseball game, but the one I think is the favorite is 'Baseball, hot dogs, apple pie'—which I do not eat—'and Chevrolet.' ").

A fan? Richard Nixon, whose secret ambition, he confessed, was to live life over as a sportswriter, was positively rabid. He munched hot dogs and (despite his denials) guzzled beer. He hooted at umpires and cheered for the home team. He kibbitzed, he swore, he exasperated, he exulted; he even sang along with "Take Me Out to the Ball Game" during the seventh-inning stretch. And if his heroes faltered, losing 4 to 0, he, perhaps better than anyone, knew that ballplayers, like politicians, lived to fight another day.

"Man for man, down the line-up, I believe the Angels can match them," Nixon advised a reporter, referring to an upcoming series with the hated Baltimore Orioles. "Now you can take all this advice and go to Las Vegas, put some money down and win yourself a trip to Hawaii, or Peking, if you want."*

Something more than baseballs was in the air. After a long and difficult dormancy, the Exile of San Clemente was beginning to stir.

Nixon's friends had been urging him to get out for more than a year, but until recently he had always resisted. Memories of Watergate and the pardon were still too fresh. He'd have reporters to contend with, demonstrators, reminders of a period he was trying hard to forget. Even so innocent an act as attending Humphrey's memorial had provoked a minor ruckus. He wasn't willing to chance it again.

Nonetheless, friends like Pat Hillings had persisted. At one point Hillings and other Nixon admirers were in his office, debating among themselves what Nixon should do. There ought to be a better system, they agreed, for utilizing the skills of former Presidents. Someone noted that John Quincy Adams had gone back to the House of Representatives. Yes, another voice said, that was true. Some former Presidents had found a role. Andrew Johnson had returned to the Senate, and William Howard Taft had been appointed to the Supreme Court. What about Truman? someone else had wondered. Well, he had had his library. And Ike? Spent his time writing books. Hillings mentioned that there was a provision in the Senate rules that said that former Presidents could address the Senate whenever they chose. No President ever had, but certainly it was an option. Nixon, who had said nothing during the discussion, finally broke in. "None of them," he said, quietly, "ever resigned."

---

* The following season, Nixon's predictions proved partially correct. With the addition of talented free agents like former Most Valuable Player Rod Carew and All-Star second baseman Bobby Grich, the once-anemic Angels won the American League's Western Division Championship, only to lose to Baltimore in the play-off series. Throughout, Nixon was their biggest fan. He bought two pairs of season tickets ("Since you've obtained Carew we know you are making every effort to bring a winner here, and we want to support you," he informed the management), listened to every away game on the radio and attended twenty home games, of which the Angels won fourteen. "Donny Baylor [an Angels outfielder] tells me he needs me here to get those hits," Nixon explained. "So if it takes me to be here, I'll drop whatever I'm doing to come out." Grateful, the Angels' players invited Nixon into the clubhouse for the championship-clinching hijinks, including the ritual pouring of a bottle of champagne over his head.

But, with his memoirs out of the way, Nixon's attitude began to change. He worried that he was becoming too comfortable, too much the golf-playing California seigneur. Already, he'd knocked ten strokes off his game. If he didn't watch it, he joked, he'd wind up like Jerry Ford. Life wasn't meant to be that easy; for Richard Nixon, it wasn't. He was "a man in the arena," he liked to say, a figure different from other men. Someone who grappled with the tough problems and made a difference. Who didn't, as he had for nearly four years, remain locked up and silent behind the walls.

In the end it was Jimmy Carter, as much as anyone, who released him. Nixon had never held out much hope for the Carter presidency, and Carter's performance in office had confirmed his worst fears. In eighteen months, as Nixon saw it, the President had done only two things right: begin the process of diplomatic normalization with the Chinese* and nudge the Israelis in the direction of restoring the Sinai to the Egyptians. The rest, Nixon thought, was a shambles. In Iran, his friend, the shah, had begun to totter. In Central America, the Marxist-leaning Sandinistas were on the verge of toppling Somoza. NATO was in disarray. The Russians had been emboldened. Almost willfully, Nixon thought, Carter had managed to antagonize virtually every important ally.

Thus far however, Nixon had said nothing publicly. In his own way he had near reverential regard for the Presidency, no matter who held it, and for months after Carter's inauguration, he refrained from criticizing him, even in private. But as Carter's miscues multiplied, Nixon grew restless. Carter, he told a friend, was not only digging himself into a political hole, he was abusing his office, squandering the presidency's prestige and credibility. He could forgive him for almost anything, even his continuing personal slights, but not that. The presidency had to be protected.

His irritation mounted as Gulley, whose love of gossip matched his own, brought him tales of what was occurring backstage at the White House. According to Gulley, Carter's younger son, Chip, had been smoking pot at Camp David, and Carter himself, for all his protestations to the contrary, was taking a drink or two. Nixon was amazed. "You mean to say he drinks?" he exclaimed, slapping his knee. "Goddam!"

Later, after Gulley had regaled him with more stories, Nixon was

---

* The establishment of full diplomatic relations between Washington and Peking, which came December 15, 1978, marked the only time Carter called Nixon in San Clemente. Nixon, Carter later recorded in his memoirs, "was most pleased and briefly discussed the worldwide impact of our accomplishment. I gave him full credit for his original move toward China and thanked him for the advice he had given me. I also offered to send [Michael] Oskenberg [Carter's White House specialist on China] to give him a personal briefing on the details of our agreement. He expressed his confidence in Mike, but cautioned me about the difficulty of maintaining secrecy and the danger of placing too much faith in subordinates!"

not as amused. "What is it about Carter?" he grumbled. "Is he intentionally misleading the American public? First, he gives everybody the idea he's against drinking, then it turns out he drinks. Then he says he doesn't remember anything about clearing the way for somebody to talk to the Justice Department on Robert Vesco's behalf—and when a memo turns up from Carter to the Attorney General doing just that, everybody's forgotten all about it. Let me tell you," Nixon went on, "when the Attorney General gets a memo from the President, he doesn't forget. He shits in his pants."

Nixon was even angrier at Carter's handling of the Defense Department. He faulted him on a number of counts, not least of which was a memo Carter had sent to Defense Secretary Harold Brown, saying that for economy reasons he wanted the number of generals and admirals reduced.

"Who gives a damn how many generals and admirals there are anyway?" Nixon griped. "When a war breaks out, right here in San Diego the Marines have got a training facility that you damn well know about. They can turn out killers every ninety days. But it's no use turning out killers if you haven't educated the generals and admirals to see the big picture and understand what has to be done."

The "big picture"—Carter's failure to grasp it, his own inability to influence it—was what was bothering him. A few weeks before the publication of his memoirs, Nixon asked a friend, "Who are the real strategic thinkers, the people who grasp what is really going on?" The friend replied, "Well, there's you."

"Of course," Nixon answered. "But who else?"

Apparently there was no one else. If the world was to be made right, it was up to him. He had the knowledge, he had the experience, he had, or so his friends kept telling him, the obligation to speak out. Nixon was still brooding over it, when in the mail from a tiny town in Kentucky came the opportunity to act.

Hyden, Kentucky, population 500, wasn't much of a place, no more than a coal-mining hamlet tucked deep in the blue-green vastitude of the Daniel Boone National Forest. The town consisted of a red-brick collection of small shops, two pool halls, a drive-in movie, one motel and the county courthouse. Housing tended to be of the aluminum variety, set up on cinder blocks. It was a tough, hardscrabble place, peopled by mountain folk who made their own liquor, fought their country's wars, and paid the outside world "no nevermind," as the local saying had it.

Except when there was a disaster at one of the mines, or the odd sociologist writing a thesis on Appalachian isolation, few strangers ever came to Hyden, and almost no Democrats. Hyden and Leslie County, its 11,623-resident political subdivision, were Republican territory—80 percent registered Republican by actual count—and had been ever since the Civil War, when slave-free Leslie decided to stick by Mr. Lincoln and the Union. During Watergate, it had stuck by another Republican President. Richard Nixon had ended the war and brought the boys back home, and, whatever the country beyond the hills thought of him, in Hyden, Kentucky, he was still a hero.

The more concrete reason for Hyden's loyalty was revenue sharing. The county had used its share of the Nixon-initiated program to build a $2.7 million recreation center, complete with swimming pool and gym. When the time came to dedicate it, the county executive and judge, a redoubtable young partisan named C. Allen Muncy, decided it was only fitting to have no less than a former President of the United States on hand. But Gerald Ford couldn't make it, so Muncy wrote to his predecessor, informing him that the county was about to name the center in his honor, and inviting him to drop on down. A week later, a letter came back from San Clemente. Nixon would be delighted to attend.

It was blisteringly hot the afternoon of July 1, 1978, but the thousand people who had gathered at London-Corbin Airport, seventy miles from Hyden, didn't seem to care. Most of them had been standing in the sun three hours, and the sweat ran down their faces in rivulets. Here and there someone adjusted an outsized 1972 Nixon campaign button on his lapel. A stand outside the airport gates had been selling them all morning, and business was brisk. Some clutched at newly purchased copies of RN, hoping for an autograph. The one intrusion on the jovial mood was a clean-cut young man toting a sign that read, NIXON: ADVOCATE OF HYPOCRISY. Several good old boys in attendance shot him a menacing look. "Get that hippie out of here," one of them said. "Or maybe we should beat hell out of him and burn his welfare check." The protester quickly departed.

The small, white executive jet bearing Richard Nixon appeared over the hills just after three. As the tanned and beaming former President disembarked, signs poked up above the crowd, proclaiming NIXON'S THE ONE FOR 1980, WE ARE GRATEFUL, and NOW MORE THAN EVER. Togged out in red satin finery and white plumage, a four-piece high-school band struck into a brassy version of "Hail to the Chief." Smiling and waving, Nixon came to the fence to press the flesh. "I came out of the hospital just to shake your hand," one woman shouted after him. "I had to thank you because my boy didn't go to war." Nixon mouthed a response— "Thank you, you are very kind"—then walked back to a waiting microphone.

He was grateful, he said, "to see so many people who, on a Saturday afternoon, could be listening to a baseball game—that's what I do, incidentally—or football, if it's on, maybe going fishing or something, come out to the airport and stand in the hot sun—that's just the nicest thing you can do. I really appreciate your coming out."

As the sun beat down, he reminisced about previous trips to Kentucky and the glories of the state, its racehorses and jockeys, its warm hospitality and political tradition. Taking note of the young men in the crowd, Nixon declared: "I'm just thankful today that after the longest, most difficult war in America's history that we were able to end it, bring our POW's home and end the draft, so that you young men will not have to fight abroad."

The crowd cheered, the band tooted and, with a last wave, Nixon climbed into his limousine for the long drive to Hyden and a reception in his honor at The Appalachia Motel, where dignitaries like Happy Chandler, the former governor and commissioner of baseball, were waiting.

Sunday dawned just as hot as Saturday had been, and even more humid. Overnight, a heavy thunderstorm had drenched the town with rain, and the air hung over the valley like a soggy blanket. In the still unair-conditioned precincts of the Richard M. Nixon Recreation Center, four thousand carefully selected Leslieites, all of them registered Republicans, fanned themselves and waited. Outside, sheriff's deputies guarded the bridge that was the only approach into town; all demonstrators had been ordered turned away.

Nixon arrived around noon, following a motorcade through town in a 1956 Cadillac convertible borrowed from an Ohio businessman for the occasion. Muncy was proud of the car—it was the same vehicle that had conveyed Lyndon Johnson through Dallas, November 22, 1963—and equally proud of the imported cannon that boomed out a twenty-one-gun salute. Nixon seemed no less enthusiastic even after waiting for an hour onstage while personages ranging from the members of the school board to the head of the Frontier Nursing Association were introduced. By the time it was his turn to speak, his blue suit was drenched in perspiration, and Nixon seemed dazed from the heat.

He recovered quickly. Gripping a lectern emblazoned with the legend THANKS FOR COURAGE UNDER FIRE, Nixon launched into a forty-two minute peroration on world events in down-home, hellfire-and-brimstone style. He denounced devils—Daniel Ellsberg, Jimmy Carter, reporters, Cubans and Communists—he extolled the faithful—Republicans, the military and the CIA—he showed that despite everything that had happened he had not changed.

Some, he said, "have given up on America . . . because they are so blinded by those things that are wrong they can't see so much that is right. They want us to turn inward and turn away from the leadership that has been imposed on us, whether we want it or not." But "let me tell you about another America," he thundered, ". . . of people who believe America should have the kind of leadership that will persist in the struggle with foreign aggression . . . who have not lost faith in America, who believe America should be strong, who believe that we should maintain our commitments throughout the world, and who believe that America should have the kind of leadership which will prevail.

"There's a spirit you'll find in great cities and small towns," Nixon told his listeners. "You'll find it in factories and mines. That is the real America, and I know that spirit is strong in the heartland of America, Leslie County, Kentucky."

The crowd roared, literally shaking the freshly painted rafters. It roared again when he told them that the occasion at which they were present was "the grandest thing that has ever happened in our lives or will ever happen again." And it roared a third time when he told them that it depended on them, their "faith and courage and will" whether "freedom survives and peace survives in the last quarter of this 20th Century." It roared and continued to roar, not so much at Nixon's words, which were predictable and banal, but at the sheer, improbable fact of his presence.

If he minded that the forty thousand admirers Muncy had been predicting failed to show up, or that the state's governor and U.S. senators found reasons not to attend, or that the band had played "The Washington Post March" as he walked offstage, Nixon never showed it. Even the remote rudeness of the setting seemed not to trouble him. Hyden, Kentucky, had provided him a platform, a place from which to utter again and in public phrases such as "I can tell you from my own experience," and "I've been to more than 90 countries." It had been four years less one month and five days since Richard Nixon had had that chance. Now, having tasted it, his exile would never be the same.*

The prospect of even a limited return by Nixon to public life did not sit well with everyone, especially when, within days of returning to California, Nixon began phoning political contacts, suggesting he might want

---

* One of the more bizarre by-products of Nixon's Hyden appearance was a supposed encounter with Dick Tuck, the political prankster who had dogged Nixon's footsteps since 1950. On assignment for *New York* magazine, Tuck arrived in Hyden the same day as Nixon, requested an interview through Jack Brennan and according to Tuck was granted it the next morning in Nixon's motel room, shortly before the motorcade through Hyden.

Tuck reported: "Nixon was sitting there at a table, in a suit and tie. I assumed he was working on his speech for the afternoon. He talked a little about Proposition 13. He mentioned the good old days of campaigning. He said Haldeman could have run a better campaign from prison at Lompoc than the one run against Proposition 13."

They talked on, Tuck recounted, chatting about Hyden and the countries— Nixon, according to Tuck, said there were thirty-five or forty of them—that had invited him to visit. At the end of their talk, Tuck claimed he told Nixon, "Of course, you understand, Mr. President, that my editors at *New York* magazine were hoping that I'd come back with a signed confession, but I'm not sure that I have much of a story." To which Nixon smiled and supposedly said, "Don't worry. You'll think of something." Tuck cracked back, "Yeah, and you'll deny you said it."

That, as it turned out, was precisely the case.

to play a role in the next congressional elections. Republican National Committee Chairman Bill Brock didn't think that was a good idea at all. Better, Brock told reporters, that Nixon remain at home; otherwise a "non-productive issue" might be injected into the campaign.

Nixon was undeterred. He had done his time, he told friends, he'd made his amends. If that wasn't enough for people like Brock, then the hell with them. He was tired of eating Watergate crow.

As if to prove it, he began laying plans for a world tour, a six-week journey that as he envisioned it would have him conferring with the leaders of a dozen nations in Asia, the Middle East and Europe. Unfortunately for Nixon, word of the trip leaked before final arrangements had been made. Doubly unfortunate, the leaders of a number of countries he planned to visit, including Australia, turned out to be less than enthralled. A spokesman for Australian Prime Minister Malcolm Fraser announced that Fraser would not be able to receive Nixon because of a "heavy program" of visiting foreign dignitaries. The spokesman added that Nixon would be granted a visa only if he provided assurances that his would be "a genuinely private visit." Unable or unwilling to get the message, Nixon said he was coming anyway—to address the Australian Cattlemen's Union.

The visa question was still pending when on August 29 Nixon's longtime friend, businessman and philanthropist Elmer Bobst died in New York. Nixon was invited to deliver the eulogy.

Despite the circumstances of the trip, Nixon was happy to be coming to New York, since it would give him the opportunity to sound out Kissinger and former Secretary of State William Rogers about his world tour. Also, Warner's, heartened by the unexpectedly strong sale of RN, wanted to sign him to do a new book. The work, which, with Ray Price's help, Nixon had already outlined, was to be a summation of his current thoughts on foreign affairs, unvarnished, hard-hitting and, or so Nixon promised his publisher, "politically controversial." If all went according to plan, it would be on the stands by the spring of 1980, just in time for the most important presidential primaries.

The news awaiting Nixon in New York was mixed. Kissinger and Rogers, it developed, were discouraging about going ahead with the trip. Press comment in several of the countries Nixon planned to visit had been negative, and the State Department, worried about the delicacy of the ongoing negotiations in the Middle East and with China, was doing nothing to smooth the way. The timing, Kissinger told him, was all wrong; make the journey, he advised, but later, after events had cooled down.

The cheering word was that Warner's was anxious to have him begin work on the new book as soon as possible. Nixon, who had been looking for a graceful exit from the world tour, had found one.

At a press conference called to announce his signing, Nixon shrugged off the "postponement" of his trip, and dwelt instead on his latest literary effort. It would, he promised, "address the whole American political system—the Presidency, Congress, the courts, the media"— and he hoped "it will be read by the opinion makers in this country." He seemed at ease during the session, and even found a few nice things to say about Carter, who was then at Camp David negotiating with Prime Minister Menachem Begin of Israel and President Anwar Sadat of Egypt. Carter, as Nixon put it, "is making every possible effort" to provide the U.S. with strong leadership.

Nixon had been back in California less than a month when two more speaking invitations arrived. The first was from the Joe Graham Post 119 of the Biloxi (Mississippi) American Legion, which wanted him to address them on Veterans' Day. The second was from an entirely different forum, the centuries-old Oxford Union, which requested his presence the next time he found himself in Great Britain. Nixon answered yes to both. He would go to Mississippi November 12 and to England three weeks later, stopping on the way in France to fulfill a longstanding invitation to appear on a television call-in show. While in England, his office announced, he would also address members of Parliament, meet with the Tory opposition and dine with the Conservative Philosophy Society.

Aboard the private jet Abplanalp lent him for the trip, Nixon arrived in Mississippi the afternoon of the eleventh. He had made two stops en route: the first in Dallas for a brief airport reception, then, the night before, in Shreveport, Louisiana, where Joe Waggonner, who had been one of his staunchest congressional allies, had hosted a barbecue for five hundred guests in his honor. Now, as he deplaned, a chorus of voices in the crowd shouted, "Keep coming out, Dick, keep coming out." Nixon flashed a grin. "Don't worry, I will. I guarantee you, this is not the last of my public appearances. This is just one of many I plan in the future." Nixon looked back toward the waiting reporters. "Officially, you can say that I'm out."

From the airport, Nixon drove on to the Broadwater Beach Hotel for a private reception organized by Frederick C. LaRue, a millionaire oil and land developer, who as deputy director of CREEP, had delivered hush money to the Watergate burglars. But on this afternoon it was all forgotten. Virtually every important Republican in the state had been gathered, and the mood was mellow. As Nixon worked his way through the room, smiling and shaking hands, nothing was mentioned of Watergate, LaRue's troubles, or his own. Here, in a congressional district that had given him 87 percent of the vote in 1972, his party was happy to have him back.

Meanwhile, at the Mississippi Coast Coliseum, the seats were filling up. The legion organizers had hoped for a full house and had nearly gotten it: nine thousand people, Middle-American, from the looks of them, and almost exclusively white. It was a Nixon crowd, and this was Nixon country. In 1969, after Hurricane Camille had devastated the area, he had made a personal inspection tour and made available millions in federal disaster relief, and the gesture hadn't been forgotten. Many in the audience sported Nixon tee shirts, showing a caricature of Nixon dressed as Superman looming over the U.S. Capitol, with the legend I SHALL RETURN.

Shortly after 7:00 P.M., Nixon walked out onstage to a three-minute standing ovation. After a series of increasingly fulsome introductions, climaxed by former Representative Bill Colmer, who declared him to be "the greatest President this section [of the country] ever had," Nixon began to speak.

He told his loyalists what they had come to hear: that the military had to be strengthened, the CIA and FBI bolstered, that, "whatever's necessary," freedom had to be defended. The crowd cheered and waved miniature American flags. It was a dangerous time, Nixon went on. At home, the economy was like "a very fat man who is about to have a heart attack." Abroad, the Soviets, "who are at least equal to us in strength and . . . moving faster than we are," were advancing on all fronts. But they could stop it. They were "the real spirit of America." They could "put government on a diet" and rally around allies like the shah. He knew Mississippians, Nixon said; he was confident that they would.

Leaning into the microphone, Nixon recalled the 1969 hurricane. "Some of the skeptics were saying it would take 25 years, if ever, for the area to come back. But as I shook hands and I spoke to you, I had a very different opinion. I knew that there was a spirit no hurricane could possibly break. I said to some, 'You can come back, and, when you do, I'll come back to see what you've done.'" Nixon paused and smiled broadly. "You've come back, and I've come back."

In Mississippi Nixon had come back, much to the perturbation of *The New York Times*. Referring to Nixon's remark about "officially being out," the newspaper commented, "Consider those simple words . . . The implication is that, beyond the formal pardon issued by President Ford, a merciful Judge Nixon has now ruled that a manly Defendant Nixon deserves to be 'out.' It is, Mr. Nixon should know, bad form to end his own sentence with, or without, a preposition."

The sniping had no more effect than did Brock's suggestion that he remain at home. After a brief Caribbean holiday with Abplanalp and Rebozo, and a quick return to California to pack his things, Nixon was on his way again, first to New York, and then by Concorde to Paris.

On arrival, Nixon phoned Tricia to learn the score of the USC–Notre Dame game, then, professing delight that Southern California had scored an upset, encamped at the Ritz. He remained there most of the next four days, fielding calls from old friends (among them, Valéry Giscard d'Estaing, who also sent an enormous bouquet of flowers), lunching on such nonnative delicacies as ham sandwiches and milk and now and again dispatching aides on shopping expeditions for the folks back home (cosmetics for Pat and his two daughters, a rag doll for his first grandchild, Jennie Eisenhower, born to Julie in August of 1978). At one point, Alexander Haig dropped by his suite for a ninety-minute chat. Nothing serious, the NATO commander told reporters waiting outside the hotel afterward, just "some reminiscing and exchanging views about the situation in Europe." When Nixon himself came down a few hours later on his way to visit the Charles de Gaulle Institute, he was grinning. Was he planning a political comeback? a reporter shouted at him. "I am," Nixon smiled, "the only American citizen above the age of thirty-five who cannot run for the presidency."

The next evening Nixon appeared on *Dossiers de l'Ecran*, French television's top-rated weekly show. He watched with evident satisfaction a 40-minute documentary the producers had prepared on his career, a bit of *cinema artifice* that, thoroughly French in its approach, barely mentioned Watergate and closed to the strains of Frank Sinatra singing "I Did It My Way." Then the phones were thrown open to questions. The 150 lines that had been set aside to handle the calls were instantly jammed. Ninety percent of the callers were friendly, and Nixon handled their questions—which ranged from the decline of the dollar to what sort of sect Quakerism was—with aplomb. With a laugh, he said no to a caller who wondered whether he had any interest in becoming secretary general of the United Nations, and, to another, confessed that "some of my best friends are members of the Eastern liberal establishment." Only once did he seem rattled, after an irate Frenchman phoned in to accuse him of lying during the cover-up investigation. "I, at times, because I did not know the facts, stated things that turned out not to be true," he faltered. Then he added, "The responsibility was mine. Mistakes were made —very grave mistakes. If one makes a mistake and does not correct it, he makes another mistake: that was my mistake in Watergate."

At a reception afterward at the Ritz, Nixon was ebullient. Spotting John Lindsay, who was covering his visit for *Newsweek*, Nixon greeted him heartily and proceeded to introduce him to the other guests as "my friend, the representative of the Washington Post Company." Later, he invited another former antagonist, John F. Kennedy's press secretary and ABC correspondent Pierre Salinger, to his suite for an hour-long post-prandial chat. Nixon spent most of the time enthusing about his television performance. He also quoted Talleyrand's famous dictum in relation to Watergate: "It was worse than a crime, it was a blunder." In reply, Salinger, who had been a Nixon opponent since the 1940s, mentioned that during the XYZ Affair, Talleyrand had attempted to extort $250,000 from the United States to resolve the two countries' difficulties. Nixon answered: "They should have paid him."

The reviews of his performance were ecstatic. "What a man!" *Figaro* headlined. "You may say he's an old crocodile," a senior French official was quoted as saying, "but his jaws are still like a steel trap." Even the American media were impressed. One newsmagazine correspondent, no admirer, wired to the home office, "It's too bad he can't run for President of France. He would win hands-down."

England, however, was an altogether different story, and from the moment Nixon's visit had been announced, it had been denounced by a grab bag of Leftist trade unions, expatriate American students, Labour MPs (one of whom rose on the floor of Parliament to demand that Nixon be barred from the country as "an undesirable alien") and most of Fleet Street, which likened him variously to Jack the Ripper, the Boston Strangler and Dracula.

But Nixon was not totally without allies. Jonathan Aitkin, a former Foreign Office official who had been a friend of Gannon's since their student days together at Oxford, and who had visited Nixon a number of times in San Clemente, had arranged for him to address a large delegation from Commons, and afterward to confer with such kindred spirits as Tory leader Margaret Thatcher and the Conservative Philosophy Society. In both sessions, Nixon was low-keyed, good-humored and, in his comments about the state of the world, typically well-informed. "An altogether likable chap," pronounced a lord who dined with him.

At Oxford, meanwhile, CREEP—"The Committee to Resist Efforts of the Ex-President"—was predicting a massive, noisy demonstration. Nixon seemed unperturbed. "In fact," he told reporters, with a grin, "I'll feel very much at home if there is one."

It was cold and drizzly outside the Oxford Union the night of Nixon's appearance, but the chill did nothing to dampen his enemies' enthusiasm. By the hundreds they had turned out, Americans most of them, with a salting of cadres from the Socialist Workers Party and the International Marxist Group. At first, the protest seemed rather festive. One student paraded back and forth draped in recording tapes; another hoisted a sign that read, NO ONE LOVES A HAS-BEEN.

But, as Nixon's black Daimler limousine came into view, an angry shout went up. Surging forward, the demonstrators broke through police lines, and, waving their fists, sprinted after it. Nixon's driver lurched down an alley—and ran smack into a dead end. Before the police could react, the car was surrounded. Cursing and spitting, the demonstrators pounded on the windows and banged on the hood. Inside the car, Nixon sat calmly, arms folded across his chest. It was Caracas, 1958, all over again. Perched on a nearby wall, an American reporter looked down and caught a glimpse of his face. The former President was smiling.

Finally, truncheons flailing, the Special Branch moved in and cleared a path. As Nixon emerged from the car, the demonstrators pressed in again, shouting obscenities. Spittle began to cover his overcoat. He paused briefly, shot his tormentors a strangely satisfied look, then, as police led the way, walked inside.

At the sight of him, the eight hundred Oxford men who had gathered in the union's wood-paneled confines, broke into whistling applause, drowning out the chanting from outside. Smiling broadly, Nixon walked to center stage and began to speak.

He went on for ten minutes, reviewing the international scene, proclaiming that world war was not inevitable and declaring himself to be "a realist, a pragmatist." Then he invited questions. By the standards of the White House press, his interrogators were exceedingly polite, and Nixon, as he had in Paris, handled them with adroitness and grace. He defended the invasion of Cambodia—"I wish I had done it sooner"—likening it to "what General Dwight D. Eisenhower did when he invaded France in 1944," and defended as well the wiretaps he had sanctioned as President. About the Soviets, he was divided: "I like the Russian people . . . I just don't like Communism." Outside, where Nixon's speech was being monitored over the BBC, the protestors erupted in catcalls and jeers. Nixon tried to begin a sentence, but the booing continued. He shrugged and tried again, but the noise remained deafening. Finally, as the din died down, Nixon gestured in the direction of the demonstrators: "Maybe they do." The union rocked with applause.

Only once was Nixon asked about Watergate, and then his interrogator was pelted with hisses. Putting up his hand for silence, Nixon said easily, "Some people say I didn't handle it properly—and they were right. I screwed it up, and I paid the price. Mea culpa. But let's get on to my achievements. You'll be here in the year 2000, and we'll see how I'm regarded then." Outside, the demonstrators chanted, "We want your head! You're dead, you're dead!"

Toward the end of the session, Nixon was asked about his future plans. "While I've retired from politics doesn't mean I've retired from life, or public life," he began. "Let me just make one thing clear. I'm not just going to fade away and live the good life in San Clemente, listening to the waves and playing golf . . . or sit and contemplate my navel by the Pacific." That would be the easy thing, Nixon went on, the option others might choose, but it was not for him. "If I did that, turned my mind off, I would be dead mentally in a year, and physically, too." He paused, as if contemplating the prospect. When he resumed, his voice had thickened with emotion. "So long as I have a breath in my body, I am going to talk about the great issues that affect the world. I am not going to keep my mouth shut. I am going to speak up for peace and for freedom."

In the hall where Disraeli and Gladstone, Hobbes, Burke and Locke had spoken, a wave of applause welled up to meet him. Richard Nixon closed his eyes and stood silent and still.

He came home to find the press, as usual, waiting for him. But there was a difference in their questions and a difference in the way Nixon answered them. What they wanted to know now was not what he had done in the past but what he might do in the future. And on that topic, at least, Nixon was at ease. When Nick Thimmesch, a syndicated columnist and former political aide, called him at his suite in the Waldorf Towers, Nixon immediately invited him up.

Thimmesch was startled at the change in him. The last time he had seen Nixon, a few months after the resignation, he had seemed exhausted and depressed, the fight drained out of him. Now, he was healthy, invigorated, fairly bursting with opinions about the world, about Carter, and—rare for Nixon—about himself.

"A man is not finished when he is defeated," Nixon said at one point. "He is finished when he quits. My philosophy is that no matter how many times you are knocked down, you get off that floor, even if you are bloody, battered, and beaten, and just keep slugging—providing you have something to live for. If you have something you believe in, something worth fighting for, the greatest test is not when you are standing, but when you are down on that floor. You've got to get up and start banging again."

Nixon threw a mock punch. "Get up," he said, "and start banging again."

15

Moving On

As Richard Nixon flew home to California triumphant, the man who had been his chief aide was preparing for a journey of a different sort. After eighteen months at Lompoc Federal Prison, Harry Robbins Haldeman, Jr., prisoner number 01489-163(B), was about to become a free man.

By the standards of most prisons, the conditions of his confinement had not been difficult. There were no iron bars or cramped cells on Lompoc's tree-shaded grounds; the guards, who wore blazers and double-knit slacks, carried no guns. Their charges, well-educated tax evaders for the most part, lived in brightly colored dormitories and passed their free time playing basketball in the well-equipped gym, attending meetings of the local chapter of the Jaycees or vying for a spot on the prison's fiercely competitive tennis team.

But prison was still prison, and the last year and a half had changed Haldeman. The Teutonic brush cut had been allowed to lengthen, and he had grown a flowing mustache. Thanks to regular games of tennis and a daily two-and-a-half-mile jog around the prison's track—relaxational pastimes he had seldom allowed himself while keeping Richard Nixon's door—he had also lost weight. But perhaps the most striking alteration was his eyes. Something there was about those eyes, so wide, so blue, so coldly relentless, that had always had the power to terrify. And so it was revealing to see what had happened to them. They were as ice-blue as ever, of course—not even prison had been able to change that—and they continued to hold whomever they fell upon in the same steady gaze, but the laserlike intensity had gone out of them. They seemed softer and more easygoing, like Bob Haldeman himself.

"Every President needs a son of a bitch, and I'm Nixon's. I'm his buffer and I'm his bastard. I get done what he wants done and I take the heat instead of him."

202

For the White House chief of staff it was a nearly perfect job description. He was a son of a bitch and he was a bastard and there were any number of his victims—from Pat Nixon to Rose Woods to cabinet secretaries to the members of his own straight-arrow, buttoned-down staff, "the Beaver Patrol"—who were willing to attest to it. Grim, unsmiling, humorless ("I cannot remember anything funny that happens," he conceded. "It's a failing of mine. Even when I was an advertising man and I needed jokes, I couldn't remember one."), intolerant of anything less than what he deemed to be perfection, "The Abominable No-Man" was the hard-ball player nonpareil. "He could be charming when time permitted," remembered Jeb Stuart Magruder, one of the young men who went to prison for doing his bidding, "but time did not often permit."

Left to his own devices, Nixon sometimes wasted time. He found it difficult to tell people no and even harder to look them in the eye. Haldeman never did. Saying no, doing the difficult, dirty jobs Nixon detested, was Haldeman's charter, and he stretched it to its limits. The symbiosis between the two of them was uncanny, almost eerie. "It was hard," John Ehrlichman said, "to tell where Richard Nixon left off and where H. R. Haldeman began."

Yet, Haldeman's relationship with Nixon was never as simple or as slavish as it was usually portrayed. Personally, they were not close (Nixon never once inquired after a single detail of Haldeman's private life and was ignorant even of the number of Haldeman's children) and there were times when Haldeman was appalled by Nixon's behavior. Only rarely, though, did he protest, and then it was, as the shorthand he favored put it, "TL 2"—too little and too late. "Well, that's his decision," he would shrug to Ehrlichman. Then, lest Ehrlichman think his devotion was slackening, he would add, "And he's right, you know."

His attitude had not changed, even after Nixon refused him a pardon and doomed him to jail. In the period between Nixon's resignation and the beginning of his prison term, he was in frequent touch with Nixon, and visited him several times at San Clemente. The pardon—neither the one that had been granted Nixon nor the one that had been denied Haldeman—was never discussed. Instead, Nixon talked about himself: his legal and financial worries, the book he was writing, the forces that had brought him down. During one such visit, November 13, 1976, Nixon made a startling admission. Haldeman later recalled the day in detail:

"I wait for the guard at the gate of Nixon's compound to admit me. The guard doesn't recognize my name. Finally, he obtains permission. I assure him I know the way. The gates open and I drive to the prefab office buildings whose construction I had once supervised.

"I found Nixon . . . in his office. . . . He was sitting beneath a

Vietnamese plaque on the same brown velvet easy chair that used to be in the Lincoln Sitting Room, books and papers all around, a yellow legal pad on his lap. . . .

"Once again, he wanted to probe my memory for details of various Watergate events for use in his book. The subject today was the Plumbers and the Ellsberg break-in.

"The more Nixon spoke, the more I realized something was strange. Nixon was worried that he had personally organized the Ellsberg break-in. This came as a surprise to me because I remembered all of those Oval Office conferences in 1973 when he appeared so stunned—and even hurt—by the Ellsberg break-in. At the time, he called it absurd, bizarre.

"Now he was implying that his hurt reaction had been a pose. Not only had he known about the 'bizarre' break-in all along, but he had ordered it, himself.

"He said, 'I was so damn mad at Ellsberg in those days. And Henry was jumping up and down. I've been thinking—maybe I did order that break-in.'

"I said that Dean had testified that Egil Krogh [the head of the Plumbers] had told Dean the orders for the break-in came right out of the Oval Office.

"That reminder bothered Nixon. He clasped and unclasped his hands beneath his chin. A bee entered the room and was executing a holding pattern over a pile of black notebooks on the floor. It buzzed off. All this time Nixon said nothing, thinking."

After Haldeman entered prison in June 1977, Nixon continued to reach out to him, writing him letters, calling him on the phone, doing everything possible, short of abject apology, to keep the relationship intact.

But by then it was already seriously flawed, undone by Nixon's performance during the Frost interviews. According to Haldeman, Nixon had misrepresented the facts, attributed to him things he had not done, while blaming him for things he had done himself. Haldeman could forgive that; what he could not abide was hearing Nixon describe himself as "not a good butcher." As he sat there in his living room, watching Nixon recount how he had told Ehrlichman the day of his firing that he had gone to bed the night before "hoping not to wake up," something inside Haldeman snapped. They were precisely the words Nixon had spoken to him at his own firing. At the time he had been moved by what he imagined was Nixon's emotional torment. Now it was apparent that the remark was merely a rhetorical device. Haldeman, who prided himself on his special loyalty, who boasted, "I'm not like John; I didn't move to the sticks, let my hair grow long, leave my wife or think of suicide," was no different than Ehrlichman. To Nixon, he was merely another troublesome aide.

Since then, Haldeman had settled accounts. The job he had taken on Ehrlichman's recommendation—maintenance man in the prison's sewage plant—had allowed him plenty of free time, and he had used it to write a book, and in its depiction of Richard Nixon, *The Ends of Power* was a scorcher.

Nixon, Haldeman claimed, had been to blame for nearly everything. It had been Nixon who authorized the break-in into Ellsberg's psychiatrist's office; Nixon who at Colson's instigation had turned loose the Watergate burglars; Nixon who had devised and directed the subsequent cover-up; Nixon who in all likelihood had personally erased the eighteen and a half minutes of incriminating tape; Nixon who had ignored his, Haldeman's, continuing caution and good advice; Nixon who had gone home to San Clemente and a government pension, leaving Haldeman and the others to take the rap.

He was not blameless, Haldeman admitted; like everyone involved in the Watergate he had done a lot of things wrong—"some criminal, some harmless, some accidental, some shrewdly calculated, some stupidly blundered, but each of them wrong." But Nixon, in whose name the acts had been committed, was wronger. He was "crude, rough . . . dirty, mean . . . coldly calculating, devious, craftily manipulative . . . the weirdest man ever to live in the White House." He didn't love Richard Nixon, Bob Haldeman said, as if it had to be stated; he never had loved him. He was his servant only, and with *The Ends of Power*, the master was getting his just deserts.

But as he prepared to leave Lompoc, Haldeman was troubled. He now regretted many of the things he had said in his book. Nixon wasn't as bad as he had portrayed him. In some respects he was actually quite decent, "like a multifaceted quartz crystal," he had written, "some facets bright and shining, others dark and mysterious." His publisher, however, had persuaded him to put all the emphasis on the latter.* The good things about Nixon—his brilliance, his mastery of foreign affairs, the

---

* After the furor that greeted the publication of *The Ends of Power*, Haldeman went to great lengths to downplay his criticism of Nixon, including writing a new, far gentler epilogue for the paperback edition. In conversation and in rare press interviews, Haldeman assigned much of the blame for the book's rough handling of Nixon to his cowriter, Joseph Di Mona, and his publisher, Times Books. As Haldeman put it to the author, "They kept emphasizing the sensational. The book was very, very substantially rewritten. They were visiting me in prison, and it was not the best time for me, so I let it ride."

Both Di Mona and Thomas Lipscomb, Haldeman's publisher, have substantially different recollections. According to Di Mona, Haldeman "wound up doing a lot of the writing himself. He got down to the straight story and put a lot of stuff in the book against Nixon." Adds Lipscomb: "He always had trouble saying things that were unfavorable to RN; he had a hard time throwing him to the wolves. [But] since he had been in advertising, he knew from a pragmatic, objective standpoint that the more he dumped on Nixon, the happier my sales manager would be."

various kindnesses he had shown him over the years, the genuine anguish he had felt about his aides going off to prison—had been ignored or omitted. Nixon hadn't called or written since the book's appearance, and the word from San Clemente was that he felt hurt and disappointed. Haldeman wondered whether Nixon could forgive and understand.

A crowd of reporters waited for him the morning he left Lompoc. Haldeman made a brief statement—"Christmas is generally considered to be a special time to rejoice, and I would like to join in that celebration by thanking all those who gave me support through their cards and letters these past 18 months. . . . Now I am leaving to rejoin my family." Then, taking his wife Jo by the arm, he walked to a waiting black Ford and slid into the driver's seat. Nervously, he tried to start the car. The engine refused to turn over. Finally, Jo switched on the ignition. Haldeman smiled faintly. The world beyond the walls would take some getting used to.

At home in San Clemente, preparing for Christmas, Nixon was pleased by Haldeman's release. Despite the book and the anger it had provoked in many of his friends, he had never given up on Haldeman, no more than he had given up on Kissinger or Haig after they had been quoted criticizing him as well.* Bob had been through a tough time, and, apart from the book, he hadn't whimpered. Many of the things he had written were true. Both of them had made mistakes. What mattered now was the future; he and Haldeman could help each other. Picking up the phone, Nixon dialed Haldeman's number in suburban Los Angeles. A moment later, Haldeman came on the line. "Merry Christmas," Nixon greeted him, "and welcome back."

The conversation moved easily. Nixon mentioned his recent travels and the new book he was writing. Haldeman said his own future was unsettled, though he had been giving some thought to going into business on his own. They discussed the possibilities, and Nixon offered to put

---

* Nixon's tolerance of former aides was not unlimited. John Ehrlichman came to be regarded with special loathing, and Nixon never spoke to him after leaving the White House.

"Ehrlichman doesn't understand politics," Nixon complained to one visitor. "He doesn't understand that sometimes it's necessary to do and say certain things about some people. Ike was the same way. If he heard that you called him a son of a bitch, he never forgave you. LBJ was different. If he heard that, then the next time he saw you, he'd say, 'You really got me that time, didn't you, you old bastard.'" Nixon shrugged. "John," he concluded, "takes things too personally."

Later, Nixon's attitude sufficiently mellowed to allow him to send Ehrlichman an autographed copy of *The Real War*. But even that gesture contained a barb. In inscribing the book, Nixon misspelled Ehrlichman's name, omitting the *h* before the *r*. When Ehrlichman told Haldeman of the incident, Haldeman laughed. "Well, at least you know it's not a forgery."

him in touch with some friends who could help. As the talk came to an end, Nixon invited him to drop by Casa Pacifica whenever he got the chance. A presidential election was coming up; he was anxious to hear Haldeman's views. Relieved by the cheeriness in Nixon's tone, Haldeman promised that he would.

The reconciliation with Haldeman further brightened Nixon's already buoyant spirits. His mood had been exceptionally good the last year, and it was showing itself in a variety of ways. He was gentler on his staff than he had been in the White House, inquiring after their troubles, praising them for work well done, going out of his way to extend small favors, like autographing a picture for an aunt back home. He relaxed more, took an occasional vacation, allowed himself unaccustomed luxuries such as lingering over a meal or savoring a fine wine. Even the mention of John Dean, which once would have driven him to fury, was now a cause for mirth. Recently, Abplanalp, Rebozo and Lasky had taken a trip to Europe aboard the liner *Queen Elizabeth II*, and to their horror discovered that Dean was aboard as well, delivering a series of lectures on Watergate. When they related the tale to Nixon, Lasky muttering how he "wanted to throw the son of a bitch over the side," he had laughed heartily.

He felt free to go out now, and apparently the public was glad to see him. According to a recent survey by the Gallup Poll, he was counted as one of the ten men Americans admired most. Two years earlier, the same survey had listed him as one of the most hated.

All in all there was good reason for him to feel better, and the invitation that arrived shortly into the New Year heartened him all the more. It was from Carter, who, having concluded the Camp David negotiations with Begin and Sadat, was in a magnanimous mood himself. Chinese strongman Teng Hsiao-ping was making a state visit, his first to the United States, and there was to be a dinner in his honor at the White House January 29. The President would be pleased if Nixon would attend.

Outside the White House the night of the Teng dinner, several dozen pickets paraded back and forth, protesting Nixon's attendance. NIXON, one of the demonstrators' signs read, YOU BELONG IN PRISON, NOT IN THE WHITE HOUSE.

Nixon, who had spent the day in the Virginia countryside, reading and preparing for a private meeting with Teng the next day, was smiling as he greeted Carter in the mansion's family quarters. Teng, whom he had never met, pumped his hand energetically. Then, flanked by the Mondales on one side, and Tip O'Neill and his wife on the other, Nixon descended the grand staircase to the room where he had said good-bye to his staff four and a half years before. When his name was announced, there was a hush followed by an audible "Oooooooooh." Mrs. O'Neill, who had threatened not to attend if she had to sit at Nixon's table, managed a grin.

At dinner, Nixon sat at a table immediately behind Carter's own. With him were Carter's national security adviser, Zbigniew Brzezinski; Richard Holbrooke, assistant secretary of state for East Asian and Pacific Affairs; Annie Glenn, the wife of the Senator/astronaut; Lorraine Percy, the wife of Senate foreign relations committee chairman Charles Percy; Leonard Woodcock, the U.S. ambassador to China and former United Auto Workers chief; their wives and Fang Yi, China's minister for science and technology. Nixon, who had left Pat at home, seemed completely at ease. As the Marine Corps string ensemble began to play, Nixon's ears perked up.

"You know they're playing the same songs, the songs they played when I was here."

Smiling, he turned to Sharon Woodcock, and asked how she had met her husband. "In a hospital," she answered. Nixon gasped, "Is there something wrong with Ambassador Woodcock?" Woodcock, who had been a prominent member of the enemies list, stared at him across the table. "No, Mr. President, I'm still fine."

As the wine flowed, Nixon chatted about U.S.–Chinese relations and offered several toasts to their continuing success. Taking out his pen, he passed it, along with his dinner menu, to the other guests, asking them to autograph it "as a souvenir for Pat." Brzezinski asked him who among the world leaders he admired most. "You won't catch me naming them," Nixon laughed, "because each one is different." Then, in spite of himself, Nixon began to list them: Charles de Gaulle, Mao, the shah of Iran. There was a pause. Fang Yi, who had been listening intently, leaned in close. "And Chiang Kai-shek."

The next morning Nixon conferred with Teng privately for two and a half hours, and afterward it was announced that Nixon would visit Peking again, possibly as early as March. Nixon himself was vague about the timing. At the moment he was more concerned about matters closer to home. With all the traveling he had been doing lately, he was wondering about home itself.

It had never been his intention to remain permanently in California. San Clemente was meant to be a temporary way station, a holding area to rest, recuperate, lay plans. One day, he always said, he would be moving on, back to the East, to New York and the center of the action. The question had always been when.

His friends, Abplanalp and Rebozo in particular, had been pressing him to make the move since 1975, but Nixon had always found a reason to resist. For all the inconvenience of living in a small town, sixty miles from Los Angeles and a continent away from power, he loved Casa

Pacifica, the beauty of its secluded grounds, the splendor of its cliff-top view of the Pacific. "Isn't this marvelous?" he asked Bryce Harlow one afternoon at sunset as the two of them stood atop the bluff overlooking the ocean. "This is a wonderful, wonderful place. I'll bet you never get this working in business." Harlow, a lobbyist for Procter & Gamble in between government assignments, replied with a laugh, "Mr. President, you sure never got it working in government."

Lately, however, Nixon had seemed less enchanted. Casa Pacifica's relatively modest proportions made it difficult to entertain overnight guests, while the spaciousness of its enormous grounds were increasingly hard to care for, particularly since his wife's stroke. He needed a house that was both smaller on the outside, and larger on the in. In late May of 1979, Nixon decided to move. In a short statement, Brennan announced that Casa Pacifica, which Nixon had once promised to bequeath as "a gift to the United States . . . [so] that future administrations and future generations can take advantage of the beautiful setting to help maintain a truly national perspective for the presidency," had been sold to three wealthy Orange County businessmen who planned to convert the property into a housing development.* The Nixons themselves were not going far—just a mile up the road to the exclusive community of Cypress Shores and a 4300-square-foot, five-bedroom, six-bathroom, ocean-front house purchased by Rebozo for $650,000 in 1975.

But almost as soon as the deal was completed, Nixon began having second thoughts. Moving to Cypress Shores would put him no closer to New York, and New York, "the fast track," as he called it, was where he wanted and needed to be.

His wife also was enthusiastic about returning East. Now nearly fully recovered from the effects of her stroke, she was anxious to get out more, and in San Clemente that was difficult, if only because there were so few places to go. Several times she'd driven to Los Angeles to visit friends like Helene Drown, but the trip was long and tiring, and, when she and Drown shopped along Rodeo Drive, people always seemed to be staring, and, or so she imagined, whispering about Watergate. At one point she had resorted to wearing a wig, but the disguise had been

* Legally, Nixon held title only to Casa Pacifica and 5.9 acres of the immediately surrounding grounds, having sold the remainder of the estate to Abplanalp and Rebozo in 1970. Abplanalp later bought out Rebozo's share. Asked once what he would do with the property, Abplanalp, who could be salty, replied, "I'm going to build a ten-story whorehouse on it."

The whorehouse, needless to say, was never erected, but even without it, Casa Pacifica had a controversial financial history. Nixon originally purchased the estate in 1969 for $1.5 million, of which $625,000 had been lent him by Abplanalp. Less than a year later he sold the bulk of the undeveloped land to Abplanalp and Rebozo for $1.2 million. How much Nixon sold the house itself for in 1979 was never disclosed, but estimates ran upward of $2 million. If true, in ten years Nixon would have realized a profit of approximately 700 percent.

quickly discovered, and during an outing to a local supermarket, someone had spat on her in a checkout line. That had brought the shopping
expeditions to an end. In New York, where people were more accustomed to celebrities, she could move about freely.

The last consideration was the grandchildren. Nixon had two of
them now—Jennie, and a boy, Christopher, born to Tricia in March
1979. Initially, Nixon had seemed apprehensive about dealing with in-
fants. When shortly before Jennie's birth Julie had asked how he wanted
the baby to address him, Nixon had thought for a long moment, then
replied, "Well, R.N. would be nice." But the formality had been put
aside (Jennie addressed him as "ba"), and in the presence of his grandchildren, Nixon was completely smitten. He bounced them on his knee,
goo-gooed and baby-talked to them, did all the things grandfathers are
supposed to do, including spoil them shamelessly. His one complaint was
that with both his daughters living in the East, he had so little time to see
them. If he were in New York, it would be different; everything would
be.

By mid-June the decision to move was final, but for the moment,
Nixon, who had begun to joke about San Clemente with his staff ("How
can you live out here? Everyone is seventy-two years old."), was keeping
his plans secret. There were a number of matters he had to attend to,
among them paying a visit to an old friend, lately fallen on hard times.
That was His Imperial Majesty, King of Kings, Light of the Aryans, Vice-
Regent of God, Reza Pahlavi, the Shah of Iran.

The shah's fall the previous January had been a blow to Nixon, who
had come to regard him as the closest of his international friends. He
was further agitated by the Carter administration's passivity, as the shah,
terminally ill with cancer, wandered from country to country, looking for
a place of refuge. Initially, however, Nixon had said nothing. He was still
being cautious in his pronouncements on foreign affairs, and was especially reluctant to criticize Carter, so long as there was a possibility
that the administration could be any help to the shah. His patience finally
unraveled, when, with no assistance from the United States and only after
the personal intervention of Kissinger, the shah came to his latest place of
refuge, the resort city of Cuernavaca, Mexico. Within days Nixon announced that "as a personal demonstration that the U.S. must stand by
its friends when they are in trouble," he would visit the shah, July 2. A
strike of the Mexican airline pushed the departure date back, but finally
on July 13, Nixon drove by car across the border to Tijuana, where he
boarded a flight for Cuernavaca.

On the plane, Nixon treated the reporters accompanying him to a
number of observations on foreign policy, his own and Carter's. He
mentioned the flood of illegal immigrants—"It is a tragedy to see these
people; you know there is a lot of hurt in them"—and what he himself

was doing about it—"At our house in San Clemente a lot of these wet-backs . . . they come down the railroad tracks and they think that they are past the Marine Corps base in Camp Pendleton. They come across the fence into our place—some of them weigh only 90 pounds—we give them a little something and they go off." Then, jaw tightening, Nixon turned to the shah's predicament. "If the United States does not stand by its own friends, we're going to end up with no friends. . . . Whether it's in Vietnam or it's Iran, you don't grease the skids for your friends."

It was nearly 2:00 A.M. by the time Nixon reached the shah's heavily guarded villa. The shah, who had insisted on staying up to greet him, seemed wan and weary, and after the briefest of pleasantries, he retired for the night.

The next day the two men ate an early lunch on the villa's terrace. Reza, the shah's eighteen-year-old son, prepared the salad and stayed on as Nixon and his father spent the next few hours talking about world events and comparing notes on their respective exiles. The shah was bitter about Carter. One day, he complained, Carter would be saying he was a great American friend of Iran, and the next day the White House would issue a statement saying it wasn't sure whether the shah could survive. All the signals he had gotten from Washington were conflicting. He didn't know whether to be tougher or relax. The shah threw up his hands. He seemed worn out and aged. Nixon tried to bolster him. "Don't fade away," he urged. "You've got to keep fighting. Make statements from time to time. Keep up your leadership role." He paused. "You could fade away, but that's the easy way out." He paused again, then smiled. "But I don't have to tell you that."

Afterward, the great iron gates of the estate were swung open and the crowd of waiting journalists were admitted to take pictures. Nixon and the shah stood side by side, grinning nervously, as a light drizzle fell over them. Neither man spoke.

In Washington, meanwhile, a minor if irritating furor had arisen over the sale of Nixon's estate. Contradicting Brennan's claims that the government had shown no interest in acquiring Casa Pacifica, a spokes-man for the General Services Administration said that the United States had been unaware of the sale until it had been completed. In Congress there were calls for Nixon to reimburse all or part of the $700,000 the government had spent improving the estate. At first Nixon reacted dis-dainfully, refusing even to comment. Then the House turned up the pressure by voting to withhold more than $60,000 from his forthcoming budget. At that point, Nixon notified the GSA that it had sixty days in which to remove the government's improvements and restore the property to its original condition, implying that if it did not, he would sue.

Finally, a panel was appointed to determine which improvements were removable and which were not, and, after several months of bickering, Nixon agreed to repay the government a total of $37,000.

Unlike 1975, when his lawyers were declaring him "almost broke," this time Nixon had no trouble coming up with the cash. The proceeds from the Frost interviews, the sale of his two Key Biscayne houses and royalties from his memoirs had made him a wealthy man; when his portion of the $2 million plus that was realized from the sale of Casa Pacifica was figured in, Nixon had an estimated net worth of well over $3 million, more than enough to buy a suitable residence in New York. Provided, that is, anyone would sell him one.

Thus far, the house hunting had been difficult. Purchase of Nixon's first choice, a nine-room, $750,000, Madison Avenue co-op, had been blocked when some of the building's residents complained of the attention and security problems Nixon's presence would bring. His next selection, a twelve-room, $925,000, Fifth Avenue condominium owned by millionaire builder and art collector Abraham Hirschfeld, fared no better. Again, the residents were worried, and, again, there were threats of lawsuits. Nixon backed out of the purchase, and in the process lost a $92,500 downpayment.

On his third try, Nixon found success, when for $750,000 he bought a three-story, brick and gray-stone town house on East Sixty-fifth Street, between Lexington and Third avenues. It was a fine house, with four bedrooms, seven bathrooms, an elevator and central air conditioning, and, on the second floor, a spacious, wood-paneled library that opened onto a terrace overlooking the garden. The neighborhood surrounding it was one of the city's most prestigious. Next door was David Rockefeller;* across the street, Theodore H. White; nearby, on Park, Ashraf Pahlavi, the twin sister of the shah; while directly behind the house, just over the garden wall, lived Kennedy historian and enemies list member Arthur Schlesinger.

With the housing situation settled, Nixon began making a series of extended good-byes. They had started in mid-July with a poolside reception for twenty astronauts and three hundred other guests to commemorate the tenth anniversary of man's landing on the moon; continued in August at a private dinner at Perino's hosted by Hillings and a cadre of old California friends, and concluded with two large gatherings over

---

* Shortly after the Nixons moved in, David Rockefeller, wanting to be neighborly, invited them over for a welcoming drink. All went well until it was time to leave and Rockefeller said, "Well, we'll have to visit you sometime." Nixon seemed taken aback. "Well, uh, I don't know," he fumbled. "Er, I'll have to consult with my staff and get back to you on that." Whether or not Nixon ever did consult with his staff, the return visitation never took place.

the Labor Day weekend, one to say thanks to everyone who had helped him in San Clemente, the other a birthday party for the man Nixon called "the last loyalist," his friend and attorney general, John Mitchell.

Life of late had not been kind to John Mitchell. About to turn sixty-six, the former chief law enforcement officer of the United States was an unemployed, indebted, painfully arthritic, convicted felon with nineteen months in prison behind him and apparently no brighter prospects ahead of him than being the tactfully described "companion" of Washington socialite Mary Gore Dean.

One thing, however, had not changed: John Mitchell was still loyal to Richard Nixon—even if Richard Nixon had not always been loyal to him.

Before Nixon's presidency, Mitchell, then the premier municipal bond salesman in the country, with an income upward of $300,000 per year, had been his law partner, the older, experienced hand who showed him the New York ropes. When Nixon ran for President, Mitchell was his campaign manager, the coolly adroit handler who allowed the "new Nixon" to emerge. Once Nixon became President, Mitchell was his attorney general, "our leader against crime and lawlessness," as Nixon called him, the architect of no-knock laws, stop and frisk and preventive detention, the "Watch what we say, not what we do" proponent of the Southern Strategy, no busing and a "restructured" Supreme Court.

They were close, John Mitchell and Richard Nixon, as close, it was said, as father and son. He was the only cabinet member with a direct line into Nixon's office, and they talked frequently, at least once a day, chewing over everything from school desegregation to White House staffing to the wisdom of invading Cambodia. During cabinet meetings, observers noticed that when Nixon was presenting his case on whatever issue happened to be at hand, he would glance out of the corner of his eye in Mitchell's direction. If Mitchell grunted and nodded, Nixon would press on; if he looked away or stopped puffing on his pipe, Nixon would backtrack or change the subject altogether.

But during Watergate, an operation personally approved and directed by Mitchell, everything changed. The White House tapes revealed Nixon not as Mitchell's friend, but as a figure eager to throw his mentor to the prosecutorial wolves. "John," he had instructed Ehrlichman, "go see Mitchell. . . . [Tell him] the boil has got to be pricked. . . . We have to prick the goddam boil and take the heat. . . . The President has said let the chips fall where they may. We are not gonna cover for anybody. . . . You're suggesting that he say, 'Look, I am responsible here. I had no knowledge, but I am responsible. And, uh, I, uh, I, and nobody else had, and, uh, that's it. I *myself*. That's it. And I want to plead, uh, this, this has got to stop—innocent people are being smeared in this thing.' "

When the tapes were played at his trial three years later, Mitchell showed no reaction. He stayed silent even after Nixon told Frost that "Watergate wouldn't have happened if John had been watching the store." And he continued to be silent throughout his imprisonment, passing his sentence quietly in the prison library, speaking only to offer his fellow convicts occasional words of legal advice and to the former President who called from San Clemente three times each week.

He was a complicated man, a gruff former PT boat commander, who, said his late ex-wife, the erratic Martha Beall, was actually "a cute, cuddly, adorable fellow." There seemed to be in him equal measures of both the cynic and romantic, and it was the latter, said his friends, that explained his tolerance for Richard Nixon. Mitchell himself put it more simply. "Richard Nixon," he told the Senate Watergate Committee, "is the greatest President our country ever had."

The Labor Day weekend birthday bash Nixon hosted for him was a fine affair, with all the merriment and gaiety of a White House ball. Two hundred and fifty guests turned out, including many of the old Nixon hands, all of them laughing and saying to each other, "What are you doing now?"

Togged out in a blue blazer and gray slacks, Nixon stood at the head of the receiving line in the inner courtyard, his wife at his left, Mitchell, looking better since surgery on his arthritic hip, on his right. As the guests filed by, Nixon had a josh and a memory for each of them. Later, while the party lingered over the catered Mexican buffet set out by the swimming pool, he conducted tours of the house, describing his late night meeting with Kissinger and Brezhnev. Finally, Nixon gathered the group near the pool to deliver a short speech. He talked affectionately of what everyone present had done for him, the history all of them had made together. Then, lifting a glass, Nixon offered a toast. "John Mitchell has friends," he said. He paused, and, in a rare moment, looked Mitchell directly in the eyes. "And he stands by them."

Nine days later, on September 12, Nixon, accompanied by Eddie Cox, Brennan and the Secret Service detail, departed on his third visit to China. His stay was a brief one, less than a week, and the airport welcome in Peking less grandiose than that which had greeted him on his previous arrivals. Nor, save for a side trip to a nearby oil refinery,* was

---

* China's vast oil reserves, and Nixon's own reservoir of Chinese contacts, was not lost on a number of major American oil producers. During the late seventies and early eighties, there was a steady procession to Peking of U.S. oilmen trying to negotiate drilling rights. The talks were long and complex, and, in an attempt to speed things along, several companies, including Atlantic Richfield, which eventually won limited drilling rights, approached Nixon to intercede on their behalf. Nixon, according to a close friend who served as an intermediary during the talks, was offered "fantastic

there any of the usual sight-seeing. The purpose of his visit, Nixon told reporters, was strictly business; he'd come to talk politics with Hua and Teng. The Chinese, nonetheless, did manage to squeeze in two banquets in his honor (where U.S. officials, including Ambassador Leonard Woodcock, were conspicuous for their absence), and while Nixon was in Peking, his picture dominated the local front pages. "There is an old Chinese proverb that applies very well in this situation," said a smiling Chinese spokesman as Nixon was being feted at the Great Hall of the People. "When drinking the water, don't forget those who dug the well." He looked in Nixon's direction. "We don't forget our friends."

While Nixon was banqueting in Peking, his wife was at home, overseeing the packing of the family belongings. Over the years the Nixons had accumulated a horde of possessions; the household furniture alone was enough to furnish not only the new home in New York, but David and Julie's big house in Pennsylvania, and still have six roomfuls left over. There were also scores of gifts from various foreign leaders, and two hundred bottles of rare wines and champagnes (among them, eight bottles from a twelve-bottle case given to Nixon by Leonid Brezhnev) that had been stocked in Nixon's cellar. When the value of everything was totaled for insurance purposes, it amounted to $325,000.

The packing continued through the fall and into the New Year. Finally, on February 9, 1980, the Nixons flew from Los Angeles to Miami, where they had scheduled a brief holiday with Rebozo, before going on to New York. In the cargo hold of the airplane, one notable item was missing. Before leaving San Clemente, Nixon had given away his golf clubs. For the life he was planning, he wouldn't have time to use them.

---

sums" in return for intervening with the Chinese. Nixon turned the offer down. "He didn't want to do anything to screw up his relationship with the Chinese," the friend explains. "Besides, by then, he didn't need the money."

16
The Fast Track

It quickly became an established routine.

At 6:00 A.M. sharp, the door of the town house at 142 East Sixty-fifth Street would swing open and out would step the former President of the United States. Turning left, he set off at a brisk pace along Sixty-fifth Street, heading toward First Avenue on the first leg of his daily two-mile walk. At First, he turned left again, uptown, in the direction of Seventy-second Street. Occasionally, a cruising cabdriver would notice him, give a double take, then flash the V-for-Victory sign. Smiling, Nixon would flash the sign back. At Seventy-second, one of his favorite thoroughfares, he turned west, merging with the waves of early-morning joggers bound for Central Park. Nixon studied them carefully. The men, he noticed, went about the routine absently, while the women seemed deep in concentration. At Third Avenue, he paused for coffee at Kasey's, then crossed the street to buy the morning papers (*Times*, *News* and *Wall Street Journal*) from Robert Vega, a blind Cuban refugee. His stride quickened the last seven blocks home. The city was coming awake; Richard Nixon didn't want to be noticed.

By 7:30, he was in his fifteen-room suite of offices at the downtown Federal Building. It was an unprepossessing place, tucked away in a corner of the thirteenth floor, down the corridor from the regional headquarters of the Immigration and Naturalization Service. Behind an unmarked door, a pair of Secret Service agents lounged in the reception area, watching a TV surveillance monitor and chatting with secretaries who answered the unlisted phone with the salutation, "President Nixon's office." On the walls around them hung a collection of enlarged photographs, most of Nixon, his family and foreign leaders, one each of Dwight Eisenhower, Gerald Ford and Abraham Lincoln.

Nixon's own office was standard government issue, a desk, a few chairs and a brace of upholstered couches, separated by a coffee table.

216

Save for a fine Oriental rug, some scattered presidential memorabilia (including a leather-bound copy of *The Poems of Mao Tse-Tung*) and a collection of beribboned flags (U.S., presidential and those of the five military services), the accouterments were typical of a middle-level bureaucrat.

Nearby, in a slightly smaller office, was Nixon's new chief of staff. Brennan had gone to work with John Mitchell as an international business consultant in Washington, and his role was now being filled by Nick Ruwe, the former advance man and scheduler who had been assistant chief of protocol in the White House. Each morning, while Ruwe sorted through the mail (104 pieces on average per day), screened calls and sifted through a growing number of speaking and social invitations, his boss worked the phones. Around eleven-thirty, having completed as many as forty calls, Nixon paused for lunch. He usually ate at his desk, nibbling on a tin of salmon and some Ry-Krisp crackers while perusing the morning mail. If, as was the case an average of twice a week, Nixon had a luncheon guest, they drove by limousine to one of the former President's two favorite restaurants: "21" or Le Circe. Nixon took whatever table was available, ordered quickly (usually the chef's special), sipped at some moderately priced wine and, after greeting any old friends who happened to be in the room, was out the door by two.

Afterward, he went back to his town house, took a brief nap and spent the remainder of the afternoon reading (a book a week, nearly always history, though occasionally a fictional thriller like Arnaud de Borchgrave and Robert Moss's *The Spike*, which Nixon judged to be "excellent, except that it has too much sex") or baby-sitting his grandchildren while his wife and daughters shopped. Three or four times a week he visited Tricia and her son Christopher at the Cox home "five shorts and three longs away," as Nixon put it, on East Seventieth. "He's very mechanical," Nixon boasted of his grandson. "He can put anything together. He has a cash register. It takes three motions to run it. *I* can't do it."

His free weekends were devoted to watching sports on television, or visiting Julie and David at their home in Berwyn, Pennsylvania. Week nights, he usually stayed at home. He had no interest in theater or opera, and loathed cocktail parties, which he termed "an invention of the devil."

"The talk, it's so loud, and people drink too much, and talk too much and think too little," Nixon explained to a visitor, a few months after moving to New York. He and Pat had "already had the best dinners, been to the best homes . . . seen them all," and he had no interest in trying to top that performance. Besides, if he went out he'd end up having to meet "The Beautiful People." They were Kissinger's type, "Harvard . . . double-domed." Personally, he didn't move much "in that art crowd." He knew who they were and what they thought of him, and, as he put it to his visitor, "I don't want to stir them up. They live in their dream world and let them rest in peace."

Instead, Nixon brought his diversion in, in the form of fortnightly issues soirees at his own dinner table. They were carefully planned, high-powered affairs, stag, intimate, off-the-record, the choice of participants seasoned to Nixon's topical taste. One evening he might invite half a dozen money people over for a round table on the economy, heavy-weights like Herb Stein and Alan Greenspan, Pete Peterson and Arthur Burns. Another night, if politics was in the news, there'd be some of the New Right types from *Commentary* and Bob Tyrrell's *American Spectator*. Still another, it might be an eclectic group, a visiting Shakespearean scholar from England, an old aide from the White House days, a friendly journalist or two.

Whatever the guest list, the format of every gathering was virtually identical. At 7:00 P.M., the guest would ring the bell, the door would open and there, in a dark blue business suit, hand outstretched in greeting, would be Nixon. Cocktails in the upstairs library would follow, Nixon mixing the drinks and joshing about being "the most expensive bartender in New York." (One of the best, too, his guests would note: his Tanqueray gin martinis were always exquisitely dry.) Over hors d'oeuvres served by two Chinese servants, there would be light conversation for half an hour. If a guest was new to the house, Nixon led him on a tour, describing the rooms and mementos. One of his favorites was a small third-century Buddha that reposed in the living room. Picking it up, Nixon would examine it and relate how it had been given to him by the recently assassinated president of Afghanistan. Matter-of-factly, he would add: "He was another of my old friends who lost his head."

Then, dinner: invariably Chinese and by all reports unfailingly superb. As his guests coped with their chopsticks, Nixon would discourse knowledgeably about the wine, linking its vintage with various political events. (Election years, he noted one night when a 1964 bottle was being served, were never good ones for wine, but, Nixon added, "1964 wasn't so bad, because we had a conservative candidate running.") Finally, the floor would be thrown open for discussion, Nixon taking the lead, Socratically probing with questions to which he already knew the answers. If the topic was West Germany, he would look meaningfully around the table and inquire, "How do you think Schmidt is doing?" After each guest had provided his assessment, Nixon would add his own, in the case of Schmidt, that he was a fine man, but, sad to say, "a prisoner of the crazies."

Afterward, the party adjourned to the living room, and over glasses of *mao-tai*—Nixon demonstrating the correct Chinese manner of toasting —Nixon would spin political war stories, usually humorous and frequently lewd.* One story he loved retelling was how, one night during the late fifties in the cloakroom of the Sulgrave Club in Washington, he prevented a drunken Joe McCarthy from strangling an equally inebriated Drew Pearson.

"There McCarthy was," Nixon recounted, holding out his hands, "with his mitts around Pearson's neck, throttling the life out of him. And there Pearson is"—Nixon affected a gagged look—"bent over and turning gray. Now, understand, I didn't agree with everything Joe said or did, but strangling Drew Pearson, that I could sympathize with."

Nixon laughed. "But in the Sulgrave Club—you know what sort of place the Sulgrave Club is, of course—well, I couldn't very well let McCarthy murder him right in front of me, could I?"

He laughed again. Then, having described and demonstrated how he had managed to pull McCarthy off, Nixon would roll his eyes. "And do you think it ever did me any good with that bastard, Pearson? Never!"

Around ten-thirty, the host would shoot a glance at the most upright of his guests and announce, "Well, I promised to get so and so to the local house of ill repute by eleven, so I guess we ought to call it a night."

His guests would head home, telling each other how much they had enjoyed the evening, how funny Nixon was, how human and how sharp. And wasn't it interesting, they would say, that Watergate had not been mentioned. Yes, they would agree, it was interesting.

Nixon was enjoying New York—"Any town that will support the Mets," he told a reporter, "is always for the underdog"—and the pleasure was evident in his schedule. He was showing up in the best restaurants, hopping back and forth to Europe, jetting off to Africa to preside at the opening of a new golf course, rooting for the Yankees from owner George Steinbrenner's box, supping at Henry Kissinger's with the cream of the media moguls,† passing off opinions on this matter and that,

---

* Nixon's vulgarity, which could be pronounced (describing his vice presidential opponent, the late Tennessee Senator Estes Kefauver, an allegedly accomplished swordsman, Nixon said, "Kefauver was going all over the state with a Bible in one hand and his cock in the other."), was the principal reason women were banned from the dinner table. One exception was Midge Decter, the neoconservative writer and wife of *Commentary* editor Norman Podhoretz. The night Decter was his guest, Nixon's conversation was squeaky-clean. At one point, though, Nixon did let slip a solitary "damn." Embarrassed, Nixon halted in midphrase, turned to Decter and apologized profusely.
† Among the media men present at the Kissinger dinner were Arthur (Punch) Sulzberger, publisher of *The New York Times;* Henry Grunwald, editor in chief of Time Inc.; Michael O'Neill, editor of the *New York Daily News;* Roone Arledge, president of ABC News and television commentator David Brinkley. Despite the fact that most of those present had favored his resignation or impeachment, Nixon seemed completely at ease as he held forth on a number of foreign policy issues. His only stumble was with David Brinkley, whom Nixon repeatedly addressed as "Chet."

doing everything possible, it seemed, to make up for lost time. LET's MAKE THIS PERFECTLY CLEAR, the *New York Daily News* headlined within months of his arrival. RICHARD NIXON IS MAKING SOMETHING OF A COME-BACK.

It was not a complete return to the life he had lived before the resignation, and in some respects the old awkwardness, especially with strangers, remained. One day, while lunching with a friend at "21," he was taken aback when a middle-aged woman with teased hair and a pink polyester pants suit approached his table, announced that she thought the world of him, and added that her husband had worked in his presidential campaign back home in Texas. Nixon seemed at a loss for words. Finally, he offered, "My, that's a wonderful outfit you're wearing; it's Oscar de la Renta, isn't it?" The woman blushed. Actually, she confessed, it was just something she had gotten off the rack. A few minutes later, another woman, young and stylish in an expensive silk dress, came up to say that she, too, was a great admirer. Again, Nixon was tongue-tied. "My," he said finally, "that's a wonderful outfit you're wearing. It's Oscar de la Renta, isn't it?"

Sometimes, Nixon seemed ill at ease, even in his own office. Once, just after having completed a two-hour interview with syndicated columnist Richard Reeves, Nixon, who had been discoursing with no difficulty on the state of the nation, began walking Reeves to the door. He grasped a handle and swung it open. "Well," he said, "here we are." Reeves smiled; Nixon had opened the door of his closet.

And yet for all Nixon's clumsiness his friends noticed a calm in him that too often had been missing in California. His conversation was not so jagged or so rambling; his comments about his enemies neither so frequent nor so barbed. The self-pitying remarks, fewer now, had a jocular tone. He seemed if not completely settled at least content, pleased by his new, more active role, and his mastery of it. The fact that there were people who liked him appeared to delight him, no matter what their age. And in response he was capable of gestures that made them like him all the more. Once, a former aide in San Clemente asked if she could bring in her eleven-year-old nephew and two of his school friends to shake his hand and get his autograph. No problem, the former President replied; he'd be happy to see the boys. When the youngsters showed up at his office, Nixon chatted with them for two hours about politics and world events, and ended the session by personally serving them cookies and milk.

A few weeks later, Nixon and Abplanalp sneaked off for a brief vacation, cruising the waters around Nantucket aboard Abplanalp's 115-foot-yacht *Star Mist*. As the boat pulled up to the wharf, a tourist named Stanley Rockwell was talking with his wife over a pay telephone. "President Nixon's here," Rockwell told her excitedly. "No, he's really here." Rockwell's wife evidently didn't believe him, and as Nixon walked by, Rockwell said, "Mr. President, would you talk to my wife?"

"What's her name?" Nixon asked.

Then, taking the receiver, Nixon cracked, "Betty, who's this woman your husband's with?"

17
Return of the Wizard

The move to New York was working out even better than Nixon had hoped. Within months, dinner and a chat with the former President had become a must for political movers and shakers, and Nixon's social calendar was chockablock with meetings from diplomats and visiting heads of state. If not yet "the peacemaker" he had talked of being ever since the resignation, he was undeniably a figure of increasing clout, and his prominence advanced another step with the publication in June of his latest book, a hard-line tome on foreign affairs entitled *The Real War*.

The reviews, like those for his memoirs, were largely negative, and, as with the memoirs, they did nothing to hurt sales; *The Real War* quickly soared to the best-seller lists. In Europe, where the press had recently quoted Nixon as saying "there's a 50-50 chance that the United States may not exist by the end of this century," the reception was even warmer. In France and England, the entire stock of copies sold out within a week, and the author was being hailed as a statesman in the Machiavellian mode. The only unkind notices came from the Soviets, whom Nixon had portrayed in *The Real War* as having "threatened, connived, conspired, subverted, bribed, intimidated, terrorized, lied, cheated, stolen, tortured, spied, blackmailed [and] murdered," all as a matter of "deliberate national policy." Wrote a commentator for *Pravda*: "One can hardly believe one's eyes when reading this mad raving, to put it mildly."

Whatever its literary merits, *The Real War* was vintage Nixon, the international high-stakes poker player who talked of "hardball-playing" and being "in the ring" with Brezhnev. "World leadership requires something that is in many ways alien to the American cast of mind," he declared. "It requires placing limits on idealism, compromising with reality, at times matching duplicity with duplicity and even brutality with brutality."

222

According to Nixon, the problem with the West was a collective failure of nerve, a reliance on the notion that "life is meant to be easy . . . coddled, pampered, truckled to." It was "America's cultural and intellectual elite" that was to blame, the "trendies"—those "guilt-ridden . . . gullible, smug . . . overglamorized dilettantes who posture in the latest idea, mount the fashionable protests, and are slobbered over by the news media"—who "castrated the CIA" and were "gun-shy about using force." They were responsible for debacles like Vietnam, which, wrote Nixon, was lost not on the battlefield, but "in the halls of Congress, in the boardrooms of corporations, in the executive suites of foundations, and in the editorial rooms of great newspapers and television networks"—not to mention "the salons of Georgetown," "the drawing rooms of the 'beautiful people' in New York" and "the classrooms of great universities."

"We are at war," Nixon warned. "We are engaged in a titanic struggle in which the fates of nations are being decided. . . . All but one of our cards [are] face up on the table. Our only covered card is the will, nerve and unpredictability of the President."

To many it sounded as if Nixon was describing himself, even plotting his own return, a prospect that, according to *Newsweek*, "most Americans would regard with as much enthusiasm as the onset of World War III." One thing was sure: Nixon wasn't talking about Jimmy Carter.

As his first term wound down, Nixon's nemesis was increasingly beset by troubles, especially in Iran, where a mob of "students" had stormed the U.S. embassy and taken hostage fifty-two Americans, after the shah had been admitted to the United States for medical treatment. Despite the shah's departure for Panama, and later, Egypt, all of Carter's efforts to free them had been unavailing.

Nixon was sympathetic, but not overly. His initial "gut reaction" to the taking of the embassy, he told a Los Angeles television interviewer, was " 'Why don't we go in there and knock these people over?' " Almost immediately, however, Nixon concluded that such an enterprise was "too dangerous perhaps," and in his subsequent public statements, expressed qualified support for Carter's attempts to resolve the crisis peacefully. But as the months dragged on, Nixon grew restless. In early April, while on a European book promotion tour, he told an interviewer that the time had come for the President to "stop giving warnings and take action." When Carter did a week later by ordering a commando raid that ended in disaster with the deaths of eight American servicemen, Nixon came to his defense, telling reporters in West Berlin that he "certainly support[ed] what President Carter did in making his decision to try to rescue the hostages." Two weeks later, during a live, hour-long interview with ABC's Barbara Walters, Nixon termed further military action "an empty cannon at this time" and proposed that the United States and its allies "provide a carrot" for negotiation by offering the Iranians massive economic assistance. He coupled his plan with a gibe at Carter.

"I regret to say this, particularly . . . with members of the hostage families perhaps listening tonight . . . but I think that one of the major errors that President Carter made at the outset was to indicate that his primary, and, in fact, it seemed to me, his only concern at the beginning, was the lives and safety of the hostages. They are important. But the moment you do that, you are inviting blackmail. They know you'll pay any price in order to save those lives and we could never do that."

In Egypt, meanwhile, the shah's health was growing steadily worse, and finally on July 27 he died quietly in his sleep. The State Department's reaction was brief, almost curt—"His death marks the end of an era in Iran, which all hope will be followed by peace and stability"—and the White House announced that no special representative would be going to the funeral.

Nixon was furious: with State, with the other governments who were declining to send delegations as well, but particularly with Carter, whose behavior during the shah's wandering exile he had yet to forgive. Within hours of the shah's death, Nixon expressed his displeasure in a manner calculated to provide Carter with maximum political embarrassment. Accompanied by his son-in-law, Edward Cox, and a detail of thirteen Secret Service men, he boarded an airliner bound for Cairo and the shah's funeral.

The long flight to the Egyptian capital did not improve his humor. In booking passage, Cox had neglected to discover that the TWA leg between Paris and Cairo did not include a first-class section, and Nixon had been forced to spend hours with his phlebitic leg cramped in tourist. When he debarked, Nixon was scowling. To a crowd of waiting reporters, he pronounced Carter's handling of the shah "one of the black pages of American foreign policy history." It was "shameful," said Nixon, that "the Administration didn't even have the grace to point out that he had been an ally and friend of the United States for 30 years." He paused to glare at the journalists. Then he added, "I think President Sadat's guts in providing a home for the Shah in his last days at a time when the U.S. turned its back on one of its friends is an inspiration to us all." With that, Nixon turned on his heel and disappeared into a waiting limousine.

The next morning, Nixon went to Abadeen Palace to pay his respects to the shah's widow and son. Sadat had already arrived and was consoling the weeping empress when Nixon entered. Nixon took hold of her hand and leaned close to murmur a few words of encouragement. He held it several minutes more, then gently guided her into an adjoining room to view the shah's closed casket. As the sound of muffled sobbing filled the room, Sadat read a verse from the first book of the Koran:

> "In the name of God, he who makes mercy, the merciful
> Praise be to God, the lord of the earth
> He who makes mercy, the merciful
> The king of the day of judgment."

Then, Nixon stepped forward and blinking back tears delivered a brief eulogy. The shah, he said, "was a real man."

A few minutes later, the shah's horse-drawn cortege began making its way through the twisting, dusty streets to el Rifai Mosque, the place of interment for Egypt's last two kings. At the head of the procession, a thousand officers from each section of the armed forces and the Presidential Guard marched in time to the dirge of the Iranian Imperial Anthem. Behind the caisson, other officers carried gold-braided, black velvet pillows bearing the shah's military decorations. A few yards farther back, Sadat, flanked by King Constantine, the former monarch of Greece, on his right, and Nixon on his left, led a small band of mourners. As the procession neared Cairo's Citadel, the hillside fortress built by Saladin after his victory over the Crusaders, a drum banged slowly. From windows and rooftops, tens of thousands of Egyptians looked down and keened an Arabic mourning. The accompanying phalanx of security men fingered their weapons. Mopping the sweat from his brow, Richard Nixon gazed up and around. The crowds were staring at him.

That night at a formal dinner in his honor, Nixon at first seemed subdued. Sitting next to Sadat, he reminisced about the shah, his role in guaranteeing the security of the Persian Gulf and their last meeting in Mexico. But as Nixon talked on, describing Carter's treatment of the shah, his tone grew more bitter, and he seemed surprised when Sadat, who had been listening without comment, did not agree with him. Realizing he was getting nowhere, Nixon finally changed the subject. Nodding in the direction of the empress and her son, he murmured, "They'll be all right. They're good people. They're strong."

Jimmy Carter was not strong, and, even before going to Cairo, Nixon had been working hard to ensure his political defeat. On his return home Nixon redoubled his efforts. His tactics were essentially those he had used on behalf of Gerald Ford: phone calls, an occasional chat with the candidate, and, as usual, a stream of handwritten memoranda.

That all this advice was being put to use by Ronald Reagan rather than John Connally continued to disappoint him. Nixon still divined, as he put it to one visitor, "Presidential greatness" in Connally and the previous fall had quietly attempted to boost his chances for the nomination. But Connally had turned out to be an inept campaigner, and despite the backing of a large segment of the business community and an expenditure of some $12 million, he had wound up with exactly one committed delegate.

By contrast, Reagan had shown himself to be not only an expert campaigner, but eager, if cautiously so, to have Nixon's advice. He had even come close to absolving Nixon of Watergate guilt, something not even Connally had done. During a 1978 appearance on the CBS interview program *Face the Nation*, Reagan, in answer to a question about whether there was a role for Nixon to play in public life, had replied, "It's going to depend on how history looks at this in the near future and what history has to say about this. Very frankly, I have always thought there's a possibility history will suddenly, or not suddenly but one day, really review the whole situation [Nixon's involvement in Watergate] and say, 'What was this all about?' "

Still, Nixon had his doubts. Reagan was certainly affable, and, if his conversations with him were any measure, far brighter than he was normally given credit. Nixon also admired his grit. The Californian, he told a reporter, was not one of "the boys," those who "want to be in high office to be somebody," but, like himself, "a man," someone who sought high office "to do something." It was what Reagan proposed to do, especially overseas, that worried him.

Since the beginning of the campaign, Reagan, a vociferous anti-Communist of long-standing, had been making a number of pronouncements about "coddling" the Soviets, charges that by implication attacked Nixon's cherished détente. To Nixon's greater alarm, Reagan was also advocating closer relations with Taiwan, seemingly at the expense of the overtures the former President had initiated with the Chinese. Nixon could live with Reagan's domestic agenda—the calls for prayers in the schools and bans on abortion, even the dismantling of the social programs proposed by his own administration—if only because domestic matters had never interested him. But foreign policy was something else entirely. Despite the rhetoric of *The Real War*, Nixon had never believed that relations between superpowers were as simplistic as Reagan portrayed them. Reagan, Nixon worried to a friend, was the mirror opposite of Barry Goldwater. Goldwater was a reasonable man who scared people by saying things in an unreasonable way; Reagan was an unreasonable man who soothed audiences by saying the same things in a reasonable way.

Nonetheless, Reagan was the party's nominee, and when the call came for help, Nixon answered it.

At first he worked through John Sears, who, as in 1976, was serving as Reagan's campaign manager. But Sears had been unable to coexist with the more dogmatic members of Reagan's inner circle, and, after the New Hampshire primary, Reagan fired him. In his place, Reagan installed William Casey, a controversial Wall Street financier who had been Nixon's chairman of the Securities and Exchange Commission. Readmitted to the Reagan fold at the same time were two aides whom Sears had banished: Michael Deaver, a California publicist whom Nixon knew socially, and Lyn Nofziger, a wisecracking right-winger who had worked as a political operative in the Nixon White House. Richard V. Allen, a former assistant to Kissinger, was already in place as Reagan's chief foreign policy adviser. In addition, there were a number of other former Nixon men in the middle and lower echelons of the Reagan camp.

All the same, Nixon was careful not to overstep. He seldom contacted Reagan directly, and any calls he placed to Reagan's aides was as much to inform himself as it was them. Usually, Nixon asked after political fine points: how, for instance, was Reagan doing south of Thirty-fourth Street in New York, or who was running the campaign in an obscure congressional district in downstate Illinois. One notable exception was the subject of the presidential debates. Nixon played a direct, important role in convincing Reagan to accept Carter's invitation to debate, and, once the debates were arranged, offered some tongue-in-cheek wisdom from his own, unhappy experience.

"I wish I could give you a lot of advice, based on my experience of winning political debates," he wrote Robert Gray, Reagan's deputy campaign manager. "But I don't have that experience. My only experience is at losing them, but I can tell you this: have the candidate ignore the fact that there are television cameras, and that there are 220 million Americans watching him, and that what he says is crucial to the outcome of the election. Just be sure he beats his opponent on points. I want to tell him how to lose."

Publicly, Nixon tried to downplay the assistance he was providing Reagan. When interviewers asked about his political involvements, Nixon smiled that he had none. "It's been six years since I left office and I have not participated in politics since that time," he insisted. "And the Republican Party seems to be very healthy and doing very well. And I don't intend to get in their way." Did that mean he thought his blessing was a political hindrance? "It isn't going to happen," Nixon answered, still smiling, if somewhat more thinly. "So you don't have to worry about that."

His caution did not prevent him from expressing his views. Carter, he told journalist Theodore H. White on the *Today* show, was "tough" and "ruthless," and, if Reagan was going to beat him, he had to "shape up" his staff. "You never knock your own man," Nixon said of Reagan's aides, who had been complaining about Reagan's frequent rhetorical gaffes. "The candidate makes a boo-boo, you go out and take the heat yourself. And that's what the Reagan staff had better learn. The Carter staff knows that, and they practice it, and I applaud them for it. It's good politics." Carter's weakness, Nixon went on, "is his record, his deeds. Reagan's weaknesses are his words, and when you run against words, I think the one that is weak on deeds is going to lose." All Reagan had to do, Nixon figured, was "win the West, which he will do; win Texas, which I think he will do; take four of the rimland states, Florida particularly, and Virginia, and maybe Tennessee and Kentucky. He's got to win Ohio, Illinois, Michigan, [and either] New York or Pennsylvania, the big five, and that, I think, is doable." Still, Nixon cautioned, Reagan should be wary. "They're a tough bunch, believe me, these Georgia boys. They may play softball down in Plains, but they play hardball in the country."

In another interview, with Barbara Walters on ABC, Nixon sized up the candidates themselves. Carter, he said, was "very intelligent," a "hard worker, very decent," an "excellent campaigner," and, Nixon added, "unfortunately, a tragedy for him, a tragedy for the country, a . . . an ineffective President."

The assessments continued:

Ronald Reagan: "Intelligent. Strong. Much younger than his years would indicate . . . and his appearance. Vigorous. And . . . in spite of the media to a certain extent, some of it painting him as being a lightweight and a kook, a very reasonable, responsible man."

George Bush: "Very attractive candidate. Admire the way that he's hung in there after the shellacking he took in New Hampshire and then in Illinois. He isn't going to make it, but nobody should try to push him out. And once Reagan is nominated, as he will be, at the convention, Bush will be a good Party man and support him."

John Anderson: "Very intelligent. Suffers a little from what some people attribute to Jimmy Carter of . . . the arrogance of moral superiority. That would be his weakness. He . . . he will start fast. He will end up with less votes, I think, than George Wallace got. And will probably hurt each candidate about the same, percentage-wise, but will probably hurt Carter more because he's going to hurt him in the big states, by taking away the liberals."

Edward Kennedy: "Suffers from comparison with both his brothers and particularly with Jack Kennedy. He's . . . I think his greatest weakness is . . . is not Chappaquiddick, although that of course has hurt him. But his greatest weakness, curiously enough, is where Jack Kennedy was strong—and I should know—television. And Teddy Kennedy, who is, some people tell me, better looking than Jack . . . was, who comes over quite well when he's speaking to a rally, comes through very hot and rasping on television. I think that is one of the things that makes him weaker."

Finally, Walters asked Nixon to rate himself. Said Nixon: "I retired from politics six years ago. But while I've retired from politics, I haven't retired from life. And perhaps I can best characterize myself by . . . recalling one of the most moving speeches I have ever heard . . . in the Congress of the United States, when Douglas MacArthur was fired by Harry Truman. And he closed the speech by saying, 'Old soldiers never die, they just fade away.' And I would paraphrase that, and this applies to me, that 'Old politicians usually die, but they never fade away.' "

As November approached, and Reagan's overwhelming lead in the polls began to diminish, Nixon grew worried. It was conceivable, he told friends, that the election might be very close; indeed, Carter might even pull a last-minute upset. "You can't underestimate this guy," Nixon told Podhoretz over dinner. Then, running his fingers in the air as if over the keys of a piano, Nixon added, "Reagan has got to learn how to play it."

Reagan's handlers, whom Nixon was calling nearly every day for the latest poll results, were not always appreciative of his counsel. At one point during the latter stages of the campaign, Nixon phoned a former aide working in the Reagan high command to report that, despite poll evidence to the contrary, Reagan was going to carry New York. When the aide put down the phone, he said to his co-workers, "The Boss says we're going to carry New York." At which point everyone in the room laughed with derision.

The story promptly got back to Nixon; it did not deter him. He was confident of his instincts (and in the case of his prediction about New York, with good reason: Reagan carried the state in November), so much so that he was becoming bolder in his public pronouncements.

When *The Times* claimed that Reagan lacked the foreign policy experience of John Anderson, who, since Reagan's nomination, was running as an independent, Nixon dispatched a letter to the editor. "In checking the record, I find that in fact Governor Reagan made four official trips abroad at the request of the White House between 1969 and 1973." Then, after listing the sixteen countries Reagan had visited, Nixon added, "I can attest to the fact that he was well-received and conducted his meetings with major foreign policy leaders with intelligence, skill and judgment."

Nixon's seeming endorsement, if only of Reagan's foreign policy skills, drew considerable attention, though not nearly as much as a comment he made to an interviewer a few months later. Revealing for the first time that he had had "very good talks" with Reagan, Nixon said, "I think he values my foreign policy judgment." That was hardly surprising, Nixon added; after all, "I've understood the foreign policy area from my early days in the House of Representatives in 1947. I've traveled more miles and known more leaders than anyone since World War II. I have a deep sense of where the world should go." While he wouldn't intrude on Reagan's campaign now—"all that Watergate crap would get dragged in"—who knew what would happen, once Reagan was in office? "Maybe," Nixon speculated, there would be a spot for him. "Something like a counselor or negotiator." In any case, "I will be available for assistance and advice."

Gerald Ford, a politician well-acquainted with the perils of Nixon's embrace, was aghast. "I think," he told reporters, "it would have been much more helpful if Mr. Nixon had stayed in the background during this campaign. It would have been much more beneficial to Ronald Reagan." A senior Reagan aide was quoted putting it more succinctly. Richard Nixon, said he, "was hallucinating."

Embarrassed by the remark, Reagan called Nixon to apologize. The aide, he said, had been talking out of school, and he had been disciplined and demoted. Nixon could be sure such gaffes wouldn't happen again. He, Reagan, was glad to have his advice, on foreign policy or any other issue, and he didn't mind saying so publicly.

Nixon thanked Reagan for his concern and advised him to relax. He shouldn't be too hard on the loose-lipped aide. Those sort of things happened in the heat of campaigns. He was an old pro; he could take it.

Despite the occasional heat, Nixon was enjoying this political season as he had few others. It wasn't like his own campaigns, when he'd been forced to weigh and modulate every word, or like that for Ford, when, with memories of Watergate and the pardon still fresh, he'd been kept from saying anything. Now he could speak his mind and, speaking it, swing from the heels. He liked that, and, to judge from the requests for speaking engagements, fund-raisers and interviews that kept coming in to Ruwe, there were others who liked it, too. A few congressmen, God bless them, had even asked for his endorsement. He'd turned them down, of course, knowing that, for all the favorable attention he was getting, it was still too early for that. But the mere fact that they had asked, that they had deemed his anointing valuable, was an unmistakable sign. The Exile was coming back.

New York, as usual, was deserted Labor Day, those with the means gone to the seashore or the mountains for a last taste of summer. Richard Nixon, however, was at home, and typically he was working. Earlier that morning, he had been rereading, yet again, the memoirs of de Gaulle, looking for appropriate quotes to use in his next book, a chatty reminiscence of various world leaders, he was entitling *Leaders*. Now, in his second-floor study, where the rice-papered walls were hung with pictures of Asian scenes, he was entertaining a former nun turned magazine journalist named Marjorie Michaels.

"Would you like some coffee?" Nixon asked. He smiled uncomfortably, as if slightly nervous being alone in the house with an attractive young woman. "The help's off. I'll make it."

Nixon disappeared into the kitchen. When he came back a few moments later, his anxiety had not eased. His halting attempts at small talk fell flat and he seemed awkward and tense. It was only after Michaels began asking him about foreign affairs that Nixon relaxed. As he discussed the state of the world, his face softened and the hesitation disappeared; the thoughts came in easy, well-rounded sentences. Then, twenty minutes into his monologue, just as he was proclaiming that "Castro couldn't even go to the bathroom unless the Soviet Union put the nickel in the toilet," the former President suddenly looked stricken.

"The coffee!" he exclaimed. "I forgot to put the water on!" He laughed. "Isn't that just like me?"

When Nixon resumed his recitation, he conducted Michaels on the by now well-worn *tour de horizon*, touching all the stops along the way. China was crucial: "If it ever joins again with the Soviet Union, we have lost World War III." But at the same time the United States mustn't forget the smaller, more out of the way countries of the world. Carter had, and the results spoke for themselves. "Angola, Ethiopia, Afghanistan, South Yemen, Mozambique, Laos, Cambodia, South Vietnam," Nixon ticked them off on the fingers of his hand, "have all been brought under Soviet control or under control of those who owe their survival to the Soviets" since he had left office. And what had the United States done in the meantime? Dropped the B-1 bomber, delayed the cruise missile, discontinued the Minuteman III production line, put the neutron bomb on hold. Nixon edged his chair closer to Michaels'. "American self-interest is not bad," he declared, voice rising. "Our masochistic intelligentsia, who run around saying that power in the hands of Americans is an evil thing, are full of crap." His chair moved closer still. Sometimes, he said, world leadership required "matching duplicity with duplicity, brutality with brutality."

More than an hour had slipped by. Mrs. Nixon and Julie would soon be returning from their shopping. It was time to go, but Michaels hesitated. She had promised not to ask him about Watergate, pledged she wouldn't inquire how he had survived it, but now, with Nixon sitting so close, so apparently at ease, the question seemed forgivable. Her words blurted out in a rush: how had he lasted? Why hadn't he cracked?

Nixon drew back as if slapped. Rising from his chair he began to pace. For a long moment he said nothing. When he looked back at Michaels, his face was flushed, and Michaels wondered whether he was going to cry. Then, in a hoarse whisper, Nixon said, "Life isn't meant to be easy. It's hard to take being on the top—or on the bottom. I guess I'm somewhat of a fatalist." He paused, trying to compose the right words. "You have to have a sense of history, I think, to survive some of these things. . . . Life is one crisis after another. Some people simply can't cope with it and they react in different ways. Some go to the bottle, some go to drugs, others simply collapse. Nervous breakdowns and the rest. . . . But once one determines that he or she has a mission in life, that it's not going to be accomplished without a great deal of pain, and that the rewards in the end may not outweigh the pain—if you recognize historically that that always happens, then when it comes, you survive it."

Nixon stopped his pacing. He looked down at Michaels. "In my life I've had ups and downs. Every campaign is a battle—each battle you get under the belt means you're ready for the next one. You realize that a lot of blood may flow—including a lot of your own—but that you just live to fight another day." He paused again. "Going through fire," he said softly, "makes what is soft iron into steel."

A few days after Michaels' interview appeared, she got a thank-you note from Nixon, expressing his appreciation for her fairness. Below, he had added a postscript. "Now," it read, "get ready to duck."

18
Into His Own

The Washington courtroom was crowded, the air fetid and still. As the gray-haired man in the blue suit took the witness stand, raised his right hand and swore to tell "the truth, the whole truth, and nothing but the truth," there was a stirring among the assembled spectators. Chief Federal District Judge William B. Bryant banged his gavel for order. If there were further demonstrations, he warned, he would clear the court. The prosecutor began his interrogation.

"How are you employed?"

"I'm retired," the witness answered quietly.

"Were you once the President of the United States?"

"Yes," the witness smiled, he had been.

It was November 1, 1980, and, after avoiding testifying in twenty other courtrooms over the last six years, Richard Nixon was on the witness stand in a criminal case. No subpoena had compelled his appearance; he had come by his own choosing, for this was an unusual—and, for Nixon, important—case.

The defendants were W. Mark Felt, former acting associate director of the FBI, and Edward S. Miller, former chief of the bureau's intelligence division. Their crime, according to the government, was conspiring to violate the civil rights of members of the radical Weather Underground suspected of planting bombs in public buildings. What they had done—and admitted doing in the name of national security—was to authorize break-ins of the suspects' homes during 1972 and 1973.

Nixon had neither known of nor authorized the break-ins in advance, which was not to say that he opposed them—far from it. In 1970, despite warnings that such activities were "clearly illegal . . . highly risky and could result in great embarrassment if exposed," he had approved a domestic intelligence-gathering program employing identical methods. Though, because of objections from Hoover, the so-called "Huston Plan" was never put into operation, Nixon continued to defend

233

its motives and tactics even after it had been listed as one of the impeachment counts against him. As he put it to Frost, during their televised
interviews, "When the President does it, that means that is not illegal."

His position had not been changed by the current case. Since
Miller's and Felt's indictments, in April 1978, Nixon had been following
the case closely and contributed money to their defense. He had also
offered to testify on their behalf, but, fearful of his impact on a largely
black jury, the FBI officials' attorneys had politely declined. The prosecution, however, had been delighted to have him, and it was as a nominal
witness for the government that Nixon had taken the stand.

As the questioning continued, however, it was apparent that Nixon
was not doing much to help the government's case. At times he seemed
more intent on lecturing than testifying. "As we sit here today," he
intoned, looking directly at the jury, "grave as our problems are, we can
be fortunate that at least the United States is at peace in the world. And
President Carter has made that point—and I think he has every right to
make the point—that during his period and term in office, we have not at
least in armed combat lost—I think what—and we have to understand
what the attitude was then.

"Now, even now, at a time of peace, we are concerned about international terrorism. We are concerned, for example, when we read what
happened in France recently, in Paris, the anti-Israeli activity resulting in
assassination, murder and bombing, what happened in Italy and so forth.
We are concerned it might happen here.

"But these concerns, I can assure you, as one who went through it,
were greatly magnified—I guess that's the proper word—by the fact that
in 1969, 1970, 1971 we were at war . . .

"I can assure you that— I think that, I hope that neither President
Carter or Governor Reagan, if he should be President, has to do what I
had to do, what Franklin Roosevelt had to do . . ."

Interrupting, Bryant instructed Nixon's interrogator to get on with
the next question. Oblivious, Nixon continued, "—what President
Truman had to do, that is, write letters to people whose sons have been
killed in war."

At length, Nixon finally came to his point: it didn't matter whether
he had specifically authorized the break-ins Miller and Felt were accused
of directing or not. The key was under what circumstances such tactics
were employed. If it was to gather information in "national security"
cases, then the bureau's authority was inherent and had been ever since
the time of Franklin Roosevelt. "It was the office, not the man," Nixon
said, tapping his finger on the witness stand for emphasis. Whoever the
President was, he had the power and he vested it in the FBI. That was
the way it had to be to contend with groups like the Weathermen and the
Black Panthers. They had pledged to "overthrow the government" and

there was "hard evidence" linking them to "foreign powers." Whatever had to be done to stop them—listen in or break in, warrant or no warrant —if it worked, it was fine with him.

From the back of the courtroom, several voices shouted, "War criminal! Liar! Thief!" Nixon's Secret Service detail rushed toward him as the protesters were hustled away. Unperturbed, Nixon turned toward the judge and lifted his eyebrows. A few minutes later he was excused from the stand.*

The appearance at the Felt and Miller trial was one more in a growing number of indications of the change that had come over Nixon during nearly ten months he had been in New York. Emotionally and physically, he was feeling better than at any time since the resignation, and there was ample reason for his mood. Time had healed a lot of wounds; it had also dulled a lot of memories. No one booed or picketed him when he appeared in public now, as they had in California. If anyone stopped him at all, it was usually to ask for his autograph (sixty requests during one outing to Yankee Stadium), or to tell him, as Jerry Turick, a Queens teenager who was ten years old at the time of the Watergate break-in, did one morning on a Manhattan street corner, that "You should be President again; you were a good President." Even the press appeared to have altered its feelings. David Broder, who had once sworn never to write about him again, was now reporting on his political comings and goings. *Time*'s Hugh Sidey, who after the pardon had written that "[Nixon] has chartered himself a course straight into the sloughs of history," was now eagerly supping at his table and proclaiming him "a strategic genius." The gentlemen of *The Times* had been pleased to have him to lunch, and Nixon in turn had been gentleman enough not to comment on the caricatures of himself that lined the corridor walls.

There was nothing surprising in all of this. Richard Nixon was once again news, and news was meant to be covered. And, almost as if he were running for office, cover him the press did. If he was spotted walking down a street, or stopping into F. A. O. Schwarz to buy a stuffed animal for his granddaughter, or declaring, during a stopover in the Magic Kingdom, that "You haven't seen the world until you've seen Disney World," it was in the paper the next morning. Meanwhile, the requests for interviews were coming in at a rate of twenty a week. One in particular caught Nixon's attention.

It came from Bob Greene, a young syndicated columnist for the

---

* Nixon's testimony failed to convince the jury. Both Felt and Miller were found guilty and sentenced to pay fines of $5000 and $3500 respectively. Within the year, while the case was on appeal, Reagan granted them both presidential pardons. Pleased by the outcome, Nixon sent each of the former FBI men a bottle of celebratory champagne. "Justice," read the accompanying note, "ultimately prevails."

Chicago Sun-Times. In his letter, Greene said that he wanted to talk to Nixon about Nixon for roughly the same reason, as he put it, as "an eight-year-old wants to go to Disney World." Nixon wrote back, saying he was flattered and thinking it over. Greene wrote again, expressing his sentiments more formally. Finally, Nixon agreed.

Greene had hoped to have a half hour with him alone; instead, Nixon kept him in his office for nearly two hours. He discussed anything and everything, from the cost of milk shakes at Rumpelmayer's ($3.40, a figure that left Nixon agog) to his impressions of New York ("You can come here and get lost if you want . . . You can find more privacy here than you can in the deserts of California.") to the prospect of having "so kind and gentle" a soul as Walter Cronkite in the White House ("God help the country"). He talked about Lyndon Johnson ("The trouble with Lyndon is that he had three television sets in the Oval Office, and he would look at them."); he talked about giving up golf ("I've broken 80, and that is as far as I'll ever go anyway."); he talked about Tom Dewey ("Somewhat of a mechanical man and I have heard that he sometimes would practice his speech before a mirror."). But mostly Nixon talked about himself.

He was wary at first. "I have never been one to do a very effective job of psychoanalysis," Nixon admitted. "I don't try to psychoanalyze others, and so I'm not good at psychoanalyzing myself. I think, frankly, that those who engage in that activity . . . much of it is superficial and contrived, and most of it is useless." But, if Greene insisted, he would try.

"I know, looking back on my own political career," Nixon began, "of a number of very able people, very intelligent, a lot of mystique, a lot of charisma, etc., who stopped at Congress. Who never went to the Senate. Never went on to become governor. Who stopped at that level. Because they didn't want to risk a safe seat. The moment people begin to think of how they can be secure, they are never going to make it clear to the top. You've got to take great risks and lose if necessary. And maybe lose twice or three times and keep coming back. That's the secret."

Nixon paused. "My public life has not been easy—for reasons we don't need to get into. And it's very tough on the family, etc. I would say, however, that if I had known what was going to happen, that I would [not] have refused or declined to get into it."

Maybe that made him different than ordinary men, Nixon conceded. But, then, he was different: distant, reserved, not an easy figure to know. Others could "reveal their inner psyche, whether they were breast-fed or bottle fed," but not he.

"You've got to retain a curtain," Nixon explained. "A President must not be one of the crowd. He must maintain a certain figure. People want him to be that way. They don't want him to be down there saying, 'Look, I'm the same as you.'

"Truman was considered to be a very down-to-earth fellow," Nixon went on, "but, believe me, he didn't want any familiarity with him, except from his close friends.

"Eisenhower with that famous grin and so forth—but he didn't want to be touched. That's right. What I mean by that is that, of course, he would shake hands and all the rest. But he didn't want people to come up and throw their arms around him and say, 'Hi, Ike.'

"Kennedy was the same way. Despite the fact that he had the reputation of being, you know, very glamorous and the rest, he had a certain privacy about him, a certain sense of dignity.

"Now Johnson was . . . Johnson was one who believed in touching the flesh, and the rest.

"I, of course, was more like Kennedy."

He was a formal man, Nixon said, and his friends, even close ones like Rebozo, treated him in formal fashion. It was always "Mr. President," never "Richard" or "Dick."

"You mean," said Greene, "that when you and Rebozo were out on a fishing boat, in casual clothes, and he wanted to offer you a beer, he actually said, 'Would you like a beer, Mr. President?'"

"Yep," Nixon answered. "That's right. That's the way."

He shrugged. "It's just the way I am. I work in a coat and tie, and believe me, believe it or not, it's hard for people to realize, but when I'm writing a speech or working on a book or dictating or so forth, I'm always wearing a coat and tie. Even when I'm alone. If I were to take it off, probably I would catch cold. That's the way it is.

"I never wanted to be buddy-buddy," Nixon continued. "Even with close friends. I don't believe in letting your hair down, confiding this and that and the other thing—saying, 'Gee, I couldn't sleep, because I was worrying about this or that or so forth and so on. I believe you should keep your troubles to yourself. That's just the way I am. Some people are different. Some people think it's good therapy to sit with a close friend and, you know, just spill your guts. Not me. No way.

"I don't allow my feelings to get hurt," Nixon concluded. "If I had feelings I probably wouldn't have even survived."

Many of his friends hadn't. "You read the obituary page and you read of people 69, 70, 65, 73, 74, 75—all of my generation. They cut off. Heart attacks, cancer, what have you. But I never get morbid about it. I never worry about it. I just figure that every day may be the last."

Greene was touched; he wanted to say something sympathetic. Seeming to sense it, Nixon suddenly cut off the interview. As the reporter got up to go, Nixon asked if he had watched the World Series game the night before. "George Brett's hemorrhoids," Nixon muttered. "They put that in the paper. Damn. They shouldn't do that. Who the hell wants to read about hemorrhoids?"

Greene began to say good-bye, but Nixon was still thinking of hemorrhoids. "Carter had them. Remember? He had them early on. It's probably the tension that causes them."

As Greene got to the door, Nixon called after him. "How old are you?"

"Thirty-three."

"Thirty-three," Nixon nodded. "Let's see, I was thirty-three years old when I was first elected to the House. It's a good time to be alive."

A few weeks later, on November 6, two days after Reagan's thrashing of Carter in the presidential election, Nixon turned up at an unexpected locale: the Russian embassy in Washington. It was the sixty-third anniversary of the Bolshevik Revolution, and the Soviets were throwing a party. A thousand guests were in attendance, the vodka was flowing, and on the receiving line waiting to shake the hand of Ambassador Anatoliy Dobrynin, Henry Kissinger was denying rumors. No, he said, he didn't want to be the new President's secretary of state or his ambassador to Peking either. He hadn't the faintest idea how those reports had come to circulate. Well, then, a reporter asked, would he like to be emissary to the Court of St. James's in London?

Kissinger was about to answer when Nixon swept into the room. Spotting his former secretary of state, Nixon grabbed him by the elbow and, propelling him toward the front of the queue, instructed, "Henry, you come with me." Dobrynin greeted the two of them with a big smile. Nixon beamed back, posed for pictures and, as reporters crowded round, delivered himself of some opinions. Washington would like the new administration, he promised. "There will be a new style—I don't mean to be critical of the current administration—[but] it will be different." Reagan was "a reasonable man, a strong man, and a man who is reliable," and, given time, the Russians would wind up liking him. He hadn't been a favorite of the Russians either—"I want to be careful how I say this," he cautioned, "because we are in the Russian embassy"—"but we made progress." According to Nixon, so would Reagan: "The President-elect will launch a real crusade for peace. He has good instincts, just like President Carter. He is a man of peace."

Accepting a glass of vodka ("I never drink the stuff," he confided), Nixon moved off, his own minireceiving line in tow. He bearded the Egyptian ambassador ("When I saw President Sadat at the Shah's funeral, I told your President that he and Reagan would hit it off very well. . . . They'll be good friends."), then a Tanzanian diplomat ("You'll like President Reagan. He's a good man. I think at some point he ought to visit Africa."), and finally an Icelandic editor ("I had a visit from eight young people of the Icelandic Independent Party this morning. They certainly play tough with their politics."). By the time he was gone an hour later, the caviar had been picked clean, the roast suckling pig demolished, and the rumors about Nixon's official reemergence thicker than ever.

It was the buzz now: Nixon was not only back, he was wheeling and dealing. He had the new President's ear, and he was whispering into it. One network reported he was even packing his bags for Peking.

None of it, or at least very little of it, was true. Nixon was neither about to become the ambassador to China, nor did he want to be any longer. He had talked to Reagan, but he was far from setting policy. What he was doing, usually indirectly, was offering a few helpful hints: set an agenda and stick to it; don't push too many programs at once— select a couple, then go all out on them; and above all don't be a Polly- anna like Carter. Give the country the bad news about the economy immediately, right after the inaugural, when presidential popularity was its highest. Later, when the economy rebounded, he could take the credit.

There was one more item: the new secretary of state. Richard Nixon had very definite views on that. "Al Haig," he told a group of guests gathered around his table one night not long after his return from Washington, "is the meanest, toughest, most ambitious son of a bitch I ever knew." Nixon paused, savoring his Tanqueray martini. "He'll make a great secretary of state."

Haig, not surprisingly, had come to the same conclusion. Since leav- ing the Ford White House he had been busily burnishing his credentials, first as commander of NATO, then as a $10,000-a-turn member of the national security lecture circuit, and finally as president of United Tech- nologies, a multibillion-dollar conglomerate that was one of the country's leading defense contractors. His only misstep had been a brief, ill-fated try for the 1980 Republican presidential nomination. Encouraged to run by Nixon, with whom he had stayed in frequent contact, Haig had made a characteristically confident go at it. "I don't mean to sound arrogant or melodramatic," he had said at the time, "but I think I have seen the office, I think I have had the experience abroad, and I think I have had the experience at home to make me believe that I am as qualified—and more—than anybody in the field." Nixon, he added, had told him the same thing.

Despite Nixon's and his own estimation of his abilities, Haig s on discovered that he had no definable political base and that without it the nomination was beyond reach. The Saturday before Christmas, 1979, he phoned Nixon to say he was dropping out of the race. Nixon was under- standing. If that was Al's conclusion, he wasn't going to argue with it.

Perhaps it was too soon. But Haig should take heart. The chance to serve would come again. Now, less than two years later, Nixon was doing his best to guarantee it.

He had been talking up Haig as a potential secretary of state even before Reagan's election. Haig might not be another Kissinger, Nixon admitted in conversation with friends, and he might lack altogether Henry's conceptual skills, but when it came to executing policy Al got the job done. That's what a strong President needed, Nixon said: someone to kick ass. Maybe Al wasn't a genius, but in that job, you didn't have to be. All that was required was knowing the score, and Al knew it. He understood the Russians, how you had to stand up to them, but at the same time talk and trade with them. He knew the importance of the China card; he wouldn't permit the right-wing "crazies" who surrounded Reagan to let Taiwan interfere with playing it. He would perform just as he, Nixon, would in the same spot.

And for Haig's chances that was the principal stumbling block. Reagan had yet to nominate him, and the Democrats in Congress already were promising a fight. Wary, Reagan let it be known that he was considering a number of other candidates as well, including George Shultz, Nixon's former treasury secretary. Haig would still find a place in his cabinet, but perhaps in another slot, say, as secretary of defense.

The news hit Nixon badly. Personally, he had nothing against Shultz, but Shultz wasn't Haig. In the crunch, well, in the crunch, George could be, as Nixon had put it on the tapes, "a candy-ass."

Quickly, Nixon began making calls: to key senators on the Hill, to foreign policy officials overseas, to close-in Reagan aides, like Mike Deaver and Ed Meese. He did not call Reagan himself. There was no need. The President-elect knew what he thought of Haig. When the time came to make a final decision, Reagan would call him.

Six weeks after the election, Nixon's telephone rang. Reagan was cordial. He had thought it over, and, after the most careful consideration, weighing every view, had all but decided to name Al Haig his secretary of state. Did Nixon think it was a good idea? Nixon told him it was and congratulated him on the wisdom of his deliberations. Al wouldn't disappoint him. He would serve his new President as faithfully as he had his old one. Reagan could be proud: it was a brilliant choice.

There remained only the hurdle of Haig's senatorial confirmation, an ordinarily routine formality that, because of Haig's association with Nixon, was proving to be a problem. A number of important Senate Democrats, including minority leader Robert Byrd of West Virginia, had expressed reservations about Haig's nomination, and the outcome of the vote in the Foreign Relations Committee was in doubt. Referring to Haig's involvement in Watergate, Rhode Island Senator Claiborne Pell, the ranking committee Democrat, told reporters, "In the 16 years I have served on this committee, I do not recall a nomination that has come before us that has caused the concern and worry in the Senate that this one has."

Initially, Haig seemed unruffled. His opening statement to the Foreign Relations Committee was courteous, if unapologetic. He had done nothing wrong during his time in the White House with Nixon, Haig insisted; he had nothing to hide. "I believe[d] that President Nixon, the duly elected and duly constituted head of the executive branch, was entitled to the presumption of innocence, until proven otherwise, accorded as a constitutional right to every American citizen. In that context, I worked hard within the boundaries of the law and the advice of the lawyers to support him."

But as the senators began to bore in, questioning his denials of involvement in Watergate and of arranging a "deal" for the Nixon pardon, Haig grew more contentious. "What do you want me to say? What are you after?" Haig demanded, during an angry exchange with Democrats Paul Tsongas of Massachusetts and Paul Sarbanes of Maryland. "There were tremendous abuses. . . . Mistakes were made. But I didn't make them. I wasn't there when they were made. I inherited a situation then and, as a consequence of those mistakes, I did my best to keep the country on an even keel." Haig glared at Sarbanes. "Nobody has a monopoly on virtue, even you, Senator."

A number of senators remained unconvinced by Haig's protestations of innocence. What they wanted was direct, corroborating evidence: the White House tapes.

Though the tapes were in the custody of the National Archives, under law, only Nixon could release them, and through his lawyers he had already made it clear he would not do so without a subpoena. The committee itself was split along party lines over whether to issue one, but eventually a compromise was arranged: the committee would subpoena not the tapes themselves but an index of them to determine their relevancy.

Nixon was still truculent. Resentful that Congress had denied him the materials in the first place, and anxious to do nothing that would embarrass Haig, he announced through his lawyers that he would contest the subpoena in court. "It's a constitutional question," Jack Miller told the press. "If Congress can go running willy-nilly through the files of former Presidents, it would be exceedingly difficult to run the government." He added that Nixon was prepared to defend his position in court no matter how long it took.

While the committee was debating how to respond, Nixon called Senator Jesse Helms, Republican of North Carolina, to assure him that there was nothing on the tapes incriminating to Haig. "Absolutely not," Helms quoted Nixon to the other committee members as saying. "And I should know more about those tapes than anyone else." A short while later, the effort to secure the tapes collapsed, and Senator Charles Percy, Republican from Illinois, the committee's chairman, moved Haig's nomination. The vote to confirm was 15 to 2.

With Reagan and Haig in office, Nixon's influence was at its post-resignation zenith, and less cautiously than before he began to use it, phoning Republican members of Congress to dispense advice, sought or not. Officially, his party had yet to welcome him back, and some of the recipients of his calls were plainly startled to hear the announcement, "Hi, this is Dick Nixon," on the other end of the line. But there were many in Washington and out of it who welcomed his help. One of them was Thomas Van Meter, the Republican president pro-tem of the Ohio State Senate.

In early February, Van Meter, who was up for reelection, invited Nixon to be the guest of honor at a fund-raiser for the GOP in Columbus. Nixon accepted immediately—to the irritation of a number of high-ranking Ohio Republicans. James Rhodes, the state's Republican governor, Earl Barnes, the state Republican chairman and the state's entire Republican congressional delegation announced they would be otherwise occupied the night Nixon was in Columbus. "It's like inviting your former mistress to your family Christmas dinner," groused one Republican county chairman who planned to absent himself from the proceedings.

Nonetheless, the entire complement of tickets sold out, $100,000 was added to the GOP's coffers, and Nixon himself seemed to have a fine time, even when, in introducing him, Ohio State football coach Woody Hayes noted that in 1974 Nixon had found "the football takes a lot of funny bounces."

After Columbus the political invitations came less self-consciously, and when Nixon accepted, Republican officeholders found fewer excuses to stay away. At Nixon's next outing, a $200-a-plate fund-raising reception at New York City's Lincoln Center in June, not only did the local party chairmen turn up, but so did the Democratic mayor, Edward Koch; the GOP national chairman, Richard Richards; the former secretary of state, Henry Kissinger; the newly elected Republican Senator Alfonse D'Amato, and three members of the Reagan cabinet—along with 1500 other Republicans, who nearly crushed him in their enthusiasm. Again, Nixon was delighted. He shook every outstretched hand, endorsed Koch for reelection ("He's a shoo-in and he deserves to be."), passed off his return to politics ("It isn't exactly like a rookie coming back to the big leagues."), used up two ball-point pens signing autographs, and, in the two hours he was on his feet, greeting and bussing the faithful, registered only one complaint: he missed listening to the ball games because of the players' strike.

All in all it had been an extraordinary eighteen months that Nixon
had spent in New York. Personally, however, he felt cramped. Grand as
the Sixty-fifth Street town house was, it afforded him little privacy, and
his grandchildren, who were becoming increasingly important in his life,
almost no place to play. In addition, Nixon, who admitted to being "a bit
square," was appalled by some aspects of city living. Directly across the
street from his house was a Catholic elementary school, and one noon-
time Nixon arrived home to find several girls perched on his stoop,
smoking marijuana.

"These were *girls*," Nixon related incredulously to a visitor. "Boys
you'd expect to engage in all sorts of shenanigans, but little girls." He
shook his head. "I don't know. I suppose that's part of the whole
women's lib movement: the girls are supposed to be as immoral and
decadent as the boys."

Whatever it was, Nixon didn't want his grandchildren part of it. It
would be better if when they came to visit he was living in the country.
And so very quietly in January he had begun looking for a new house. He
had a number of requirements. His new residence had to have space, the
more the better; he also wanted a big yard, a pool, and for his privacy, it
should be heavily wooded and set well back from the road. A library was
also a must, along with a wine cellar to house his growing collection of
choice vintages. Finally, the house had to be within a fifty-minute drive
of his Manhattan office. Fifty minutes in the backseat of his limousine
would be time enough to go through the morning papers and catch up on
the mail. Anything more, and he would be bored, and, if there was one
thing Richard Nixon did not want to be, it was a bored, commuting
suburbanite.

Ruwe found a house in the exclusive bedroom community of Saddle
River, New Jersey, that filled all the stipulations. Set on four and a half
wooded acres at the end of a quiet cul-de-sac, the low-slung fieldstone
and redwood contemporary had fifteen rooms, a lighted tennis court, a
nine-hundred-square-foot swimming pool, three built-in stereo systems, a
winding staircase descending through the foyer, separate guest quarters
and a wine cellar with space enough for a thousand bottles. The owner, a
retired stockbroker, had had it on the market at $1.25 million. After a
personal inspection tour by the Nixons and Rebozo, and what the real-
estate broker characterized as "very gentlemanly and swift bargaining"
the seller let it go for just over $1 million. "We haven't had a Democrat
in office since time began," said Saddle River's mayor. "The Nixons will
be welcome here."

It was harder for Nixon to find accommodations for the materials he
prized most, his White House papers and tapes. Though legally they still
belonged to the government, the new administration had let it be known
that Nixon could have them back, provided he found a suitable place to

house them. The obvious solution, as it had been for Presidents since Franklin Roosevelt, was a presidential library.

Nixon had been making plans for the library since 1971. The original scheme called for building it on a large hillside tract of ocean-view property within the boundaries of the San Clemente marine base. It was to be a lavish edifice, even more opulent, Haldeman promised John Dean, who was dispatched to inspect the site, than the recently opened archival mausoleum Lyndon Johnson had erected on the campus of the University of Texas. "Lyndon Johnson grabbed every paper and file cabinet in the executive branch and hauled it down to Texas," Haldeman told Dean. "LBJ did it first class, and with grand style, but we'll do it better, you just wait and see."

In short order, a Nixon Library Foundation was set up, a distinguished board of trustees, headed by the U.S. ambassador to Belgium, Leonard K. Firestone, enlisted, and a fund-raising campaign put into operation. At Nixon's instruction, White House lawyers began investigating how to amend the tax code to make it possible for friends like Annenberg to buy Kissinger's personal papers and donate them to the projected library, while claiming a multimillion-dollar tax deduction in the process. According to Dean, Nixon also wanted legislation to enable him to claim tax deductions for the donation of his own papers, which were conservatively valued at more than $3 million. He wanted other changes in the tax code that would allow him to sell his papers outright with no tax consequences. His plan, he told Dean, was to use the money thus raised to provide an annuity for his children and grandchildren.

During meetings in the Roosevelt Room of the White House, proposals were discussed for making the library a center for conferences of world leaders. Peace treaties would be signed there. Approved scholars would use its facilities for the writing of books and papers celebrating the Nixon presidency. There was even talk of including a film studio for the production of movies that would present the Nixon message to high schools and colleges.

But before matters could progress further, Watergate intervened, and soon after Nixon's resignation, the library foundation was dissolved. Plans for the library itself, however, remained active, and in April 1975, during a holiday at Annenberg's Palm Desert estate, Nixon promised to donate "the papers and materials of my Presidency as well as the materials from other periods in my life" to the University of Southern California, Pat's alma mater, and home of his favorite college football team. But to build the library, USC had to have the papers, and while they remained in government custody, stored at the National Archives, plans for the library had languished.

Lately, however, there had been renewed interest in the project from

USC. Then in late July, 1981, Nixon received a visit from Terry Sanford, the president of Duke. A former North Carolina governor who had made two tries at the Democratic presidential nomination, Sanford was no admirer of Nixon's, but he was keen on acquiring his papers, which Sanford regarded as of academic value. Sanford told Nixon that Duke would donate the land on which a combination library-museum would be built. The $25 million it would cost to erect the library itself would come from private contributors.

Nixon still had warm feelings about Duke, which had given him a scholarship to law school during the depths of the Depression, but he was not prepared to commit himself on the spot. He had had trouble with Duke's promises before; in 1954, the university had said it would grant him an honorary degree, then backed out after the faculty had voted against it. Leery of another snafu, Nixon instructed Sanford to have his trustees come up with a firm proposal and forward it back to him by August 19. As Sanford prepared to depart, Nixon gave him one other bit of advice: hire George Allen as the university's football coach.

Sanford returned to Raleigh to find a rebellion awaiting him. He had neglected to inform either the trustees or the faculty of his intentions before going to New York, and they were livid. Two trustees, Democratic presidential adviser Charles Murphy and novelist William Styron, resigned in protest, and disgruntled professors began circulating petitions of condemnation. "You don't have to hate Nixon to worry about linking up with him and his friends in a long and deep relationship," presidential scholar James David Barber advised the faculty in an open letter. "I don't want to spend the rest of my life at this place correcting the record regarding Nixon. As of now, I say it's broccoli and I say to hell with it." The university's Academic Council agreed and voted unanimously to "categorically reject the creation of any museum or memorial designed to foster the glorification of the former President." A few days later, the same body, by a margin of one vote, disapproved of the library altogether.

While the search continued for a new site,* Nixon departed for

---

* When negotiations between Nixon and Duke foundered, a number of other locations, including Harry Truman's hometown of Independence, Missouri, and Leavenworth, Kansas, the site of the federal penitentiary, began vying for the Nixon library. Finally, in April 1983, after nearly a dozen communities and institutions had expressed varying degrees of interest, the library question was settled. The winner was San Clemente, California. If, as expected, Congress approves, Nixon's papers and tapes will be stored in an 80,000-square-foot building (a fourth smaller than either the Ford or Kennedy libraries) to be constructed on a thirteen-acre, $6.5 million site, immediately adjacent to Chapman College. Funds for building the library are to be privately raised. The estimated $1.4 million annual cost of maintaining and operating the library will be borne—as it is for other presidential libraries—by the National Archives.

Europe and a two-week vacation, sailing along the Danube and touring the vineyards of the Baron Phillipe de Rothschild. He came home to both good and bad news.

The former was that, in what the *New York Daily News* termed "the sweetest real estate deal since the Indians sold Manhattan island for $24," his New York town house had been purchased by the Syrian Mission to the United Nations for $2.6 million. The latter was that his friend, the secretary of state, was in trouble again.

Sinister forces had been conspiring against Alexander Miegs Haig, and his stock in the Reagan administration was dwindling. The problem wasn't Watergate or his continuing relations with Nixon; it was Haig himself. In ten months on the job, he had clashed with the vice president, the President's national security adviser, the U.S. special trade representative, the White House staff and most of the members of the Reagan cabinet, including the secretaries of defense, treasury and agriculture. His arguments over policy—from the neutron bomb to relations with Israel to the importation of Japanese automobiles—were incessant. He had blustered, he had bullied, he had threatened—more than once—to resign, and Reagan at last was growing weary of it. "His departure is kind of like our view of the Soviet invasion of Poland," an exasperated White House aide told a reporter, not long after Haig had announced "I am in control here," following an attempt on Reagan's life. "It is inevitable but not imminent. Then, on the other hand, it may occur tomorrow."

Nixon was trying hard to prevent it. Though Haig had fallen out with Kissinger and many of the other old Nixon hands, he had remained close to his former commander in chief, and as his troubles mounted, their relationship grew stronger. They talked frequently, at least several times per week, Nixon dispensing advice not only about Haig's internecine difficulties, but on a broad range of policy questions. The moves—or lack of them—Reagan was making around the world worried Nixon. Tough talk about the Soviets was one thing; acting even tougher was quite another. Reagan was going too far, taking the counsel of *The Real War* too much to heart. There had to be the stick, yes, and Reagan had done admirably at wielding it, but there had to be the carrot as well, and thus far Reagan hadn't been offering it. Instead of negotiating with the Russians, as Nixon had recommended, he was continually threatening them, and the Russians had responded in kind. That was bad policy, Nixon thought, and it was dangerous. Good policy, smart policy—*his* policy—was to keep the channels of communication open.

Al had to do something about it, Nixon urged him, keep the ship on course. He didn't give a good goddam what Reagan did in Latin America, but the Soviet Union, Europe and China were important, and relations with all of them were menaced. Haig mustn't let that happen. He was the last bastion, the only same one around. Didn't Reagan realize it? Nixon demanded. He was courting disaster.*

Haig listened sympathetically, but he could do very little. His position within the administration was precarious, and he was worried about enlisting Nixon as too public an ally. He had taken great pains to keep their relationship secret, including withholding the contents of their conversations from his closest aides. In the current atmosphere, no one could be fully trusted. Later, provided he survived, Nixon might play a more open and useful role. Reagan himself had hinted at it. Time, the new President had said, would tell. It depended on events, on how the history of the next few months flowed.

The summer passed. At his new home in New Jersey, Richard Nixon picked out wallpaper and played with his grandchildren. The world might be heading toward chaos, but his own life was going well. Mrs. Nixon had redecorated the house, giving it new openness and light. He liked the touches she had lent it, the pale yellow coziness of the living room, the Chinese landscapes on the wall. It was a place he could come home to and be at peace. And, more than he ever had been in his life, Nixon was at peace. He was surer of himself now, confident that when people looked back, in fifty or seventy-five years, it wouldn't be Watergate or Henry Kissinger they'd remember, but Richard Nixon.

He wanted them to remember his wife, too, and he was taking steps to ensure it. Wherever and whenever his library was built, it would contain a section dedicated to the life and accomplishments of Patricia Ryan Nixon. Everything else had changed through the years, but she hadn't. Forty-one years they had been married now, forty-one often difficult years, and Pat had remained steadfast. It was, he'd lately been telling friends, the ideal pairing, a real love match. Others didn't know that, still snickered about their marriage, but it didn't matter. He knew it, and in her way Pat knew it. She must.

---

* Besides Reagan's foreign policy moves, Nixon was also critical of the President's supply-side economics, and the whopping budget deficits that came with it. In private conversations, Nixon, who had been schooling himself on the economy, sometimes referred to Treasury Secretary Donald T. Regan as "that asshole," and expressed worries that the administration's tax cutting in combination with massive new outlays for defense was weakening the U.S. vis-à-vis the Soviets.

"He would have been smarter to go slower," Nixon told his former commerce secretary, Peter G. Peterson, referring to Reagan's plan to increase defense spending 10 percent beyond inflation. "If he had gone for, say, five percent, he could have sold it on the Hill. Now, he can't, and the Soviets know it. We'd be better off politically unified behind a smaller figure. That would scare the hell out of them [the Russians]." Nixon shook his head. "In a funny way," he continued, "you can almost say he [Reagan] is bad for defense."

He hoped that the two of them would soon go to Washington for the unveiling of their official portraits in the White House. His family had teased him about his own portrait, how, when he had examined it, he had asked the artist to "take a little off the jowls" and he had taken the ribbing well. So, if everything fell into place, they'd make the trip. It all depended on his schedule and the flow of events. Everything hinged on events.

19
Funeral in Cairo

It began, like many great events, with a parade, a very special celebration for the president of Egypt.

Anwar Sadat was in the reviewing stand, as he always was on October 6, watching proudly the armed forces of his country pass in review. There were many parades in Egypt, but none so important to him as the one on the anniversary of his country's lightning strike across the Suez Canal at the start of the 1973 Yom Kippur War. The parade October 6 marked the beginning of the war that had made the peace possible. Other occasions the president of Egypt could ignore; not this one. Today, October 6, 1981, would be the eighth straight year he had taken his soldiers' salute.

It had been a grand show. Fireworks had exploded overhead; sky divers had leaped to the earth in intricate formation; mortars had sent aloft miniature parachutes that drifted down bearing tiny Egyptian flags and portraits of Sadat. For two hours, the president had watched it all with obvious delight.

Now, a few minutes before 1:00 P.M., the festivities were about to come to an end. In the brick and concrete stands alongside of him, a thousand diplomats and guests looked up as a formation of French-made Mirage 5-E fighters screamed earthward, spewing contrails of colored smoke. At that moment, a column of seventy-two Soviet-made Zil-151 flatbed trucks, arrayed four abreast and each towing a North Korean–made 130-millimeter armor-piercing gun, rumbled into view. Just in front of Sadat's position, one of the last trucks in the procession halted. The doors opened and half a dozen uniformed men began sprinting toward the reviewing stand.

All at once the air was rent with the chatter of automatic weapons. A grenade arced toward the reviewing stand and exploded, sending deadly shrapnel spraying in all directions. Sadat's security men froze in stunned surprise. Another grenade landed at the feet of the defense minister but did not explode; a third struck the armed forces chief of staff in the face and bounced off. "Get your head down! Get your head down!" Sadat's personal bodyguard yelled, drawing his pistol and squeezing off six shots. Heedless, Sadat rose to face his assassins directly, as if daring them to kill him. A second later, a fusillade of steel flung him to the floor. Still firing, and crying "Glory to Egypt! Attack! Attack!" two gunmen reached up over the edge of the reviewing stand and sprayed the fallen president and his party with bullets at point-blank range.

In forty-five seconds, the attack was over. His face bathed in blood, his body punctured by five bullet wounds, Anwar Sadat, president of Egypt and architect of peace, lay dying under a pile of broken bodies and chairs.

Richard Nixon was at home, going over the manuscript of his latest book, when the call came in from Alexander Haig. The news of Sadat's assassination stunned him; the first reports he had heard of the incident had said that Sadat was only slightly wounded. Recovering from his surprise, Nixon began discussing what Sadat's death would mean for the Middle East. His tone was analytic and dispassionate; though they had had a number of friendly dealings, he and the Egyptian president had not been close. At the moment he was far more worried about the implications of Sadat's murder. Apart from warm feelings toward the West, Sadat's successor, Vice President Hosni Mubarak, who had been slightly wounded in the attack himself, was a largely unknown quantity. Whether he would continue the peace process Sadat had initiated was a mystery. It was a worrisome time and a worrisome event.

Nixon asked, "Has the President appointed a delegation?"

Haig answered that the question was still up in the air. Reagan's instinct was to attend Sadat's funeral personally, but with the unsettled climate in Cairo and memories of the attempt on his own life still fresh, the Secret Service was urging him not to go.

Nixon said, "Well, whatever the President does, I am going to go."

Early the next morning Nixon and Haig talked again. Nixon confirmed his intention to attend the funeral and revealed that he had decided to use the occasion to accept long-standing invitations to meet with the leaders of Saudi Arabia, Jordan, Tunisia and Morocco. He asked Haig to pass along the information to Reagan, but otherwise to keep it secret. "I don't want everyone finding out about it," Nixon said. "This is a trip to a funeral, and for the moment I want to keep it at that. I don't want anything to detract from Sadat."

Haig agreed, and promised to have briefing books on each of the countries Nixon would visit waiting for him at the plane.

Meanwhile, at the White House, the debate was continuing on the makeup of the U.S. delegation to the funeral. Reagan had decided to accept the Secret Service's advice and forgo traveling to Cairo himself. Who to send in his place, however, was proving tricky. Sadat had been a head of state, and to dispatch a representative of lesser rank, such as Haig or Vice President George Bush, would seem a slight, especially when a number of U.S. allies were sending their own heads of state. Complicating matters was that, in addition to Nixon, Carter and Kissinger had already made plans to attend. Haig devised a solution. "Why don't we just send them all?"

After a phone call to Ford to enlist his participation, the question was settled. Led by Haig, the U.S. delegation would include, in addition to various congressional leaders, all three former living Presidents—"the Presidential hat-trick," Haig called it.

The arrival at Andrews Air Force Base, Thursday, the eighth, had been timed with military precision. Each of the three Air Force planes bearing the former Presidents wheeled up to the tarmac simultaneously. On command, their hatches opened up and out stepped three very different men who shared only one thing in common.

Their greeting to each other was notably chilly, and the reserve remained as Marine One ferried them to the White House. As the chopper settled onto the lawn, Ford tried to break the ice. "Look," he said, "for the trip, at least, why don't we make it just Dick, Jimmy and Jerry?" Nixon and Carter nodded their assent.

Standing at the end of a red carpet, the man who had followed them into the White House waited, his face uncharacteristically grim. Carter, taking his wife's hand, emerged from the helicopter first, as a crowd of several hundred White House staffers broke into polite applause. The clapping grew louder when Ford stepped out. When at last Nixon appeared in the hatchway, there were cheers and whistles. Reagan's face began to brighten. He pumped the former Presidents' hands, then smiled broadly as Nixon kissed Mrs. Reagan on the cheek.

Afterward, at a small reception inside the White House, Nixon sipped at a martini, nibbled hors d'oeuvres and appeared grave as he discussed the Middle East with George Bush. Carter and Ford avoided looking at each other. Each of the Presidents seemed relieved when the time came to depart.

On the lawn, Reagan eulogized Sadat as "a man of peace in a time of violence." Those who "choose violence over brotherhood" feared Sadat when he was alive, he said, "but in death you must fear him more, for the memory of this great and good man shall vanquish you." He then wished his predecessors well with an Irish expression: "Until we meet again, may God hold you in the hollow of his hand." The photographers moved forward to take a group portrait. Carter at first drew back, then took his place in line and flashed a smile.

A moment later the helicopter lifted off. As it began swinging in the direction of Andrews, Nixon looked down at the White House and said softly, "I kind of like that house down there." He grinned at Carter and Ford. "Don't you?" In spite of themselves, they began to smile.

On board SAM 26000, the plane that had brought John Kennedy's body back from Dallas, the preflight preparations were complete. The White House transportation office had rustled up a supply of matches with the names of each of the Presidents printed on their covers, and Terry Yamada, the chief Air Force steward, had laid in two quarts of butter-pecan ice cream for Ford and some Don Diego cigars for Nixon. Briefing books on the funeral and the political dangers following Sadat's death were neatly laid out on every President's seat. Photographs of the current occupant of the White House peered down from the bulkhead walls. On the tables, there were jars of his favorite brand of jelly beans.

Haig, as leader of the delegation, was assigned what was normally the presidential cabin. His staff took up the next cabin, ordinarily reserved for the First Lady. That left the presidential staff compartment for the three former Presidents. The Carters were to sit on the left; facing them across a table would be Egypt's ambassador to the United States, Ashraf Ghorbal, and his wife. On the right side of the aisle, Nixon and Ford would face, respectively, Kissinger and Secretary of Defense Caspar Weinberger. Farther back in the airplane, other seats were reserved for the rest of the delegation (Charles Percy, chairman of the Senate Foreign Relations Committee; Senator Strom Thurmond, Republican from South Carolina; Sol Linowitz, Carter's special Middle East ambassador; Congressmen Clement Zablocki, Democrat of Wisconsin; William Broomfield, Republican of Michigan; and Jim Wright, Democrat of Texas). In the last compartment were to be billeted members of the former Presidents' staffs and a three-member press pool.

Precisely on schedule, at 7:45 P.M., SAM 26000, gleaming under a fresh application of Turtle Wax, took off and headed out over the Atlantic, bound for Madrid, first stop on the twelve-hour flight. A few minutes later the stewards began laying out the evening meal. As the Presidents dined on crab claws and beef tenderloin, talking about Sadat and speculating about the motives of his assassins, the strain among them was apparent. Ford and Nixon were not getting along, and Ford and Carter were barely speaking. Finally, as the dishes were being cleared away, Nixon turned to Rosalynn Carter and complimented her on her dress. "It matches the color of your eyes."

Smiling, Carter got up, took off his suit coat and, slipping on a tan cardigan, perched on the edge of his seat and began chatting with Nixon. Soon Ford got up as well, and he, too, slipped off his coat. Taking his cue, Nixon finally rose, stripped off his jacket and donned a navy blue cardigan. He signaled for a martini and began munching handfuls of peanuts. The conversation began to move more easily as they traded stories about Sadat. The day he heard of Sadat's death, Carter said, was one of the worst in his life. "The only time I had that bad a day," he added, "was when my daddy died."

Eventually, the talk turned to the Middle East and the hazards that lurked for Arab moderates like the Saudis. Nixon noted the importance of selling AWACS planes to the Saudis, and Carter and Ford concurred. As the miles slipped by, they began discussing the presidential libraries each of them was planning, the books they were writing, of what life was like for them since leaving the White House. Then, as Ford moved back to the aft compartment to talk Michigan politics with Broomfield, Nixon began regaling Carter with tales of China and various Washington personalities, punctuating his points with sweeps of his glass. Carter seemed rapt as Nixon spun stories about Mao and Chou, Eisenhower and Kennedy, Hiss and Helms. Even Rosalynn Carter, to whom Nixon continued to play flattering deference, was impressed. Nixon, she confided to a fellow passenger, was so much more charming than she had imagined; he was, well, almost nice.

The more Nixon talked, the more charming he became. Seeing him at ease, holding forth on this crisis or that, sent a current of electricity through the plane. Cameras appeared. Old pols began grabbing up souvenirs. In one of the rear compartments, Sol Linowitz fought to stay awake, afraid that if he slept, something historic might occur in the seats in front of him. Like eager groupies, Haig's aides began drifting back to ask Nixon for his autograph. "You're the spokesman," Nixon said to Dean Fischer, when Haig's press aide came out to shake his hand. "I've seen you on television." Fischer blushed.

After an hour, Nixon began working his way back through the plane. To some, he still seemed hesitant, as if unsure whether to reach for a hand or wait until it was offered to him. The hands were all outstretched. As Nixon grabbed hold of each one, he paused for a moment, recalled some obscure personal detail of its owner, then moved on, to the next, and the next, never missing a name or a beat. He lingered longer with Jim Wright, telling the House majority leader how grateful he was for a resolution Wright had sponsored years before, calling for a peaceful settlement of the Vietnam War, and longer still with Percy, who had been one of the first members of his party to call for his resignation. Ignoring the past, Nixon talked with the Foreign Relations Committee chairman about NATO and Japan, defense and the Middle East. In the midst of the conversation, Nixon suddenly grasped Percy's hand. "Chuck Percy has stood by Presidents in foreign policy," he said. Watching the exchange, Kissinger felt good. Nixon was saying all the right things.

Haig appeared in the passageway. "Well," he boomed, "this is quite a planeload." Then quietly he beckoned Kissinger aside and informed him that after the funeral in Cairo, Nixon was going to Saudi Arabia. Kissinger was startled; Nixon had said nothing to him about the trip. Haig, without mentioning his conversations with Nixon, assured him it was true. The embassy in Jidda was already cabling, inquiring whether it should host a dinner in Nixon's honor. Kissinger said he would ask Nixon about it.

Nixon, in the meantime, had become huddled in another conversation with Carter and Ford. Zablocki approached, asking for an autograph. Grinning, Nixon obliged. Then Zablocki asked the Presidents to pose together for a picture. Momentarily, Nixon seemed embarrassed. "You don't want my picture with them." Zablocki assured him that he did, and, without further prompting, Nixon slipped his arms around Carter's and Ford's waists. His was the biggest smile of all.

It disappeared as soon as he stuck his head in the last compartment and spotted Haynes Johnson, a *Washington Post* reporter whom he had cursed on the White House tapes. Nixon's eyes widened in surprise. "Oh," he said, "how are you?" Before Johnson could answer, Nixon mumbled to himself, "This is all," and turned away.

Kissinger was waiting for him back in the staff compartment. Was it true? Kissinger wondered. Was he really going on to Saudi Arabia? Nixon threw up his hands. The Saudis had invited him, yes, but nothing had been set. He wasn't at all sure that the trip would actually come off. Kissinger studied him thoughtfully. He knew that Nixon was lying.

After a brief refueling stop at an air base outside Madrid, the party continued on, increasingly weary. Nixon in particular seemed exhausted. Soon after takeoff, he stretched out on a bench outside Haig's cabin, and, pulling a blanket up over his head, quickly dropped off to sleep.

In the rear of the plane, the talk continued about Egypt and the Middle East. The reports that had been received since leaving Washington were not encouraging. Libyan radio was urging the Egyptians to take up arms and there had been scattered instances of trouble. While Cairo itself was quiet, largely because of the celebration of the Moslem Id Al Ahba feast of sacrifice, the armed forces had been placed in an extreme state of readiness, and troops had been drawn up along the Libyan border.

Weinberger, who was going over the latest cable traffic with Haig in the secretary of state's cabin, was worried. A week before Sadat's assassination, Mubarak had come to Washington, and the two of them had had several long conversations, focusing on Egypt's defense needs and the threat it faced from its unpredictable neighbor to the west, Libyan strong man Muammar Qaddafi. Mubarak had emphasized the seriousness of the situation, and Weinberger was prepared to take him at his word. Even in the best of circumstances, Qaddafi was a volatile commodity; with Sadat dead, there was no telling what he would do.

"Jesus," one of Haig's aides mumbled. "Can you imagine it? All those world leaders drawn up for the funeral. What an opportunity for a single terrorist with a grenade. Qaddafi must be licking his chops."

Several rows behind him, Gerald Ford was pacing nervously. Like everyone else on the plane, he was tired, but he had not been able to sleep. Bob Barrett, his military aide, had briefed him on the security precautions that were going to be taken in Cairo, including the wearing of bulletproof vests. Ford had already survived two assassination attempts, and Betty and the children had argued against his coming. But, with Nixon and Carter committed, and Reagan asking him personally, he really had had no choice. Now, whether he liked it or not, he was about to become a target in a potential shooting gallery. The thought kept him pacing.

In the tail section of the airplane, Carter, seemingly at ease, was talking with the press. He mused about Libya—"If Libya goes beyond Chad, the consequences will be very severe; this is one time the United States ought to be ready to use muscle if necessary"—then about his distinguished traveling companions. "I've never known another ex-President," Carter said.

"How's it going?" Haynes Johnson asked. "Haig says you're all on your best behavior. Any problems with Ford?"

Carter shrugged. "Oil and water, you know."

"And Nixon?"

Carter smiled. "We're getting along."

They put down early afternoon Cairo time at an airport swarming with security men, automatic weapons at the ready. At the nearby El Salam Hotel, where they paused to freshen up, there were more troops in evidence, and more still flanking their motorcade and parade route as they later paid calls on Mubarak and the acting Egyptian president, speaker of the parliament Sufi Abu Taleb.

By the time the American Presidents' motorcade crossed the Nile on the way to Giza and the residence of Sadat's widow, the capital was quiet. Too quiet, Ruwe thought; like a Western town, waiting for a shootout. Sitting alongside of him, in the backseat of the limousine, Nixon seemed unconcerned. As the deserted blocks flashed by out the window, he looked for reminders of his last trip to Cairo in June 1974. Then he and Sadat rode in triumph through crowds packed a hundred deep. More than a million Egyptians had come out to welcome him, the largest assemblage ever for a foreign guest, all of them crying at the top of their lungs, "Nik-son! Nik-son! Nik-son!" In the car, Sadat had turned to him and said, "This is a great day for Egypt. These people are here because they want to be here. You can bring people out, but you can't make them smile." Now, Sadat was gone, Nixon was no longer President, and the streets were dusty and deserted.

"Memories," he said to Ruwe. "The memories this brings back."

Sadat's children were waiting to greet them in the courtyard of their father's home. At the sight of Kissinger, one of Sadat's younger sons broke down and began to weep. Kissinger gathered him up in a burly hug, then, blinking back tears of his own, accompanied the other Americans inside.

One by one, Nixon, Carter and Ford embraced Jihan Sadat and whispered words of consolation. Ford told her, "We know how great this loss was to you, but it is our great loss as well. America looked upon him as a beautiful man." Jihan thanked him and then she began to weep.

At the hotel that night, U.S. Ambassador Alfred L. Atherton, Jr., hosted a dinner in the delegation's honor. Seated around the ballroom were members of the U.S. Mission and their wives. After the meal had been served, each of the Presidents delivered a toast. Carter's was in a religious vein, about the blessings God would bestow to peacemakers like Sadat. Equally in character, Ford rambled on earnestly about Sadat's human traits. Then it was Nixon's turn to speak. He seemed self-conscious and nervous as he launched into an extended congratulation to the foreign service officers on their "typically fine work and dedicated service." Next, he thanked the crew of the plane that had brought him to Egypt. Then the hotel staff. Then the waiters for "serving us this delicious food." He paused, and half-laughed, for no apparent point. Around the room, people began shifting in their seats. It was the little people, the unknown, the unrecognized, who deserved credit for the success of this trip, he went on, "not the famous . . . or the infamous." He smiled again; Jody Powell noticed that he was beginning to sweat. Nixon's last words came in a rush, "And so we thank you for letting us be here." He then sat down so quickly that he nearly missed his chair. Carter looked down the table at Ford. Ford merely shook his head.

Ruwe awoke early the next morning. Getting up, he pulled back the blinds of his hotel room window and peered out. Cairo was still quiet; if anything, even quieter than the day before. He looked down and saw part of the reason: stationed every ten feet, as far as he could see, were men in civilian garb, AK-47s at port arms.

He went in to see Nixon a few minutes later and found him shaved and showered and going over a State Department briefing book, outlining the morning's events. The schedule called for the American delegation to link up with those of other countries at a military parade ground in the industrial suburb of Nasr City, not far from the spot where Sadat had been assassinated. From there, the mourners were to follow Sadat's horse-drawn caisson nine hundred yards to the place of interment, the tomb of Egypt's Unknown Soldier. As soon as the ceremonies were complete, the American Presidents were to be driven immediately back to the airport for the flight home to Washington.

Nixon, too, would be leaving for the airport as soon as the services were complete, but on a different flight to a different destination. The Royal Saudi jet that would take him to Jidda was fueled and waiting, and he instructed Ruwe to tell Kissinger of his plans.

Kissinger was struggling to get into a bulletproof vest when Ruwe knocked on his door. He seemed neither surprised nor upset by the announcement of Nixon's trip and with a grunt agreed to pass along word to Ford.

At the staging area where the foreign delegations were to gather, the Egyptians had erected an enormous yellow-and-white-striped tent, beneath which in the style of the desert had been laid scores of Oriental rugs. The several hundred dignitaries mingled easily, exchanging gossip and greetings. It was an imposing aggregation. From England had come Prince Charles; from France, the new president, François Mitterrand, and his Gaullist predecessor, Valéry Giscard d'Estaing; from Germany, Helmut Schmidt; from Norway, King Olav; from Italy, President Alessandro Pertini—leaders from virtually every corner of the globe except the Arab world. Save for Sudan and the tiny sheikdom of Oman, the Arabs had sent no one.

The American Presidents arrived sitting side-by-side in the backseat of an armor-plated limousine flown in from Washington. "My," Percy said, noting their peculiarly erect posture, "aren't we looking upright."

Nixon tapped his chest. "It's this," he said, referring to the bulletproof vest beneath his shirt. Percy, who was not so equipped, cracked, "I'm walking behind you."

The helicopter bearing Sadat's body settled down in a swirl of sand and dust. Solemnly, the honor guard stepped forward, and, to the sound of muffled drums, transferred the flag-draped casket to a caisson drawn by six black stallions. Then slowly the procession moved off: caisson in the lead, trailed by Sadat's family, then a coterie of high Egyptian officials, then contingents of the various armed forces, and, finally, the delegations of foreigners, flanked on each side by cordons of troops.

At first the foreigners walked along in silence, occasionally whispering among themselves about the lack of Egyptian mourners, who had been banned from the ceremonies as a security precaution. Then, as the procession stretched out, Giscard called out after Carter.

"Jimmy! Are you working in Washington now?"

"No," Carter replied, "I have an office in Atlanta."

Giscard seemed momentarily puzzled.

"Atlanta, Georgia," Carter explained.

Giscard fell in beside him and began talking about dinner parties, the problems involved in entertaining four hundred guests at once. Spotting Ford, Giscard greeted him as well, and Ford could be heard saying, "July 14, yes, yes, that's my birthday, too."

The coincidence of having his birthday on Bastille Day made Ford laugh. "Mine won't live in history as long."

Eyes straight ahead, face mournful, Nixon joined in none of the banter until Menachem Begin waved him over. The Israeli prime minister seemed tired and drawn; he brightened when Nixon approached. "Mr. President," he said, "every time I make a speech I say we owe our thanks to three Presidents. Truman for recognition, Nixon for help in the 1973 war and Carter for Camp David." When Nixon fell back into line, he commented to Ruwe, "You know, I don't think Begin is that intractable. Tough, yes, but not hopeless."

As they approached the reviewing stand where Sadat had been shot, Carter asked Ghorbal, "Where was the assassination?"

"It was right there," the Egyptian ambassador answered, gesturing toward the pavilion. "They ran from the truck from over there."

They proceeded into the pavilion, Ford, Carter, Ghorbal and the first ranks of the foreign dignitaries. Behind them, Nixon, who had begun talking with Kissinger, was about to follow with the rest of the delegation when suddenly a group of rifle-waving soldiers cut them off. "What is going on?" Kissinger stuttered nervously. "What is going on?"

A Secret Service man whispered into his radio, "Pace, there is a silver vehicle off to the right. It is armed. If anything goes down, bring it over to the left."

Nixon remained ice-calm. Finally, after conversations between American and Egyptian security men, the rank of soldiers melted away and Nixon, Kissinger and the remaining Americans moved into the pavilion. Nixon's eyes swept over the scene. In the box where Sadat had been gunned down, the bullet holes had not yet been patched. He could still see the bloodstains on the floor.

The foreigners filed through, pausing to pay their final respects to Mubarak and Sadat's family. After they and the other non-Moslem guests had gone, Jihan, her children and a few close friends walked to the Tomb of the Unknown. On a black stone that would cover Sadat's underground crypt a verse had been inscribed from the Koran: "Do not consider those killed for the sake of Allah dead but alive and blessed by the side of the Almighty." Beneath the words was Sadat's name, the date of his birth and death, and the words, "Hero of war and peace. He lived for the sake of peace and was martyred for the sake of principles."

By the time taps was being played over Sadat's grave, the American delegation had returned to the airport. It was there that the press noticed that Nixon was missing. Briefly, there was speculation that something had happened to him. As Carter and Ford were boarding the presidential jet, Haig's spokesman revealed the truth, stressing that Nixon was traveling on a "private visit" and would not be delivering messages for either Reagan or Haig.*

Nixon arrived in Jidda† a few hours later, and that night attended a banquet in his honor hosted by King Khalid and Crown Prince Fahd. After two days of talks about the pending AWACS sale and the recently devised Saudi peace plan ("A very positive step and a progressive one," Nixon called it), he flew on to Amman, and another banquet presided over by King Hussein, an old friend whom Nixon described as having "very useful ideas." Twenty-four hours later he was off again, bound to Tunis and a meeting with President Habib Bourguiba. From the Tunisian capital, Nixon flew on to Fez, Morocco, and his fourth "summit" in as many days, this time with King Hassan, to whom he provided tips on investing in New Jersey real estate.

On reaching Paris, Nixon encamped at the Crillon Hotel, the traditional headquarters for visiting heads of state. In between visits with French dignitaries, Nixon readied a report of his travels for submission to Reagan and Haig ("No written report or anything like that," he emphasized. "Nor am I going to take two hours talking to the President. That used to bore the dickens out of me."), as well as a four-page summary for release to the press.

The latter's contents were unremarkable. Nixon expressed support

---

* Initially, the White House claimed that it had learned of Nixon's travel plans only when the press did. Later, presidential spokesman Larry Speakes conceded that Nixon had informed Haig in advance, but that Haig, who according to Speakes had helped Nixon arrange his trip—an allegation promptly denied by Haig's spokesman—had not notified the White House. Other sources in the White House reported that presidential counselor Edwin Meese and chief of staff James Baker were furious with Haig for not telling Reagan. That was denied by Baker, who through Speakes insisted, "I am not angry." The State Department then muddled the actual sequence of events further by claiming that before departure for Cairo Nixon had intended to tell Haig but, unable to find him, had notified Deputy Secretary of State William Clark. Clark, State went on, then passed the news on to White House deputy chief of staff Michael K. Deaver. Not so, said Deaver; he recalled no such thing. Finally, after a series of frantic communications, State, the White House and Haig's spokesman got the story straight: Nixon had informed Haig, and Haig, who had helped arrange the trip, had passed the word on to Reagan, who had, the White House said, "forgotten" about it.

† The Royal Saudi 727 that conveyed Nixon to Jidda is perhaps the world's most luxurious aircraft, featuring, among other accouterments, solid-gold bathroom fixtures. For all the splendor, however, Nixon fell prey to the standard tourist-class nightmare: a piece of his luggage was lost and with it his favorite pair of pajamas. "Gosh," said the understandably mortified Saudi chief of protocol when he heard of Nixon's predicament, "I bought some new ones at Sulka's in London and never wore them. Be my guest." Nixon accepted and wore them the rest of the trip. Returning home, Nixon called the New York branch of Sulka's and had the store dispatch an identical pair (white with blue piping) to the helpful Saudi official. With them, Nixon attached a note. "Above and beyond the call of duty," it read.

for Arab moderates, endorsed the sale of AWACS aircraft to the Saudis, and, taking a passing swipe at Libya's Qaddafi ("He is more than a desert rat. He is an international outlaw."), called for direct talks between the Israelis and the PLO, terming them "inevitable" unless additional progress came out of the Camp David Accords. Substantively, it was no more than what Ronald Reagan had said as a candidate. Never before, though, had Nixon reported publicly on his postresignation travels, and certainly never before had he been accorded the treatment he received in Paris. The American embassy was put virtually at his disposal. Embassy press officers duplicated his statement on embassy machines, and made calls on embassy phones to the bureaus of the major news organizations, alerting reporters to the statement's release. As the press was quick to note, a change had come over him and in the regard for him.

Time, which devoted a full page to his thoughts, termed him "the world's unique and ubiquitous elder statesman without portfolio." The *Washington Post* talked of "Nixon's redemption" and said that in going to Egypt and the Middle East, he had furthered his "rehabilitation."

"There was both a poignancy and a fascination at seeing him standing at attention with the other presidents on the steps of that plane, taking the Egyptian salute on their Cairo arrival," Haynes Johnson wrote. "God knows what hurts he must hold inside, or what thoughts his return to that ceremonial public duty must have prompted. . . . [But] here he was, back in the full glow of the presidential spotlight as an official state funeral emissary. . . . What greater repatriation, what ultimate way back from Elba, than to perform as a peacemaker, whatever lack of official sponsorship, at so critical a juncture in the Mideast?"

Nixon lost no time in capturing the moment. Within days of his return to the United States, he began laying new plans: a trip to China in the spring, Eastern Europe in the summer, Africa in the fall. There'd also be another book, a political fund-raiser or two, a dash, when the time was right, back to Europe and Morocco, maybe even Russia. He'd like to return to Russia, he told friends, help reassemble the now-shattered détente. He wasn't worried about the Russians—"We can beat the hell out of them"—and Brezhnev had been pestering him to come. He knew Brezhnev, understood how his mind worked; indeed, for all their differences the two of them were practically old friends. Experience like that was valuable. Sometimes a leader like Brezhnev would say things to someone like himself that he wouldn't to an ambassador or secretary of state. He could be a transmission belt, perhaps even contribute an idea or two of his own.

He talked on expansively as he always did in discussing the greats. "The men in the arena," he called them, quoting Theodore Roosevelt. Teddy, he told a visitor, had had it right. Leaders, the Brezhnevs, the

Sadats, the de Gaulles, were different, not quite like their fellowmen. He pulled out the manuscript of his latest book, flipped it open to a passage he had taken from a speech Roosevelt had delivered at the Sorbonne in 1910 and putting on his glasses began to read aloud:

> It is not the critic who counts; not the man who points out how the strong man stumbles, or where the doer of deeds could have done them better. The credit belongs to the man who is actually in the arena, whose face is marred by dust and sweat and blood; who strives valiantly; who errs and comes up short again and again; because there is not effort without error and shortcoming; but who does actually strive to do the deeds; who knows the great enthusiasms, the great devotions; who spends himself in a worthy cause, who at the best knows in the end the triumphs of high achievement and who at the worst, if he fails, at least fails while daring greatly; so that his place shall never be with those whose cold and timid souls know neither victory nor defeat.

Finishing, Richard Nixon seemed pleased. He had come out of the desert. He was back in the arena again.

20

Never Looking Back

Like a force suddenly let loose, Nixon was a blur of activity the next several months.

In January, he put the finishing touches on his manuscript and submitted it to his publisher.

In February, he flew to Jamaica for two weeks of vacationing and conferences with the newly elected conservative prime minister, Edward Seaga.

In March, he traveled again to Morocco for talks with King Hassan.

In April, he granted a long interview to *Time* on his current thoughts on the state of the presidency.

In May, he delivered a foreign policy address to a Republican fund-raiser in Orange County, California.

And there was more ahead. In the next year, he would deliver seven major speeches, appear on eleven network interview shows, attend seven GOP fundraisers, travel to nine foreign countries (meeting the heads of state of each), confer with the editorial boards of several major publications, and, if he got around to it, perhaps grant interviews to the 150 reporters with standing requests. Such was his prominence that even hated Harvard was asking him to come.

Confident was not the word for Richard Nixon's mood. He was ebullient, and, with the reception he had been getting of late, there was cause for it. When he addressed the party faithful in Orange County, denouncing proponents of the nuclear freeze and warning that the next year was going to be "tough politically," he was introduced as "truly one of our great Presidents" and a band played "Hail to the Chief." Afterward, the Republican autograph-hunters, many of whom had paid $1000 a piece to shake his hand, stood in queues thirty-deep. In Morocco, where the king hosted one banquet in his honor and the U.S. ambassador another, 75,000 people gathered outside his Marrakech hotel on the chance they might get a glimpse of him. When Nixon rewarded them by wading into the crowd to shake hands and hold up babies, a chant went up in Arabic, "You should still be President." Nixon responded by flinging out his arms in his V-for-Victory campaign salute, and shouting into the din, "*Hasta luego!*"

The only bit of unpleasantness in all of this came from an unexpected source. In late May, as Nixon was setting his plans for a three-week trip to Eastern Europe, Diane Sawyer called, asking for an interview. Since leaving San Clemente, Sawyer had become a television star for CBS, first as the network's State Department correspondent, and later as cohost of the CBS *Morning News*. Throughout, her relations with Nixon had remained friendly, and Nixon agreed to the interview request. He coupled his acceptance with an invitation to dinner.

At first, the session went well. Nixon was in a relaxed, almost playful mood, gently poking fun at himself ("My media critics consider that—that I'm rather the one who probably was behind the barn door when the brains were handed out."), advising Teddy Kennedy to lose twenty pounds and "get some new ideas" ("I'm sure he will; he's a very practical man.") and terming former Vice President Walter Mondale ("Mondale, blah!") "just a warmed-over Carter." As for Reagan, Nixon had nothing but praise.

"Now," Nixon said, "if—if—if you ask whether he's smart in terms of IQ, in terms of whether or not he would be accepted as a full professor at Harvard, the probabl—the answer is, probably not, and thank God we don't have a full professor at Harvard as President."

His tone sharpened when Sawyer asked him about the press. "Now let's talk about the ladies in the press for a moment," Nixon replied. "We have to realize that men reporters can be tough, but women reporters think they have to be tougher; they've got to prove something. . . . A delightful fellow, Manolo Sanchez, who worked for us when we were in the White House years—walking by the press quarters, he used to refer —he'd look in there, and he says, 'There you have the vultures and the witches.' Now [by] the vultures he referred to the men, [by] the witches he referred to the women." Nixon shrugged. "My views are a bit old-fashioned, I must admit. . . . But . . . like the little ditty from the song, 'Why can't a woman be like a man?' . . . I want women to be like women. I want men to be like men."

"Maybe . . . the press has a visceral reaction against me," he went on. "Maybe it was my manner, I don't know. But it was there, and, as far as I am concerned, it's now live and let live." He smiled at Sawyer. "They usually have underestimated me. And—but I've done reasonably well, except for some unfortunate events which we won't go into at the moment."

But it was precisely those events Sawyer did want to go into. Noting that the tenth anniversary of the Watergate break-in was approaching, she asked what it now meant to him.

"It happened a long time ago," Nixon answered, eyes narrowing. "I've said everything I—I can on the subject. I have nothing to add, and I'm looking to the future rather than the past. . . . I've always said this: 'Remember Lot's wife. Never look back.' "

Sawyer continued to press. "But a lot of people say, and these are common people, ordinary people, people in the street, say that you never just said, 'I covered up and I'm sorry.' "

"Well, that—is, of course, not true," Nixon replied with apparent agitation. "As a matter of fact, if you—if you go back and look at the Frost broadcast, and if you read my memoirs, I've covered all that in great, great detail. And I've said it all, and I'm not going to say anything more in the future."

Sawyer was not so easily put off. "Do you think about it when you're just sitting alone, when some—when it's—you're not working?"

"Never," Nixon snapped. "No. If I were thinking about it, I wouldn't be able to—do I—what is some of the constructive work I've been doing on my new book, and also preparing for the travels I'm going to be doing. You see, I understand—I—I—I—understand the obsession with this subject. It's understandable. But people who are obsessed with it don't understand me. I went through it, I know what went wrong, I know that I have a responsibility, I'm not trying to excuse myself. But I'm not going to spend my time just looking back and wringing my hands about something I can't do anything about."

The exchange grew increasingly hostile.

SAWYER: You don't even sit sometimes and think to yourself, once again, as everyone thinks you must, "Why didn't I burn those tapes?"

NIXON: I've covered that also, of course, in my—in my memoirs, and I must say that if—I must get—I must get a—oh, a half a dozen letters a week even now. "Why didn't you burn those tapes?" And the answer is, of course, I should. It should have been done. But the main part is, they should never have been started.

SAWYER: You did say to David Frost, you said that you made horrendous mistakes, ones not worthy of a President, ones that did not meet the standard of excellence that you dreamed of as a young boy. What was the worst one, the thing that you're most sorry about?

NIXON: Oh—oh—oh, the worst one—the—the—I've—covered this in great detail, and I'm not going to go into it any further.

SAWYER: There's no one thing that you had in mind when you were saying that?

NIXON: Well, the—the—well—well, the—if—if—well, it—I th—I've—I've covered it already, but it's—it perhaps is—on reflection, the thing that was the greatest mistake was in failing to concentrate on it the moment I got word on it.

SAWYER: What's it like to be Richard Nixon, and go out and walk into a room? Do you—what do you sense when you walk into a room? Do you ever think, these people are looking at me because I resigned, or that—you—

NIXON: No, I never look back. I never did look back. And people are very friendly. You—you have to realize that people who reach the highest levels in public life don't become obsessed with themselves, and thinking, "Oh, my God, what are people going to be thinking of me," and all that sort of thing. If they do, they're never going to be great leaders.

SAWYER: You also said to David Frost, you said, "I let down my friends, I let down the country, I let down an opportunity I had for projects that would have built a lasting peace; and I let the American people down, and I have to carry that burden with me the rest of my life." Does that burden get heavier or lighter?

NIXON: Now that says it all, right there, and, as far as I am concerned, having said it then, I'm not going to say it again now.

SAWYER: Could I get some phrases again? John Mitchell.

NIXON: Well, I think I've covered enough now, so we'll—I—I think we'll—

SAWYER: How about John Dean?

NIXON: No comment.

SAWYER: You won't even say whether the burden, year by year, gets heavier or lighter?

NIXON: No (pauses) I've—I've already pointed out that I'm not looking back.

The camera switched off. Nixon smiled tightly at Sawyer and rubbed his hands together, as he did when he was nervous. "Well," he said, "you got it?"

When Sawyer returned to her office, a message was awaiting her. The dinner was canceled.

In Washington, meanwhile, the man who had done so much to make Nixon's reemergence possible was on the verge of losing his job.

Alexander Haig, it had become increasingly obvious, had never been cut out to be one of the team players of the Reagan administration. He had tried to get along, to swallow his ego and be the good soldier Nixon had wanted him to be. And for a time the lowered-voices approach seemed to be working. With the departure from the White House of Richard Allen, and his replacement as national security adviser by William Clark, a California judge who was both Reagan's longtime friend and Haig's deputy at State, the waters that had been so turbulent the whole of 1981 temporarily calmed. But nothing substantively had changed, and during the last few weeks, there had been a series of new disputes, some petty, some serious, and Reagan had at last decided that he had had enough.

The breaking point came during a state visit by Menachem Begin in late June, not long after the Israeli invasion of Lebanon, and when U.S.–Israeli relations were at an all-time low. Despite the troubles with the Israelis, Haig, alone among Reagan's foreign policy advisers, urged that the United States refrain from public criticism, lest Begin become even more intransigent. Reagan agreed. But within twenty-four hours the White House issued a statement calling on the Israelis not to attack Beirut and to resume talks on West Bank autonomy as soon as possible.

Enraged, Haig summoned Clark to the State Department to read him a long list of grievances, covering everything from Clark's private meetings with the Saudi ambassador to the naming of George Bush as the head of the U.S. delegation to the recent funeral of King Khalid. A line had to be drawn somewhere, Haig said, and he was drawing it. In fact, he might just resign when he saw the President the next morning.

While Clark returned to the White House to report to Reagan what had transpired, Haig phoned Nixon in New York.

Since the onset of Haig's most recent round of troubles, the two of them had been talking even more frequently than usual. Recently they had also met secretly in New York at Tricia's apartment. All of their conversations were nearly the same. Haig would complain, say how he couldn't take it anymore and was thinking of resigning. Then, soothingly, Nixon would assure him and convince him to stay on. So it went this time. Again Haig railed against his enemies in the White House, recounting how he had told Clark he might quit, and again Nixon advised him to be patient. Grudgingly, Haig agreed, and by the next morning, Thursday, June 24, he had decided to remain at his post.

In the meantime Reagan had been thinking things over as well. He was disturbed by Clark's report of Haig's threats and weary of the troubles from his secretary of state. If, as Clark predicted, Haig submitted his resignation at their next meeting, he had decided he would accept it.

He was thus taken aback when Haig came into the Oval Office Thursday morning and announced that while he had a letter of resignation in his pocket, he had decided not to submit it. Instead, he handed Reagan a four-page letter outlining the same complaints he had made to Clark the day before.

The rest of that day and into the night, Reagan puzzled over what to do. So long as Haig remained it was apparent that the situation was not going to improve. Reluctantly he decided to force the issue.

Early the next morning, Friday, June 25, the President called Baker, Deaver and Clark into his office and instructed them to begin immediately drafting a statement accepting Haig's resignation. Reagan said he would inform Haig of his fate after the weekly NSC lunch that afternoon. In the meantime, Deaver was to contact George Shultz, who was attending a business meeting in London, to ask whether he would agree to be Haig's replacement.

Unaware of what was about to occur, Haig was good-humored and bantering during the NSC lunch. As the meal was breaking up, Reagan motioned him aside. Still unsuspecting, Haig followed Reagan into the executive chamber and settled himself into a chair. Reagan reached across the desk and handed him the statement accepting his resignation. Haig read it in silence. When he finished he told Reagan he accepted his decision with no rancor. The secretary then got up, shook hands and walked out of the room. As the door closed behind him, Reagan buzzed for his secretary and asked her to get Nixon on the phone.

He reached him in Paris, where Nixon was stopping over on the way to Eastern Europe. Nixon expressed no surprise when Reagan informed him of Haig's firing. He told Reagan he understood, and, if that was the President's decision, he was not going to second guess it. Shultz, perhaps, was more plodding than Haig, but he was nothing if not a team player. Reagan wouldn't have the problems with him that he had had with Haig.

Afterward, Nixon phoned Haig to commiserate. He then called in the press. "I happen to be one of the few who know both Shultz and Haig, perhaps better than anyone else," Nixon announced. "Secretary Shultz will carry on. He will have his differences from Haig's policy, perhaps a shade of a difference in the Mideast, although not nearly as great as some have indicated. But he's going to carry on and be a very effective Secretary of State. If there has been any sniping or guerrilla warfare against the Secretary of State, as Secretary Haig has indicated, let me tell you, you're not going to see anything publicly about it from Secretary Shultz. He will not tolerate it. That will stop."

Having conferred his blessings on Shultz, Nixon departed for Prague, where Haig had helped arrange a series of meetings for him with senior government officials. From there, he went on to Bucharest, then Sofia, Budapest, Vienna and London, before heading home, a total of seven countries in thirteen days.

A month later Nixon was on the go again, bound for China and five days of talks with the newest set of Peking leaders. For the Chinese, there was an element of nostalgia to his journey—September marked the tenth anniversary of Nixon's first visit—but, as far as Nixon was concerned, the trip was strictly business. Mrs. Nixon, whose health had taken a mild turn for the worse, had remained at home, and Nixon kept the sightseeing and banqueting to a diplomatic minimum. Instead, he spent virtually all of his time in Peking closeted in talks, urging the Chinese to be more patient with Reagan and explaining the realities of right-wing

American politics. "They [the Chinese] know very well we have no designs on them [like] the Soviet Union [does], and consequently, they know they need us," Nixon told a reporter after one of the sessions. "They aren't stupid. They know we are still the richest country in the world. They know that potentially we are the most powerful country in the world. And they know that without us, they would be down the tube."

By the time Nixon returned to New York, the first copies of his latest book, *Leaders*, were on the stands. Apart from such tidbits as the brand of Brezhnev's masseuse's perfume (Arpege) and a colloquy with Khrushchev over which smelled worse, pig or horse manure, Nixon's portraits of various postwar figures revealed little about them that was not already known. Stylistically, his aphorisms on leadership were more in the manner of Curt Gowdy than Charles de Gaulle. "Many good hitters hit for the averages, trying for singles in order to push their averages toward .300," a typical passage went. "But these are not the great hitters who make headlines and draw thousands into the park. The great hitters, the Reggie Jacksons, are the ones who hit in the clutch, who go not for the averages but for the game-winning home-runs." So, too, Nixon continued, "The leader must organize his life and concentrate his energies with one overriding goal in mind: to make the big plays."

Leaders itself may have been a cheap hit, but it was revealing about Nixon. The leaders he had singled out for admiration, the de Gaulles and Adenauers, Yoshidas and Nkrumahs, Sukarnos and Churchills, had like himself "walked in the wilderness," been turned out of power, exiled or imprisoned.* But like himself they had been strengthened by the very circumstances of their adversity. They had waited, plotted, planned and reflected—behaved as Richard Nixon.

"The greats," as Nixon termed them, were not "the guy down the street or the man next door." Frequently, they were "cold . . . remote . . . brutally tough at times in order to do [their] job[s] . . . never informal, even with [their] close friends . . . mysterious . . . contradictory . . . enigmatic." They attained their positions by "struggling" and "fighting" for them, and they aroused "great controversies" and made "bitter enemies." They took "bold but calculated" risks and they didn't "spend much time fretting about decisions once they are past, wondering whether they were right." Because of who they were and what they did, they realized that mistakes were inevitable, and having made them, learned

---

* Among the briefer profiles Nixon sketched was that of Italy's first postwar prime minister, Alcide de Gaspari. He included de Gaspari, Nixon told an associate, for two reasons: first, because he had thwarted the Communists from taking power, and second, as Nixon put it, "Having him in will be a plus for the few Italians who can read."

from them without being "compulsive or guilt-ridden." Like Nixon, they put their misdeeds "firmly behind [them]."

Nixon had little use for figures who were "paralyzed" either by contrition or morality. Leadership, he insisted, was "morally neutral" and those to whom it was entrusted "not necessarily good." Approvingly quoting Churchill's maxim that "Those who do not stoop, do not conquer," Nixon noted that even Lincoln, the "supreme idealist," was also a "cold pragmatist" and "total politician" who "broke laws," "violated the Constitution," "usurped arbitrary power" and "trampled individual liberties" in order to save the Union. "His justification," Nixon wrote, "was necessity." Then, in a line reminiscent of the smoking gun conversation with Haldeman, June 23, 1973—"*I don't give a shit what happens; I want you all to stonewall it, let them plead the Fifth Amendment, cover-up or anything else, if it'll save it, save the plan*"—Nixon added, "Whatever the field, the crucial moral questions are, in effect, those of the bottom line."

In other passages, particularly when he seemed to be referring to his own plight, Nixon's tone was less combative. Sorrowfully, he wrote of the "aching" and "yearning," the "almost physical pain," of the leader out of power "who believes that his own judgment is best, even though fallible, and who chafes at seeing lesser men mishandle the reins."

"The final verdict of history is not rendered quickly," Nixon concluded. "It takes not just years but decades or generations to be handed down. Few leaders live to hear the verdict." Referring to Herbert Hoover, another American President who had been "viciously vilified, deserted by his friends and maligned by his enemies," Nixon added: "In the twilight of his life, he stood tall over his detractors. His life illustrated the truth of de Gaulle's favorite line from Sophocles: 'One must wait until the evening, to see how splendid the day has been.' "

The publication of *Leaders* brought with it another promotion campaign, and throughout the fall, Nixon was more active and publicly visible than ever, making the rounds of the morning news shows, dispensing wisdom to the Sunday supplements, arguing foreign policy with the editors of *The Times*. More quietly, he also sent off a number of autographed copies of his book, including one to a former opponent the voters had not treated kindly. The thank-you note that came back was not expected. "History," it read, "will remember you as one of the great peacemakers of the twentieth century." The letter was signed, "George McGovern."

Meanwhile, Nixon continued to be in demand. With an important midterm election coming up, and the Democratic presidential contenders beginning to stir, the appetite for his opinions seemed inexhaustible and so, too, his willingness to provide them. One day he'd been on *Good*

Morning America, praising Jerry Brown's "ruthlessness," and terming Walter Mondale "a bottle of champagne the day after—just dead, nothing comes out." Another morning, he'd be on *Today*, analyzing the recent election returns and assuring viewers that "[Reagan's] not stupid. . . . He isn't going to just dig in his feet and be remembered as the veto President." Still another, he'd be chatting with a newspaper reporter, giving Reagan pointers on foreign affairs and saying of the President, "He gives me a call. I criticize him privately and praise him publicly." During one especially eventful day, following Brezhnev's death, he appeared on six separate network telecasts, including one hosted by his old adversary, Dan Rather, with whom Nixon teased and joked.

Provided the audience was sufficiently large, Nixon seemed willing to discuss almost anything, even Watergate. Yes, he conceded, in an interview with the twelve-million-circulation *Family Weekly*, he should have burned the tapes, and, looking back, he guessed he was "very naive" not to have destroyed them. But, Nixon added, "The tapes were put in there for the purpose of being available to the Presidential Library, for historical reasons. As you know," he went on, launching into a familiar refrain, "Eisenhower had some tapes; Kennedy . . . there are 200 reels of tapes at the Kennedy Library; Johnson had a huge taping system there, in the Johnson Library. And we had ours, only for the last two years." Nixon stopped to laugh, as if suddenly struck by the absurdity of his rationale. "But I suppose that's the last taping there will be."

Inevitably, there were moments, usually when he was alone, when Nixon's mood was not as good. One day while doing errands in Saddle River for his wife, he stopped into Oluf Hansen's candy store. As he selected his purchases—a pound of handmade chocolate-walnut fudge for himself, a box of soft-center creams for Pat—Nixon seemed dejected. Hansen looked up from the packages he was wrapping and said, "Mr. President, for what it's worth, I voted for you, and I'd vote for you again." Nixon broke into a smile, reached across the counter and gave Hansen a bear hug.

The year now passing had marked for Nixon several decade anniversaries: the Watergate break-in in June; the first trip to China in September and now, in November, the reelection to the presidency. To celebrate the occasion, Ron Walker, a former Nixon advance man, began putting together a reunion.

Originally, he intended the gathering only for "the roadrunners," as the former advance men called themselves. But, as knowledge of the party spread, more and more veterans of the Nixon wars asked to attend, until Walker decided to throw it open to everyone. He sent Nixon an invitation, and to his surprise the former President immediately accepted.

. . . .

Togged out in their tuxedos and evening gowns, two hundred of the men and women who had made the Nixon administration what it was gathered in the grand ballroom of the Washington Marriott the night of November 6, ten years to the day since Nixon's reelection. Nearly everyone who had been someone appeared to be there, from Henry Kissinger and John Mitchell, to Gordon Strachan and Dwight Chapin, to Charles Colson and Egil Krogh.

Under a huge blue banner that read WELCOME CLASS OF '72, the guests embraced and backslapped, gossiped and swapped tales. Pat Buchanan related that he had interviewed Nixon that afternoon for Ted Turner's Cable News Network, and that "the old man" had seemed fine. Sharp as ever, Buchanan said he was, telling Reagan to stick by his guns on the tax cut and advising Cap Weinberger to "bite the bullet" on defense. In another part of the room, Ed Nixon, the youngest of the Nixon brothers, was describing how Dick had changed the last few years. "Writing has done a great deal for him," Ed said. "For anyone who's had the experience of the sort he's been through, you reflect. And, once it's written down, you don't have to look at it anymore."

Suddenly, at the bottom of an escalator, there was Nixon himself. He smiled broadly as a cheer went up, and continued smiling and waving as the escalator carried him to the ballroom floor. Nixon grabbed an outstretched hand, then another. *Good to see you. Good to see you. Hi. Thanks for coming.* One of his former aides, recently divorced, approached with a date. "A new girl, huh?" Nixon gibed. Then, looking at the aide's young woman, he added, "Your friend here was a real stand-up guy." He looked back at the aide and winked. "His only problem was that he wasn't tough enough."

Ziegler, double-chinned and fatter than his White House days, spotted his former deputy, Jerry Warren, standing at that bar. Warren was still trim and athletic, and his job—editor in chief of the *San Diego Union*—was one of the most important in American journalism. Ziegler had not been so lucky. He was a lobbyist now in suburban Virginia, promoting the virtues of the National Association of Truck Stop Operators. When he greeted his ex-subordinate, there was a trace of envy in his voice.

"Look at this," boomed Ziegler, "the editor of the *San Diego Union* is leaning over the bar."

Warren smiled wanly. "Ron," he said, "you were never this loose before. What happened?"

"Well," Ziegler smirked, "I have a better staff now."

Ordering a drink, Ziegler walked over to a roped-off area where the press was confined. He was fine, Ziegler said; no, he didn't miss the action of the old days at all. "There's nothing more exciting than a truck stop," he smiled. Finally, someone asked him about Watergate. "I don't think Watergate is ever really put behind any of us," Ziegler answered, making a play on the words he had repeated so often to the White House press. "It occurred. It's a fact. But some of the duplicity of the period is past, some of the hypocrisy of the period is past. People are beginning to put it in a different light."

The meal was about to begin. Ziegler walked back toward the now-jammed tables, looking for a place to sit. Brennan, with whom he'd nearly come to blows during a recent meeting of former Nixon aides, turned his back to him. Others in the room began looking at their plates. Warren felt sorry for him. Ron seemed very lost; his wife Nancy was knotting her hands nervously. Clearing a place, Warren motioned him over.

Almost immediately he regretted it. Ziegler was caustic throughout the meal. Several times Warren tried to steer the conversation in more placid directions, recalling some of the jollier times that had occurred in the White House, but Ziegler would have none of it. He was drinking, and the alcohol was not improving his mood. He belittled Warren, recounting his various screw-ups. Angrily, he talked of the press, how it had always been out to get them. They were bastards, sons of bitches; none of them, himself especially, ever had a chance. A pall fell over the table. It was a night for fellowship and celebration. Around the rest of the room, people were laughing and merry. The bad old days were behind them; only Ron wouldn't let them go.

When dinner was over, Walker delivered a short speech. After congratulating Nixon for being "one of the greatest statesmen of our time," he looked down the dais at Kissinger and added playfully, "I hope you will agree with that, Henry." The crowd, including Kissinger and Nixon, roared. Later, Rose Woods took a turn at the mike. "To Richard Nixon," she said, offering a toast. "The most honorable man this country has ever produced."

Finally, Nixon rose to speak. He began by thanking all of them for everything they had done for him through the years. "Thirty-two years ago," he joked, "I could never have gone anywhere, even the bathroom, without an advance man." Turning serious, he talked about the challenge they faced in the West, the various dangers that menaced them every day. But they should take heart; life was never as dark as it appeared to be. The Democrats had given the Republicans a licking in the last congressional elections, but it could have been worse. "Instead of getting a knockout," as Nixon put it, "all they got was a split decision." It was a sign, he continued, that things were turning up. By 1984, when they went out to advance again, interest rates, taxes, inflation and unemployment would all be down.

He concluded by reading Teddy Roosevelt's speech to the Sorbonne, the same passage he had read to them that morning in the White House East Room, August 9, 1974.

> . . . The credit belongs to the man who is actually in the arena, whose face is marred by dust and sweat and blood; who . . . at best knows in the end the triumphs of high achievement and who at the worst, if he fails, at least fails while daring greatly; so that his place shall never be with those cold and timid souls who know neither victory nor defeat. . . .

As Nixon took off his reading glasses, the room was very still. Many of those who had been listening had tears in their eyes. Nixon paused and looked out over the room. "None of you are timid souls."

At the piano someone began playing "God Bless America." Joining hands, the Class of '72 stood and began singing, rocking gently to the beat of the music. Nixon, who had been singing along with the rest of them, went to the piano and played the hymn again. Then, flashing a smile, Nixon called out, "Is it anyone's birthday?" It was, so Nixon played "Happy Birthday." He asked for requests, heard one he liked and struck into an up-tempo version of "Let Me Call You Sweetheart." "More!" they shouted. "More!"

The sound of the cry carried out into the night: more, more, more.

Years before, while still in exile in San Clemente, Nixon had told David Frost that resignation was "worse than death."

"After a man is President," he had said, "there is nothing he can do."

Time and his own grit had proved him wrong. Against the odds, against virtually every prediction, Richard Nixon had survived and, in enduring, found there was, after all, something he could do.

The role he had carved out for himself—that of occasional sage and elder statesman—did not put him at the center of power, but at its periphery. He advised on rather than created policy; suggested actions rather than ordered them; hoped for outcomes instead of willing them. And even then the ringing telephone bearing his counsel was not always answered.

It was an unaccustomed position for a man who had struggled so long to attain, and fought so hard to keep, "the ultimate," as in boyish awe he described the office he had occupied and abused. And yet in his own, curious, peculiar way, Richard Nixon was content. He joked about being "the only American over thirty-five" ineligible to run for President, and laughed at the rumors that he might be appointed to fill out the term of New Jersey's ABSCAM-convicted senator, Harrison Williams. "I'm not running for any office," he grinned at an interviewer in late 1982.

"I'm not seeking any office. And I have no obligations to any office." What he had, Richard Nixon said, was freedom, and "I prefer that."

The wasted, beaten figure who returned to California in August of 1974 had not felt such ease, nor would he have allowed himself to confess it to a reporter. That he did now was a measure of how far he had come, of how much he had changed. He was less driven, more reflective and relaxed, not so haunted by the sound of passing trains that whistled in the night. In other respects though, Nixon remained the same, still awkward and jealous, still a trifle unsure, still all those things that made him so different from other men.

With friends, he railed about his enemies—the "liberal establishment," the "goddam Ivy Leaguers," the "fucking academics"—no less fiercely or self-pityingly than he had on the White House tapes. They were "hypocrites," he told one visitor, "little bastards . . . trash . . . sanctimonious frauds . . . people who couldn't butter a piece of toast." And because he wasn't one of them, because he wasn't "pampered, rotten, spoiled," because he hadn't been "brought up to ask people to comfort or do things for me," because he was, as he put it, "culturally different," he believed, as he always had, that they hated him.

He claimed, as ever, that it didn't bother him, that he didn't worry about being detested by those who, he said, mocking them with every syllable, "always cloaked their opposition in such *high* and *mighty*, such *lofty, idealistic* terms." He was who he was, a "tough guy" who understood "the real world," who didn't agonize over "this stupid business about there being 'good wars' and 'bad wars,'" or, indeed, any of "all that mumbo-jumbo the trendies focus on and mutter about and which amounts to absolute zero." He was a leader who simply did, and having done it, didn't "confide and whimper and spill everything." "I prefer the Catholic way," Nixon told one visitor in 1982. "Go to a priest and confess your frailties, but do it quietly, no flim-flam. I think you should be responsible, keep your troubles to yourself."

He could have changed, "taken the easy way," as he put it, been more approachable, likable and contrite. But he rejected that—"these empty, slobbering show-biz gestures" he called them—as he did anything which, by his lights, seemed less than "manly" and "strong." "What in the hell is admirable about that?" he demanded of a friend who suggested that he surrender to his gentler impulses. "It's being weak and, even more, self-centered."

It was that "refusing to grovel" that framed his attitudes about the scandal that had cost him the presidency. Of his essential blamelessness he remained convinced, as sure as ever of the words he had spoken to his aides in 1973. "Ten years from now," he had said then, "Watergate will be a few paragraphs in the history books. Fifty years from now, it will be a footnote." Nothing that had occurred since the resignation shaded his opinion. He was not troubled by the evidence, or by the overwhelming vote to impeach him, or even by the polls that showed that a decade after the break-in, the same margin of Americans thought him guilty as ever and unworthy of playing a role in public life.* "Remember Lot's wife," he always said. "Never look back."

January 9, 1983, was a normal day in the life of Richard Nixon. He rose early, as was his custom, and by 9:00 A.M. was in his library, reading and going through papers. That afternoon he watched on television as his old favorites, the Washington Redskins, beat the Dallas Cowboys for the Eastern Division Championship of the National Football League. The Redskins' triumph left him in an exceptionally good mood; among other things it helped ease the realization that today was his seventieth birthday.

* The poll, commissioned by *Newsweek* magazine and ABC News to commemorate the tenth anniversary of the Watergate break-in, revealed that if anything most Americans' attitudes had hardened about Nixon's guilt. When the question was asked, "Do you think that Nixon's actions regarding Watergate were, or were not, serious enough to warrant his resignation?" 75 percent answered that they were—versus 65 percent who thought so in August 1974. Significantly, most of that increase derived from the "don't know" column, indicating a growing perception of Nixon's guilt, rather than a shift in previously formed attitudes.

Conversely, the poll also recorded more sympathy for Ford's decision to pardon Nixon. In June 1976 when the question was asked, "Do you think that Ford did the right thing [in pardoning Nixon] or the wrong thing?" 55 percent answered that he had done the wrong thing. When the same question was asked five years later, the percentage had shrunk to 46 percent.

As for whether Nixon should play an active role in public life, either as an adviser or ambassador, 32 percent answered that yes, he should, while 62 percent replied that no, he shouldn't.

But perhaps the most interesting finding of the poll was the general cynicism it uncovered. More than a third of those questioned said they believed it "very likely" that another Watergate-style scandal could erupt again, and an even higher proportion said such a recurrence was "somewhat likely." Only one person in five said that the extensive, high-level corruption typified by Watergate was "not at all likely" to happen again.

On the question of whether Nixon's culpability was worse than that of other Presidents, respondents split along party lines. By a margin of 51 to 35, Democrats agreed with the statement that "what Nixon did in the Watergate affair was worse than what other Presidents have done," while Republicans, by a margin of 67 to 23, thought the statement "other Presidents engaged in the same kind of activities that forced Nixon out of office" was correct. There was less partisanship on the question of whether Nixon should return to public life. Here, the overall response was yes, 28 percent; no, 64 percent. Among Republicans, 53 percent opposed a Nixon return, while 38 percent favored it. When the same question was put to Democrats, 76 percent answered no while 16 percent answered yes. Independents opposed Nixon's return to public life by a margin of 2 to 1.

The poll also found that majorities continued to believe that Nixon should have been tried for his alleged crimes (56 percent to 35 percent), and more narrowly (47 percent to 45 percent) that Ford was wrong in granting Nixon a pardon. Here again, though, there was considerable partisanship. When the pardon question was asked of Republicans, 62 percent favored it, versus the 60 percent of Democrats who opposed it. Independents were evenly divided.

He didn't like birthdays and even less the fuss that was always made over them, but reluctantly he had agreed to mark this one. It wasn't every day that a man celebrated a seventieth birthday, especially when not many years before there were doubts whether he'd live to see another one. True, the years had taken a toll. His hair was far grayer than it had been when he was in the White House, his jowls heavier, his waistline just a bit thicker. But still and all he looked and felt improbably well. He intended to remain that way, he told the callers who phoned their congratulations. He still had plans and a lot of living to do. He wanted to be around to see what the twenty-first century was like, he said. Come the year 2000, he'd "only be eighty-seven" and the Nixons were a sturdy bunch. He had a grandmother on his mother's side who lived to be ninety-four, a great-grandmother who'd survived till ninety-six. If he took care of himself, followed his doctor's orders, there was no reason why he wouldn't make it. He'd like that, living until then. The world would be so much different; it would be interesting to see.

That evening, Pat hosted a dinner party in his honor: small and intimate, just the girls, their husbands and the grandchildren. There was good food and fine wine and easy conversation. Afterward, when the guests were gone, the former President went through some of his birthday cards. Pat Hillings, his old chum from Whittier, had written an especially touching note, and later, Nixon penned a reply.

"Always dream of the future," the difficult, gifted man who had been thirty-seventh President of the United States wrote. "Never think of the past."

A Note on Sources

Richard Nixon did not cooperate in the making of this book, insofar as he did not grant me an interview. At the same time, he put no barriers in my path. On numerous occasions, sources checked with him or his staff before agreeing to talk to me. And, so far as I am able to discover, the President neither encouraged nor discouraged their participation. Likewise, it was with his at least tacit acquiescence that a number of members of his senior staff, past and present, consented to be interviewed.

The interviews themselves were conducted over a two-year period between the summer of 1981 and the summer of 1983. In all, over three hundred persons were contacted, and, of that number, some 174 provided their insights and reminiscences. Geographically, the scope of the inquiry encompassed twenty-one states and six foreign countries. Of those who were interviewed, roughly three-quarters spoke either on the record or on a not-for-attribution basis, while the remaining quarter spoke on background only. (A complete listing of those sources who allowed their names to be used is contained in the Acknowledgments.) In several cases, sources were offered the option of having their quotes read to them in context before publication, with the right to strike quotes from the final typescript, if they wished. No quotations were thus deleted.

In addition to interviews, I relied, sometimes heavily, on previously published materials. This included the running account of President Nixon's post-resignation activities as reported in *The New York Times*, the *Washington Post*, the *Los Angeles Times*, the *San Diego Union* and *Tribune*, the *San Clemente Sun-Post*; the wire services of The Associated Press and United Press International and *Time* and *Newsweek* magazines. Other periodicals that proved useful in accounting for certain portions of the President's life since the resignation were: *The New Republic*; *The National Review*; the *Christian Science Monitor*; *The Wall Street Journal*; the *New York Daily News*; the *New York Post*; the *Bergen (NJ) Record*; *The Economist*; *Le Monde*; *Congressional Quarterly*; *Facts on File*; *Parade*; the *Ladies' Home Journal*; *McCall's*; *Life*; *The Atlantic Monthly*; *The Village Voice*; the *Daily Telegraph* (London); *The Times* (London); and *New Times*. Transcripts of the President's major postresignation television interviews were provided by CBS, ABC

and NBC. The quoted exchanges during the Halperin and Dobrovir depositions were taken from court records of each proceeding. Finally, I had access to
unpublished notes and materials from one major news organization, which has
requested anonymity. (A detailed accounting of how all these materials were
employed is contained in the following notes section.)

A number of books and government documents (listed separately in the
Bibliography) were of enormous value throughout the manuscript. A good
portion of my knowledge of the pardon, for instance, was drawn from Gerald
Ford's memoirs, A Time to Heal, and from Robert Hartmann's account of the
Ford presidency, Palace Politics, while David Frost's "I Gave Them a Sword"
helped lay much of the groundwork for my understanding of the Frost interviews. The Watergate material was drawn from a number of sources, including Carl Bernstein and Bob Woodward's All the President's Men and The
Final Days, as well as J. Anthony Lukas' Nightmare, which is unmatched in
pulling all the narrative threads of the scandal together.

Both during and after the writing of the manuscript, extraordinary care
was paid to fact checking, not only against the written record, but with princi-
pals themselves. Portions of the manuscript were shown to several friends and
associates of the President prior to publication, with the understanding that
their comments would be advisory only. In addition, President Nixon himself
responded to checking queries through Nick Ruwe, his chief of staff. Finally,
Edward Cox, the President's son-in-law, graciously offered to resolve, so far as
he was able, any questions I might have as to fact or tone. Though Mr. Cox
did not grant me a formal interview, his assistance in this regard helped clear
up several important matters.

Frequently in this book, I write of persons, including President Nixon,
"thinking" or "wondering" or "feeling" without direct attribution as to source.
This narrative technique raises an obvious question: how do I know what
people were thinking, wondering or feeling, especially when they were alone?
The simple answer is that they either told me, or, in a number of instances,
told others, who subsequently related those emotions to me. So far as con-
fidentiality allows, I have reported the source of these conversations in the
notes.

Though this is not an "investigative" book per se, I have followed
standard reportorial procedures in reconstructing events that by their nature
are either controversial or embarrassing to the parties involved; namely, by
relying on the recollections of at least two sources. In certain instances, notably
President Nixon's revealing conversation with Kenneth Clawson, this was impossible, and, like any reporter, I have had to trust my instincts. In the Clawson
case, the contents of the conversation were reported by Clawson himself in a
long article for the Washington Post. Though Clawson declined to grant me
an interview, his respect, loyalty and affection for the President have long been
a matter of public record, and I had no reason to doubt the accuracy of his
account. Moreover, aides and friends of the former President reported similar
exchanges to me.

Finally, except where explicitly stated, the judgments and opinions rendered in this volume are my own.

Notes

1. HOMEWARD

13
The words were sharp, almost a shout: Woodward and Bernstein, *The Final Days*, 453.
13
"I don't know if I'm going to be able": author's interview with senior Nixon aide, not for attribution, February 11, 1983.
13
Mrs. Nixon's appearance: described, Woodward and Bernstein, *Final Days*, 453.
13–14
Nixon's farewell to the staff in the East Room: transcript quoted, UPI, August 9, 1974.
14
Sawyer background, feelings on Air Force One: author's interview with senior Nixon aide, not for attribution, July 19, 1983.
14
Grier and Quinlin crying: author's interviews with Anne Grier Willard, December 20, 1982, June 3, 1983.
14
Gannon watching: author's interview with Frank Gannon, July 12, 1983.
14–15
Albertazzie's flight preparations: terHorst and Albertazzie, *The Flying White House*, 35–43.
15
"Don't bother the President": quoted, terHorst and Albertazzie, 38.
15
"The balls of him": author's interview with Colonel Ralph Albertazzie, August 15, 1983.
15
Description of disembarkation from helicopter: author's interview with Ronald Ziegler, August 4, 1983.
16
Air Force One takeoff: terHorst and Albertazzie, 41.

16

Traces of his presence already were being stripped away: *Time*, August 19, 1974.

16

Ford's feelings about suitability of inaugural address: author's interview with Robert Hartmann, August 5, 1983.

16

"You won't have a lot of spare time"; "You look like you need a drink"; "To the President": quoted, Hartmann, 169–70.

17

Johnson's encounter with Jarriel; Brokaw soothes her: author's interview with Judy Johnson, April 9, 1983.

17

Ziegler's conversations with Haldeman and Warren: quoted, terHorst and Albertazzie, 45, 47; author's interview with Gerald Warren, July 1, 1982.

17

Bull sipped on a bourbon: terHorst and Albertazzie, 46.

17–18

Brennan's feelings about Nixon's resignation: terHorst and Albertazzie, 46.

18

Bull tells Cox papers will be shipped to California: terHorst and Albertazzie, 48.

18

"I'm quitting": quoted, terHorst and Albertazzie, 48.

18

Gannon's letterwriting: Gannon interview.

18

Marine Band was playing mood music: Hartmann, 171.

18

Haig gives Kissinger Nixon letter of resignation: *Time*, August 19, 1974.

18–19

Simmons' encounter with Nixon: author's interview with Sergeant Lee Simmons, August 24, 1983; also quoted by terHorst and Albertazzie, 48–49.

19

Air Force One's position at noon: terHorst and Albertazzie, 51.

19

Bible opened to third chapter of Proverbs: Reeves, *A Ford, Not a Lincoln*, 63.

19

Air Force One lunch menu: terHorst and Albertazzie, 51.

20

Ziegler's meeting with Nixon: author's interview with senior Nixon aide, not for attribution, July 19, 1983.

20

Poor Ron: Bull interview, June 28, 1982.

20–21

Nixon's conversation with Albertazzie: Albertazzie interview; quoted, terHorst and Albertazzie, 54–55.

21

"I see you remembered . . .": Gannon interview.

21

"It certainly smells better back here": quoted, terHorst and Albertazzie, 55.

21

Albertazzie considers future: terHorst and Albertazzie, 55.

21
"Al, what do you think of that?": quoted, Reeves, *A Ford, Not a Lincoln*, 67.
22
"Look out your window": Gannon interview.
22
Description of El Toro crowd: author's interview with Patricia Reilly Hitt, January 18, 1983.
22
"it appears that we're here": author's interview with senior Nixon aide, not for attribution, September 1, 1982.
22
Crowd sings "God Bless America": Hitt interview.
22
Bull and Simmons embrace: author's interview with Simmons; terHorst and Albertazzie, 59.
22
"I was with him"; "Tell him we still love him": Gannon interview.
23
Nixon's remarks to El Toro crowd: quoted, terHorst and Albertazzie, 59.
23
"We covered a lot of miles"; "I am, too": quoted, terHorst and Albertazzie, 60.
23
TerHorst press briefing: quoted, transcript, Press Office of the President, August 9, 1974.
23–24
Nixon arrival at Coast Guard station: author's interviews with Paul Presley, July 22, and August 5, 1983; Johnny Grant, January 11, 1983.
24
Smell of burned paper: Hartmann, 173.
24
Hillings, Sears and Ruwe at Lafayette Park: author's interview with Pat Hillings, August 14, 1982.
24–25
Mrs. Nixon arranging personal possessions in Nixon bedroom: author's interview with senior Nixon aide, not for attribution, April 6, 1983.
25
Nixon walks to the bluff: author's interview with senior Nixon aide, not for attribution, April 6, 1983.

2. THE FIRST MONTH

26
Abplanalp and Rebozo visit Nixon: *San Diego Tribune*, August 12, 1974.
26
Rebozo and Nixon take drive: *San Clemente Sun-Post*, August 13, 1974.
26
Nixons and Rebozo picnic on the beach: AP, August 13, 1974.
27
"a lot has happened": quoted, author's interview with Robert Finch, August 28, 1982.

27
"I appreciate how you handled that business"; "Think nothing of it"; "I really mean it": quoted, author's interview with Herb Klein, January 21, 1983.

27
Nixon meeting with Hitt: Hitt interview.

28
Gulley's transport of materials and visit to San Clemente: author's interview with Bill Gulley, June 10, 1983.

28
Gulley meets with Ziegler: Gulley interview.

28
Gulley meets with Brennan and Bull: Gulley interview.

29
Brennan promises to have marines meet each of the flights: Gulley interview.

29
Ziegler's predeparture instructions to staff: Gannon interview.

29
Activities of staff on Monday: Gannon interview.

29
"There is no news": quoted, report from correspondent to major news organization, August 12, 1974.

29–30
History and description of Casa Pacifica: report from correspondent to major news organization, January 30, 1975.

30
"Handsome and kind": quoted, David, *The Lonely Lady of San Clemente*, 13–14.

30
Nixon calling aides at home: author's interview with senior Nixon aide, not for attribution, July 9, 1983.

30
"I've called you here to discuss": author's interview with senior Nixon aide, not for attribution, July 9, 1983.

30
"hurt people's feelings": quoted, Reeves, *A Ford, Not a Lincoln*, 75.

30
"I think we have a fine team here": quoted, Ford, *A Time to Heal*, 131.

30
Hartmann fires speechwriters: Ford, *A Time to Heal*, 148.

30
"You don't suspect ill motives": quoted, Ford, *A Time to Heal*, 148.

31
Nixon papers stored at Andrews hangar: Gulley interview.

31
Gulley's shipments and Marsh's interception: Gulley interview; see also Gulley, *Breaking Cover*, 229.

31
"Nixon people burning crap like crazy": Hersh, "The Pardon," *The Atlantic Monthly*, August 1983.

31
Becker discovers trucks, meets with Haig: Hersh, "The Pardon."

31–32
Gulley's meeting with Nixon: Gulley interview; see also Gulley, 115–17.

32

Nixon's reaction to Ford on Rockefeller nomination: Ford, 146; Persico, *The Imperial Rockefeller*, 246.

32–33

Nixon's dislike of Rockefeller: Persico, 242.

33

Phone call to Reagan: report from correspondent to major news organization, October 16, 1974.

33

Nixon was put on hold; "Those who served you best": quoted, White, *Breach of Faith*, 342.

33

young people . . . gave Nixon the finger: report from correspondent to major news organization, August 20, 1974.

33

HOME OF THE WESTERN WHITE HOUSE signs stolen: *Time*, August 26, 1974.

33

Bull's search for appropriate stationery: Bull interview.

33

"That depends on who writes the history": quoted, Nixon, *RN: The Memoirs of Richard Nixon*, 1084.

34

Financial difficulties; Cox going over family budget: Hitt interview.

34

a number of literary proposals had already come in: Gannon interview.

34

Description and background of Lazar: *Time*, February 2, 1962; see also Allen, "Swifty Lazar Is a Big Deal," *New York*, July 18, 1983.

34

"The legendary ability to enter a revolving door behind you": Frost, "*I Gave Them a Sword*," 19.

34

Nixon's meeting with Lazar: report from correspondent to major news organization, September 5, 1974.

35

"completely in command": quoted, report from correspondent to major news organization, September 5, 1974.

35

"I just wish the rest of us felt half as up": author's interview with Ken Reich of *Los Angeles Times*, December 23, 1982.

35

Nixon's brooding: author's interview with senior Nixon aide, not for attribution, July 19, 1983.

35–36

Meeting between Gulley and Nixon: Gulley interview; see also Gulley, 230–31.

36

"There are worse things than jail": quoted, Woodward and Bernstein, *The Final Days*, 450.

36

Jaworski explains why he didn't indict Nixon: Jaworski, *The Right and the Power*, 100–101; see also Hersh, "The Pardon."

36

naming him an unindicted coconspirator instead: *The New York Times*, August 11, 1974.

37

"regardless of the position or status of any individual alleged to have violated the law": quoted, *Time*, August 26, 1974.

37

"Would it be just to permit [Nixon] to go untried": *Time*, August 26, 1974.

37

Brooke introduces "sense of the Congress" resolution: *Washington Post*, August 9, 1974.

37

crimes that were punishable . . . by more than thirty years' imprisonment: *Time*, September 2, 1974.

37

Final Judiciary Committee report: *Time*, September 2, 1974.

37

Conversation with Montgomery: author's interview with Congressman G. V. ("Sonny") Montgomery, February 7, 1983.

37

Conversation with Kuykendall: author's interview with Dan Kuykendall, March 1, 1983; see also Doyle, *Not Above the Law*, 349.

38

Nixon weeping: Jaworski, *The Right and the Power*, 222.

3. THE PARDON

39

Ford not Nixon's first choice for vice president: Reeves, *A Ford, Not a Lincoln*, 39–40.

39

"great on the tube": quoted, Stein, "Richard Nixon Goes to a Party," *Esquire*, November 1976.

39

Nixon's assistance to Connally: author's interviews with Harry Dent, December 16, 1982, and June 20, 1983.

39

"A plodder": quoted, Reeves, *A Ford, Not a Lincoln*, 41.

39

"could not fart and chew gum at the same time": quoted, Reeves, *A Ford, Not a Lincoln*, 25.

39

"Can you imagine": quoted, Reeves, *A Ford, Not a Lincoln*, 42.

39

"the damn pen": Woodward and Bernstein, *The Final Days*, 28.

40

"He's been my friend": quoted, Reeves, *A Ford, Not a Lincoln*, 44.

40

"I can say from the bottom": quoted, Reeves, *A Ford, Not a Lincoln*, 55.

40

Buzhardt orders staff to draw up list of all current and potential Watergate defendants; calls Nixon: Hersh, "The Pardon."

40
Buzhardt's meeting with Haig: Woodward and Bernstein, *Final Days*, 325–26.
41
Meeting between Haig and Ford: Woodward and Bernstein, *Final Days*, 326.
41–42
Ford's meeting with Harlow and telephone conversation with Haig: Hartmann, *Palace Politics*, 136–37.
41
"should have taken Haig": quoted, Hartmann, 131.
42
"For God's sake, enough is enough": quoted, Hartmann, 249.
42
Rockefeller appearance on *Meet the Press*: Hartmann, 249.
42–43
Ford's mock press conference with staff: Hartmann, 250–51.
43–44
Price and Garment's conversation, Garment's memo, Price's pardon proclamation, Haig's and Buchen's reaction: *Washington Post*, December 18, 1975; see also Hersh, "The Pardon."
44–45
Ford's press conference: described and quoted, Ford, *A Time to Heal*, 157–58; see also *Report, Watergate Special Prosecution Force*, October 1975, 129–30.
45
Haig talks to Ford after press conference: *Washington Post*, December 18, 1975.
45n
Ford's testimony before the House Judiciary Subcommittee on Criminal Justice: transcript quoted, *U.S. News & World Report*, October 28, 1974.
45n
"Haig spent the day in the White House": quoted, Hersh, "The Pardon."
46
Haig and Kissinger's meeting with Ford: *The New York Times*, September 17, 1974.
46
Laird's phone call to Buchen: author's interview with Melvin Laird, December 1, 1982.
46
"Watergate addiction": quoted, Ford, 160.
46
Eisenhower appeal, "off the deep end": quoted, *The New York Times*, September 14, 1974.
46–47
Ford's meeting with Buchen, Hartmann, Marsh, and Haig: Hartmann, 257–61.
48–49
Jaworski keeping low profile, following opinion polls: Doyle, *Not Above the Law*, 355, 357.
49
"He's in bad shape": quoted, Jaworski, *The Right and the Power*, 222.
49
Jaworski anxious to return to Texas; financial strain of being special prosecutor: Doyle, 349; see also Hersh, "The Pardon."

49
Jaworski examined by doctor; promises staff to stay on until "the big decision" is made: Doyle, 349, 356.
49
more than sufficient evidence: Hersh, "The Pardon."
49
"There are conflicting factors": quoted, Hersh, "The Pardon."
49
Jaworski instructs spokesman to prepare press analysis: Doyle, 355.
49
Jaworski asks Miller to write brief: Ben-Veniste and Frampton, *Stonewall*, 301.
49
Jaworski meets with Buchen: Ben-Veniste and Frampton, 306.
50
"require a delay": quoted, Jaworski, *The Right and the Power*, 241–42.
50
Ruth's memorandum stating areas of potential criminal liability: *The New York Times*, September 11, 1974.
50
Ruth memorandum: quoted, Jaworski, *The Right and the Power*, 229.
50
Quantity of papers and tapes: Ford, *A Time to Heal*, 164.
50
Nixon's illegal claim of $432,000 tax deduction: *The New York Times*, October 29, 1975.
50
Nixon's letter to GSA administrator: quoted, unpublished manuscript by James Reston, Jr.
50–51
TerHorst's August 14 press briefing: quoted, Hartmann, 244–45.
51
Jaworski complains to White House; terHorst admits "error": Hartmann, 246.
51
Ford anxious to get rid of materials: author's interview with Robert Hartmann, August 5, 1983.
51
worries whether the floor would stand the weight: Ford, *A Time to Heal*, 165.
51
Saxbe's recommendation: Ford, *A Time to Heal*, 164.
51
"history will record this": quoted, Hersh, "The Pardon."
51
Buchen and Becker meet with Miller: Ford, *A Time to Heal*, 165.
51
"Look, I think it's important": quoted, Ford, *A Time to Heal*, 165–66.
52
"technical points": Hartmann, 262.
52
"You'll never get it": quoted, Hersh, "The Pardon."
52
"Be very firm out there": quoted, Ford, *A Time to Heal*, 168.

52
Ford's meeting with Buchen, Hartmann, Marsh and Haig: Hartmann, 262.
52–53
"Let's get one thing straight"; Becker threatens to return to Washington: quoted, Ford, *A Time to Heal*, 168–69.
53
Papers and tapes agreement: Hersh, "The Pardon."
53
Becker suspects a leak: Hersh, "The Pardon."
53
Ford accepts papers agreement: Hartmann, 262.
53–54
Nixon's debate with Miller over accepting pardon: the Frost interviews, transcript quoted, *The New York Times*, May 26, 1977.
54
"In accordance with the law": quoted, Hersh, "The Pardon."
54–55
Becker's meeting with Nixon and description to Ford: Ford, *A Time to Heal*, 170–72.
55
Ford refuses to accept Ziegler's telephoned changes in "statement of contrition": Ford, *A Time to Heal*, 173.
56
"You know what this means?": author's interview with Jerald F. terHorst, December 3, 1982; see also terHorst, *Gerald Ford and the Future of the Presidency*, 225–40.
56
Ford attends church, returns to White House: Ford, *A Time to Heal*, 175.
56
Ford additions concerning Nixon's health in pardon speech: Hartmann interview; see also Hartmann, 266; Ford, *A Time to Heal*, 175.
56
"don't you think it's a little early?": quoted, Ford, *A Time to Heal*, 175.
56
TerHorst's resignation: terHorst interview; see also terHorst, 226–27.
56
"Are you set?": Sidey, *Portrait of a President*, 70.
57
"How do you think it went?" "don't ask me"; "I had to get it out of the way": Laird interview; see also Hersh, "The Pardon"; Ford, *A Time to Heal*, 178.

4. FIRE STORM

58
Demonstrators protest against Ford: *Time*, September 16, 1974.
58
"Difficult to understand": quoted, *Time*, September 16, 1974.
58
"Why were we ever stupid enough": quoted, *Time*, September 22, 1974.

58
"embraced the demon"; "a sour smell": quoted, Reeves, A *Ford, Not a Lincoln*, 107.

58
The Times reaction: *The New York Times*, September 9, 1974.

58n
Gallup Poll results: *Time*, September 16, 1974.

59
"If a man who almost wrecked": quoted, *Time*, September 23, 1974.

59
"I have never seen a tournament": quoted, *The New York Times*, September 12, 1974.

60
"The pardon was a big relief": quoted, *San Diego Union*, September 10, 1974.

61
"I don't know if I can make it": quoted, Ziegler interview.

61
"It's amazing my health": quoted, Nixon, *RN: The Memoirs of Richard Nixon*, 1027.

62
"I'll never get out of there alive"; "a ravaged man"; "severe physical strain": quoted, *The New York Times*, September 15, 1974.

62
"not get under any more pressure": quoted, *The New York Times*, September 16, 1974.

62
"The pardon did him no damn good": quoted, UPI, September 16, 1974.

62
"It will require a miracle": quoted, *Newsweek*, September 16, 1974.

62
"Right at the moment": quoted, *Washington Post*, September 13, 1974.

62
"fine, really well": quoted, UPI, September 4, 1974.

62
"still way down": quoted, AP, September 12, 1974.

62–63
"in good health and spirits"; "distraught"; "good"; "super": quoted, *The New York Times*, September 10, 1974.

63
"tanned, invigorated": quoted, *Time*, September 16, 1974.

63
Ford's original budget request: *The New York Times*, August 30, 1974.

63
Shipment of Pat Nixon's jewels: *Washington Post*, August 22, 1977.

65
"Do you feel good?": quoted, Reeves, A *Ford, Not a Lincoln*, 77.

65
Briefing book incident: Hartmann, 203.

65
Buchanan appointment: Hartmann, 205–6.

65

Bugging of Ford's Oval Office: Hartmann, 198–99.

65

"Fuck Haig": quoted, Reeves, *A Ford, Not a Lincoln*, 75.

65

"If you have any influence": quoted, Hersh, "The Pardon."

66

"Had I been asked": quoted, *Time*, September 30, 1974.

66

Ford considers appointing Haig Army chief of staff: Ford, *A Time to Heal*, 185.

66

Resentment of Haig within the Army: Hartmann, 206.

66

Ford appoints Haig commander in chief of NATO: Ford, *A Time to Heal*, 185–86.

66–68

Meeting between Nixon and Clawson: Clawson, "A Loyalist's Memoir," *Washington Post*, August 9, 1979.

68–69

Lungren's visit, September 16; results of examination: *Time*, October 7, 1974.

68

Lungren's background: report from correspondent to major news organization, September 26, 1974; see also *Washington Post*, November 3, 1974.

69

Sirica turns down request to drop charges against Haldeman, Ehrlichman and Mitchell: *The New York Times*, September 12, 1974.

69

Description of Nixon embolism: AP, September 25, 1974; see also *Time*, October 7, 1974.

69

"This is a potentially dangerous situation": quoted, *Long Beach Independent-Press-Telegram*, September 25, 1974.

69

Nixon's mood according to Lungren: quoted, AP, September 25, 1974.

70

"Mr. Nixon's staff has allowed the Medical Center to release the following information": report from correspondent to major news organization, September 25, 1974.

70

The remaining tidbits: UPI, September 25, 1974.

70

a bomb threat and a promise of "salvation": report from correspondent to major news organization, September 25, 1974.

70

Ziegler denies Nixon's depression: quoted, report from correspondent to major news organization, September 26, 1974.

70

Confrontation with photographer: *Washington Post*, October 4, 1974.

70–71

Visit to Nixon from Timothy Cardinal Manning; cardinal's comments: *Long Beach-Independent Press-Telegram*, September 29, 1974.

71

"physically extremely fatigued": quoted, *The New York Times*, October 5, 1974.

71

"I feel great": quoted, *The New York Times*, October 5, 1974.

5. SHOCK

72

following his doctor's orders: *Newsweek*, November 11, 1974.

72

Nixon "pissed": author's interview with Nixon friend, not for attribution, July 22, 1982.

72

"goddam Marine Corps": author's interview with Nixon friend, not for attribution, November 16, 1982.

73

Nixon opinions about Johnson: quoted, Gulley, *Breaking Cover*.

73

"Put a few Jews on your staff": quoted, *Newsweek*, November 11, 1974.

73

$2.5 million memoirs advance: *Time*, August 11, 1975.

73

"He sleeps beautiful": quoted, AP, September 9, 1974.

74

Jesus . . . in the Garden of Gethsemane": Ehrlichman, *Witness to Power*, 411.

74

"deceived, misled and lied": quoted, *Time*, October 28, 1974.

74

"John, you have been my conscience": quoted, Ehrlichman, 390.

74

Lungren affidavit: *San Diego Union*, October 28, 1974.

75

Lungren October 23 visit with Nixon: *Washington Post*, October 30, 1974.

75

Sanitationman greets Nixon: *Newsweek*, November 4, 1974.

75

"99 and $^{44}/_{100}$'s percent blocked": quoted, *Time*, November 11, 1974.

75n

"feeling low"; "poor surgical risks": quoted, *Los Angeles Times*, September 30, 1974.

75n

"pardons can kill": quoted, *Time*, September 30, 1974.

76

Nixon's skin color: report from correspondent to major news organization, October 24, 1974.

76

"This hospital admission was imperative": quoted, *Washington Post*, October 24, 1974.

76
Venogram test results: *The New York Times*, October 24, 1974.
77
Nixon's conference with Barker: author's interview with Dr. Wiley F. Barker, July 27, 1983.
78
"I feel a little silly being here": quoted, *Newsweek*, November 11, 1974.
78
Description of Miles clip: *Los Angeles Times*, October 30, 1974.
78
Account of Nixon surgery: *Newsweek*, November 11, 1974.
78
"The doctors are looking rather pleased": quoted, *Time*, November 11, 1974.
78
"doing well, post-op": quoted, *Time*, November 11, 1974.
78
Account of Nixon slipping into shock: author's interview with senior Nixon aide, not for attribution, December 9, 1982.
79
Tubes inserted into Nixon: *Time*, November 11, 1974.
79
"Richard Nixon received his first liquid nourishment today": quoted, report from correspondent to major news organization, November 6, 1974.
79
"fighting for that man's life": quoted, *Los Angeles Times*, October 30, 1974.
79
Hospital's eleven-line statement: *Los Angeles Times*, October 30, 1974.
80
Medical bulletin from Lungren and Hickman: quoted, *Washington Post*, October 29, 1974.
80
"There is no question about the fact that we almost lost President Nixon": quoted, *San Diego Union*, October 30, 1974.
80
"Are we going to do the surgery now?": author's interview with senior Nixon aide, not for attribution, July 18, 1983.
80
Nixon's postshock condition: *San Diego Union*, November 1, 1974.
80
"There is very real danger lurking": quoted, *Washington Post*, November 1, 1974.
80
"Don't get your hopes up": Gannon interview.
80
Nixon dictation: Gannon interview.
81
Nixon's condition improves: *Long Beach Independent-Press-Telegram*, November 1, 1974.
81
"He is alert": quoted, *Long Beach Independent-Press-Telegram*, November 1, 1974.
81
Ford's visit to Calvin College: Ford, *A Time to Heal*, 200.

81
"If there's no place in politics for human compassion": quoted, Nessen, *It Sure Looks Different from the Inside*, 36.
81–82
Ford telephone conversation with Pat Nixon: Nessen, 34.
82
"He's a very sick man": Ziegler interview.
82
"Nixon squirming uncomfortably in his bed": Nessen, 35.
82
Bull turned the doorknob: Bull interview.
82
"It looks like we're going to do fine": quoted, Ford, *A Time to Heal*, 201.
82
Ford wonders whether he will see Nixon again: Ford, *A Time to Heal*, 202.
82–83
Ziegler's instructions to Nessen: Nessen, 35.
83
"He's obviously a very, very sick man": quoted, *San Diego Union*, November 2, 1974.
83
Nixon's recovery; "terribly physically weak"; develops pneumonia: *Washington Post*, November 8, 1974.
83
"physically quite ill": quoted, *Washington Post*, November 4, 1974.
83
Nixon's blood pressure immediately soared: report from correspondent to major news organization, November 14, 1974.
83–84
Results of doctors' panel examination of Nixon: AP, December 1, 1974.
84
Neal's summation to Watergate jury: quoted , Doyle, 387.
84
Nixon's recollections of slipping into shock: author's interview with senior Nixon aide, not for attribution, July 9, 1983.

6. TRANSITION

85
"If I had known Nixon was taping my conversations": quoted, *Washington Post*, January 3, 1975.
85
Nixon's reaction to Haldeman, Ehrlichman, Mitchell convictions: *Washington Post*, January 3, 1975; *The New York Times*, January 10, 1975.
85
"poor, poor woman": quoted, Gulley, 240.
85n
Trial results for Parkinson and Mardian: *The New York Times*, January 2, 1975.
86
"this business"; "what they are going through"; quoted, Gulley, 240.

86
"this fulfills your doctor's requirements for good health": quoted, Feldman, "The Quiet Courage of Pat Nixon," *McCall's*, May 1975.
86
Haldeman's treatment of Pat Nixon: *The New York Times*, August 14, 1974; see also Smith, "Ordeal! Pat Nixon's Final Days in the White House," *Good Housekeeping*, July 1976.
86
Mrs. Nixon blames Haldeman for troubles: *Newsweek*, March 3, 1975.
86
"I never had time to think about who I wanted to be": quoted, Steinem, *Outrageous Acts and Everyday Rebellions*, 241.
86
Brennan joke about instructing Nixon how to kiss wife: Woodward and Bernstein, *The Final Days*, 165.
86
"the thief": quoted, author's interview with senior member of Nixon staff, not for attribution, July 19, 1983.
87
"Nobody could sleep with Dick": quoted, David, "Pat Nixon's Life Story: 'I Gave Up Everything I Ever Loved . . . ,' " *Good Housekeeping*, August 1978.
87
Nixon plays with yo-yo at Grand Ole Opry: Smith, "Ordeal: Pat Nixon's Final Days in the White House"; see also *Time*, October 7, 1974.
87
"I keep it all in": quoted, Thimmesch, "The Unsinkable Pat Nixon," *McCall's*, April 1979.
87
"You have ruined my life": quoted, Hersh, "The Pardon."
87
"I used to catch myself resenting": quoted, Feldman, "The Quiet Courage of Pat Nixon."
88
"Well, goddam!": author's interview with Victor Lasky, April 3, 1983.
88–89
Account of birthday party for Nixon: Lasky interview.
89
Nixon's fatigue and poor health: *Los Angeles Times*, January 10, 1975.
89
"After all, she is both a Nixon and an Eisenhower": quoted, *The New York Times*, February 9, 1975.
89–90
Nixon's comments to Gulley about Goldwater: quoted, Gulley, 247–48.
90
Korff's background: *The New York Times*, July 28, 1974.
91
"lynch-mob psychosis": quoted, *The New York Times*, January 6, 1974.
91
Teamster contributions to Korff: *The New York Times*, July 23, 1974.
91
Korff denounces White House for withholding Nixon mail: *Los Angeles Times*, January 10, 1975.

91
Korff appeal for suspension of legal harassment: UPI, December 17, 1974.

91
"nothing but love and admiration for Jerry Ford": quoted, *Washington Post*, June 6, 1975.

92
Nixon financial appropriations: *U.S. News & World Report*, February 10, 1975; see also *Los Angeles Times*, February 9, 1975.

92
Nixon financial problems: *Time*, February 10, 1975; see also *Washington Post*, January 10, 1975; *Los Angeles Times*, February 9, 1975.

92
Nixon back taxes: *Los Angeles Times*, February 9, 1975.

93
Condition of Casa Pacifica's grounds: *The New York Times*, February 9, 1975.

93
Boy Scout clean-up: *Los Angeles Times*, August 30, 1974.

93
Abplanalp managing Nixon budget: *The New York Times*, February 9, 1975.

93
Two hundred long-distance phone calls before Christmas: *The New York Times*, February 9, 1975.

93
Laird and Connally urge Nixon to fire Ziegler: *The New York Times*, July 23, 1974.

93
"Ron knows nothing about public relations": quoted, *The New York Times*, July 23, 1974.

94
shouting tirades over the phone to Washington: author's interview with Gerald Warren, July 1, 1982.

94
life was "pretty much shattered": author's interview with senior Nixon aide, not for attribution, August 19, 1983.

94
Ziegler speaking tour: *The New York Times*, January 8, 1975.

94
"We conducted probably the worst public relations and press program in the history of the United States": quoted, *The New York Times*, February 14, 1975.

94
"morally wrong": quoted, *The New York Times*, January 23, 1975.

95
Nixon relationship with Ziegler: *The New York Times*, July 23, 1974.

95
"They will never get that pound of flesh": *The New York Times*, July 23, 1974.

95
Ziegler realizes he has become expendable: author's interview with senior Nixon aide, not for attribution, August 19, 1983.

95
"Ron, Jack has something to tell you": quoted, author's interview with former Nixon aide, not for attribution, March 12, 1983.

95–96

Ziegler conversation wth reporters at San Clemente Inn: quoted, *Los Angeles Times,* January 12, 1974; also, Reich interview.

96–97

Dismantling of Western White House complex: report from correspondent to major news organization, January 30, 1975.

97

Babcock sentenced to four months: *Time,* February 10, 1975.

97

"Ich kann nicht Englisch sprechen": quoted, *Time,* February 10, 1975.

97

"I can't let them leave and take with them a state of frustration": quoted, *San Clemente Sun-Post,* February 9, 1975.

97–98

Account of staff farewell party: *The New York Times,* February 9, 1975.

98

"Can you hear me?": quoted, report from correspondent to major news organization, February 10, 1975.

7. WATERGATE REDUX

99–100

Account of Annenberg dinner party: *Time,* March 10, 1975; AP, February 23, 1975; *Los Angeles Times,* February 24, 1975; UPI, February 22, 1975; author's interview with Herman Kahn, January 8, 1982.

100

Cost of Nixon's lawyers: *Los Angeles Times,* January 10, 1975.

100

Price paid to Haldeman for interview with CBS: *Newsday,* July 19, 1975.

101

Nixon dinner with Johnny Grant and Paul Presley: Presley and Grant interviews; see also, *The New York Times,* August 27, 1975.

101

Opposition to Nixon selling interview: *The New York Times,* August 27, 1975.

101

"in a mood of acceptance for what [Nixon] would have to say": quoted, *The New York Times,* August 27, 1975.

101

Nixon working on memoirs: Gannon interview.

101

"She's a little like the choir member in the Baptist Church": quoted, Ephron, "Rose Mary Woods—The Lady or the Tiger?" *New York,* March 18, 1974.

102

"Rose . . . is our kind of people": quoted, Ephron, "Rose Mary Woods."

102

Rose Woods background: Ephron, "Rose Mary Woods"; see also *The New York Times,* November 9, 1973; *New York Daily News,* November 18, 1968; *Los Angeles Times,* April 24, 1960; *The New York Times,* November 11, 1968; *New York Post,* November 16, 1968; *Washington Post,* October 26, 1968.

102–3

Woods transcribing tape at Camp David: Ephron, "Rose Mary Woods—The Lady or the Tiger?"

103

He told her not to worry: Ephron, "Rose Mary Woods—The Lady or the Tiger?"

103

"Maybe I'm out of line for saying this": quoted, Ephron, "Rose Mary Woods—The Lady or the Tiger?"

103

White House handling of Woods during tape erasure controversy: Ephron, "Rose Mary Woods—The Lady or the Tiger?"

103

baby-sat for his children and exchanged clothes with his wife: *New York Post*, November 16, 1968.

103–4

Ford administration treatment of Woods after Nixon resignation: Stroud, "The Sad New Life of Rose Mary Woods," *McCall's*, June 1975.

104

Connally acquitted in milk-fund case: *Report, Watergate Special Prosecution Force*, 82.

104

Conviction of appraiser: *The New York Times*, November 16, 1975.

104

Consortium of editors and reporters bring suit to block release of Nixon papers and tapes: *The New York Times*, December 6, 1975.

104

Korff "physically tired" and "mentally exhausted": quoted, *Los Angeles Times*, May 29, 1975.

104n

Dobrovir deposition: author's interview with William Dobrovir, January 15, 1983; see also transcript of deposition proceedings.

105

Korff resigns from Justice Fund: *The New York Times*, May 29, 1975.

105

Nixon persuades Korff to stay on: AP, July 26, 1975.

105

"doing what I can . . . to help solidify the cause of peace": quoted, *The New York Times*, June 8, 1975.

105

"Our day will come again": quoted, *Los Angeles Times*, August 8, 1975.

105

"South Vietnam would not have gone down the drain": quoted, *Time*, August 11, 1975.

105

"If they want me, fine": quoted, Gulley interview.

105

Charles Evers visit: *Los Angeles Times*, March 26, 1975.

105

"Things may be heating up too quickly": quoted, Fine, "Sunday with Richard Nixon," *Ladies' Home Journal*, December 1975, 52; author's interview with William Fine, October 22, 1982.

105
"Okay . . . but he's too accessible": quoted, Fine, "Sunday with Richard Nixon."

105
"I would ask five or six of the best brains around me": quoted, Fine, "Sunday with Richard Nixon."

105–6
"You ought to write about Watergate": quoted, *Time*, August 11, 1975.

106
"There was some wrong in what I did": quoted, *Newsweek*, October 20, 1975.

106
"This Watergate thing was ridiculous": quoted, *The New York Times*, October 23, 1975.

106
"To this day . . . he does not know the full story": quoted, *Washington Post*, June 6, 1975.

106
Nixon mistakenly believes former aide went to jail: author's interview with former Nixon White House aide, not for attribution, November 4, 1982.

106
Unresolved Watergate mysteries: *The New York Times*, June 28, 1975.

107–8
Rebozo background: Safire, *Before the Fall*, 613–16; see also Lukas, *Nightmare*, 362–63.

108
Rebozo financial history: "The Story of Bebe Rebozo: The Making of a Millionaire," six-part series in *Newsday*, October 6–13, 1971.

108
Nixon investment in real estate: Brodie, *Richard Nixon: The Shaping of His Character*, 484; Lukas, 361.

108
his wealth increased sevenfold: *Washington Post*, August 25, 1974.

108
Rumored $1 million contribution from Arab oilmen: AP, March 5, 1978.

108
Rumored multimillion slush fund in Bahamas bank: AP, March 5, 1978.

108
Scope of inquiry into Rebozo's activities: *Report, Watergate Special Prosecution Force*, 82–84.

108–9
Background of Rebozo and the $100,000 "campaign contribution" from Howard Hughes: *Report, Watergate Special Prosecution Force*, 82–84; see also Anderson, *The Anderson Papers*, 28–30; Lukas, 364–68.

109
as much as $790,000: *The New York Times*, December 9, 1974.

109
a set of platinum and diamond earrings: Senate Watergate Hearings, 26: 12692–94; see also Lukas, 367.

109
$45,621 for improvements and furnishings: Lukas, 367–68.

109
"I'm not going to nit-pick with the President": quoted, Lukas, 368.

109–10
"Let me ask you this": quoted, Lukas, 366.
110
"We could get a million dollars": quoted, Brodie, 550.
110
Ruth calls Miller: author's interview with Henry Ruth, April 6, 1983.
110
"a legal circus": Ruth interview.
110n
Nixon tells Haldeman about Rebozo fund: Haldeman, *The Ends of Power*, 20.
110n
"Well, as a matter of fact, I had in mind the contribution he [Rebozo] received from Hughes": David Frost interview with Nixon, quoted, *Washington Post*, March 25, 1977.
110n
Rebozo court deposition: quoted, *Washington Post*, February 18, 1978.
111
"This is history, you know": Ruth interview.
111
he seemed in excellent spirits: *Newsweek*, July 7, 1975.
111
Nixon grew increasingly testy: *Time*, July 7, 1975.
111n
"After all investigation was completed": *Report, Watergate Special Prosecution Force*, 84.

8. END OF A YEAR

112
Total of Nixon's legal bills: *Time*, August 11, 1975.
112
Lazar's negotiations with the networks: *Christian Science Monitor*, August 1, 1975.
112
NBC offered $300,000: Frost, *"I Gave Them a Sword,"* 19.
112
Frost background: "David Can Be a Goliath," *Time*, May 9, 1977.
112
"This is a vast question, I know": quoted, unpublished manuscript by James Reston, Jr.
113
"In the words of David Schoenbrun": quoted, Frost, 15.
113
Frost contacts Herb Klein: Frost, 16; author's interview with Herb Klein, January 21, 1983.
113
Minoff has breakfast with Klein: Frost, 17.
113
Felker informs Frost of Lazar negotiations: Frost, 18–19.
113
"Swifty believed in coming right to the point": Frost, 19.

113
Frost's conditions for doing the interview: Frost, 19–21.
114
In return for $600,000 plus 20 percent of any profits: Frost, 21.
114
Account of Frost and Ziffren's meeting with Nixon: Frost, 27–30; author's interview with Paul Ziffren, May 22, 1983.
114
Frost had to scramble to borrow the money: Frost, 31–32.
115
"Can I have the check please?": quoted, Frost, 29.
115
"This is where Brezhnev and I met": quoted, Frost, 30.
116
Nixon telephone conversation with Kissinger: Gulley interview.
116
Nixon's security worries: *Time*, August 9, 1975.
116
"It puzzles me a bit": quoted, *Newsweek*, October 20, 1975.
116
Nixon attends staff party at beach house: Willard interview.
116
"My God, Ken, I can't go in there": author's interview with Ken Allan, September 29, 1982.
117
John Wayne gives Nixon horse: Allan interview.
117
Brennan restores the golf greens: Hillings interview.
117n
Nixon's involvement with the Teamsters: Sheridan, *The Fall and Rise of Jimmy Hoffa*, 157, 159, 436–37, 487, 515–16.
118
"I don't wear hats": quoted, *The New York Times*, October 10, 1975.
118
"I'm just fine": quoted, *The New York Times*, October 10, 1975.
118
"Those others were for practice": quoted, *The New York Times*, October 10, 1975.
118
"This is nice": quoted, *The New York Times*, October 10, 1975.
118
Background of Teamsters who met with Nixon: *The New York Times*, October 10, 1975.
119
The New York Times editorial denouncing Nixon for playing golf with Teamsters: *The New York Times*, October 13, 1975.
119
Account of Halperin deposition of Nixon: author's interview with Morton Halperin, August 26, 1982; *Washington Post*, January 19, 1976; *Newsweek*, March 22, 1976; *Los Angeles Times*, January 15, 1976.
119–20
Disposition of Halperin and Fitzgerald cases: *Washington Post*, August 14,

1981 (Nixon bet); June 25, 1982 (Supreme Court ruling on presidential immunity); *Time*, July 5, 1982.
120
"there are still people out there who love us!": quoted, author's interviews with Harry Dent, December 16, 1982, and June 20, 1983.
120
"Didn't you hear?": quoted, Dent interview.
121
"What did I do wrong?": Walters, *Silent Missions*, 609.

9. China Passage

122
Description of Nixon's office: author's interview with senior Nixon aide, not for attribution, April 1, 1983.
122
"The roots are so shallow": author's interview with William Fine, October 22, 1982.
122
Message from Chou en-Lai: *San Clemente Sun-Post*, August 6, 1975.
122
Mao calls Nixon in the hospital: Osborne, "White House Watch: The China Caper," *The New Republic*, March 20, 1976.
122
personal messages conveyed by Huang Chen: *Washington Post*, February 20, 1976.
122
second invitation from Mao: Jack Anderson column, *Washington Post*, August 13, 1975.
123
Kissinger was discouraging: Hillings interview; see also Osborne, "The China Caper."
123
Ford's China trip: Ford, *A Time to Heal*, 335–37.
123
Preparations for David and Julie's trip to China: Eisenhower, *Special People*, 135.
123–24
Account of David and Julie's meeting with Mao; couple's reception in China: Eisenhower, 134, 138–43.
124
"The Chinese do not forget *their* friends": quoted, Eisenhower, 144.
124
Nixon was euphoric: Gulley interview, June 10, 1983.
124–25
Nixon tells Gulley about China trip: Gulley interview.
125
"Jerry's got New Hampshire anyway": quoted, Gulley, *Breaking Cover*, 265.
125
"You won't believe this, and you can't tell anybody": Gulley interview.

125

Kissinger visits Nixon February 2: Osborne, "The China Caper."

125

Han Hsu meets with Scowcroft: Osborne, "The China Caper."

125

Nixon's phone call to Ford two weeks before: Ford, A *Time to Heal*, 360.

125–26

Ford's telephone conversation with Nixon: Ford, A *Time to Heal*, 360.

126

Kissinger's reaction; tells Ford Nixon is lying: Ford, A *Time to Heal*, 360.

126

Ford's advisers meet; Kennerly curses Nixon: Osborne, "The China Caper." *The New Republic*, March 20, 1976.

126

Ford's New Hampshire trip went well: Ford, A *Time to Heal*, 361–62.

126n

The Chinese were not easily bluffed: Gulley interview; author's interview with State Department official, not for attribution, February 19, 1983.

127

"If he wants to do this country a favor": quoted, *Time*, March 8, 1976.

127

"A sleazy act": Joseph Kraft column, *Washington Post*, February 17, 1976.

127

"Any other man might have delayed the many-squalored thing": Mary Mc-Grory column, *Washington Star*, cited by Witcover, *Marathon*, 392.

127

"The utter shamelessness of the man": David S. Broder column, *Washington Post*, February 25, 1976.

127

"He has to offer only sycophancy": William F. Buckley, "Nixon to China," *The National Review*, March 19, 1976.

127

Nixon's letter to Safire: quoted, *The New York Times*, February 9, 1976.

127–28

Nixon arrives at LAX; departs for Peking: *Newsweek*, March 1, 1976.

128

Nixon's arrival in Peking: *Newsweek*, March 1, 1976.

128

"Wow, . . . what memories this brings back": quoted, AP, February 22, 1976.

128

"You must be tired after your long journey": quoted, AP, February 22, 1976.

128

Nixon pays condolence call on Chou's widow: *Toronto Globe and Mail*, February 23, 1976.

128

Nixon confers with Hua: *Toronto Globe and Mail*, February 23, 1976.

128–29

Description of banquet in Nixon's honor: *Toronto Globe and Mail*, February 23, 1976.

129

"The future of all the people in this world": quoted, *Toronto Globe and Mail*, February 23, 1976.

129
"My God, I've used that statement a dozen times": quoted, *Time,* March 8, 1976.

129
Nessen's icy reaction: *Newsweek,* February 16, 1976.

129
Question from New Hampshire high-school student; Ford's response: *Newsweek,* March 1, 1976.

129
"We'll make an even trade": quoted, *Toronto Globe and Mail,* February 24, 1976.

129
"a wide range of matters on the international scene": quoted, *The New York Times,* February 24, 1976.

129
Nixon's gift to Mao; Mao's toast: report from correspondent to major news organization, February 25, 1976.

129–30
Nixon's meeting with reporters: described and quoted, report from correspondent to major news organization, February 27, 1976.

130
Nixon attends cultural program at the Great Hall of the People: *Toronto Globe and Mail,* February 24, 1976.

130
Text of Taiwan song: quoted, *The New York Times,* February 24, 1976.

130
Nixon nearly falls into orchestra pit: UPI, February 24, 1976.

130
Additional conferences with Hua, sight-seeing: *The New York Times,* February 24, 1976.

130
Nixon's colloquy with tour guide about large character posters: quoted, UPI, February 25, 1976.

131
Nixon's conversation with Chinese foreign minister: quoted, UPI, February 25, 1976.

131
Nixon's exchange with Chinese man over birth control: quoted, UPI, February 25, 1976.

131
"We have not finished the bridge": quoted, *Time,* March 8, 1976.

131
"This . . . is a slap in the belly of Kissinger with a big wet fish": quoted, report from correspondent to major news organization, March 1, 1976.

131
Kissinger's flip-flop reaction to Nixon trip: UPI, February 22, 1976.

131–32
Ford's victory in New Hampshire primary: Witcover, 396.

132
Nixon limping during sight-seeing in Kweilin: UPI, February 27, 1976.

132
Description of Nixon boat ride, difficulty with pill: author's interview with John Lindsay, August 3, 1982.

132

"It must be easy to be a reporter": quoted, Lindsay interview.

132

Nixon's reception in Canton: report from correspondent to major news organization, March 3, 1976.

132

Posing with reporters for picture: author's interview with Saul Pett, November 26, 1982.

132–33

Phone call from Kissinger: *The New York Times*, March 4, 1976; see also Osborne, "The China Caper."

10. INTERVAL

134

Miller's brief, challenging Court of Appeals decision on papers: *The New York Times*, January 11, 1976.

134

"Our meatball President": quoted, Woodward and Bernstein, *The Final Days*, 188.

134

Characterization of Nixon in *The Final Days*: Woodward and Bernstein, *The Final Days*, 104, 167, 329 (emotionally unstable); 343, 395, 403–4, 431, 436 (potentially suicidal); 103–4, 395, 424 (frequently drunk).

134

Nixon's relationship with his wife: Woodward and Bernstein, *Final Days*, 165–66.

134

Nixon considers suing for libel: Finch interview.

134–35

Nixon's complaints to Gulley about *The Final Days*: quoted, Gulley, 241–42.

135

Nixon's meeting with Frost: Frost, *"I Gave Them a Sword,"* 36.

135

"You can put that in your apartment in New York": quoted, Frost, 36.

135

"Marry that girl": quoted, Frost, 36.

135

"Not since Ed Sullivan": *Time*, May 9, 1977.

135–36

Frost's liabilities, cross-examination technique: *Time*, May 9, 1977.

135n

Nixon prays with Kissinger: Frost interviews transcript; quoted, Nixon, *RN: The Memoirs of Richard Nixon*, 1077.

136

"The aim of everything I do": quoted, *Time*, May 9, 1977.

136

Frost erects ad hoc "network": Frost, 46.

136

Frost's financial backers: Frost, 32; see also *Time*, May 9, 1977.

136

Frost's editorial staff: Frost, 38–39; also, author's interviews with James

Reston, Jr., February 4, 1983; Marvin Minoff, July 28, 1983; and Robert Zelnick, June 20, 1983.
136
Account of Frost's meeting with editorial team in Washington: Frost, 44–45; also, Reston and Minoff interviews.
136
Purported homosexual relationship with Bebe Rebozo: Frost, 44; also, Reston interview, Reston manuscript.
137
Description of Brennan's phone call from California; Gannon's comments; Frost's departure for Iran: Frost, 47–49.
137
Reston's research; discovery of Colson conversations: Reston interview.
137–38
Reston's interview with Charles Colson: Reston manuscript.
138
Transcript of Colson conversation with Nixon: Reston manuscript.
138
Nixon's dinner at the El Adobe: *Newsweek*, July 19, 1976.
138
Bicentennial dinner dance: *Newsweek*, July 19, 1976.
139–41
Account of Julie Eisenhower's birthday party: Stein, "Richard Nixon Goes to a Party," *Esquire*, November, 1976; author's interview with Benjamin Stein, April 6, 1983.
141
Mrs. Nixon's taste in literature: David, *The Lonely Lady of San Clemente*, 3.
141
She was reading *The Final Days*: Hitt interview; see also Thimmesch, "The Unsinkable Pat Nixon," *McCall's*, May 1979.
141
Suddenly she felt weak: *Time*, July 19, 1976.
141
Nixon noticed she was having trouble: *Time*, July 19, 1976.
141
"I can't believe this is happening to me": McClendon, "Pat Nixon Today," *Good Housekeeping*, February 1980.
141
"a dinky lesion . . . the size of a pea": quoted, *The New York Times*, July 9, 1976.
142
"My wife is one who has been through a great many difficult experiences": quoted, *Washington Post*, July 10, 1976.

11. THE WIZARD

143
Two weeks before Pat was sufficiently well: *The New York Times*, July 23, 1976.
143
months of painful therapy: Hitt interview; see also *Newsweek*, July 26, 1976. 1976.

143
Ford, Nixon's feelings about each other; relations between respective staffs: *Washington Post*, April 30, 1976.
143–44
Nixon's conversations with Gulley about presidential politics: Gulley interview.
144
Nixon's code name, "The Wizard": Warren interview.
144
"The minute you start getting familiar with people": quoted, Gulley, 238.
144
"One of Jerry's biggest problems": quoted, Gulley, 257.
144
"Nancy Reagan runs Ronald Reagan": quoted, Gulley, 248.
144–45
Nixon's relations with Reagan: Hitt interview; also, Hillings interview.
145
"Maybe that will satisfy the lynch mob": quoted, *Los Angeles Times*, October 30, 1974.
145
"a dinner invitation was dispatched": Hillings interview.
145
Connally's work on the Ash Council: author's interviews with H. R. Haldeman, April 9, 1983; also, Dent interviews.
145
"John Connally . . . is a gut-fighter and total politician": quoted, Ehrlichman, *Witness to Power*, 259.
145–46
Connally's standing in Nixon administration: Safire, *Before the Fall*, 498–508; see also Dent, *The Prodigal South Returns to Power*, 272–74.
146
"I brought him up from the Texas League": quoted, Safire, 507.
146
Nixon's plans to reshape Republican party: Ehrlichman, 259–60; also, Haldeman interview.
146
Nixon's plan to appoint Connally vice president, nominate Agnew to Supreme Court: Ehrlichman, 136.
146–47
Dent role in devising "Southern Strategy": Dent interviews.
147
Nixon sends Dent to Camp David: Dent interviews.
147
Nixon tries to recruit Dent on Connally's behalf: Dent interviews.
147
Nixon's conflicting comments on whom he prefers for President: *The New York Times*, June 6, 1976.
147
Nixon's conversation with Haldeman: Haldeman interview.
147
"his name was not uttered from the podium": *Facts on File*, August 21, 1976, 615.
147
"a cover-up of virtue": quoted, *Newsweek*, August 30, 1976.

147
"People speak of events": quoted, *Newsweek*, August 30, 1976.
147
Reference to Nixon deleted from party platform: *Newsweek*, August 30, 1976.
147
Nixon trying to arrange Connally's selection as vice president: Dent interviews.
147–48
Ford tactics with Mississippi delegation: Dent interviews.
148
At Cheney's instruction, Gulley pleaded ignorance: Gulley interview.
148
"They're going to have trouble with that guy": quoted, Gulley interview.
148
Nixon lists states each candidate will win: Gulley, 249.
148
"We know who our guy is": quoted, Gulley, 249.
148
"because the Republicans [there] hate him": quoted, Gulley, 265.
148
"Kissinger's talking too much about black Africa": quoted, Gulley, 264.
148
"I don't give a shit what Max Fischer": quoted, Gulley interview.
148
Nixon's advice to Ford about television debates: Gulley, 250.
149
"Don't worry about what you say about Nixon": quoted, Gulley, 264.
149
"There is no Soviet domination of Eastern Europe": quoted, Witcover, *Marathon*, 597.
149
"Well, goddam it, I checked": quoted, Gulley interview.
149
Nixon advises Ford to spend less time in New York and concentrate on California and Texas: Gulley, 251; also, author's interview with Congressman Richard Cheney, August 2, 1982.
149
"Jerry's running for President of the United States now": quoted, Gulley, 264.
149
"An international incident could be useful to Ford": quoted, Gulley, 264.
149
"the Nixon-Ford Administration": quoted, *Washington Post*, August 4, 1976.
149
"The American people wouldn't accept it"; quoted, Gulley, 268.
150
Watergate special prosecutor investigating Ford campaign contributions: *The Wall Street Journal*, September 21, 1976.
150
Ford's discussions with White House about blocking Watergate inquiry: Hersh, "The Pardon."
150
The transcript of one of the Nixon tapes was resurrected: cited by Witcover, 585.

150

"The spirit of this country has been damaged": quoted, Witcover, 589.

150

"I could just see myself waking up in the morning": quoted, Witcover, 639.

150

Nixon votes by absentee ballot: Witcover, 643.

150

"the exit polling conducted by the Republicans": author's interview with former Nixon aide, not for attribution, December 8, 1982.

150

Correctness of Nixon's predictions: Gulley, 249.

12. THE FROST INTERVIEWS

151

"Be sure you pay your taxes"; following conversation: quoted, Frost, 51.

151

"It's the way you look that I'm really worried about": quoted, Frost, 75.

151–52

Frost-Brennan argument: quoted, Frost, 82.

152

Sale of Key Biscayne: *The New York Times*, July 24, 1976.

152

Nixon reneges on promise to pay back taxes: *The New York Times*, May 2, 1976.

152

Alleged Nixon "love letters": *The New York Times*, June 4, 1976.

152

Alleged Nixon liaison with Hong Kong tour guide: *The New York Times*, June 22, 1976.

152

New York disbars Nixon: *The New York Times*, July 9, 1976.

152

Nixon's papers soaked in Maryland: *The New York Times*, August 5, 1976.

153

"It is like he is in training for a heavyweight fight": quoted, Murphy, "Inside the Nixon-Frost TV Interviews," *New York*, April 25, 1977.

153

Frost compared to Watergate special prosecutor: unpublished manuscript by James Reston, Jr.

153

waiters at Rive Gauche whisper words of encouragement: Frost, 73–74.

153

"The Frost-Nixon sessions represent another typical Nixon deal": quoted, Frost, 50.

153

"A cascade of candor?": quoted, Frost, 131.

153

Frost barters free lodging at Beverly Hilton: author's interview with James Reston, Jr., February 4, 1983.

153
"to take television by storm": quoted, Reston interview.
153
145 independent stations agree to carry interviews: author's interview with Marvin Minoff, July 28, 1983.
153
Frost could expect to realize a profit of well over $1 million: *New York Post,* May 2, 1977.
153
Reston and Zelnick had interviewed scores of sources: Reston interview.
153
The Watergate prosecutors had opened their files: Reston interview.
153
Lists of scripted questions had been prepared: author's interview with Robert Zelnick, June 20, 1983.
153
Zelnick playing Nixon: Zelnick interview.
153
"Assuming the worst": quoted, *Washington Post,* May 1, 1977.
154
the great bulk of his education came at the eleventh hour: Reston and Minoff interviews.
154
Frost recently returned from Australia: unpublished manuscript by James Reston, Jr.
154
He was woefully uninformed: Minoff, Reston interviews.
154
drinks with Tony Ulasewicz: Frost, 77.
154
"Don't worry": quoted, Reston manuscript.
154
Nixon conversation with Jörn Winther: author's interview with Jörn Winther, March 8, 1983.
154
Nixon had been cramming and rehearsing: author's interview with senior Nixon aide, not for attribution, February 9, 1983.
154
"or so Frost later suspected": Reston manuscript.
154
Nixon calls Kissinger: *Time,* May 9, 1977.
154–55
Nixon fails to prepare fully for Watergate; R.N.'s view of Frost's Watergate questioning technique: author's interview with senior Nixon aide, not for attribution, August 19, 1983.
155
Khachigian's dealings with Zelnick and Reston: Zelnick interview; also, Gannon interview.
155
Staff estimate of how Frost will approach Watergate: author's interview with senior Nixon aide, not for attribution, August 19, 1983.
155
"a rented blue Mercedes": Frost, 91.

155
Site of the tapings switched: *Time*, May 9, 1977.
155
Frost up past midnight; jotting notes on blue question sheets: Reston interview.
155
Frost's conversation with Zelnick: Frost, 91.
155–56
Furnishings on the set: *Time*, May 9, 1977; Reston manuscript.
156
Nixon, Frost pretaping banter: quoted, Reston manuscript.
156
"Mr. President," Frost began: quoted, Frost, 93.
156
Nixon appears startled, gives disjointed reply: Frost, 93.
156
"It is true": quoted, Reston manuscript.
156
"Move in, tear the son of a bitch to pieces": quoted, Frost, 97.
156
Nixon talks about Dean, Haig, Wallace; reminisces about various personalities: Frost, 94–97.
156–57
Nixon describes final days in White House: quoted, Frost, 97.
157–58
"political activities which led to the resignation": quoted, Frost, 102.
158
"a double standard": quoted, Frost, 102.
158
happy to "demolish": quoted, Frost, 100.
158
"a mitigated disaster": quoted, Frost, 103.
158
Joseph Kraft views tape, gives reaction: Frost, 104–5.
158
" 'Henry,' I said, 'we've done it' ": quoted, Frost, 164.
158
"I hated every minute of it": quoted, Frost.
158
Frost asks about Nixon watching *Patton*; Nixon's reply: Frost, 116.
158–59
"What we have to understand": quoted, Frost, 168.
159
"Did you do any fornicating this weekend?" quoted, Frost, 171.
159
Reston leaking transcripts to Fawn Brodie: Reston interview.
159
"This program does the one thing": quoted, Frost, 196.
159
Minoff becoming increasingly worried: Minoff interview.
159
Felker falls asleep during tape viewing: Frost, 195–96.
159
"too PBS": quoted, Frost, 196.

159
Staff members threatening to quit: Minoff interview.

159
"When the President does it": quoted, Frost, 183.

159
The answer startled even Nixon's staff: author's interview with senior Nixon aide, not for attribution, April 19, 1983.

159–60
Zelnick argues with Frost: quoted, Frost, 187.

160
"It hasn't been easy": quoted, Frost, 192.

160
Brennan bounded into the room: Frost, 192.

160
Nixon signs autographs: *Time*, May 9, 1977.

160
"If that guy runs for President again": quoted, *Time*, May 9, 1977.

160
"Frost and Nixon, Frost and Nixon": quoted, *Time*, May 9, 1977.

160–61
Zelnick and Birt criticize Frost's interrogation: quoted, Frost, 197–201; also, Zelnick, Reston and Minoff interviews; Reston manuscript.

161
Frost immerses himself in the research: Reston manuscript; see also Frost, 203–5.

161
Frost asks for conspiracy to obstruct justice statute: quoted, Frost, 215.

161
Nixon's conversation with his barber: Allan interview.

161
Frost and Nixon chat on the set: Reston manuscript.

161
Frost begins interrogation, Nixon feints: Frost, 219–22.

162
". . . And so you knew, in terms of intent": quoted, Frost, 224.

162
"An obstruction of justice is an obstruction of justice": quoted, Frost, 224–25.

163
Frost quotes from Colson transcript, Nixon expresses surprise: quoted, Frost, 232–33.

163
Frost's recitation of Watergate quotes, Nixon's response: quoted, Frost, 238–39.

164
Frost and Nixon staff reactions to interview session: Frost, 242.

164
Nixon arrives late for next taping, appears haggard: Frost, 246.

164
The Colson tapes had jolted him: Gannon interview.

164
Light bulb explodes; Nixon makes comment about assassins: Reston manuscript.

164
"Let the bad come out": quoted, Frost, 251.
164–65
Nixon recounts firing of Haldeman and Ehrlichman: quoted, Frost, 261–62.
165
Frost encourages Nixon to go further: Frost, 262; also, Reston manuscript.
165–66
Brennan holds up sign; taping halted; conversation between Brennan and Frost staff: Frost, 264–65.
166
Nixon talks about sand dabs in the kitchen: Minoff interview.
166–68
Resumption and conclusion of interview: described and quoted, Frost, 266–72.
168
"This is gold": Minoff interview.
168
Description of Nixon and staff after interview; "that should make you happy": Minoff interview.
168
Ratings for first Frost telecast: *Newsweek*, May 16, 1977.
168
Jaworski's reaction: quoted, *Newsweek*, May 16, 1977.
168
Bernstein's reaction: quoted, *Newsweek*, May 16, 1977.
168
Ehrlichman's reaction: quoted, *New West*, May 23, 1977.
168–69
Hunt's reaction: quoted, *Newsweek*, May 16, 1977.
169
Ervin's reaction: quoted, *Newsweek*, May 16, 1977.
169
Goldwater's reaction: quoted, *Newsweek*, May 16, 1977.
169
Carter's reaction: *Washington Post*, May 14, 1977.
169
Price's reaction: quoted, *Newsweek*, May 16, 1977.
169
Buchanan's reaction: quoted, *Newsweek*, May 16, 1977.
169
Gallup Poll findings: *Newsweek*, May 16, 1977.
169
Frost party at Chasen's: *Newsweek*, May 16, 1977.
169
Salant's comments about telecast: *Newsweek*, May 16, 1977.
169
Nixon activities day of telecast: *Newsweek*, May 16, 1977.
169
He made it a practice never to watch himself on TV: *Newsweek*, May 16, 1977.
169
He thought he had handled himself well: author's interview with senior Nixon aide, not for attribution, July 19, 1983.

169
Kissinger and Tricia phone their congratulations: *Newsweek*, May 16, 1977.
169–70
Nixon phones Khachigian: *Newsweek*, May 16, 1977.

13. MEMOIRS

171
Public comments from Warner's about memoirs progress: quoted, *Publishers Weekly*, March 14, 1977.
171–72
Gannon photocopies thirty thousand pages: Gannon interview.
171n
Supreme Court upholds government seizure of Nixon tapes, papers: *Washington Post*, June 29, 1977.
171n
Supreme Court sides with Nixon on privacy issue: *Newsweek*, May 1, 1978.
172
Supplementary interviews conducted by staff: Gannon interview.
172
Nixon had dictated a total of 1.5 million words: Gannon interview.
172
Kaminsky's reaction to material: author's interview with Howard Kaminsky, February 8, 1983.
172
"All provable expenses": *The New York Times*, September 29, 1976.
172
as many as twenty separate drafts: Gannon interview.
172
unedited words filled forty black binders: Gannon interview.
172
Warner's sells hardcover rights to Grosset & Dunlap: *Publishers Weekly*, March 14, 1977.
172
Markel background: author's interview with Robert Markel, November 4, 1982.
172–73
Markel and Roth fly to California: author's interview with Herbert Roth, November 23, 1982.
173
Markel reads rough draft; his reaction: Markel interview.
173
Existence of Nixon diaries: Gannon interview.
173
Markel's conversation with Sawyer and Gannon about Watergate material: Markel interview.
174
Sawyer describes Nixon's mail: quoted, Markel interview.

174
Gannon resists cuts: quoted, Markel interview.
174
Gannon's joke about Don Nixon: quoted, Markel interview.
174–75
Publisher's meeting with Nixon: Markel, Roth interview.
175–76
Markel, wife, daughter meet with Nixon: Markel interview.
176
Copy-editor Frost's background: author's interview with David Frost, November 9, 1982.
176
Brooks's background: author's interview with Nancy Brooks, December 16, 1982.
176
"It must not, it cannot, it will not": quoted, Brooks interview.
176
Working schedule of Nixon staff: author's interview with senior Nixon aide, not for attribution, July 26, 1983.
176
Nixon's routine: author's interview with senior Nixon aide, not for attribution, July 26, 1983.
176–77
Nixon's taste in literature, feelings about de Gaulle: Gannon interview.
177
Nixon's television viewing: author's interview with Nixon friend, not for attribution, February 4, 1983.
177
Nixon walks Irish setter at night: Brooks interview.
177
Nixon's golf with Brennan: author's interview with Nixon friend, not for attribution, January 8, 1983.
177
Rules of "presidential golf": Presley interview; author's interview with former Congressman Charles Wiggins, February 10, 1983.
177–78
Nixon's feelings about football; lessons learned from "Chief" Newman: Nixon, *RN: The Memoirs of Richard Nixon*, 19–20.
178
Nixon discusses weekend football games with Brooks and Frost: Brooks interview.
178
Frost argument with Gannon over memoirs' opening line: Frost interview.
178
Markel discovers that Nixon reveals intelligence methods: Markel interview.
178
Nixon's comments about "Jewish press"; Markel's recommendation to Gannon: Markel interview.
178
"It was like a gnat buzzing in front of my eyes": author's interview with Dewey Clower, October 30, 1982.

179–80
Gannon, Sawyer backgrounds: Gannon interview; see also, Sawyer profiles in *Winnipeg Free Press*, February 20, 1982, and *The New York Times*, September 30, 1981.
180
Sawyer's work on Watergate material: Gannon interview.
180
"the key . . . to *Finnegans Wake*": quoted, Gannon interview.
180
Nixon's reaction to Sawyer's background paper on Watergate: author's interview with senior Nixon aide, not for attribution, December 4, 1982.
180
"I don't even *know* Donald Segretti": Gannon interview.
180
Sawyer termed "the Jill Wine Volner of San Clemente": author's interview with senior Nixon aide, not for attribution, December 4, 1982.
180–81
Nixon's relations with Sawyer: author's interview with senior Nixon aide, not for attribution, February 23, 1983.
181
Nixon's defensive comments about Watergate: Nixon, *RN*, various.
181–82
Markel reads the Watergate rough draft; complains to Gannon and Sawyer about tape gap explanation: quoted, Markel interview.
182
Markel raises tape gap with Nixon: quoted, Markel interview.
182
Nixon works with Brooks on tape gap: Brooks interview.
182
Nixon's final explanation of tape gap: Nixon, *RN*, 948–52.
183
Nixon's dinner invitation to Markel; account of dinner; Nixon's remarks about nuclear war: described and quoted, Markel interview.
183–84
Nixon's conversation with Hubert Humphrey; instructions to Brennan about preparing for funeral: Hillings interview.
183–84n
Nixon's feelings about Humphrey: Markel interview; see also Nixon, *RN*, 655–56.
184
Nixon's conversation with Humphrey's widow: *Washington Post*, January 16, 1978.
184
Nixon's ride with Dewey Clower: Clower interview.
184
Nixon's opinion of the Super Bowl; activities rest of the day: quoted and described, *People*, January 30, 1978.
184–85
Nixon attends reception in Howard Baker's office: *Time*, January 30, 1978.
185
Nixon attends Humphrey memorial: *Washington Post*, January 16, 1978.
185
Dispute over memoirs' title: Markel interview.

185
"That's how I want it": quoted, Gannon interview.
185
"It's Pat. She can't bear to look at them": quoted, Markel interview.
185–86
Galleys reset: Brooks interview.
186
Markel insists that book be published: Markel interview.
186
Sales campaign for *RN*; size of first printing; rises to best-seller list: Markel interview; see also *Publishers Weekly*, May 29, 1978.
186
Staff scatters; changes in Frost and Brooks: Frost, Brooks interviews.
186–87
Nixon toasts Sawyer and Gannon: Gannon interview.

14. STIRRINGS

188–89
Nixon's conversation with Dick Enberg: quoted, *New Times*, July 24, 1978.
189
Friends urging Nixon to get out, his resistance: Hillings interview.
189
"None of them ... ever resigned": quoted, Hillings interview.
189n
Nixon as Angels' fan: *Time*, October 8, 1979.
190
Nixon worried about getting too comfortable: Stein interview.
190
Nixon's opinion of Carter administration, private criticisms: Hillings interview.
190–91
Nixon's discussion with Gulley: Gulley, 239.
190n
Carter's phone call to Nixon: Carter, *Keeping Faith*, 199–200.
191
"Who are the real strategic thinkers": author's interview with Nixon friend, not for attribution, November 7, 1982.
191–92
Description of Hyden, Kentucky: *Newsweek*, July 17, 1978; *The New York Times*, June 5, 1978.
192
Nixon's revenue sharing, Hyden's recreation center: *The New York Times*, June 5, 1978.
192
Muncy's invitation: Nixon's acceptance: *The New York Times*, June 5, 1978.
192
Description of Nixon's arrival in Hyden: *Newsweek*, July 17, 1978; *Washington Post*, July 2, 1978.
192
"Get that hippie out of here": quoted, *Newsweek*, July 17, 1978.

192
"I came out of the hospital": quoted, report from correspondent to major news organization, July 7, 1978.
192-93
Nixon's arrival speech: *Washington Post*, July 2, 1978.
193
Reception at Hyden motel: *Newsweek*, July 17, 1978.
193
Sunday audience waiting for Nixon in the heat: *Newsweek*, July 17, 1978.
193
Nixon motorcade, convertible, cannon salute, introductions on stage: *Newsweek*, July 17, 1978.
193-94
Lectern, Nixon's speech, crowd reaction: *Newsweek*, July 17, 1978; report from correspondent to major news organization, July 5, 1978; *The New York Times*, July 3, 1978.
194-95
Brock's objections: *The New York Times*, July 19, 1978.
194n
Purported Dick Tuck encounter with Nixon: *New York*, July 17, 1978.
195
Nixon confiding to friends that he'd done his time: Hillings interview.
195
Plans for world tour, unenthusiastic response from Malcolm Fraser and other world leaders, Nixon's decision to visit anyway: *Washington Post*, September 3, 1978; *Los Angeles Times*, September 7, 1978.
195
Bobst's death, invitation to Nixon to deliver eulogy: *The New York Times*, August 29, 1978.
195
Nixon's plan for new book: UPI, September 13, 1978.
195
Kissinger's and Rogers' discouragement of world tour: author's interview with Nixon friend, not for attribution, January 7, 1983.
195
Warner's encouragement of new book: Kaminsky interview.
195-96
Press conference: UPI, September 13, 1978.
196
Invitation from Biloxi: author's interview with Frederick C. LaRue, August 8, 1983.
196
Invitation from Oxford: AP, November 13, 1978.
196
Nixon stopovers in Dallas and Shreveport: *Biloxi Sun Herald*, November 6, 1978.
196
Nixon's arrival in Biloxi; crowd remarks; Nixon's response: *The New York Times*, November 11, 1978.
196
Reception at Broadwater Beach Hotel: LaRue interview; author's interview with Jack Nelson of *Los Angeles Times*, June 27, 1983.

196
LaRue as CREEP official: Lukas, *Nightmare*, 279, 299.
197
Nixon and Hurricane Camille: *Los Angeles Times*, November 12, 1978.
197
Nixon appearance onstage, *Los Angeles Times*, November 12, 1978.
197
Nixon's speech: *Los Angeles Times*, November 12, 1978.
197
Times critique: *The New York Times*, November 14, 1978.
197
Caribbean holiday, return home: *Washington Post*, April 12, 1978.
197
Nixon's departure for Europe: *The New York Times*, November 26, 1978.
197
Nixon's call to Tricia: *Newsweek*, December 11, 1978.
198
Phone call from Giscard: *Newsweek*, December 11, 1978.
198
Sandwiches, shopping: *Newsweek*, December 11, 1978.
198
Haig's visit; "some reminiscing": *The New York Times*, November 27, 1978.
198
"the only American citizen": quoted, Lindsay interview.
198
Appearance on *Dossiers de l'Ecran: Washington Post*, November 29, 1978; *The New York Times*, November 29, 1978.
198
Nixon's introduction of Lindsay: Lindsay interview.
198–99
Chat with Salinger: author's interview with Pierre Salinger, May 4, 1983.
199
"What a man!" "You may say he's an old crocodile": quoted report from correspondent to major news organization, November 29, 1978.
199
"It's too bad he can't run for President of France": report from correspondent to major news organization, November 30, 1978.
199
Nixon visit to England denounced; termed "undesirable alien": AP, November 17, 1978.
199
Nixon's address to members of Parliament; meeting with Thatcher and Conservative Philosophy Society: author's interviews with Jonathan Aitkin, April 19 and May 4, 1983; Lord Longford, April 11, 1983; and Peregrine Worsthorne, April 1, 1983.
199
British CREEP: *The Village Voice*, December 11, 1978.
199
"I'll feel very much at home": quoted, Lindsay interview.
199–200
Demonstration on night of Nixon's appearance, attack on car and Nixon:

Lindsay interview; *The Village Voice*, December 11, 1978; *London Daily Telegraph*, December 1, 1978.
200
Applause from Oxford men: *Time*, December 11, 1978.
200
Nixon's speech, reaction, demonstrators: *Time*, December 11, 1978; *The New York Times*, December 1, 1978.
201
Thimmesch interview with Nixon: author's interview with Nick Thimmesch, October 15, 1982; Thimmesch, "Richard Nixon Speaks His Mind," *Saturday Evening Post*, March 1979.

15. MOVING ON

202
Description of Lompoc: *Time*, July 4, 1977.
202
Changes in Haldeman: Haldeman interview.
202
"Every President needs a son of a bitch": Lukas, *Nightmare*, 225.
203
"Beaver Patrol": Rather and Gates, *The Palace Guard*, 225.
203
"I cannot remember anything funny that happens": Lukas, 224.
203
"The Abominable No-Man": Rather and Gates, 280.
203
Haldeman saying no when Nixon couldn't: Safire, 278–93.
203
"It was hard . . . to tell where Richard Nixon left off": quoted, Ehrlichman, 78.
203
Nixon and Haldeman not as close as portrayed: Haldeman interview.
203
"Well, that's his decision": quoted, Ehrlichman, 80.
203
Nixon in frequent touch with Haldeman following resignation and during prison term: Haldeman interview.
203–4
Haldeman's visit to Nixon: Haldeman, 113–14.
204
Haldeman's anger over Nixon's remarks during Frost interviews: *The New York Times*, May 27, 1977; Haldeman, 294.
204
"I'm not like John": quoted, Haldeman interview.
205
"some criminal, some harmless, some accidental": Haldeman, xiv.
205
"crude, rough . . ." Haldeman, 72.
205
Haldeman's regret over critique of Nixon: Haldeman interview.

205n
Haldeman's attempt to downplay criticism, assigning blame to Di Mona and publisher; "They kept emphasizing the sensational": Haldeman interview.
205n
Di Mona's and Lipscomb's recollections: author's interview with Joseph di Mona, April 19, 1983; author's interview with Thomas Lipscomb, May 11, 1983.
206
Haldeman's departure from Lompoc, "Christmas is generally considered to be a special time": *The New York Times*, December 21, 1978.
206
Nixon's forgiveness of Haldeman: Haldeman interview.
206–7
Nixon's phone call to Haldeman: Haldeman interview.
206n
Nixon's dislike of Ehrlichman; "Ehrlichman doesn't understand politics": quoted, Gulley interview.
206n
Nixon's misspelling of Ehrlichman's name; "at least you know it's not a forgery": author's interview with John Ehrlichman, October 26, 1982.
207
Nixon's buoyant spirits: author's interview with senior Nixon aide, not for attribution, January 8, 1983.
207
Nixon's reaction to Lasky's story about Dean: Lasky interview.
207
Gallup survey: *The New York Times*, December 21, 1978.
207
Invitation from Carter: *Washington Post*, January 16, 1979.
207
Pickets outside the White House: *The New York Times*, January 30, 1979.
207
Nixon's day in Virginia countryside: *The New York Times*, January 30, 1979.
207–8
Meeting with Teng and Carter, descent to East Room, reaction to announcement of name: *The New York Times*, January 30, 1979.
208
Seating arrangements at dinner: author's interview with Richard Holbrooke, March 1, 1983.
208
"You know they're playing the same songs": *New York Post*, January 30, 1979.
208
Conversation with Woodcock; toasts; autographing of menu; discussion of world leaders: Holbrooke interview.
208
Private conference with Teng: *The New York Times*, January 31, 1979.
208
San Clemente as a temporary home: Hillings interview.
208
Friends pressing Nixon to return East: *Los Angeles Times*, May 30, 1975.
209
"Isn't this marvelous?": quoted, author's interview with Bryce Harlow, December 10, 1982.

209
Later dissatisfaction with Casa Pacifica: author's interview with senior Nixon aide, not for attribution, March 26, 1983.
209
Brennan's statement about sale of house: UPI, May 25, 1979.
209
"a gift to the United States": quoted, The New York Times, May 29, 1979.
209
"the fast track": quoted, Brodie, 479.
209
Nixon's desire to return to New York: Hillings interview.
209–10
Pat Nixon's infrequent outings: Hitt interview.
209–10
Wig as disguise: Thimmesch, "The Unsinkable Pat Nixon."
209n
Abplanalp and Rebozo's partial ownership of estate: San Diego Union, May 25, 1979.
209n
"Ten-story whorehouse": quoted, Brodie, 482.
210
Spitting incident: author's interview with Robert Markel, November 4, 1982.
210
Birth of grandchildren and Nixon's affection for them: Hitt and Stein interviews.
210
Nixon's discussion with Julie about how grandchild should address him: author's interview with Julie Nixon Eisenhower, November 24, 1983.
210
"How can you live out here?": author's interview with junior Nixon aide, not for attribution, August 13, 1983.
210
Nixon's initial caution over criticizing Carter's handling of shah: Hillings interview.
210
"as a personal demonstration": quoted, AP, July 4, 1979.
210
Mexican airline strike: UPI, July 3, 1979.
210
Nixon's journey to Mexico: AP, July 13, 1979.
210–11
Nixon's comments to reporters: San Diego Union, July 13, 1979.
211
Nixon's arrival at Shah's villa: Armao interview.
211
Nixon and Shah's lunch and conversation: Armao interview; Pahlavi, Answer to History, 16.
211
Shah's complaints about Carter; "Don't fade away": quoted, Armao interview.
211
Picture taking outside the shah's villa: Washington Post, July 14, 1979.
211
Dispute with government over sale of estate; resolution: The New York Times,

May 27, 1979; AP, July 18, 1979; *San Diego Tribune*, September 6, 1979; *Los Angeles Times*, July 23, 1979.

212
Nixon's improved financial status: *Los Angeles Times*, January 25, 1979.

212
Nixon's failure to purchase Madison Avenue co-op: AP, August 3, 1979.

212
Nixon's failure to purchase Fifth Avenue condominium: *Washington Post*, October 3, 1979.

212
Nixon's purchase of Sixty-fifth Street town house; description; neighbors: *New York Daily News*, February 6, 1980.

212
Poolside reception for astronauts: *Los Angeles Times*, July 16, 1979.

212
Dinner at Perino's: Haldeman, Hillings interviews.

212n
Nixon's visit to David Rockefeller: author's interview with friend of David Rockefeller, not for attribution, September 22, 1982.

213
Mitchell's troubles: *The New York Times*, June 6, 1975 (disbarment); *The New York Times*, December 12, 1977 (arthritis); *New York Post*, May 20, 1975 (debts).

213
Mitchell's relationship with Mary Gore Dean: *Newsweek*, May 5, 1975.

213
Mitchell background, relations with Nixon: Rather and Gates, 243–47; Safire, 263–71.

213
"John, . . . go see Mitchell": quoted, Lukas, 314.

214
"Watergate wouldn't have happened": quoted, *Los Angeles Times*, September 4, 1977.

214
Mitchell's behavior in prison: *The New York Times*, January 20, 1979.

214
Nixon's calls to Mitchell: *Washington Post*, January 26, 1978.

214
"a cute, cuddly, adorable fellow": quoted, Lukas, 5.

214
Description of Mitchell party: author's interview with Michael-Raoul Duval, December 22, 1982.

214
Nixon visit to China: *San Diego Tribune*, September 22, 1979.

214–15n
Offer to Nixon to intercede on oil drilling rights, Nixon refusal: Hillings interview.

215
Purpose of visit: *Los Angeles Times*, September 13, 1979.

215
"There is an old Chinese proverb": quoted, *Los Angeles Times*, September 23, 1979.

215
Packing of family belongings, worth: *New York Post*, February 25, 1980.
215
Nixons fly to Miami: *The New York Times*, February 10, 1980.
215
Nixon giving away golf clubs: Baumgold, "Nixon's New Life in New York," *New York*, June 9, 1980.
215n
"He didn't want to do anything to screw up his relationship": quoted, author's interview with Nixon friend, not for attribution, December 11, 1982.

16. The Fast Track

216
Nixon's morning routine: *New York Daily News*, May 27, 1980.
216–17
Nixon's office: author's visit to Nixon office, January 26, 1983.
217
Nick Ruwe's and Nixon's office routine: author's interview with Nick Ruwe, January 26, 1983.
217
Nixon's visits to restaurants: author's interview with Sirio Maccioni, January 5, 1983.
217
Nixon's afternoon routine: Ruwe interview.
217
"five shorts and three longs": Baumgold, "Nixon's New Life in New York," *New York*, June 9, 1980.
217
"He's very mechanical": Baumgold, "Nixon's New Life in New York."
217
Nixon's weekend and week-night routine: Baumgold, "Nixon's New Life in New York."
217
"an invention of the devil": Bob Greene column, "What Can an Unemployed President Do?" *New York Daily News*, October 23, 1980.
217–18
"The talk, it's so loud"; "already had the best dinners"; "The Beautiful People"; "Harvard"; "in that art crowd"; "I don't want to stir them up": quoted, Baumgold, "Nixon's New Life in New York."
218–19
Description of typical Nixon dinner: author's interviews with journalist Tom Bethel, December 2, 1982; former Nixon aide T. Harding Jones, November 11, 1982; journalist Joseph Sobrin, November 11, 1982.
218
"How do you think Schmidt is doing?" "prisoner of the crazies": Blum, "Dinner with Nixon: The Talk Is Private, the Drinks Are Fine," *The Wall Street Journal*, July 2, 1981.
219
Cloakroom story; "There McCarthy was"; "bent over and turning gray"; "And do you think it ever did me any good": author's interview with Nixon dinner guest, not for attribution, August 26, 1983.

219
"Any town that will support the Mets": quoted, Baumgold, "Nixon's New Life in New York."

219
Nixon's European trip: *Washington Post*, April 19, 1980.

219
Nixon in Africa to preside at opening of new golf course: *Washington Post*, March 9, 1980.

219
Rooting for the Yankees from Steinbrenner's box: Baumgold, "Nixon's New Life in New York."

219n
Nixon's vulgarity: author's interview with Nixon dinner guest, not for attribution, February 26, 1983.

219n
"Kefauver was going all over the state": author's interview with Nixon dinner guest, not for attribution, February 26, 1983.

219n
Midge Decter as guest: author's interview with Norman Podhoretz, February 26, 1983.

219n
Kissinger dinner: author's interviews with Mike O'Neill, November 22, 1982; David Brinkley, April 9, 1983.

220
LET'S MAKE THIS PERFECTLY CLEAR: *New York Daily News*, January 19, 1981.

220
Incident at lunch at "21": author's interview with Nixon friend, not for attribution, August 4, 1983.

220
Reeves interview: author's interview with Richard Reeves, September 22, 1983.

220
Friends' perception of Nixon's new calm: author's interview with Nixon friend, not for attribution, August 31, 1983; Gannon, Haldeman interviews; see also Allen, "Richard Nixon Is Making Something of a Comeback," *New York Daily News*, January 19, 1981.

220
Nixon visits with former aide's nephew and friends: author's interview with former Nixon aide, not for attribution, August 19, 1983.

220–21
Nixon's conversation with tourist's wife: *Washington Post*, September 15, 1980.

17. RETURN OF THE WIZARD

222
Nixon's calendar full of meetings with diplomats and heads of state: Ruwe interview.

222
Sales of *The Real War*: Kaminsky interview.

222
"there's a 50-50 chance": quoted, *Newsweek*, May 19, 1980.

222

"One can hardly believe one's eyes": quoted, *The New York Times*, May 20, 1980.

222

"World leadership requires something": Nixon, *Real War.*

223

"life is meant to be easy"; "trendies"; "guilt-ridden": "castrated the CIA": "gun-shy about using force"; "in the halls of Congress": Nixon, *Real War.*

223

"We are at war": Nixon, *Real War.*

223

"most Americans would regard with as much enthusiasm as the onset of World War III": *Newsweek*, May 19, 1980.

223

"gut reaction"; "Why don't we go in there and knock these people over?" "too dangerous": quoted, *Los Angeles Times*, November 27, 1979.

223

"certainly support[ed] what President Carter did": quoted, *The New York Times*, April 26, 1980.

224

"an empty cannon at this time"; "provide a carrot"; "I regret to say this": transcript, *20/20*, May 8, 1980.

224

State Department's response to shah's death: quoted, *Newsweek*, August 4, 1980.

224

Nixon's anger at response, decision to go to Cairo: *New York Post*, July 28, 1980.

224

Description of flight to Cairo: Gulley interview.

224

"one of the black pages"; "shameful"; "I think President Sadat's guts": quoted, *Washington Post*, July 29, 1980.

224–25

Nixon's visit with empress: Armao interview.

225

"In the name of God": quoted, Sadat, Armao interview.

225

Nixon eulogy; "a real man": Armao interview.

225

Description of Shah's funeral procession: *Washington Post*, July 30, 1980.

225

Nixon's behavior at dinner; reminiscences about the shah; bitterness about Carter; "They'll be all right": Armao interview.

225

Nixon's efforts to defeat Carter: author's interview with senior member of Reagan campaign staff, not for attribution, October 23, 1982.

225–26

Nixon's support of Connally; "Presidential greatness": *Christian Science Monitor*, August 23, 1980.

226

Connally's unsuccessful campaign: Germond and Witcover, *Blue Smoke and*

Mirrors: How Reagan Won and Carter Lost the Election of 1980, 138; see also Stacks, *Watershed,* 150.

226
Reagan's eagerness for Nixon's advice: author's interview with senior member of Reagan campaign staff, not for attribution, October 23, 1982.

226
"It's going to depend on how history looks at this in the near future": quoted, UPI, May 14, 1978.

226
"the boys"; "want to be in high office"; "a man"; "to do something": Bob Greene column, "Nixon: 'I'm Not Buddy-Buddy with Anybuddy,' " *New York Daily News,* October 21, 1980.

226
Reagan attacking détente by implication; statements about "coddling" the Soviets: Stacks, 49.

226
Reagan advocating closer relations with Taiwan: Germond and Witcover, 212.

226
Nixon's view of relations between superpowers as more complex than Reagan's: Charlotte Curtis column, "Nixon and the Russians," *The New York Times,* November 23, 1982.

226
Nixon's view of Reagan as the mirror opposite of Barry Goldwater: *Christian Science Monitor,* August 23, 1980.

226
Nixon working through John Sears: author's interview with senior member of Reagan campaign staff, not for attribution, October 23, 1982.

227
Reagan firing Sears, taking on Casey, Deaver, Nofziger, Allen and other former Nixon aides in Reagan camp: Germond and Witcover, 137–40.

227
Nixon's practice of placing calls to Reagan's aides, inquiring after political fine points: author's interview with senior member of Reagan campaign staff, not for attribution, October 23, 1982.

227
Letter to Robert Gray on debates: author's interview with Robert Gray, May 7, 1983.

227
"It's been six years since I left office"; "It isn't going to happen": transcript, *20/20,* May 8, 1980.

227–28
Nixon's comments on the *Today* show: quoted, *The New York Times,* September 8, 1980.

228–29
Nixon's assessments of various candidates: transcript, *20/20,* May 8, 1980.

229
Nixon's daily calls for poll results: author's interview with senior member of Reagan campaign staff, July 1, 1982.

229
Nixon's letter to the editor of *The Times: The New York Times,* July 17, 1980.

229–30
"very good talks"; "I think he values"; "I've understood the foreign policy

area"; "Something like a counselor"; "I will be available": quoted, Michaels, "Why Nixon Believes We Are Losing the Race on Land, on Sea and in the Air," *Parade*, October 5, 1980.
230
"it would have been much more helpful": UPI, August 8, 1980.
230
"hallucinating": quoted, UPI, October 3, 1980.
230
Reagan calls to apologize for aide's remarks: author's interview with senior member of Reagan campaign staff, July 1, 1982.
230
Requests for speaking engagements, fund-raisers, interviews: Ruwe interview.
230
Congressmen's requests for endorsements: Ruwe interview.
230–32
Account of Nixon interview with Marguerite Michaels, and thank-you note: author's interview with Marguerite Michaels, February 27, 1982; see also Michaels, "Why Nixon Believes We're Losing the Race on Land, on Sea and in the Air."

18. INTO HIS OWN

233
Description of Washington courtroom: *Washington Post*, November 2, 1980.
233
"How are you employed?" "I'm retired"; "Were you once the President of the United States?" "Yes": quoted, *Washington Post*, November 2, 1980.
233
Background of Felt and Miller case: *The New York Times*, September 20, 1980.
233
Nixon's ignorance of break-ins: *The New York Times*, October 30, 1980.
233
"clearly illegal . . . highly risky": quoted, Lukas, 33.
233
Nixon's authorization of "Huston Plan": *The New York Times*, October 30, 1980.
233–34
Nixon's defense of Huston Plan tactics: *Washington Post*, October 30, 1980.
234
"When the President does it, that means that is not illegal": Frost interviews; quoted, Frost.
234
Nixon following the case, contribution of money: author's interview with Nixon friend, not for attribution, March 27, 1983.
234
Nixon's offer to testify; defense attorneys decline; prosecution calls Nixon as witness: *Washington Post*, November 2, 1980.
234–35
Nixon's testimony: *Washington Post*, October 30, 1980.

235
Demonstrators interrupt court proceedings: *Washington Post*, October 30, 1980.
235
Requests for autographs at Yankee Stadium: Baumgold, "Nixon's New Life in New York."
235
"You should be President again": quoted, Allen, "Richard Nixon Is Making Something of a Comeback."
235
David Broder reporting on Nixon again: *Washington Post*, February 25, 1976.
235
"chartered himself a course straight into the sloughs of history": *Time*, September 23, 1974.
235
Sidey as dinner guest; "a strategic genius": author's interview with Hugh Sidey, December 11, 1982.
235
Nixon's lunch at *The Times*; caricatures of him on corridor walls: author's interview with Max Frankel, February 4, 1983.
235
"You haven't seen the world": quoted, *Washington Post*, May 6, 1982.
235
Twenty interview requests a week: Ruwe interview.
235–36
Nixon and Greene's correspondence, Nixon's final acceptance: Greene, "Reflections in a Wary Eye," *Esquire*, February 1981.
235–38
Greene's interview with Nixon: Greene, "Reflections in a Wary Eye"; extended version of same interview published as five-part series, *New York Daily News*, October 18–23, 1980.
235n
Outcome of Miller-Felt trial: *Washington Post*, December 24, 1980.
235n
Miller and Felt pardoned; receive note and champagne from Nixon: *The New York Times*, April 30, 1981.
238
Reagan's thrashing of Carter in election: Stacks, *Watershed*, 249.
238–39
Description of party at Russian embassy; Nixon's comments quoted: *Washington Post*, November 7, 1980.
239
Nixon's helpful hints: author's interview with Robert Gray, May 7, 1983.
239
"Al Haig . . . is the meanest, toughest": quoted, *Time*, July 5, 1982.
239
Haig burnishing credentials: Morris, *Haig*, 370–78.
239
Haig's attempt at 1980 Republican nomination: *The New York Times Biographical Service*, December 1980.
239
Nixon's support of Haig nomination: Morris, 381.

239
"I don't mean to sound arrogant or melodramatic": quoted, Ungar, "Alexander Haig: Pragmatist at State," *The Atlantic Monthly*, March 1981.
239
Haig's phone call to Nixon when dropping out of race: Ungar, "Alexander Haig: Pragmatist at State."
240
Nixon's assessment of Haig to friends: quoted, author's interview with Nixon friend, not for attribution, March 1, 1983.
240
Democrats in Congress promising to oppose Haig's nomination: *Washington Post*, December 6, 1980.
240
Reagan saying he was considering other candidates, including Shultz: Barrett, *Gambling With History*, 68.
240
Nixon's assessment of Shultz: cited by UPI, June 28, 1982.
240
Nixon phone calls to Senators and officials: author's interview with senior Reagan campaign aide, not for attribution, March 11, 1983.
240
Reagan informs Nixon of Haig's pending appointment: author's interview with senior Reagan campaign aide, not for attribution, March 11, 1982.
240
Senate Democrats' opposition to Haig, including Byrd's: *Washington Post*, January 7, 1981.
240–41
"In the 16 years I have served on this committee": quoted, *Washington Post*, January 10, 1981.
241
Haig's opening statement to Foreign Relations Committee: text quoted, *Washington Post*, January 10, 1981.
241
"What do you want me to say?" "There were tremendous abuses"; "Nobody has a monopoly": quoted, *Washington Post*, January 14, 1981.
241
Senators insisting on White House tapes: *Washington Post*, January 7, 1981.
241
Nixon's possession of and refusal to surrender tapes: *Washington Post*, January 13, 1981.
241
Committee split; eventual compromise to subpoena index: *Washington Post*, January 9, 11, 1981.
241
Nixon's decision to contest subpoena; Miller's statement: AP, January 17, 1981.
241–42
Nixon's phone call to Helms; Helms's description to committee; collapse of effort to secure tapes: Morris, 381–82.
242
Foreign Relations Committee recommends Haig's confirmation: *Washington Post*, January 16, 1981.

242

Nixon's phone calls to Capitol Hill: *Newsweek*, December 29, 1980.

242

Van Meter's invitation: author's interview with Thomas Van Meter, August 3, 1982.

242

State officials' decision not to attend fund-raiser: UPI, February 23, 1981.

242

"It's like inviting your former mistress": quoted, *The New York Times*, February 19, 1981.

242

Sold-out tickets; Nixon's enjoyment: *Columbus Citizen-Journal*, February 20, 1981.

242

"the football takes a lot of funny bounces": *Columbus Citizen-Journal*, February 19, 1981.

242

Description of Lincoln Center fund-raiser: author's interview with Richard Rosenbaum, June 16, 1983; see also *New York Daily News*, June 16, 1981.

242

"He's a shoo-in": quoted, *Washington Post*, June 16, 1981.

242

"It isn't exactly like a rookie": quoted, *The New York Times*, June 16, 1981.

243

Nixon feeling cramped, wanting more room for grandchildren: Ruwe interview.

243

"a bit square": quoted, Bob Greene column, *New York Daily News*, October 23, 1980.

243

marijuana incident: "These were *girls*": quoted, Bob Greene column, *New York Daily News*, October 23, 1980.

243

Nixon's requirements for new house: Ruwe interview.

243

Description of New Jersey house; cost: *The New York Times*, June 12, 1981.

243

"very gentlemanly and swift bargaining": quoted, *Bergen Record*, June 12, 1981.

243

"We haven't had a Democrat": quoted, *The New York Times*, June 12, 1981.

243–44

New administration willing to give Nixon papers and tapes: *The New York Times*, May 1, 1983.

244

Plans for Nixon library: Dean, *Lost Honor*, 105–8.

244

"Lyndon grabbed every paper and file cabinet": Dean, 107.

244

"Nixon Library Foundation": Dean, 108.

244

Nixon instructing lawyers to investigate tax code and legislation for papers donations: Dean, 107.

244
Discussions in Roosevelt Room about library: Dean, 108.
244
Library foundation dissolved: *Washington Post,* January 2, 1975.
244
Nixon's public plan to donate papers to USC: *Washington Post,* April 21, 1975.
245
Sanford's interest in library and proposal to Nixon: Duke University Public Relations Department document, "Initial Chronology of Duke–Nixon Negotiations" (Summer 1981).
245
Nixon's ambivalence, request for firm proposal: author's interview with Don Seaver, Duke University public relations, October 22, 1982.
245
1954 honorary degree incident: *The New York Times,* April 5, 1954.
245
Nixon's football advice: *Washington Post,* August 31, 1981.
245
Negative reaction at Duke; Murphy and Styron resignations: *Washington Post,* August 27, 1981.
245
"You don't have to hate": "Statement of Professor James David Barber, James B. Duke Professor of Political Science and Policy Studies, to the Academic Council of Duke University," September 3, 1981.
245
"categorically reject": *The New York Times,* September 12, 1981.
245–46
Nixon's European vacation: report from correspondent to major news organization, August 25, 1981.
245n
Potential new library sites: *Los Angeles Times,* April 11, 1983.
245n
San Clemente selected for library: *The New York Times,* May 1, 1983.
246
Sale of town house; "the sweetest real estate deal": *New York Daily News,* July 23, 1981.
246
Haig's clashes with Reagan officials, threats to resign, Reagan's weariness; "His departure is kind of like our view of the Soviet invasion": described and quoted, *New York,* April 20, 1981.
246
"I am in control here": *Newsweek,* April 13, 1981.
246
Haig fallen out with Kissinger and other old Nixon hands: *Newsweek,* May 11, 1981.
246
Nixon and Haig's closer relationship: author's interview with State Department official, not for attribution, July 19, 1982.
246
Nixon's criticisms of Reagan's hard-line policy: author's interview with State Department official, not for attribution, July 19, 1982.

247
Haig's worry about keeping his relationship with Nixon private: author's interview with State Department official, not for attribution, July 19, 1982.
247
Reagan hinting at broader role for Nixon: quoted, *Newsweek*, December 29, 1980.
247
New wallpaper, grandchildren, redecoration: Ruwe interview.
247
Section in library dedicated to Pat: Hitt interview.
247
Nixon's praise of Pat to friends: author's interview with Nixon friend, not for attribution, January 18, 1983.
247n
Nixon's criticisms of supply-side economics: author's interview with Peter G. Peterson, August 16, 1983.
247n
"that asshole": quoted, Peterson interview.
247n
"He would have been smarter": quoted, Peterson interview.
248
Possible trip to Washington for portrait unveiling: Hillings interview.
248
"a little off the jowls": author's interview with John Sanders, November 29, 1982; see also "The 'Vasari' Diary," *ARTnews*, March 1982.

19. FUNERAL IN CAIRO

249–50
Description of parade and assassination: *Time*, "Murder of a Man of Peace," October 19, 1981; *Newsweek*, " 'An Act of Infamy,' " October 19, 1981.
250
Call to Nixon from Haig; Nixon's reaction; discussion of delegation and Nixon's decision to attend funeral: author's interview with Nick Ruwe, January 26, 1983.
250
Nixon informs Haig of decision to travel to other countries: Ruwe interview.
250–51
White House debate over makeup of delegation: author's interview with Major Bob Barrett, April 19, 1983; see also *Washington Post*, October 8, 1981.
251
Description of three Presidents' arrival at Andrews; journey to White House; meeting with Reagan; and reception: Barrett interview.
251
"for the trip, at least, why don't we make it just Dick, Jimmy and Jerry": quoted, Barrett interview.
251
"a man of peace in a time of violence"; "in death you must fear him"; "Until we meet again": quoted, *Washington Post*, October 9, 1981.

251
Photographs, reboarding helicopter: *Washington Post*, October 9, 1981.
252
"I kind of like that house down there": quoted, *Time*, October 26, 1981.
252
Preflight preparations, seating plans: Barrett interview.
252
Early part of flight tension among Presidents: "Three Presidents," *Time*, October 26, 1981.
252
"It matches the color of your eyes": quoted, *Newsweek*, October 26, 1981.
252–53
Presidents changing coats for cardigans; Nixon with martini and peanuts: *Time*, October 26, 1981.
253
"The only time I had that bad a day": quoted, *Washington Post*, October 10, 1981.
253
Presidents discuss Middle East, libraries, books: Sidey, *Time*, October 26, 1981.
253
Ford with Broomfield: Sidey, *Time*, October 26, 1981.
253
Nixon and Carter's conversation; Nixon gesturing with glass; Rosalynn impressed: *Time*, October 26, 1981.
253
Passengers' reaction to Nixon: Barrett interview.
253
"You're the spokesman": quoted, *Washington Post*, October 10, 1981.
253
Nixon working the plane: Barrett interview.
253
"Chuck Percy has stood by Presidents": *Time*, October 26, 1981.
253–54
"Well, . . . this is quite a planeload": quoted, *Washington Post*, October 10, 1981.
254
Haig talks to Kissinger about Nixon's travels: *Time*, October 26, 1981.
254
Zablocki requests autographs and photos: Johnson, *Washington Post*, October 10, 1981.
254
"You don't want my picture with them": quoted, *Time*, October 26, 1981.
254
Nixon encounters Johnson: author's interview with Haynes Johnson, February 24, 1983.
254
Nixon misleads Kissinger about travels: *Time*, October 26, 1981.
254
Nixon asleep: Barrett interview.
254
Alarming reports from Cairo: author's interview with Dean Fischer, March 11, 1983.

254–55
Weinberger's worries: *Washington Post*, October 10, 1981.
255
"Can you imagine it?": quoted, author's interview with State Department official, May 6, 1983.
255
Ford's thoughts: Barrett interview; also, *Time*, October 26, 1981.
255
Carter's conversation with press: Johnson interview.
255
Scene in Cairo after arrival: Barrett, Ruwe interviews.
255
Ruwe's thoughts: Ruwe interview.
255
Nixon looking for reminders of last trip to Cairo: Ruwe interview.
255–56
Description of Nixon's 1974 trip to Cairo: Nixon, RN, *The Memoirs of Richard Nixon*, 1010–12.
256
"The memories this brings back": quoted, Ruwe interview.
256
Presidents and Kissinger at Sadat's home: Barrett interview.
256
"We know how great this loss was to you": quoted, *The New York Times*, October 10, 1981.
256
Description of dinner and toasts; Nixon's comments: Barrett, Fischer interviews.
256–57
Scene when Ruwe awoke; Ruwe's meetings with Nixon and with Kissinger: Ruwe interview.
257
Description of staging areas for foreign delegations: Barrett interview.
257
"My, . . . aren't we looking upright"; "It's this"; "I'm walking behind you": quoted, *Time*, October 26, 1981.
257
Arrival of Sadat's body, procession: *Time*, October 26, 1981.
257–58
Giscard's conversation with Carter: quoted, *Washington Post*, October 10, 1981.
258
Giscard's conversation with Ford: quoted, *Washington Post*, October 10, 1981.
258
"every time I make a speech": quoted, *Washington Post*, October 10, 1981.
258
"I don't think Begin is that intractable": quoted, *Time*, November 2, 1981.
258
"Where was the assassination?": quoted, *Washington Post*, October 10, 1981.
258
Delegation is cut off by soldiers: Ruwe, Barrett interviews.

258
American delegation moves into pavilion, files past Mubarak and Sadat family: Ruwe, Barrett interviews.

258
Family and friends walk to Tomb of the Unknown; verse on stone: *Newsweek*, October 19, 1981.

258
Delegation arrives at airport; notices Nixon is missing: Johnson interview.

259
"private visit": quoted, *Washington Post*, October 10, 1981.

259
banquet in Jidda; talks: UPI, October 12, 1981.

259
"A very positive step": quoted, UPI, October 14, 1981.

259
Banquet in Amman: Reuters, October 13, 1981.

259
"very useful ideas": quoted, Reuters, October 13, 1981.

259
Visit to Tunis, Fez: UPI, October 14, 1981.

259
"No written report": quoted, *Time*, November 2, 1981.

259–60
Contents of press summary: quoted, *Washington Post*, October 18, 1981.

259n
White House flap over Nixon's visit: *Washington Post*, October 19, 1981.

259n
Description of Saudi 727; pajama incident: *Washington Post*, December 1, 1981.

260
"He is more than a desert rat": quoted, *Washington Post*, October 18, 1981.

260
Treatment of Nixon in Paris: *Washington Post*, October 18, 1981.

260
"the world's unique and ubiquitous elder statesman": *Time*, November 2, 1981.

260
"Nixon's redemption"; "rehabilitation": Johnson, "Nixon's Redemption," *Washington Post*, October 13, 1981.

260
"There was both a poignancy and a fascination": Johnson, "Redemption."

260
Nixon's new plans: Ruwe interview.

260
"We can beat the hell out of them": quoted, *Time*, November 2, 1981.

260–61
Nixon discusses Roosevelt and de Gaulle and reads passage from book: author's interview with Nixon friend, not for attribution, November 25, 1982.

20. NEVER LOOKING BACK

262
Finishing touches on manuscript: *Washington Post*, February 14, 1982.
262
Jamaica vacation and conferences: *New York*, February 14, 1982.
262
Moroccan trip: AP, March 27, 1982; *Washington Post*, March 27, 1982.
262
Orange County address, crowd reaction: *The New York Times*, April 23, 1982.
262
Nixon's upcoming schedule: Ruwe interview.
262
"tough politically": quoted, *Washington Post*, April 25, 1982.
262
"one of our great Presidents": quoted, *The New York Times*, April 23, 1982.
262–63
Moroccan trip and crowd reaction: author's interview with U.S. Ambassador Joseph Reed, July 29, 1983.
263–65
Nixon interview with Sawyer: transcript, *CBS Morning News*, June 1–June 4, 1982.
265
Dinner invitation retracted: Hillings; Ehrlichman interviews.
266
Haig's anger over White House criticism of Israel; grievances voiced to Clark; and threat to resign: *Time*, July 5, 1982.
266
Haig's phone calls to Nixon; meetings at Tricia's apartment; and June 23 conversation: *New York Daily News*, September 21, 1981.
266
Reagan's decision to accept resignation; Haig's decision not to resign but submit grievances: *Time*, July 5, 1982.
266–67
Reagan's decision to force the issue; meetings with aides; decision to appoint Shultz: *Time*, July 5, 1982.
267
Reagan fires Haig: *The New York Times*, June 26, 1982.
267
Reagan calls Nixon: UPI, June 28, 1982.
267
Nixon calls Haig: UPI, June 28, 1982.
267
Nixon makes statement to the press: UPI, June 28, 1982.
267
Nixon's travels to seven countries: Ruwe interview.
267
Description of Nixon's visit to China: *Washington Post*, September 9, 1982; AP, September 11, 1982.
268
"They [the Chinese] know very well we have no designs on them"; "They aren't stupid": quoted, *Washington Post*, September 9, 1982.

268
"Many good hitters": Nixon, *Leaders*, 337.
268–69
"The greats"; "cold"; "struggling"; "fighting"; "great controversies"; "bitter enemies"; "bold but calculated"; "spend much time"; "compulsive"; "firmly behind them"; "paralyzed"; "morally neutral"; "not necessarily good": Nixon, *Leaders*, "In the Arena" chapter, 320–45.
268n
"Having him in will be a plus": quoted, author's interview with Nixon friend, not for attribution, February 5, 1983.
269
"Those who do not stoop": cited by Nixon, *Leaders*, 331.
269
"violated the Constitution"; "usurped arbitrary power"; "trampled individual liberties"; "His justification": Nixon, *Leaders*, 326.
269
"I don't give a shit what happens": quoted, *Time*, June 14, 1982.
269
"Whatever the field": Nixon, *Leaders*.
269
"aching"; "yearning"; "almost physical pain"; "who believes that his own judgment": Nixon, *Leaders*, p. 321.
269
Nixon's characterization of Herbert Hoover: Nixon, *Leaders*, 345.
269
" 'One must wait until the evening' ": cited by Nixon, *Leaders*, 345.
269
Thank-you note from George McGovern: Gannon interview.
269–70
Nixon comments on *Good Morning America*: quoted, Reuters, October 30, 1982.
270
Nixon comments on *Today*: quoted, UPI, November 4, 1982.
270
"He gives me a call": quoted, Charlotte Curtis column, *The New York Times*, November 30, 1982.
270
Appearance on six network telecasts, including with Dan Rather: Ruwe interview.
270
Comments to *Family Weekly*: Cooper, "An Exclusive Interview with Richard Nixon," *Family Weekly*, November 26, 1982; also, author's interview with Arthur Cooper, December 1, 1982.
270
Incident at Hansen's candy store: *Newsweek*, June 14, 1982.
270–73
Planning of advance men reunion; description: author's interview with Ron Walker, February 10, 1983; see also *The New York Times*, November 8, 1982; *Washington Post*, November 8, 1982.
271
Buchanan's comments: quoted, *Washington Post*, November 8, 1982.
271
Ed Nixon's comments: quoted, *Washington Post*, November 8, 1982.

271

Nixon's appearance: described, *Washington Post*, November 8, 1982.

271

"A new girl"; "Your friend here"; "His only problem": quoted, Warren interview.

271

Ziegler's conversation with Warren: Warren interview.

271–72

Ziegler's comments to press: quoted, *Washington Post*, November 7, 1982.

272

Ziegler isolated, behavior at Warren's table: Warren interview.

272

Walker's and Rose Woods's speeches: quoted, *Washington Post*, November 8, 1982.

272–73

Nixon's speech: quoted, *The New York Times*, November 8, 1982.

273

Nixon playing piano: *The New York Times*, November 8, 1982.

273

"After a man is President": quoted, Bob Greene column, *New York Daily News*, October 23, 1980.

273

"the ultimate": quoted, Bob Greene column, *New York Daily News*, October 21, 1980.

274

Nixon's comments about enemies: quoted, Smith, *Long Time Gone*, 213.

274

"Ten years from now . . . Watergate will be a few paragraphs": quoted, Pat Buchanan column, *New York Post*, November 9, 1982.

275–76

Activities on seventieth birthday: Ruwe, Eisenhower interviews.

275–76

Results of *Newsweek* and ABC News Poll: *Washington Post*, July 17, 1982.

276

Nixon comments about longevity: quoted, *San Jose Mercury-News*, October 27, 1978.

276

Note to Pat Hillings: Hillings interview.

Bibliography

SELECTED BOOKS

Abrahamsen, David, M.D. *Nixon vs. Nixon: An Emotional Tragedy.* New York: Farrar, Straus & Giroux, 1976.

Barrett, Lawrence I. *Gambling with History.* Garden City, N.Y.: Doubleday, 1983.

Ben-Veniste, Richard, and Frampton, George, Jr. *Stonewall.* New York: Simon and Schuster, 1977.

Bernstein, Carl, and Woodward, Bob. *All the President's Men.* New York: Simon and Schuster, 1974.

Brodie, Fawn. *Richard Nixon: The Shaping of His Character.* New York: W. W. Norton & Co., 1981.

Carter, Jimmy. *Keeping Faith: Memoirs of a President.* New York: Bantam Books, 1982.

Cohen, Richard M., and Witcover, Jules. *A Heartbeat Away: The Investigation and Resignation of Vice-President Spiro T. Agnew.* New York: Viking Press, 1974.

Colson, Charles W. *Born Again.* Old Tappan, N.J.: Fleming H. Revell Co., 1976.

Cooney, John. *The Annenbergs: The Salvaging of a Tainted Dynasty.* New York: Simon and Schuster, 1982.

David, Lester. *The Lonely Lady of San Clemente: The Story of Pat Nixon.* New York: Thomas Y. Crowell Co., 1978.

Dean, John W., III. *Blind Ambition.* New York: Simon and Schuster, 1976.

————. *Lost Honor.* Los Angeles: Stratford Press, 1982.

Dent, Harry S. *The Prodigal South Returns to Power.* New York: John Wiley & Sons, 1978.

Doyle, James. *Not Above the Law: The Battles of Prosecutors Cox and Jaworski.* New York: William Morrow & Co., 1977.

Ehrlichman, John. *Witness to Power: The Nixon Years.* New York: Simon and Schuster, 1982.

Eisenhower, Julie Nixon. *Special People.* New York: Simon and Schuster, 1977.

Evans, Rowland, Jr., and Novak, Robert D. *Nixon in the White House: The Frustration of Power.* New York: Random House, 1971.

339

Ford, Betty. *The Times of My Life.* New York: Harper & Row, 1978.

Ford, Gerald R. *A Time to Heal: The Autobiography of Gerald R. Ford.* New York: Harper & Row, 1979.

Frady, Marshall. *Billy Graham: A Parable of American Righteousness.* Boston: Little, Brown, 1979.

Frost, David. *"I Gave Them a Sword": Behind the Scenes of the Nixon Interviews.* New York: William Morrow & Co., 1978.

Gulley, Bill. *Breaking Cover.* New York: Simon and Schuster, 1980.

Haldeman, H. R. *The Ends of Power.* New York: Times Books, 1978.

Hartmann, Robert T. *Palace Politics: An Inside Account of the Ford Years.* New York: McGraw-Hill, 1980.

Hersh, Seymour. *The Price of Power: Kissinger in the Nixon White House.* New York: Summit Books, 1983.

Jaworski, Leon. *Confession and Avoidance: A Memoir.* Garden City, N.Y.: Anchor Press/Doubleday, 1979.

———. *The Right and the Power: The Prosecution of Watergate.* New York: Reader's Digest Press, 1977.

Klein, Herbert G. *Making It Perfectly Clear: An Inside Account of Nixon's Love-Hate Relationship with the Media.* Garden City, N.Y.: Doubleday, 1980.

Lukas, J. Anthony. *Nightmare: The Underside of the Nixon Years.* New York: Viking Press, 1976.

Magruder, Jeb Stuart. *An American Life: One Man's Road to Watergate.* New York: Atheneum, 1974.

Mazlish, Bruce. *In Search of Nixon: A Psychohistorical Inquiry.* New York: Basic Books, 1972.

Mollenhoff, Clark. *The Man Who Pardoned Nixon.* New York: St. Martin's Press, 1976.

Morris, Roger. *Haig: The General's Progress.* New York: Playboy Press, 1982.

Nessen, Ron. *It Sure Looks Different from the Inside.* New York: Playboy Press, 1978.

Nixon, Richard. *RN: The Memoirs of Richard Nixon.* New York: Grosset & Dunlap, 1978.

———. *The Real War.* New York: Warner Books, 1980.

———. *Leaders.* New York: Warner Books, 1982.

Osborne, John. *The Last Year of the Nixon Watch.* Washington: New Republic Books, 1975.

Pahlavi, Mohammad Reza. *Answer to History.* Briarcliff Manor, N.Y.: Stein and Day, 1980.

Persico, Joseph E. *The Imperial Rockefeller: A Biography of Nelson A. Rockefeller.* New York: Simon and Schuster, 1982.

Rather, Dan, and Gates, Gary Paul. *The Palace Guard.* New York: Harper & Row, 1974.

Reeves, Richard. *A Ford, Not a Lincoln.* New York: Harcourt Brace Jovanovich, 1975.

———. *American Journey: Traveling with Tocqueville in Search of Democracy in America.* New York: Simon and Schuster, 1982.

Report, Watergate Special Prosecution Force. U.S. Government, 1975.

Safire, William. *Before the Fall: An Inside View of the Pre-Watergate White House.* Garden City, N.Y.: Doubleday, 1975.

Schell, Jonathan. *The Time of Illusion.* New York: Random House, 1975.

Sheridan, Walter. *The Fall and Rise of Jimmy Hoffa*. New York: Saturday Review Press, 1972.

Sidey, Hugh. *Portrait of a President*. New York: Harper & Row, 1975.

Sirica, John J. *To Set the Record Straight*. New York: W. W. Norton & Co., 1979.

Smith, Curt. *"Long Time Gone": The Years of Turmoil Remembered*. South Bend, Ind.: Icarus Press, 1982.

Stacks, John. *Watershed: The Campaign for the Presidency, 1980*. New York: Times Books, 1982.

Stans, Maurice H. *The Terrors of Justice: The Untold Side of Watergate*. New York: Everest House, 1978.

Steinem, Gloria. *Outrageous Acts and Everyday Rebellions*. New York: Holt, Rinehart and Winston, 1983.

terHorst, J. F. *Gerald Ford and the Future of the Presidency*. New York: Okpaku Communications, 1974.

————, and Albertazzi, Colonel Ralph. *The Flying White House: The Story of Air Force One*. New York: Coward, McCann & Geoghegan, 1979.

Ungar, Sanford J. *FBI: An Uncensored Look Behind the Walls*. Boston: Atlantic Monthly Press, 1975.

U.S. Congress. Senate. Select Committee on Presidential Campaign Activities. *The Senate Watergate Report*. The final report of the Senate Select Committee on Presidential Campaign Activities (the Ervin Committee), 1974.

Walters, Vernon. *Silent Missions*. Garden City, N.Y.: Doubleday, 1978.

Washington Post, staff of. *The Presidential Transcripts*. New York: Dell, 1974.

White, Theodore H. *The Making of the President, 1960*. New York: Atheneum, 1961.

————. *The Making of the President, 1964*. New York: Atheneum, 1965.

————. *The Making of the President, 1968*. New York: Atheneum, 1969.

————. *The Making of the President, 1972*. New York: Atheneum, 1973.

————. *Breach of Faith: The Fall of Richard Nixon*. New York: Atheneum, 1975.

————. *America in Search of Itself: The Making of the President, 1956–1980*. New York: Harper & Row, 1982.

Wills, Garry. *Nixon Agonistes: The Crisis of the Self-Made Man*. Boston: Houghton Mifflin Co., 1969.

Witcover, Jules. *Marathon: The Pursuit of the Presidency, 1972–1976*. New York: Viking Press, 1977.

Woodward, Bob, and Bernstein, Carl. *The Final Days*. New York: Simon and Schuster, 1976.

SELECTED ARTICLES

Allen, Jennifer. "Swifty Lazar Is a Big Deal." *New York*, July 18, 1983.

ARTnews. " 'A Little Off the Jowls,' " March 1982, 13.

Axthelm, Pete. "A Different Sort of Notoriety." *Newsweek*, July 17, 1978, 30–31.

Baumgold, Julie. "Nixon's New Life in New York." *New York*, June 9, 1980, 22–28.

Broadcasting. "Ready to Roll: Court Rules Nixon Tapes Should Be Made Available to All," November 11, 1976, 34–35.

Brown, Thomas M. "The Exile." *The New York Times Sunday Magazine,* August 3, 1975, 7ff.

Buckley, William F. "Nixon to China." *The National Review,* March 19, 1976, 9.

Coffee, Helen. "A Very Special Bi-Centennial Party." *Orange County Illustrated,* August 1976, 63–66.

Congressional Quarterly Almanac. "Congress Votes to Retain Nixon Tapes," 1974, 654.

Cooper, Arthur. "An Exclusive Interview with Richard Nixon." *Family Weekly,* December 26, 1982, 4–8.

David, Lester. "Pat Nixon's Life Story: 'I Gave Up Everything I Ever Loved . . .' " *Good Housekeeping,* August 1978, 113–15.

Duka, John. "The House that Dick Bought." *New York,* September 3, 1979, 47–48.

Economist, The. "The Last Lap," January 17, 1976, 74–75.

————. "Whose Property?" February 19, 1977, 47.

————. "The Ghost Walks," July 15, 1978, 38.

————. "The Unreal Statesman," May 24, 1980, 117.

Ehrlichman, John. "The Top Aide Tells How Nixon Sold Him Out." *New West,* May 23, 1977, 76.

Eisenhower, David. "The Last Days in the Nixon White House." *Good Housekeeping,* September 1975, 89–91.

Eisenhower, Julie Nixon. "My Mother." *Newsweek,* May 24, 1976, 13.

Ephron, Nora. "Rose Mary Woods—The Lady or the Tiger?" *New York,* March 18. 1974, 33–37.

Erdstein, Ehrich. "The Long, Lonely Fall from the Peacock Throne." *Macleans,* July 9, 1979, 24.

Facts on File. "Public Hears Watergate Tapes," July 27, 1979, 460.

Feldman, Trude B. "The Quiet Courage of Pat Nixon." *McCall's,* May 1975, 74–75.

Fleming, Standish M. "Celebrity Scissors." *Orange County Illustrated,* May 1980, 45–47.

Fox, Frank, and Parker, Stephen. "Is the Pardon Explained by the Ford-Nixon Tapes?" *New York,* October 10, 1974, 41–45.

————. "The Skeleton in Gerald Ford's Closet." *New York,* April 21, 1975, 42–43.

Getelin, Frank. "Crook Books: Vol. VI." *Commonweal,* May 26, 1978, 324–26.

Greene, Bob. "Reflections in a Wary Eye." *Esquire,* February 1981, 13–15.

Hersh, Seymour. "The Pardon." *The Atlantic Monthly,* August 1983, 55–78.

Horner, Charles. "Hindsight." *Commentary,* August 1980, 64–65.

McClendon, Winzola. " 'Bebe': An Intimate Look at President Nixon's Closest Friend." *Ladies' Home Journal,* November 1973, 30–35.

————. "Martha Mitchell's Lonely Dream House." *McCall's,* March 3, 1974, 68.

————. "Pat Nixon Today." *Good Housekeeping,* February 1980, 128–29.

Michaels, Marguerite. "Why Nixon Believes We're Losing the Race on Land, on Sea, and in the Air." *Parade,* October 5, 1980, 4–8.

Murphy, Mary. "Inside the Nixon-Frost TV Interviews." *New York*, April 25, 1977, 17–18.

Nation, The. "The Nixon Special," February 26, 1977, 228.

National Review, The. "Nixon's Fourth Comeback." December 22, 1978, 1579–80.

Newsweek. "Special Issue," August 19, 1974.

———. "Nixon's Fight for Life," November 11, 1974, 26–29.

———. "Haldeman's Tale," March 31, 1975, 37.

———. "At Last, Nixon Under Oath," July 7, 1975, 12–13.

———. "Nixon Speaks," September 1, 1975, 17–18.

———. "Nixon's New Life," October 20, 1975, 22–29.

———. "Back to China," February 16, 1976, 21.

———. "Citizen Nixon in Peking," March 1, 1976, 16–17.

———. "Richard Nixon's Final Days," April 5, 1976, 25–28.

———. "Pat Nixon's Latest Crisis," July 19, 1976, 35–36.

———. "Pat Nixon's Therapy," July 26, 1976, 78.

———. "Ghosts in the Hall," August 30, 1976, 44–45.

———. "Nixon Speaks," April 9, 1977, 35–39.

———. "Grilling Nixon," May 16, 1977, 22–38.

———. "Nixon's Tapes—Someday," July 11, 1977, 17.

———. "Haldeman Speaks Out," February 27, 1978, 29–31.

———. "Now, It's 'Deep Book,' " February 27, 1978, 75.

———. "Nixon Wins One," May 1, 1978, 29.

———. "Richard Nixon on World War III," May 19, 1980, 48.

———. "Richard Nixon Calling," December 29, 1980, 15.

———. " 'An Act of Infamy,' " October 19, 1981, 31–40.

———. "Presidential Hat-Trick," October 26, 1981, 30.

———. "Nixon: 'Never Look Back,' " June 14, 1982, 38.

New Times. "Nixon Kicks Off '80 Campaign Before 29,289 in Anaheim Stadium," July 24, 1978, 5.

New York. "A Report on the Current State of Richard Nixon's Wit," April 25, 1977, 66.

Nixon, Richard. "Needed: Clarity of Purpose." *Time*, November 10, 1980, 33–35.

Osborne, John. "White House Watch: The Pardon." *The New Republic*, September 28, 1974, 9–11.

———. "White House Watch: Settling In." *The New Republic*, October 5, 1974, 8–9.

———. "White House Watch: Ghosts." *The New Republic*, October 12, 1974, 11–12.

———. "White House Watch: Troubles." *The New Republic*, October 19, 1974, 10–11.

———. "White House Watch: Shake-Out." *The New Republic*, October 26, 1974, 9–10.

———. "White House Watch: On the Stump." *The New Republic*, November 2, 1974, 11–12.

———. "White House Watch: Ruffles and Shuffles." *The New Republic*, December 28, 1974, 9–10.

———. "White House Watch: Rocky at Work." *The New Republic*, January 25, 1975, 11–12.

———. "White House Watch: More About Rocky." *The New Republic*, February 1, 1975, 13–14.

————. "White House Watch: Nixon Then and Now." *The New Republic*, February 22, 1975, 12–13.

————. "White House Watch: The China Caper." *The New Republic*, March 20, 1976, 8–10.

————. "White House Watch: Nixon's Good Guy." *The New Republic*, October 8, 1977, 8–11.

————. "White House Watch: Shabby Piece of Work." *The New Republic*, March 4, 1978, 15–18.

People. "The Death of His Old Political Foe Brings Unhappy Warrior Nixon Briefly Out of Exile." January 30, 1978, 18.

————. "His Memoirs Behind Him, Citizen Nixon Ponders Travel, A New Book and the Difficulties of Re-Entry." May 15, 1978, 48.

Publishers Weekly. "Nixon Memoirs Sold to Warner Paperback Library." October 4, 1974, p. 13.

Purnick, Joyce. "It's Better in the Bahamas." *New York*, May 21, 1979, 10–11.

Ravenal, Earl C. "Nixon's Challenge to Carter: No More Mr. Nice Guy." *Foreign Policy*, Winter 1977/1978, 27–35.

Reinert, Al. "Zen and the Art of John Ehrlichman." *Esquire*, July 1976, 64–69.

Reuter, Madalynne. "G & D Buys Hardcover Rights to Nixon Memoirs." *Publishers Weekly*, March 14, 1977, 40–41.

Rosenheim, Andrew. "All the President's Boys." *The Village Voice*, December 11, 1978, 67.

Rovere, Richard. "Richard the Bold." *The New Yorker*, June 19, 1978, 96–97.

Schlesinger, Arthur. "Playing Politics." *Saturday Review*, June 1980, 67–73.

Schmidt, Benno C., Jr. "Why We Haven't Heard the Nixon Tapes." *Columbia Journalism Review*, September/October 1975, 53–54.

Schorr, Daniel. "Nixon: Wrestling with Himself." *The Progressive*, August 1978, 39–40.

Seligman, Daniel. "A Postmortem on Detente." *Fortune*, July 28, 1980, 88–99.

Sendler, David. "A New Plan for Presidential Debates." *TV Guide*, March 8, 1980, 4–10.

Shearer, Lloyd. "Frank Gannon—He's Researching Nixon's Autobiography." *Parade*, 4–5.

Sherrill, Robert. "The Sound of One Hand Clapping." *The Nation*, July 8, 1978, 53–57.

Sidey, Hugh. "An Illustrious Kaffeeklatsch." *Time*, January 30, 1978, 26.

————. "Nixon as Grandfather." *Time*, August 28, 1978, 16.

————. "Drum Rolls and Lightning." *Time*, September 10, 1979, 27.

————. "The Genie That Got Away." *Time*, July 5, 1982, 14.

Smith, Helen McCain. "Ordeal! Pat Nixon's Final Days in the White House." *Good Housekeeping*, July 1976, 83.

Steel, Ronald. "Perfectly Clear." *The New York Review of Books*, June 26, 1980, 18–20.

Stein, Benjamin. "Richard Nixon Goes to a Party." *Esquire*, November 1976, 106–11.

Steinberg, Sybill. "Conn. Bookseller Refuses to Sell Nixon's 'Memoirs.' " *Publishers Weekly*, May 5, 1978, 46.

Stroud, Kandy. "Pat Nixon Today." *Ladies' Home Journal*, March 1975, 76.

————. "The Sad New Life of Rose Mary Woods." *McCall's*, June 1975, 46–50.

Thimmesch, Nick. "The Nixons' Closest Friend." *McCall's*, July 1974, 18–25.

————. "David Eisenhower: 'Our Hardest Year.' " *McCall's*, August 1975, 24–28.

————. "Richard Nixon Speaks His Mind." *Saturday Evening Post*, March 1979, 55–56.

————. "The Unsinkable Pat Nixon." *McCall's*, April 1979, 89.

Time. "Swifty the Great," February 2, 1962, 54–55.

————. "The Healing Begins" (Special Issue), August 19, 1974.

————. "Not Hounded Out of Office," September 2, 1974, 24–25.

————. "The Pardon That Brought No Peace," September 16, 1974, 10–19.

————. "The Fall-Out from Ford's Rush to Pardon," September 23, 1974, 11–22.

————. "Nixon: Depressed and Ill," September 23, 1974, 17.

————. "A Question of Fitness," September 30, 1974, 15.

————. "Psychosomatic Phlebitis?" September 30, 1974, 65.

————. "Nixon's Reclusive Recuperation," October 7, 1974, 22–23.

————. "The Trial Begins Minus Its Star," October 14, 1974, 15–16.

————. "The End Begins with Bitter Fratricide at the Trial," October 21, 1974, 13–16.

————. "Trying to Get at the T-R-U-T-H," November 4, 1974, 21.

————. "Nixon: Surgery, Shock and Uncertainty," November 11, 1974, 15–16.

————. "A Quiet, Private Dinner," March 10, 1975, 28.

————. "The Man Who Walks the Beach," August 11, 1975, 15–18.

————. "Frost's Big Deal," August 25, 1975, 58.

————. "Evading the Questions," September 1, 1975, 10–12.

————. "A Questioning of Conduct," October 10, 1975, 43.

————. "Nixon's Embarrassing Road Show," March 8, 1976, 22–25.

————. "Still More Pain for the Nixons," July 19, 1976, 26–27.

————. "Nixon Talks," May 9, 1977, 22–33.

————. "No One Knows How It Feels," June 6, 1977, 11.

————. "Nos. 24171–157 and 01489–163(B)," July 4, 1977, 11.

————. "Sorry . . . Sorry . . . Sorry," October 17, 1977, 19.

————. "The Case of the Purloined Pages," February 27, 1978, 20.

————. "Much Ado About Haldeman," February 27, 1978, 16–20.

————. "Tape Tie-Up," May 1, 1978, 80.

————. "Nixon's Memoirs; 'I Was Selfish.' " May 8, 1978, 26–27.

————. "Trading Down." June 4, 1979, 24.

————. "The Fan from San Clemente," October 8, 1979, 90.

————. "The Real Nixon," June 9, 1980, 22.

————. "Reagan Sticks with Haig," December 29, 1980, 8–10.

————. "The Watergate Role," December 29, 1980, 12.

————. "Murder of a Man of Peace," October 19, 1981, 12–35.

————. "The Private Travels of Nixon," November 2, 1981, 30.

————. "Reflections of a China Hand," November 1, 1982, 56.

Travis, Neal. "The Nixon-Tuck Encounter." *New York*, July 17, 1978, 6.

Trillin, Calvin. "Variations." *The Nation*, April 5, 1980, 391.

U.S. News & World Report. "Ford's Own Story of the Nixon Pardon: 'No Deal—,' " October 28, 1974, 20–25.

————. "Why Nixon Claims Right to Tapes," September 1, 1975, 41.

————. "Nixon Comes Back into the Limelight—and Controversy," March 1, 1976, 24.

————. "Nixon in China—The Trip That Kicked up a Storm," March 8, 1976, 20.

————. "Why Nixon Went on the 'Witness Stand,' " April 16, 1977, 27–29.

————. "An $800,000 Yearly Tab for Nixon, Ford." April 16, 1979, 30–31.

Weighart, James. "The Exile of San Clemente." *Sunday* (New York) *News Magazine*, August 5, 1979, 21–23.

Wills, Garry. "Why All of Us Should Read Nixon's Memoirs." *New York*, July 3, 1978, 58–59.

Acknowledgments

Like all works of nonfiction, this book owes its creation to an extraordinary number of people. That is particularly so in this case, and, however inadequately, I would like to thank some of them.

Foremost is Jeanne O'Connor, a gifted young journalist who served as my principal research associate on the project. Jeanne conducted many of the secondary interviews; organized the notes and waded through countless library stacks and clipping files, all with unfailing precision, humor and good grace. In her case, the cliché—"without whose help this book would not have been possible"—describes reality.

Others involved in the research effort were Hollis Evans and Robert Boggs in California; Tina Crenshaw and Cara Morris in New York; and Dennis Rini and Bob Lyford in Washington, and to them goes my appreciation as well.

I would also like to thank my agent, Peter Shepherd, of Harold Ober Associates, and my editor, Alice Mayhew of Simon and Schuster. They are friends and professional colleagues both. My gratitude goes as well to Ann Godoff and Michael Gast of Ms. Mayhew's staff; to Sophie Sorkin, Simon and Schuster's copy chief, and to Mary Solak, whose copy editing of this book "saved" the author on a number of occasions.

To James Reston, Jr., who provided access to an unpublished manuscript on the Frost interviews, I owe a special debt, as I do to the other journalists whose time and contacts helped make this book possible. They include John Lindsay of *Newsweek*; Marge Michaels of *Parade*; Bob Greene of the *Chicago Sun-Times*; Art Cooper of *Family Weekly*; Richard Reeves of the Universal Press Syndicate; Godfrey Sperling of the *Christian Science Monitor*; Haynes Johnson of the *Washington Post*; John Stacks of *Time*; Jennifer Allen of *New York* and Jack Nelson and Ken Reich of the *Los Angeles Times*.

Not all who contributed to the making of this book can be named, some because of who they are, others because of who they were. Many others, though, can be identified, and for giving of their memory and themselves, I would like now to thank them. They include: Jonathan Aitkin, Ralph Albertazzie, Ken Allan, Jennifer Allen, Robert Armao, Peter Aschkenasy, Wiley F. Barker, Bob Barrett, Pat Beard, Jeffrey Bell, Tom Bethel, Reid Boates,

347

David Brinkley, Tom Brokaw, Nancy Brooks, Thomas W. Brown, William F. Buckley, Steve Bull, Lou Cannon, George Champion, John Chancellor, Joseph Chappell, Richard Cheney, George Clark, Dewey Clower, Bill Codus, T. Eugene Coffin, Kenneth Cole, Clement Conger, Art Cooper, Harry Dent, John Dean, Jeremiah F. Denton, Joseph Dimona, William Dobrovir, Bob Dole, Michael-Raoul Duval, Julie Nixon Eisenhower, John Ehrlichman, Robert Ellsworth, Charles Evers, Henry Fair, Robert Finch, William Fine, Dean Fischer, Max Frankel, David Frost, Frank Gannon, Brigidio Garcia, Leonard Garment, Suzanne Garment, Johnny Grant, Robert Gray, Sidney Gruson, Bill Gulley, H. R. Haldeman, Morton Halperin, Bryce Harlow, Jeffrey Hart, Robert Hartmann, Eldon Hickman, Pat Hillings, Patricia Hitt, Richard Howard, Richard Holbrooke, Roman Hruska, Henriette Wyeth Hurd, Haynes Johnson, Judy Johnson, Meredith Johnson, Merrill Johnson, T. Harding Jones, Herman Kahn, Howard Kaminsky, Herb Klein, Irving Kristol, Dan Kuykendall, Melvin Laird, Victor Lasky, Howard Lebengood, John Lindsay, Thomas Lipscomb, John Lofton, Lord Longford, Sirio Maccioni, John McLaughlin, Frank Mankiewicz, Stanford Manning, Robert Markel, Jack Marsh, Elias Meza, Marge Michaels, Robert Michel, Hack Miller, Marvin Minoff, G. V. ("Sonny") Montgomery, Jack Nelson, Lyn Nofziger, Robert Odle, Mike O'Neill, Mary Neiswender, Charles Palmer, Otto Passman, Norman Vincent Peale, Susan Pescar, Jim Perrin, Peter G. Peterson, Saul Pett, Milton Pipps, Norman Podhoretz, Jody Powell, Paul Presley, William F. Price, Joseph Reed, Ken Reich, James Reston, Jr., John Rhodes, Charles Riley, James Roosevelt, Richard Rosenbaum, Barry Roth, Harold Roth, Russ Rourke, Henry Ruth, Nick Ruwe, William Safire, Pierre Salinger, John T. Sanders, William Sarnoff, Gerrold Schecter, Arthur Schlesinger, John Sears, Don Seaver, Gloria Seelye, Frank Shakespeare, Hugh Sidey, Lee Simmons, William Simon, Helen Smith, Joe Sobrin, Stu Spencer, Godfrey Sperling, John Stacks, Maurice Stans, Benjamin Stein, Connie Stuart, Kandy Stroud, Stobe Talbott, Gannon Taylor, Jerald terHorst, Nick Thimmesch, Strom Thurmond, Thomas Van Meter, Richard Viguerie, Joe Waggonner, Ron Walker, Gerald Warren, Paul Weyerich, Charles Wiggins, Anne Grier Willard, Jörn Winther, Leonard Woodcock, Peregrine Worsthorne, Bob Zelnick, Ron Ziegler and Paul Ziffren.

Index